The COMPLETE GARDEN EXPERT

Dr. D. G. Hessayon

Published by Expert Books
a division of Transworld Publishers

Copyright © Expert Publications Ltd 2012

TRANSWORLD PUBLISHERS
61-63 Uxbridge Road, London W5 5SA
a division of the Random House Group Ltd

EXPERT BOOKS
www.expertbooks.co.uk

Contents

The Random House Group Limited supports The Forest Stewardship Council (FSC®), the leading international forest certification organisation. Our books carrying the FSC label are printed on FSC® certified paper. FSC is the only forest certification scheme endorsed by the leading environmental organisations, including Greenpeace. Our paper procurement policy can be found at www.randomhouse.co.uk/environment

Reproduction by Spot On Digital Imaging Ltd, Gomm Road, High Wycombe, Bucks HP13 7DJ
Printed and bound in Great Britain by Butler, Tanner & Dennis Ltd, Frome & London

MIX
Paper from responsible sources
FSC® C023561

ISBN 978 0 903505 98 7

CHAPTER 1

INTRODUCTION

*"I haven't a garden. You see I ..." She gave me a swift keen look,
sharp as an eagle. "You haven't a garden!" she cried scornfully.
"Then why are you an Englishman?"*

Gone Rustic *(Cecil Roberts 1934)*

A little exaggerated, of course, but it is an undeniable fact that no other
nation on earth can match our interest in and love of gardening. About 30
million people in Britain work in the garden attached to their homes or in
a nearby allotment, and you must be one of them ... or you would not be
reading this book.

There are many facets to the joy of gardening. There are the
satisfaction of seeing the results of one's labours, the healthy exercise
derived from the varied tasks involved, the peace of mind away from the
stresses of the workaday world and perhaps the pleasure of being able to
pick your own fruit and vegetables.

But there is another side to the picture. We are not born with an
inherent knowledge of gardening to help us answer all the questions
which arise and to solve the problems which occur. For thousands of
years people had to rely on experienced gardeners for guidance, and
today this remains a widely used path to problem solving.

In 1400 along came an additional guide, the first gardening book in
English — *The Feat of Gardening* by Master Ion Gardener. In 1730 the first
illustrated plant catalogue was published and in 1826 the first magazine
appeared. The 20th century saw the arrival of the radio gurus such as
Mr Middleton and later the TV gardening celebrities appeared.

Today there are so many sources of information. Books, magazines,
newspapers, DVDs, the Internet, flower shows, radio programmes — the
list goes on and on. One of the cornerstones, however, remains as firmly
established as ever — the comprehensive manual which covers all the
aspects of the garden.

In the middle of the 20th century the first *Garden Expert* appeared and
subsequent editions have had to keep up with the changing scene. And
now here is the latest *Garden Expert*, much larger and far more
comprehensive than ever before, providing information and guidance for
the second decade of the 21st century.

You will find many rules, hints, design and planting suggestions etc,
but never forget it is *your* garden.

*"A garden is for its owner's pleasure, and whatever the degree or
form of that pleasure, it is right and reasonable."*

Gertrude Jekyll

Choosing a plant

You might think that the choice is entirely up to you — just a matter of liking the picture in the catalogue or the specimen at the garden centre. No, it isn't — there are a number of factors to be considered if you are not going to waste a lot of money and time. Follow the steps described below to avoid the pitfalls.

1. PICK THE RIGHT PLANT TYPE FROM PAGE 5

"Do I want a permanent or temporary display?"
Trees and shrubs are used to form the permanent living skeleton of the garden. Hardy perennials will live in the garden for years, but die down in the winter. Annuals are for temporary display only.

"Do I want a labour-saving plant?"
Border perennials and 'hobby plants' such as dahlias and chrysanthemums involve a lot of work — staking, feeding, dead-heading, dividing etc. Most shrubs and trees involve little annual maintenance, but well-timed pruning may be a requirement.

"Do I want the leaves to stay on over winter?"
Choose an evergreen, but it is not always the best plant to grow. A garden filled with evergreens can look dull and unchanging — deciduous plants add an extra dimension with fresh leaves opening in the spring and changing colours in autumn.

2. PICK THE RIGHT EXAMPLE OF THE PLANT TYPE

"What shape and size would be suitable?"
One of the commonest mistakes in gardening is to buy a plant which at maturity is far too large for the space available. Chopping back every year means that both natural beauty and floral display can be lost. Always check the expected height before buying.

"What will the growing conditions be like?"
Check if the plant has clear-cut requirements with regard to sunshine, temperature, soil texture, lime tolerance, drainage and soil moisture. Some plants are remarkably tolerant of climatic and soil conditions — others are not. Nearly all annuals need full sun, rockery perennials demand good drainage and some shrubs (e.g rhododendron) hate lime.

3. PICK THE MOST SUITABLE PLANT MATERIAL OF THE CHOSEN VARIETY

"Is money the main consideration?"
Seed bought in packets or saved from your own plants is inexpensive, but it may take years to raise a shrub or border perennial by this method. Rooted cuttings taken from plants in the garden are another inexpensive source of plant material.

"Is simplicity the main consideration?"
After the War, plants in containers from a local garden centre transformed planting out. Just choose a container-grown specimen at any time of the year, dig a hole in the garden and pop it in. The work involved is not quite that easy (see page XX), but container-grown plants are the most convenient and 'instant' of all plant materials.

4. BUY FROM THE RIGHT SOURCE OF SUPPLY

A 'bargain offer' from a mail order nursery may be the right choice if you are short of money and have a large space to fill, but in most cases it is preferable to see what you are buying and it is always wise to seek out a supplier with a good reputation.

ROSES

Deciduous Shrubs and Trees of the genus *Rosa*, usually listed seperately in the catalogues because of their importance and great popularity

A **Half Standard** is a Rose tree with a 75 cm (2¹/₂ ft) stem

A **Full Standard** is a Rose tree with a 1 m (3¹/₂ ft) stem

WOODY PLANTS

Perennial plants with woody stems which survive the winter

A **Shrub** bears several woody stems at ground level

A **Tree** bears only one woody stem at ground level

A **Climber** has the ability when established to attach itself to or twine around an upright structure. Some weak-stemmed plants which require tying to stakes (e.g Climbing roses) are included here

A **Hedge** is a continuous line of Shrubs or Trees in which the individuality of each plant is partly or wholly lost

EVERGREEN SHRUBS & TREES

Woody plants which retain their leaves during winter

Conifers bear cones and nearly all are Evergreens

Semi-evergreens (e.g privet) retain most of their leaves in a mild winter

DECIDUOUS SHRUBS & TREES

Woody plants which shed their leaves in winter

Top Fruit are Trees which produce edible fruit (e.g apple, pear, peach, plum)

Soft Fruit are Shrubs and Climbers which produce edible fruit (e.g blackcurrant, gooseberry). A few are Herbaceous plants (e.g strawberry)

A **Ground Cover** is a low-growing and spreading plant which forms a dense, leafy mat

TURF PLANTS

Low-growing carpeting plants, nearly always members of the Grass family, which can be regularly sheared and walked upon

VEGETABLES

Plants which are grown for their edible roots, stems or leaves. A few are grown for their fruits (e.g tomato, cucumber, marrow, capsicum)

HERBS

Plants which are grown for their medicinal value, their culinary value as garnishes or flavourings, or their cosmetic value as sweet-smelling flowers or leaves

HERBACEOUS PLANTS

Plants with non-woody stems which generally die down in winter

BULBS

Bulbs (more correctly Bulbous plants) produce underground fleshy organs which are offered for sale for planting indoors or outdoors. Included here are **True Bulbs, Corms, Rhizomes** and **Tubers**

BIENNIALS

Plants which complete their life span, from seed to death, in two seasons

A **Hardy Biennial** is sown outdoors in summer, producing stems and leaves in the first season and flowering in the next

Some Perennials are treated as Biennials (e.g wallflower, daisy)

PERENNIALS

Plants which complete their life span, from seed to death, in three or more seasons

A **Border Perennial** will live for years in the garden — the basic plant of the herbaceous border

A **Rockery Perennial** is a dwarf Hardy Perennial suitable for growing in a rockery. **Alpine** is an alternative name, although some originated on the shore rather than on mountains. Some delicate True Alpines need to be grown indoors

A **Half-hardy Perennial** is not fully hardy and needs to spend its winter in a frost-free place

A **Greenhouse Perennial** is not suitable for outdoor cultivation

ANNUALS

Plants which complete their life span, from seed to death, in a single season

A **Hardy Annual** is sown outdoors in spring

A **Half-hardy Annual** cannot withstand frost, and so they are raised under glass and planted outdoors when the danger of frost is past

A **Greenhouse** (or **Tender**) **Annual** is too susceptible to cold weather for outdoor cultivation, but may be planted out for a short time in summer

A **Bedding Plant** is an Annual or Biennial set out in quantity in autumn or spring to provide a temporary display

Naming the parts

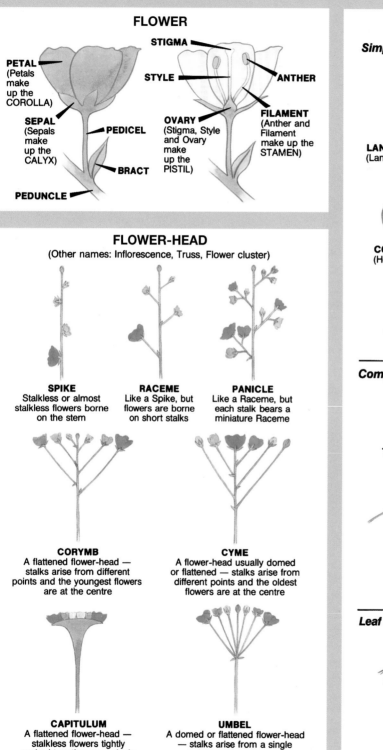

FLOWER

STIGMA

PETAL
(Petals make up the COROLLA)

STYLE

ANTHER

SEPAL
(Sepals make up the CALYX)

PEDICEL

OVARY
(Stigma, Style and Ovary make up the PISTIL)

FILAMENT
(Anther and Filament make up the STAMEN)

BRACT

PEDUNCLE

FLOWER-HEAD
(Other names: Inflorescence, Truss, Flower cluster)

SPIKE
Stalkless or almost stalkless flowers borne on the stem

RACEME
Like a Spike, but flowers are borne on short stalks

PANICLE
Like a Raceme, but each stalk bears a miniature Raceme

CORYMB
A flattened flower-head — stalks arise from different points and the youngest flowers are at the centre

CYME
A flower-head usually domed or flattened — stalks arise from different points and the oldest flowers are at the centre

CAPITULUM
A flattened flower-head — stalkless flowers tightly packed together on a single disc

UMBEL
A domed or flattened flower-head — stalks arise from a single point and the youngest flowers are at the centre

FOLIAGE

Simple leaves

LANCEOLATE
(Lance-shaped)

OVAL

CORDATE
(Heart-shaped)

OVATE

LOBED

Compound leaves

TRIFOLIATE

PALMATE

PINNATE

BIPINNATE

Leaf edges

ENTIRE

CRENATE

SERRATE

CHAPTER 2
GARDEN SOIL

Pick up a handful of soil in your garden. It is ordinary, unexciting earth, yet your success as a gardener largely depends upon its condition. You should therefore get to know your soil and then set about improving its quality.

All soils are composed of four basic elements — mineral particles, organic matter, air and water. The physical nature of this blend is described as the soil's texture or structure. These two terms mean quite different things as explained on page 9 — you can do little to change its texture (the relative proportion of each ingredient), but you can improve the structure (the way these ingredients bind together).

Your soil may be nothing like the crumbly loam described at the bottom of this page. It can be back-breaking clay or sandy stuff which needs frequent watering and feeding. Don't despair — the purpose of this chapter is to explain the four steps to take in order to improve the structure and quality of your soil. Follow these steps and you cannot fail to create a better crumb structure and an increase in the helpful population of micro-organisms.

This improvement may be spectacular, but you cannot change the basic texture unless you add vast quantities of the mineral particle which is deficient. So your soil will remain basic clayey, sandy etc which means you should wherever possible choose plants which are recommended for your soil type.

Sufficient plant nutrients, both major and minor, to ensure vigorous and healthy growth, flowering and fruiting

Soil structure is crumbly — crumbs range from lentil- to pea-sized. Both large and small pores are present

Sufficient organic matter to ensure high bacterial activity and humus production

The ideal garden soil

Soil texture is medium loam with few or no stones

Sufficient lime to counteract soil sourness

Sufficiently free-draining to prevent waterlogging of the topsoil during periods of heavy rain

Step 1 : Get to know the words

MINERAL PARTICLES

The non-living skeleton of the soil which is derived from the decomposition of rocks by weathering. The fertility and size of these particles are governed by the type of parent rock.

Particle name is based on size. All **SANDS** have a gritty feel — **COARSE SAND** (0.6–2.0 mm in diameter) is distinctly gritty, **MEDIUM SAND** (0.2–0.6 mm) feels like table salt and **FINE SAND** (0.02–0.2 mm) has a grittiness which is not easy to feel.

SILT (0.002–0.02 mm) has a silky or soapy feel.

CLAY (less than 0.002 mm) feels distinctly sticky.

AIR

Air is essential for the support of plant life and desirable soil life — it is also required for the steady breakdown of organic matter which releases nutrients. Movement of air is necessary to avoid the build-up of toxic gases – this air movement takes place through the soil pores.

HUMUS

Plant and animal remains are gradually decomposed in the soil. The agents of decay are the bacteria and other microscopic organisms. They break down dead roots and underground insects as well as fallen leaves carried below the soil surface by worms. Partially decomposed organic matter with the horde of living and dead bacteria is known as **HUMUS** to the gardener. For the scientist this word has a much narrower meaning. True humus is the dark, jelly-like substance which binds mineral particles into crumbs — see page 14.

LIVING ORGANISMS

Millions of living organisms can be found in every gram of soil. Most are microscopic — bacteria, fungi, eelworms etc. Others are small but visible — insects, seeds and so on. Worms and beetles are easily seen — the largest and least welcome living thing you are likely to find is the mole.

DEAD ORGANIC MATTER

The soil is the graveyard for roots, fallen leaves, insects etc as well as the organic materials (humus makers) we add to enrich it. Dead organic matter is not humus until it has decomposed. It does, however, serve as the base material for high bacterial activity and humus production. With this decomposition both major nutrients and trace elements are released into the soil. Some types of dead material may take many years to decompose.

STONES & GRAVEL

These are particles larger than 2 mm in diameter. **STONES** usually refers to sizeable pieces of rock whereas **GRAVEL** describes the smaller weathered fragments — but there is no precise distinction.

WATER-BASED SOLUTION

This is often shortened to **SOIL WATER** but it is in fact a solution containing many dissolved inorganic and organic materials. Some (e.g nitrates, phosphates and potassium salts) are plant nutrients.

CRUMB

Crumbs range from lentil- to pea-sized. The spaces between them are known as **PORES**.

TOPSOIL is the fertile and living part of the soil. It is fertile because it contains nearly all of the humus, and it is living because it supports countless bacteria. These bacteria change various materials into plant foods. This layer varies from 5 cm in chalky soils to a metre or more in well-tended gardens. **When digging, this layer should be turned over, not buried under the subsoil.**

SUBSOIL lies under the topsoil. It can be recognised by its lighter colour, due to lack of humus. Soil structure is poor.
When digging, it should not be brought to the surface.

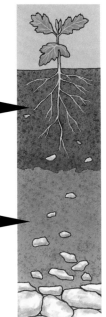

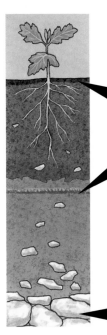

A **SOIL PAN** is a horizontal layer, on or under the soil surface, which prevents the free movement of air and water to the region below. A **SURFACE PAN** is formed by the action of heavy rain on certain soil types — remove by hoeing or forking. Cultivating to the same depth year after year can cause a **SUB-SURFACE PAN** — another cause is the leaching down of iron, aluminium and manganese salts to a level where they form a chemical pan. Break through sub-surface pans by double digging (page 13).

BEDROCK is the mineral base below the subsoil. Usually it is the parent material of the soil above.

SOIL TEXTURE refers to the proportions of different-sized mineral particles which are present in the soil. When coarse (sand) particles predominate the texture is **LIGHT**. When minute (clay) particles are plentiful the soil is described as **HEAVY**. **It is not practical to change the soil texture.**

SOIL STRUCTURE refers to the way the mineral particles are joined together in the soil. They may be almost unconnected as in a very light soil with little organic matter or they may be grouped in clods, plates or crumbs in a heavy soil. A crumb structure is the ideal — such soil is described as **FRIABLE**. **It is possible to change the soil structure** by following step 3 in the soil improvement plan — see page 12.

COLD Clay-rich soil which warms up slowly in spring due to the high water and low air pocket content. In general cold soils produce late crops.

COMPACTION Damaged crumb structure due to heavy rain or foot traffic in wet weather.

FALLOW Soil which has been neither cultivated nor planted for a period of time.

FERTILE Soil which has a good crumb structure, adequate nutrients and an organic matter content of 3-7%.

LEACHING The loss of plant nutrients as a result of rainfall or watering. The amount of leaching depends on soil type and organic matter content.

MOR Humus formed under acid conditions.

MULL Humus formed under alkaline conditions.

PH A measure of the acidity or alkalinity of the soil. pH 7 is neutral. A figure under 5 indicates acid soil — a pH over 8.5 means that the soil is alkaline.

SHALLOW Soil which has an undesirably thin layer of topsoil above the subsoil.

SOIL PROFILE A cut-away section of soil from topsoil to bedrock — see illustrations above.

TILTH Fine and crumbly surface soil produced by cultivation.

WARM Sand-rich soil which warms up quickly in spring due to the low water and high air pocket content. In general warm soils produce early crops.

WATER TABLE The upper level of waterlogged soil.

Step 2 : Put a name to your soil

Improving the structure of your soil begins with knowing the type you have. The three important tests are the walkover, hand and pH tests — the pit test is necessary only if the soil remains abnormally wet after heavy rain.

The walkover test

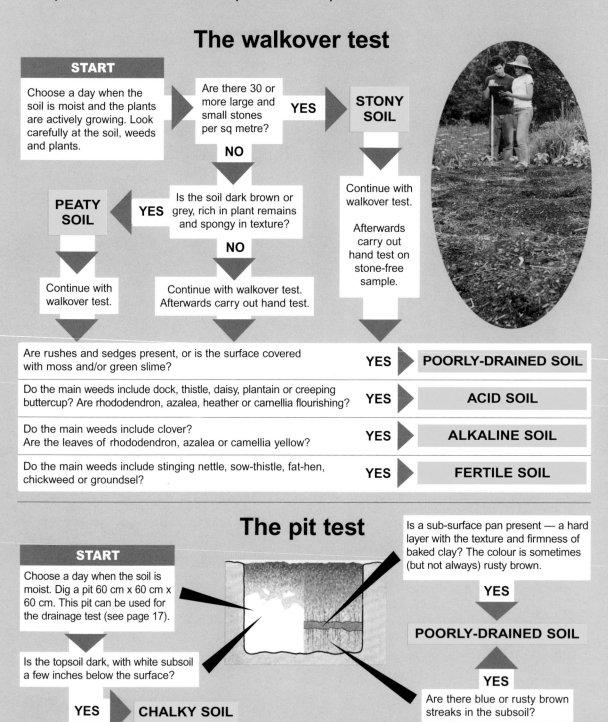

START

Choose a day when the soil is moist and the plants are actively growing. Look carefully at the soil, weeds and plants.

Are there 30 or more large and small stones per sq metre?

YES → **STONY SOIL**

NO

Is the soil dark brown or grey, rich in plant remains and spongy in texture?

YES → **PEATY SOIL**

NO

Continue with walkover test.

Afterwards carry out hand test on stone-free sample.

Continue with walkover test.

Continue with walkover test. Afterwards carry out hand test.

Are rushes and sedges present, or is the surface covered with moss and/or green slime? — **YES** → **POORLY-DRAINED SOIL**

Do the main weeds include dock, thistle, daisy, plantain or creeping buttercup? Are rhododendron, azalea, heather or camellia flourishing? — **YES** → **ACID SOIL**

Do the main weeds include clover? Are the leaves of rhododendron, azalea or camellia yellow? — **YES** → **ALKALINE SOIL**

Do the main weeds include stinging nettle, sow-thistle, fat-hen, chickweed or groundsel? — **YES** → **FERTILE SOIL**

The pit test

START

Choose a day when the soil is moist. Dig a pit 60 cm x 60 cm x 60 cm. This pit can be used for the drainage test (see page 17).

Is the topsoil dark, with white subsoil a few inches below the surface?

YES → **CHALKY SOIL**

Is a sub-surface pan present — a hard layer with the texture and firmness of baked clay? The colour is sometimes (but not always) rusty brown.

YES

POORLY-DRAINED SOIL

YES

Are there blue or rusty brown streaks in the subsoil?

The hand test

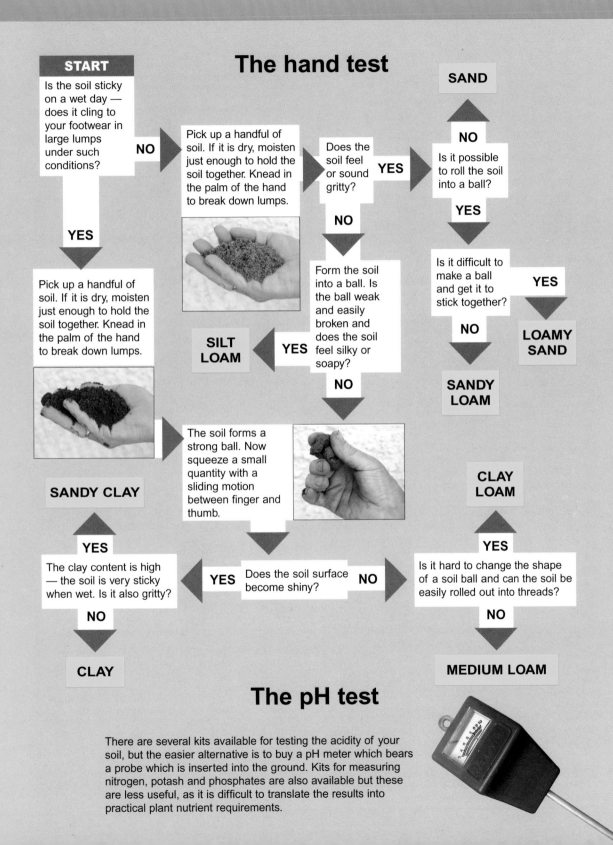

START
Is the soil sticky on a wet day — does it cling to your footwear in large lumps under such conditions?

NO →

Pick up a handful of soil. If it is dry, moisten just enough to hold the soil together. Knead in the palm of the hand to break down lumps.

Does the soil feel or sound gritty?

YES →

SAND

NO
Is it possible to roll the soil into a ball?

YES

Is it difficult to make a ball and get it to stick together?

YES →

LOAMY SAND

NO

SANDY LOAM

YES (from START, going down)

Pick up a handful of soil. If it is dry, moisten just enough to hold the soil together. Knead in the palm of the hand to break down lumps.

NO

Form the soil into a ball. Is the ball weak and easily broken and does the soil feel silky or soapy?

YES →

SILT LOAM

NO

The soil forms a strong ball. Now squeeze a small quantity with a sliding motion between finger and thumb.

CLAY LOAM

SANDY CLAY

YES

The clay content is high — the soil is very sticky when wet. Is it also gritty?

YES ←

Does the soil surface become shiny?

NO →

Is it hard to change the shape of a soil ball and can the soil be easily rolled out into threads?

YES

NO

CLAY

NO

MEDIUM LOAM

The pH test

There are several kits available for testing the acidity of your soil, but the easier alternative is to buy a pH meter which bears a probe which is inserted into the ground. Kits for measuring nitrogen, potash and phosphates are also available but these are less useful, as it is difficult to translate the results into practical plant nutrient requirements.

Step 3 : Improve the structure

It is worth repeating the point made on page 9 that you can do nothing to change soil texture (the content of mineral particles of different sizes) but you can change soil structure (the way the particles are grouped together to form crumbs and air spaces).

If you are lucky you will have a loamy soil. It will hold water, but not too much. It will drain, but not too quickly. But most soils are either sandy or clayey. In order to create a crumb structure a combination of techniques may be required and it cannot be done overnight or in a single season — there is no magic formula.

DIG if necessary
page 13

Add ORGANIC MATTER
page 14-15

Add LIME if necessary
page 16

Tackle DRAINAGE if necessary
page 17

The improvement plan for your soil

LOAMY SOIL

Good points: Good crumb structure — possesses all the advantages, to a lesser degree, of both heavy and light soils.

Bad points: Surface capping takes place in wet weather if the silt content is high.

•

Try to keep it as it is, with regular dressings of humus-making materials and nutrients. Occasional applications of calcium will be necessary — dig only if the soil is compacted.

SANDY SOIL

Good points: Easy to work, even when wet. Free-draining in winter. Warm — suitable for early flowers and vegetables.

Bad points: Usually short of plant foods. Frequent watering is necessary in summer or shallow-rooted plants may die. Cools down rapidly at night.

•

Water and food shortage are regular problems during the growing season. The structure is generally poor — lack of organic matter means that the soil is not crumbly. Digging is not the answer — if you decide to dig do it in spring, not autumn. The solution is to incorporate plenty of humus-making material into the top 10 - 15 cm (4 - 6 in.) in late winter or early spring — tread down the soil after cultivating. Mulching is vital to conserve moisture and reduce the leaching of nutrients.

CLAYEY SOIL

Good points: Generally well supplied with plant foods. Good water retention.

Bad points: Difficult to cultivate under most conditions. Cakes and cracks in dry weather — may waterlog in wet weather. Cold — flowers and vegetables appear later than average.

•

If the plot has not been cultivated before then dig thoroughly in autumn to expose the clods to winter frost — a generous quantity of bulky organic matter should be incorporated at this time. Apply lime if the soil is acid or gypsum if it is not in order to improve the structure. Do not plant out until the soil is reasonably dry. Mulch established plants. Each autumn fork organic matter into the top 15 cm (6 in.) of soil. Do not expect miracles — it will take 3 - 5 years to create a crumbly structure.

CHALKY SOIL

Good points: Best soil type for some shrubs and many alpines. Usually free-draining and warm.

Bad points: Sticky and soft in wet weather — often parched in summer. Nutrients may be deficient. Too alkaline for many plants.

•

Digging must be kept shallow — add plenty of organic matter. Regular feeding will be necessary. Add topsoil if the area is small. Although the bedrock is chalk, the soil is occasionally acid.

DIG if necessary

The benefits of digging are well known. Clods are exposed to the elements, roots of perennial weeds can be removed and so on. But the drawbacks are less well known. It is obvious that if you dig in the wrong way you can hurt yourself, but it is not quite so obvious that you can harm the soil. Do not dig too early in the season and never dig land which is frozen or waterlogged. In shallow soil the fertile topsoil can be buried.

Dig if the ground has not been cultivated before or if the soil has become compacted. An important virtue of digging is that it allows organic matter to be incorporated with the soil below the surface. Then follow a no-dig programme — in future years top up the humus content with an annual dressing of organic matter to the surface (see page 14).

A word of warning. Work for only 10 minutes between rest periods if you are reasonably fit but out of condition — extend to 20 minute stints if you are fit and used to physical exercise. For most people 30 minutes digging is enough for the first day.

① Choose the right season — early winter for most soils and early spring for light land. Choose the right day — the ground should be moist but not water-logged nor frozen

② Use the right equipment — a spade for general work or a fork if the soil is very heavy or stony. Carry a scraper and use it to keep the blade or prongs clean

③ Dig out a trench about 30 cm (1 ft) wide and 1 spade spit deep. Transport the removed soil to the other end of the plot. You will need this soil to fill in the final trench

④ Spread a layer of bulky organic material all along the bottom of the trench. Use a bucketful per 3 m (10 ft) of trench. A sprinkling of bone meal can be added

⑤

Drive the spade in vertically. Press (do not kick) down on the blade. This should be at right angles to the trench

⑥
Make a cut parallel to the trench 15 - 20 cm (6 - 8 in.) behind the face. Do not take larger slices to save time

⑦

Pull steadily (do not jerk) on the handle so as to lever the soil on to the blade. Lift up the block of soil

⑧

With a flick of the wrist turn the earth into the trench in front — turn the spadeful right over to bury the weeds

Double Digging
A strenuous task which has fallen out of favour, but it has its place where serious waterlogging is a problem. Fork over the bottom of the trench to the full depth of the prongs at the end of stage 4.

Large Areas
Think twice before lifting a spade if you have a large area of compacted earth to turn over — a typical example is the ground left by builders. Hire a cultivator which can work to a depth of 20 cm (8 in.), or call in a contractor.

Add ORGANIC MATTER

Soil bacteria are the key to soil fertility. When alive they produce heat and transform organic materials into simple chemicals. When dead they release these nutrients plus colloidal gums. It is these gums and not decomposing plant remains which are **humus** — the magical material which cements clay, silt and sand particles together to form soil crumbs.

Under natural conditions the organic level remains roughly balanced — in a fertile soil there is an average of 5 per cent organic matter. Under cultivation this organic content decreases and the humus level falls. This means that you have to add **humus makers**. All are bulky organic materials which add to the humus content of the soil.

The humus makers are not the only type of organic matter used in the garden. There are also **non-humus makers** which hold water and air but do not stimulate bacterial activity and finally there are the **decorative organic mulches** such as chipped bark which keep down weeds and reduce water loss but do little to improve the soil.

The Humus Makers

RAW HUMUS MAKERS stimulate bacterial growth. Both heat and true humus are produced in the soil. Examples include fresh dung and grass clippings.

Using a raw humus maker is a good way of warming the soil and raising its humus content, but there are drawbacks. The rapid build-up of bacteria robs the soil of nitrogen, so a nitrogen-rich fertilizer should be added. Allow some time before planting and keep it well away from roots.

MATURED HUMUS MAKERS do not stimulate bacterial growth. They are made from raw humus makers by composting. Examples include garden compost and well-rotted dung.

The humus produced by composting promotes crumb formation. The warming effect is lost, but this is outweighed by the advantages — tender roots are not damaged and nitrogen is not locked up.

The Non-humus Makers

NON-HUMUS MAKERS do not stimulate bacterial growth. Rich in cellulose — they act as sponges, improving air- and water-holding capacity. Examples include peat and coir.

The use of peat is frowned upon as its removal from its natural habitat is undesirable. Avoiding peat is not a problem as it decomposes very slowly and is of no value as a humus maker.

When to apply organic matter

A humus maker can be added to the soil in three ways:

(1) **At digging time** The instructions on page 13 recommend that the organic matter should be spread in the trench at stage 4. Some people prefer to spread garden compost or well-rotted manure over the surface before digging begins.

(2) **Before planting** A matured humus maker is spread over the soil in late winter or early spring and forked into the surface.

(3) **Around plants** Mulching is one of the most important jobs you can do in the garden, but its virtues are often neglected or touched on only briefly in the textbooks. The organic matter is spread over the surface in late spring when the soil is moist and warm.

Other sections to read

MAKING COMPOST   page 55
MULCHING   page 61

PEAT

Peat is no longer recommended for forking into the soil or for mulching. There are much better organic materials to use for these purposes, but some gardeners still prefer to use potting compost which contain peat because of its excellent water-holding capacity.

BARK or COCOA SHELL

Bark is a better choice than peat for mulching. The chips should be 1-5 cm (1/2-2 in.) long. Cocoa shell is a good alternative but can be smelly when wet. Use them in the way described on page X — they are the most attractive mulches for use around trees and shrubs. Both will last on the surface for 2-3 years.

WELL-ROTTED MANURE

Manure is less attractive than bark as a surface cover, but it is available very cheaply at the farm or stable gate and is the best soil improver of all. It must be well-rotted and quality from an unknown source can be a problem — weed seeds may be present. Annual topping-up is necessary.

GARDEN COMPOST

Garden compost is not only free — it also gets rid of grass clippings, soft cuttings, old stems etc. Like manure it provides nutrients and improves the soil structure as well as acting as an insulator, but it is usually less effective. Poor quality compost is unpleasant to handle and may contain abundant weed seeds and roots.

STRAW

Straw is easy and cheap to obtain in rural areas, and is widely used as a mulch both in grand estates and tiny allotments. It is rather unsightly, however, around the plants in a bed or border in the front garden. Two problems — weed seeds are often present and it requires the use of a nitrogen-rich fertilizer.

OLD GROWING COMPOST

Spent peat compost has the virtues and limitations of peat with the added value of having some nutrients present. Examples include the contents of used growing bags, spent tomato compost (suitable for nearly all plants) and spent mushroom compost (not for use around lime-hating plants).

LEAF MOULD

Fallen leaves should not be wasted. Collect leaves in autumn (oak and beech are the favourites) and build a heap — 15 cm (6 in.) layers of leaves separated by 2.5 cm (1 in.) layers of soil. Composting is slow — leave for a year before using for digging-in or mulching around plants.

Add LIME if necessary

Tiny particles of clay group together in the presence of calcium to form crumbs which improve soil structure. **To supply calcium use either lime or gypsum** — which one depends on the acidity of the soil and the plants you grow. This improvement is short lived and these crumbs must be 'fixed' by humus.

LIME

(calcium hydroxide or calcium carbonate) This calcium source reduces acidity.

Various forms are available. **Chalk** and **ground limestone** are slow-acting. **Dolomite limestone** contains magnesium — this is the recommended type. **Calcified seaweed** (coral) is the 'organic' form — long-lasting and expensive. **Hydrated lime** (slaked lime) is by far the most popular type. It is cheaper, stronger and quicker-acting than the others.

Do test your soil before liming — see page 11. If an excessive amount is used, humus breaks down too quickly and some plant leaves turn yellow because of the lock-up of iron and manganese.

Benefits

Improves structure of heavy soil
Calcium binds clay particles into soil crumbs.

Serves as one of the plant foods
Calcium is needed in moderate amounts by plants.

Frees nutrients
Elements locked up by clay particles are freed.

Discourages some soil pests
Examples include club root, slugs and wireworms.

Neutralises acidity
Very few plants grow well in acid soil and bacteria and earthworms decline in acid soil.

GYPSUM (calcium sulphate)

This calcium source does not reduce acidity.

Sold under various trade names — sometimes used as a gypsum/ dolomite limestone mixture.

It is used where heavy soil is not acid, or where the soil is acid but is used for lime-hating plants such as rhododendrons.

TIMING

Lime every 3 years
•
Leave at least 2 months after compost or fertilizers
•
Leave at least 1 month before compost, fertilizers or seeds

| | pH | TO LIME OR NOT TO LIME | HYDRATED LIME | |
			Sandy Soil	Clayey Soil
	4.5 – 5.5 VERY ACID Seriously short of lime	Ideal for azaleas, camellias, blue hydrangeas, most heathers, rhododendrons and blueberries. For other plants liming is essential, but never plant lime-loving plants. Add little or no lime if preparing the ground for a new lawn — fine-leaved lawn grasses thrive in acid soil.	500 g/sq.m (1lb/ 10 sq.ft)	1 k/sq.m (2 lb/ 10 sq.ft)
	5.5 – 6.5 ACID Short of lime	Ideal for most fruit trees and bushes, including apples, pears, raspberries and strawberries. It is also suitable for some vegetables such as potatoes, tomatoes, marrows and cucumbers. Liming is not necessary for roses or lawns, but nearly all other garden plants benefit from liming.	250 g/sq.m (8 oz/ 10 sq.ft)	750 g/sq.m (1½ lb/ 10 sq.ft)
	6.5 – 7.3 NEARLY NEUTRAL Correct amount of lime	Suitable for nearly all flowers, shrubs, trees and vegetables but not for plants listed as acid lovers. Liming is not necessary as a regular treatment, but liming may be needed every few years as rain steadily washes lime out of the soil. Test with a pH meter.	125 g/sq.m (4 oz/ 10 sq.ft)	500 g/sq.m (1lb/ 10 sq.ft)
	7.3 – 8.0 ALKALINE Too much lime	Satisfactory for carnations, wallflowers, delphiniums, cabbages, Brussels sprouts, some shrubs and many rockery plants. Too much lime or chalk in the soil is generally undesirable as some plant foods are locked up. Never lime soil of this type.	do not lime	do not lime

Tackle DRAINAGE if necessary

Faulty drainage is more than a nuisance — it is a plant killer. Stagnant water around the roots starves them of air. Helpful bacterial activity is slowed down and harmful organisms flourish. Toxic gases build up and the overall result is poor growth at first and possibly the eventual death of the plants. **Poor drainage** is associated with heavy topsoil. Water moves very slowly through clay, and so the answer is to improve the structure by cultural means. **Impeded drainage** is a more serious problem, as the downward movement of water is blocked. There are three prime causes — non-porous rock below the soil, a sub-surface pan (see page 9) or a high water table (see page 9). Some remedial action is essential.

Cultural aids

The crumbs created by digging provide only temporary relief — you must build up a permanent crumb structure by adding organic matter (page 14). Add calcium — see page 16.

Poor drainage caused by a heavy clay content can be improved by double digging in autumn (page 13). Never break up the clods. Double digging with a spade will break through a thin soil pan (page 9) but a sub-surface pan may require a pickaxe or steel bar plus sledge hammer.

Cultural aids cannot help if non-porous rock near the surface or an abnormally high water table is the cause. There are structural aids (see below) but adding topsoil to the surface is a simpler answer.

Drainage Test

A vital job in soil improvement is to find out whether drainage is satisfactory. The simple test outlined below will give you the answer.
Dig a hole 60 cm (2 ft) square and 60 cm (2 ft) deep at the lowest part of the garden — see page 10. Look inside the hole after heavy rain and see how much water is present at the bottom.

An hour after rain — no water in the hole	**Excessive drainage** If topsoil is sandy — addition of humus is essential (page 12)
A few days after rain — no water in the hole	**Satisfactory drainage** No help is needed
A few days after rain — some water still present at the bottom of the hole	**Poor drainage** One or more cultural aids (see adjacent column) are needed
A few days after rain — water has seeped in from surrounding soil; hole partly filled	**Impeded drainage** A structural aid (see below) as well as cultural aids may be needed

Structural aids

The traditional method for overcoming impeded drainage is to lay drains below the surface — a feature of large Victorian gardens, but far too expensive these days for the ordinary gardener. Soakaways and raised beds are sometimes recommended for small areas.

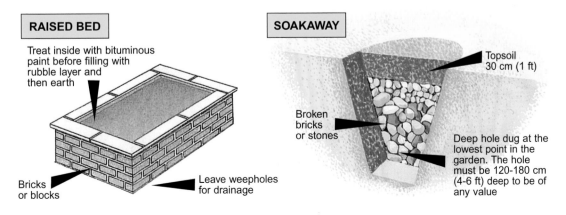

RAISED BED

Treat inside with bituminous paint before filling with rubble layer and then earth

Bricks or blocks

Leave weepholes for drainage

SOAKAWAY

Topsoil 30 cm (1 ft)

Broken bricks or stones

Deep hole dug at the lowest point in the garden. The hole must be 120-180 cm (4-6 ft) deep to be of any value

CHAPTER 3
GARDEN WEATHER

DECEMBER	
JANUARY	Winter
FEBRUARY	
MARCH	
APRIL	Spring
MAY	
JUNE	
JULY	Summer
AUGUST	
SEPTEMBER	
OCTOBER	Autumn
NOVEMBER	

Weather is the combination of rainfall, temperature, wind, sunshine and air humidity which affects your garden at a particular point in time. **Climate** is the summary of the weather from past years. The climatic maps of your area should be used as rough guides only. They provide averages over many years rather than telling you the extremes of weather conditions which you are likely to enjoy (or suffer) during a particular year. In addition, the general climate of your region will be much modified by the factors around the garden (the local climate) and the factors around each plant (the microclimate).

CLIMATE

General climate

The general climate provides a rough guide to the weather you can expect in your garden. In Britain it varies from nearly sub-tropical (S.W. coastal areas) to nearly sub-arctic (N. Scottish highlands). The general climate is controlled by latitude, altitude, direction of the prevailing wind and the closeness to the sea. The effect of latitude is obvious to everyone — southern gardens are warmer than northern ones. The effect of being close to the sea is equally well known — western coastal gardens are kept virtually frost-free by the Gulf Stream. Less well known is the effect of small increases in altitude (page 20) and the plant-damaging effect of salt in coastal areas for as much as 5 miles inland.

Local climate

The local climate is the modified form of general climate. It is controlled by

- Slope — a south-facing sloping site starts its growing season about 1 week before a level plot.
- Openness — nearby trees and bushes will cast shade and reduce solar energy, but they will also reduce the damaging effect of high winds.
- Proximity of buildings — town gardens are affected in many ways by the closeness of walls, houses etc. Walls cast shadows and so reduce solar energy — they can also cast rain shadows and so reduce rainfall. Walls affect the temperature — heat is released at night and south-facing walls can form a sun-trap.
- Soil type — frosts are more likely to occur over sandy soils than over heavy ones.
- Proximity to water — a nearby large lake can have a cooling effect on hot summer days.

Microclimate

The microclimate is the modified form of local climate in the immediate vicinity of a plant. Large variations can occur from one part of a garden to another. Nearby walls and hedges or overhanging plants will of course result in less light and less rainfall than in the open garden — the effect of this rain shadow can be to cut the water supply to only 25 per cent of the rainfall in the open garden. On the credit side the effect of nearby walls and plants is to cut the risk of frosts on clear, still nights and to reduce the harmful effect of wind. The general climate cannot, of course, be changed. The local climate is usually impossible to alter but the microclimate can often be changed by moving nearby plants or features, or by introducing cloches or windbreaks.

THE GROWING SEASON

STARTS
when the soil temperature reaches 6°C (43°F)

The **Growing Season** is the period of the year when most plants (including grass) are in growth. This growth may be slow at the start and finish of the growing season, and may cease altogether if there is an unseasonal frost.

FINISHES
when the soil temperature falls below 6°C (43°F)

Growing Season in Britain	
Average	250 days
Longest (Extreme S.W.)	330–360 days
Shortest (Scottish Highlands)	150–180 days

FROST

Hardy Plants will survive in the garden during the period between the first frosts in autumn and the last frosts in spring. **Half-hardy Plants** are killed during this period if left unprotected outdoors.
The damaging effect of frost occurs when thawing takes place — a rapid thaw on a sunny day is more harmful than a slow one.

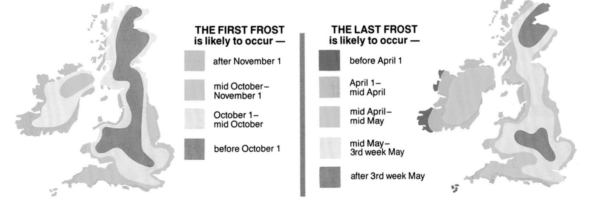

THE FIRST FROST
is likely to occur —

- after November 1
- mid October– November 1
- October 1– mid October
- before October 1

THE LAST FROST
is likely to occur —

- before April 1
- April 1– mid April
- mid April– mid May
- mid May– 3rd week May
- after 3rd week May

A frost occurs when the temperature falls below 0°C (32°F). It is damaging to plants in two ways — water is rendered unavailable to plant roots and the cells of sensitive plants are ruptured. The damage is governed by the severity and duration of the frost as well as the constitution of the plant — in Britain we leave our roses unprotected over winter whereas in some parts of Scandinavia and N. America straw or sacking protection is essential.

Late spring frosts which occur after growth has started are the most damaging of all. The danger signs are clear skies in the evening, a northerly wind which decreases at dusk and a settled dry period during the previous few days. The risk to a plant is reduced if there are overhanging branches above, other plants around, heavy soil below and the coast nearby.

In frost-prone areas avoid planting fruit trees and delicate shrubs. Provide some form of winter protection for choice specimens.

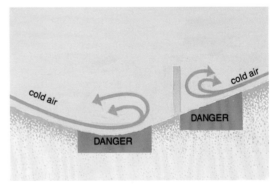

A frost pocket is an area which is abnormally prone to early autumn and late spring frosts. It occurs where there is a solid barrier on a sloping site — replace with an open barrier which allows air through. A frost pocket is also formed in the hollow at the bottom of a sloping site.

WIND

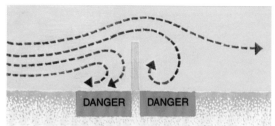

DANGER DANGER

The spectacular effects of a gale are well known — broken branches, knocked-over pots etc. But the effects of persistent winds are less well known — lop-sided development due to the death of buds on the windward side, and stunted growth due to the cooling and drying effect on the growing point. On exposed sites a windbreak may be necessary, but never use a solid screen. A wall or closed fence will create down-draughts on either side (see above) and plants will be harmed, but a hedge will gently reduce wind speed for a distance of 15-30 times its height.

RAINFALL

The average annual rainfall is 86 cm (34 in.) in England, 105 cm (41 in.) in the British Isles. Unlike some other areas of the globe there is no distinct rainy season, but October-January is usually the wettest period.

A drought is a period of 15 consecutive days without measurable rainfall, and droughts do occur at fairly regular intervals in Britain. Thorough watering is necessary at such times, otherwise plants will suffer or die. Snow is a mixed blessing — a blanket of snow can protect plants which would otherwise be damaged by arctic-like winds, but heavy snowfalls can damage or break the branches of evergreens.

ALTITUDE

The height of your garden has an effect on the general climate. For every 180 m (600 ft) increase in altitude, the average annual temperature falls by 1°C (2°F) and the start of the growing season is delayed by 3 days. Solar energy decreases whereas both rainfall and wind speed increase.

TEMPERATURE

- Temperatures of -12°C (10°F) occur occasionally during still, clear nights in winter — prolonged spells of abnormally cold weather can lead to the death of some plants normally regarded as hardy.

- High summer temperatures are necessary for the satisfactory ripening of tomatoes, sweet corn and many fruits which originated in warmer climates. Hot weather (27°C/80°F and above) has its drawbacks — soils dry out quickly, bloom life is shortened, transplanting is made difficult and the germination of some seeds (e.g lettuce) is impaired.

WINTER TROUBLES

Frost is a threat to the life of non-hardy plants — you must wait until the danger of frost is over before sowing or transplanting them. A hard frost can damage new growth on some hardy plants. Spraying frosted leaves with cold water in the morning will reduce the damage. Horticultural fleece is a godsend for preventing frost damage to susceptible plants. The worst effect of frost is seen in the fruit garden, especially when the frost is followed by an unusually mild spell. Once again horticultural fleece is the answer. In the flower garden use a mulch to cover the crowns of plants which are not completely hardy. The weight of snow on large conifer branches can cause them to break. After a heavy fall knock off snow from the branches with a cane.

Rain can be a problem. Some evergreen rockery plants are killed by persistent rain and not by frost. Use a sheet of glass on bricks to protect a choice specimen — use open-ended cloches if there are numerous plants.

SUMMER TROUBLES

Drought is the most serious summer problem. Regular watering of pots, hanging baskets and newly planted stock is a routine task during dry weather, but drought puts many more garden plants at risk. For many gardeners the answer is to rush around with a watering can or hosepipe, but watering is an art and can do more harm than good if not done properly. Read the Watering section on page XX, where you will also learn that the defence against drought should begin before summer arrives.

Heat stroke and scorching by the sun's rays are not general problems in the garden, but in summer your greenhouse can become a death trap for plants when the temperature stays over 30°-32°C/85°-90°F. In addition some plants such as begonia, African violet and gloxinia are scorched by summer sunshine. The ideal answer is to instal outside blinds — inside ones do not reduce the temperature in the house. Most people use some form of shading — use a shading paint which is wiped off in autumn.

CHAPTER 4

FLOWERS

Garden flowers range in size from tiny alpines peeping through the soil to man-sized giants in the border, but they all share three features. Firstly, they can all be grown outdoors during their flowering season. Some are too delicate to survive the frosts of winter, but all are sold for growing in the garden for all or part of the year. Secondly, garden flowers do not have a framework of permanent woody stems and finally all produce sufficient bloom to provide a noticeable display, although a few (e.g ajuga) are grown principally for their foliage. All these plants are divided into a number of major groups — see page 5.

Annuals and Biennials are used as bedding or container plants, and the usual practice is to plant out seedlings in the place where they are to flower. Some of the annuals are **Hardy annuals** which can withstand frosts, and so seeds may be sown outdoors whenever the soil is suitable. However, most people prefer to buy them as bedding plants for setting out in May. **Half-hardy annuals** cannot withstand frosts, and so they are treated as bedding plants — seedlings are raised under glass and set out in late May-early June. **Hardy biennials** are sown outdoors in summer for a floral display in the following season after which they die.

An enormous number of plants are classified as hardy perennials, and depending on their height are referred to as border or rockery perennials. These are plants which come up year after year, although the leaves and stems of most of them die in winter. To see **Border perennials** at their best look at a well-planned herbaceous border in midsummer, although these days a mixed border made up of perennials, bulbs, shrubs etc is preferred to a plot devoted entirely to border perennials. The **Rockery perennials** are dwarf hardy perennials which are suitable for growing in a rock garden — there is no more precise definition. Finally, there are the **Half-hardy perennials** which cannot withstand frost. Because of this lack of hardiness they have to spend winter indoors and then be returned to the garden once the danger of frost has passed. The way plants are overwintered varies — pelargoniums are kept under glass as green plants, dahlias are stored as tubers and chrysanthemums as roots.

Bulbs make up another large group and it is a pity that so many gardeners restrict themselves to a handful of favourites such as tulip, crocus and narcissus when there are varieties which can provide all-the-year-round colour. **Bog plants** make up the final group — non-woody flowering plants which need a constantly damp, humus-rich soil. And so on to the A-Z guide, where you will find some out-of-the-way plants as well as established favourites.

ACANTHUS
Bear's Breeches

Border
perennial

A. spinosus

Flower time: July—September
Location: Sun or light shade
Propagation: Divide clumps in autumn

A handsome plant grown for its flowers and foliage. The arching leaves are deeply divided. Good drought tolerance. Dislikes disturbance and heavy soil. Cut back to near-ground level when flowering is over. *A. spinosus* is the popular one — height 1.2 m (4 ft). *A. mollis* is taller with soft spines.

ACHILLEA
Yarrow

Border
perennial
•
Rockery
perennial

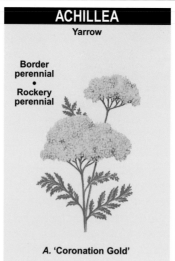

A. 'Coronation Gold'

Flower time: June—September
Location: Best in full sun
Propagation: Divide clumps in spring

Easy to recognise — flat plates of tiny flowers (usually yellow) above ferny foliage. Easy and not fussy about soil type. Good for cutting and drying. Stake tall varieties. The favourite border variety is *A. filipendula* 'Gold Plate' — height 1.2 m (4 ft). *A. tomentosa* is a rockery species.

AGAPANTHUS
African Lily

Border
perennial

A. 'Headbourne Hybrids'

Flower time: July—September
Location: Best in full sun
Propagation: Divide clumps in spring

Clusters of trumpet-shaped flowers appear on long stems above the strap-like leaves. Each flower is about 5 cm (2 in.) long and blue is the usual colour. The most popular types are the Headbourne hybrids — height 75 cm (2½ ft). Not fully hardy — cover crowns over winter.

AGERATUM
Floss Flower

Half-hardy
annual

A. houstonianum 'Blue Mink'

Flower time: June—October
Location: Sun or light shade
Propagation: Sow seeds in Feb-March

The small powderpuff flower heads have long been a familiar sight in floral bedding schemes, but it has lost its popularity. There are several colours available but blue and mauve remain the favourite ones. The problem with the white varieties is that they turn brown with age.

AJUGA
Bugle

Border
perennial

A. reptans 'Multicolor'

Flower time: April—June
Location: Sun or light shade
Propagation: Divide clumps in autumn

An easy-to-grow perennial which is planted for its evergreen colourful leaves rather than its heads of small flowers which are borne on short stalks in late spring. The brightest floral display is provided by *A. reptans* 'Alba' — height 15 cm (6 in.). Any reasonable soil will do.

ALCHEMILLA
Lady's Mantle

Border
perennial
•
Rockery
perennial

A. mollis

Flower time: June—August
Location: Sun or light shade
Propagation: Divide clumps in spring

A useful ground cover, producing clumps of lobed leaves and sprays of tiny greenish-yellow flowers. *A. mollis* is the one you will see in herbaceous borders — height 45 cm (1½ ft). After flowering cut down the plant to just above ground level. For the rockery there is *A. alpina* 15 cm (6 in.).

ALLIUM
Flowering Onion

Bulb
•
Border perennial

A. albopilosum

Flower time: May—July
Location: Best in full sun
Propagation: Divide clumps in autumn

The popular varieties belong to the Ball-headed group, bearing clusters of tightly-packed flowers on upright stalks. For really large heads measuring 20 cm (8 in.) across grow *A. albopilosum*. The Tufted alliums are smaller with loose flower clusters. Alliums are sold as bulbs or growing plants.

ALTHAEA
Hollyhock

Border perennial
•
Hardy annual or biennial

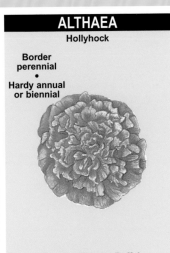

A. rosea 'Powder Puffs'

Flower time: July—September
Location: Sunny sheltered site
Propagation: Sow annuals in Feb

The tall spires are a familiar sight in herbaceous borders — Hollyhocks are still grown by some gardeners as perennials. The problem is that rust disease weakens the plant and after a couple of years it becomes a sorry sight, so grow it as an annual or biennial. Height 75-180 cm (2½-6 ft).

ALYSSUM
Sweet Alyssum

Hardy annual

A. maritimum 'Rosie O'Day'

Flower time: June—September
Location: Best in full sun
Propagation: Sow under glass in Feb

The traditional partner for Lobelia to provide a white and blue edging around flower beds. Nowadays there are pink, red and purple varieties of the basic species *A. maritimum* providing dwarf cushions which are covered with tiny blooms. Avoid rich soil and trim off dead blooms. Water copiously in dry weather.

ALYSSUM
Alyssum

Rockery perennial

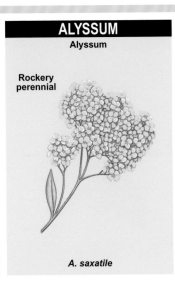

A. saxatile

Flower time: April—June
Location: Best in full sun
Propagation: Cuttings under glass in June

You will find *A. saxatile* (Gold dust) growing in rockeries everywhere. In spring the large heads of tiny flowers cover the grey foliage which persists year round. A fine splash of colour, but it can spread rapidly. It grows 20 cm (8 in.) high — *A. montanum* is an excellent 15 cm (6 in.) miniature.

Raised flower beds were once an unusual feature but are now becoming more popular as people realise the advantages they bring to the garden. Drainage is improved in heavy soil, the plants are brought closer to the eye which is important with small plants such as alpines, and closer to the hand which makes weeding, planting, dead-heading etc much easier. Finally, a third dimension is added to flat sites.

AMARANTHUS
Love-lies-bleeding

Half-hardy annual

A. caudatus

Flower time: July—October
Location: Best in full sun
Propagation: Sow under glass in Feb

A plant for a large container or as the centrepiece in a formal bedding scheme. In summer 45 cm (1½ ft) long tassels of tiny blooms are an eye-catching feature. Water regularly during dry spells and support the stems if the site is exposed. Any well-drained non-acid soil will do.

ANCHUSA
Alkanet

Border perennial

A. azurea 'Loddon Royalist'

Flower time: June—August
Location: Best in full sun
Propagation: Divide clumps in spring

The perennial anchusa is not an attractive plant — the straggly branches need support, the large leaves are coarse and it is short-lived. Few flowers, however, can match the vivid blue of anchusa in the border. The most popular variety is *A. azurea* 'Loddon Royalist' — height 90 cm (3 ft).

ANEMONE
Anemone

Bulb

A. coronaria 'de Caen strain'

Flower time: March—April
Location: Sun or light shade
Propagation: Divide clumps in summer

The bulb varieties are grown from rhizomes or tubers. Daisy anemones have a yellow disc and narrow petals — the popular one is *A. blanda* — height 15 cm (6 in.). Florist anemones have poppy-like single or double flowers. The usual ones are varieties of *A. coronaria* — height 15-30 cm (6-12 in.).

ANEMONE
Japanese Anemone

Border perennial

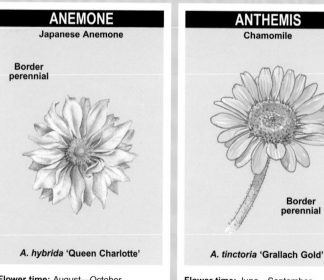

A. hybrida 'Queen Charlotte'

Flower time: August—October
Location: Sun or light shade
Propagation: Plant rooted sections

Unlike the low-growing bulb anemones these are tall-growing border perennials which produce white or pink 5 cm (2 in.) wide blooms. The leaves are deeply lobed. The usual choice is a variety of *A. hybrida* — height 90 cm-1.5 m (3-5 ft). Cover crowns with mulch in winter.

ANTHEMIS
Chamomile

Border perennial

A. tinctoria 'Grallach Gold'

Flower time: June—September
Location: Best in full sun
Propagation: Divide clumps in autumn

A bright plant for the front of the border. The foliage is finely-divided and the daisy-like flowers appear intermittently all summer long. Each bloom has a central golden disc and the petals are white or yellow. *A. tinctoria* is the Golden marguerite — height 60 cm (2 ft).

ANTIRRHINUM
Snapdragon

Half-hardy annual

A. 'Rembrandt'

Flower time: June—October
Location: Best in full sun
Propagation: Sow under glass in Feb

The ordinary snapdragon is known to everyone — 45 cm (1½ ft) upright stems with spikes of lipped tubular flowers which open when squeezed. Nowadays there are all sorts of variations, including dwarfs and open-faced types. Pinch out tips when the plants are about 8 cm (3 in.) high.

AQUILEGIA
Columbine

Border perennial
•
Rockery perennial

A. 'McKana Hybrids'

Flower time: May—June
Location: Best in partial shade
Propagation: Sow seeds in April

A. vulgaris has been grown in cottage gardens for centuries and has white or blue short-spurred flowers. These days there is a wide range of brightly-coloured long-spurred varieties, and there are also dwarf rockery species. The most popular aquilegias are the McKana hybrids.

ARABIS
Rock Cress

Rockery perennial

A. albida

Flower time: March—April
Location: Sun or light shade
Propagation: Divide clumps in autumn

A basic component of most rockeries — the grey-leaved carpet is covered with flowers in the spring. The usual one is *A. albida* — height 25 cm (10 in.), spread 60 cm (2 ft) with white flowers. For large double blooms look for the variety 'Flore Pleno'. Pink and red types are available.

ARMERIA
Thrift

Rockery perennial
•
Border perennial

A. maritima

Flower time: May—July
Location: Best in full sun
Propagation: Divide clumps in spring

The grassy leaves are packed into neat mounds and are a common sight in rock gardens and around the seashore. The flower stalks bear globular heads of papery blooms. The native thrift is A. maritima — height 20 cm (8 in.), spread 30 cm (1 ft). There are pink, red and white varieties.

ARUNCUS
Goat's Beard

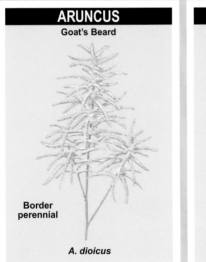

Border perennial

A. dioicus

Flower time: June—July
Location: Needs partial shade
Propagation: Divide clumps in autumn

A. dioicus is a tall, impressive plant, reaching a height of 1.8 m (6 ft). Feathery plumes of tiny cream flowers tower above the sprays of pale green leaves. For most gardens a more compact type is preferable — look for *A. d. 'Glasnevin'* — 1.2 m (4 ft) or *A. aethusifolius* — 30 cm (1 ft).

ASTER
Michaelmas Daisy

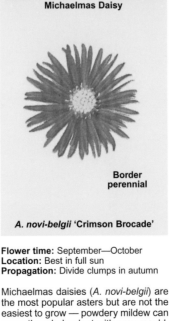

Border perennial

A. novi-belgii 'Crimson Brocade'

Flower time: September—October
Location: Best in full sun
Propagation: Divide clumps in autumn

Michaelmas daisies (*A. novi-belgii*) are the most popular asters but are not the easiest to grow — powdery mildew can cover the whole plant with grey mould. The usual height is 60-90 cm (2-3 ft). The New England aster (*A. novae-angliae*) group are similar but have good mildew resistance.

ASTILBE
Astilbe

Border perennial
•
Rockery perennial

A. 'Bressingham Beauty'

Flower time: June—August
Location: Best in light shade
Propagation: Divide clumps in autumn

Tiny flowers are borne in showy plumes — the foliage is deeply cut and often coppery in spring. A large number of hybrids in a variety of colours are available in the 30-90 cm (1-3 ft) range. Moist, humus-rich soil is necessary. There are several dwarf hybrids — height 15 cm (6 in.) for the rockery.

AUBRETIA
Aubretia

Rockery perennial

A. deltoidea

Flower time: March—June
Location: Best in full sun
Propagation: Divide clumps in autumn

The most widely grown of all rockery plants. The grey-green downy leaves are covered with masses of flowers in spring. *A. deltoidea* is the basic species — height 8-12 cm (3-5 in.), spread 60 cm (2 ft), but this form is not grown. It has produced many garden varieties in pale purple, pink, red or blue.

BEGONIA
Tuberous-rooted Begonia

Bulb

B. tuberhybrida

Flower time: June—September
Location: Best in light shade
Propagation: Plant sprouted tubers

The best known plant in this group is the large-flowered *B. tuberhybrida* with 5-15 cm (2-6 in.) wide rose-like blooms. *B. multiflora* — height 20 cm (8 in.) bears masses of smaller flowers. *B. pendula* — length 30-60 cm (1-2 ft) is the one to choose for hanging baskets. Water thoroughly in dry weather.

BEGONIA
Bedding Begonia

Half-hardy annual

B. semperflorens

Flower time: June—October
Location: Best in light shade
Propagation: Plant plugs or seedlings

A bedding plant to grow where most others would fail, in beds or containers which are in shade for most of the day. The fleshy leaves are in shades ranging from pale green to chocolate brown. There are many varieties of *B. semperflorens*, from 10 cm (4 in.) dwarfs to 30 cm (1 ft) giants.

BELLIS
Daisy

Hardy annual

B. perennis

Flower time: June—August
Location: Sun or light shade
Propagation: Sow seeds in May

The familiar daisy on the lawn has given rise to a large number of garden varieties. The basic species is *B. perennis* — height 8-20 cm (3-8 in.) and the garden varieties are generally doubles in which the central yellow disc is absent. Usually grown as a biennial — plant out in autumn.

BERGENIA
Elephant's Ear

Border perennial

B. cordifolia

Flower time: March—April
Location: Sun or partial shade
Propagation: Divide clumps in autumn

This ground cover thrives under trees, spreads rapidly, keeps down weeds and provides leaf colour all year round. In spring there are hyacinth-like flowers. The type species is *B. cordifolia* — height 45 cm (1½ ft) — choose one of the white, pink or red hybrids. Remove dead leaves in spring.

BIDENS
Bidens

Half-hardy annual

B. ferulifolia 'Golden Goddess'

Flower time: June—October
Location: Sun or light shade
Propagation: Sow under glass in Feb

A bedding plant introduced in the 1990s which has lived up to its promise. It grows vigorously and the ferny-leaved spreading stems are studded with large yellow flowers. The basic type is *B. ferulifolia* 'Golden Goddess' — stem length 45-60 cm (1½-2 ft). Use as ground cover or in hanging baskets.

CALENDULA
Pot Marigold

Half-hardy annual *(on Callistephus)*

Hardy annual

C. officinalis 'Orange King'

Flower time: June—September
Location: Sun or partial shade
Propagation: Sow under glass in Feb

It may be old fashioned but this bedding plant is easy to grow, does not mind poor soil and does not need a sunny site. There are many varieties of the basic species *C. officinalis* — height 22-60 cm (9 in.-2 ft). The colours range from cream to mahogany. Pinch out tips of young stems.

CALLISTEPHUS
China Aster

Half-hardy annual

C. chinensis 'Ostrich Plume'

Flower time: July—October
Location: Best in full sun
Propagation: Sow under glass in Feb

The basic species is *C. chinensis*. You will find a wide range of varieties in the seed catalogues — giants and dwarfs, singles and doubles, whites to near-blacks. The chrysanthemum-like flowers are of various types — incurved, plumed, ball-like and pompons.

CAMPANULA
Bedding Campanula

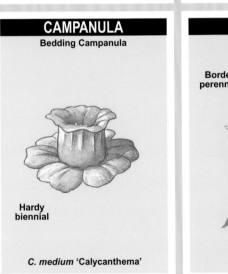

Hardy biennial

C. medium 'Calycanthema'

Flower time: May—July
Location: Sun or light shade
Propagation: Sow seeds in May-June

The most popular one is *C. medium* (Canterbury bell) — single, semi-double or double in colours ranging from white to purple. 'Calycanthema' (Cup and saucer) is the old favourite — height 45 cm (1¹/₂ ft). For single flowers choose 'Bells of Holland'. The giant is *C. pyramidalis* — height 1.8 m (6 ft).

CAMPANULA
Border Campanula

Border perennial

C. latifolia

Flower time: June—August
Location: Sun or light shade
Propagation: Divide clumps in spring

You will find examples of this bell- or starry-flowered group for the front, middle and back of the border. There are *C. lactiflora* 'Loddon Anna' — height 30 cm (1 ft), *C. persicifolia* — height 60-90 cm (2-3 ft) and *C. latifolia* — height 1.2-1.5 m (4-5 ft). The usual colours are blue and lavender. Watch out for slugs.

BORDER PERENNIALS FOR SHADY SITES

Alchemilla mollis
Anemone japonica
Aquilegia hybrids
Astilbe species
Bergenia species
Dicentra spectabilis
Digitalis species
Doronicum excelsum
Euphorbia species
Helleborus species
Hosta species
Monarda hybrids
Polygonum affine
Ranunculus species
Saxifraga urbium
Tradescantia andersoniana
Viola species

BEDDING PLANTS FOR DRY, SUNNY SITES

Alyssum
Calendula
Eschscholzia
Helichrysum
Mesembryanthemum
Petunia
Phlox
Salvia
Tagetes
Tropaeolum
Zinnia

FLOWERS TO ATTRACT WILDLIFE

Alyssum ....Bu
Aster ....Bi, Bu
Aubretia ....Bu
Calendula ....Bu
Centaurea ....Bi
Chrysanthemum ......Bu
Dianthus ....Bu
Echinacea ....Bu
Echinops ....Bi
Helianthus.................Bi
Helichrysum ....Bu
Iberis ....Bu
Muscari ....Bu
Myosotis ....Bi, Bu
Papaver.....................Bi
Scabiosa ....Bu
Solidago ....Bi

KEY: Bi — Birds   Bu — Butterflies

CANNA
Canna Lily

Bulb

C. generalis

Flower time: July—October
Location: Sunny sheltered site
Propagation: Cut up sprouted rhizomes

A canna in flower provides an eye-catching focal point for the centre of a bedding plant display. The bright blooms are up to 10 cm (4 in.) across and the paddle-shaped leaves are often coloured. *C. generalis* — height 60 cm-1.2 m (2-4 ft) has produced many varieties. Plant rhizomes in June.

CENTAUREA
Cornflower

Hardy annual

C. cyanurus

Flower time: June—September
Location: Sun or light shade
Propagation: Sow seeds in April

The thistle-like flower heads of this old favourite attract bees and butterflies — blue is the usual colour but shades from white to maroon are available. *C. cyanurus* — height 30-90 cm (1-3 ft) is the usual species, an easy plant to grow which is usually sown where it is to flower.

CENTRANTHUS
Red Valerian

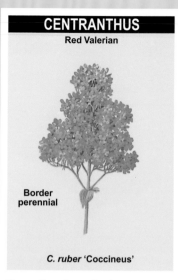

Border perennial

C. ruber 'Coccineus'

Flower time: June—October
Location: Best in full sun
Propagation: Sow under glass in March

A fine cottage garden plant — you will find it growing on old walls and in stony ground. *C. ruber* — height 45 cm (1½ ft) has pink flowers, but there are red and pink varieties. The plants are short-lived but nearby self-sown seedlings are generally abundant. Not a good choice if drainage is poor.

CERASTIUM
Snow-in-summer

Rockery perennial

C. tomentosum

Flower time: May—July
Location: Best in full sun
Propagation: Divide clumps in spring

A popular rockery plant which has few friends among the experts — the silvery-leaved sheets which flower in early summer can quickly spread and choke out nearby delicate plants. *C. tomentosum* — height 10 cm (4 in.) is the usual one. *C. alpinum* is more restrained but less free-flowering.

CHEIRANTHUS
Wallflower

Hardy biennial

C. cheiri 'Vulcan'

Flower time: Spring
Location: Best in full sun
Propagation: Sow seeds in May

Millions are planted out every October. Wallflowers (*C. cheiri*) — height 20-60 cm (8 in.-2 ft) flower in March-April, Siberian wallflowers (*C. allionii*) — height 30 cm (1 ft) flower in May-June. Yellow, orange and red are the basic colours. Pinch out tips of seedlings before planting.

CHIONODOXA
Glory of the Snow

Bulb

C. sardensis

Flower time: February—April
Location: Sun or light shade
Propagation: Divide clumps in May

A popular spring-flowering bulb, but not a universal favourite like crocuses and snowdrops. The six-petalled flowers are borne in dainty sprays above the strap-like foliage. *C. luciliae* is the usual one — height 15-25 cm (6-10 in.) with white-eyed blue flowers. *C. sardensis* has a blue flower with a tiny white eye.

CHRYSANTHEMUM
Annual Chrysanthemum

Hardy
annual

C. carinatum 'Court Jesters'

Flower time: June—July
Location: Best in full sun
Propagation: Sow seeds in April

A small group of chrysanthemums are easily-grown hardy annuals which are sown in spring where they are to flower. *C. carinatum* — height 60 cm (2 ft) is the Painted daisy with banded petals. *C. coronarium* — height 30-90 cm (1-3 ft) is the yellow-flowered Crown daisy.

CHRYSANTHEMUM
Garden Chrysanthemum

Border
perennial

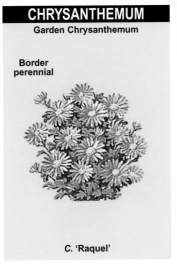

C. 'Raquel'

Flower time: Generally Sept—Oct
Location: Best in full sun
Propagation: Divide clumps in spring

These small-flowered chrysanthemums are hardy, but cut down and cover crowns with a mulch in autumn. There are the Korean hybrids — height 60-90 cm (2-3 ft), the Rubellum hybrids — height 90 cm (3 ft) and finally the Cushion mums which produce leafy mounds 45 cm (1½ ft) high.

CHRYSANTHEMUM
Florist Chrysanthemum

Half-hardy
perennial

C. 'Fairweather'

Flower time: September—October
Location: Sun or light shade
Propagation: Plant cuttings in late May

Here are the best-known and the showiest chrysanthemums — decorative types for cutting and the smaller-flowered ones for garden display. Called Dendranthema by botanists, but still Chrysanthemum in the catalogues. Lift and store rootstocks over winter — take cuttings in February-April.

CLARKIA
Clarkia

Hardy
annual

C. elegans

Flower time: June—September
Location: Best in full sun
Propagation: Sow seeds in April

Small, hollyhock-like flowers are borne on upright spikes — it is available in white, pink, red or mauve. An easy plant, but where possible it should be sown where it is to grow. Pinch out the growing tips of seedlings. *C. elegans* — height 30-60 cm (1-2 ft) is the basic species.

COBAEA
Cup & Saucer Plant

Half-hardy
annual

C. scandens

Flower time: July—October
Location: Best in full sun
Propagation: Sow under glass in Feb

The stems of this climber attach themselves to supports by means of tendrils borne by the leaf stalks. Useful where a quick-growing but temporary screen is needed. *C. scandens* — height 3 m (10 ft) is the only species — bell-like 8 cm (3 in.) long flowers appear all summer long.

COLCHICUM
Autumn Crocus

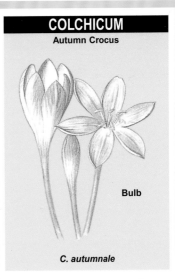

Bulb

C. autumnale

Flower time: September—November
Location: Sun or light shade
Propagation: Divide clumps in July

Surprisingly this bulb is not related to the true crocus. In autumn the long tubes at the base of the petals extend down into the ground. *C. autumnale* — height 15 cm (6 in.) bears lilac flowers. There are also numerous varieties with double flowers and colours ranging from white to violet.

CONVALLARIA
Lily of the Valley

Bulb

C. majalis

Flower time: April—May
Location: Best in partial shade
Propagation: Divide clumps in October

Dainty bells on arching stems appear at the same time as the lance-shaped leaves — an excellent choice for spring-flowered ground cover in shady areas. *C. majalis* — height 25 cm (10 in.) has many varieties. 'Prolificans' has double flowers, 'Rosea' has pink flowers and 'Albostriata' blooms have green stripes.

CONVOLVULUS
Convolvulus

Hardy annual

C. tricolor 'Royal Ensign'

Flower time: July—September
Location: Best in full sun
Propagation: Sow under glass in March

A bushy plant, unlike its close relative the common bindweed. *C. tricolor* — height 30 cm (1 ft) is the popular species, but a mixture of varieties is usually offered. Yellow-hearted 5 cm (2 in.) wide trumpets are borne all summer long, but each flower lasts for only a day.

COREOPSIS
Tickweed

Border perennial

C. verticillata

Flower time: July—October
Location: Best in full sun
Propagation: Divide clumps in spring

Yellow flowers are borne in profusion on slender stems — an excellent choice if flower arranging is an interest. *C. verticillata* — height 60 cm (2 ft) and its varieties are the popular choice. 'Grandiflora' is a larger-flowered type — 'Moonbeam' is lemon-yellow. *C. rosea* 'American Dream' has pink blooms.

CORTADERIA
Pampas Grass

Border perennial

C. selloana

Flower time: August—October
Location: Sun or light shade
Propagation: Divide clumps in spring

The only grass grown for its floral display rather than its foliage. The silvery silky plumes are about 45 cm (1½ ft) long — female plants produce the best flower heads. *C. selloana* — height 1.8 m (6 ft) is the basic species. Choose 'Sunningdale Silver' for the tallest plants and largest plumes.

COSMOS
Cosmea

Half-hardy annual

C. bipinnatus 'Sensation'

Flower time: July—October
Location: Best in full sun
Propagation: Sow under glass in March

A popular bedding plant which is easy to recognise — single dahlia-like flowers are carried on slender stems above ferny foliage. Thrives best in poor sandy soil. *C. bipinnatus* — height 90 cm (3 ft) is the basic species and has many varieties. 'Hot Chocolate' petals look and smell like chocolate.

CROCOSMIA
Montbretia

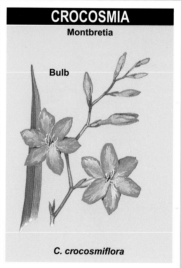

Bulb

C. crocosmiflora

Flower time: July—August
Location: Best in full sun
Propagation: Divide clumps in autumn

A plant to grow for flower arranging and for colour in the border. Arching stems carry tubular or starry flowers above sword-like leaves. *C. crocosmiflora* — height 60 cm (2 ft) has produced numerous hybrids. Red-flowered 'Lucifer' is hardy, but some like the yellow 'Solfaterre' are semi-tender.

CROCUS
Crocus

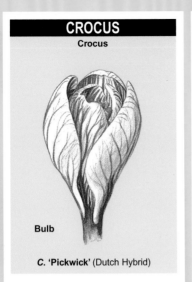

Bulb

C. **'Pickwick'** (Dutch Hybrid)

Flower time: Depends on variety
Location: Sun or light shade
Propagation: Divide clumps in autumn

There are four groups of this ever-popular bulb. Dutch hybrids with the largest flowers (March-April), Chrysanthus hybrids with medium-sized flowers (Feb-March), Spring-flowering species with small flowers (Jan-Feb) and Autumn-flowering species with small flowers (Sept-Dec).

DAHLIA
Garden Dahlia

Half-hardy perennial

D. **'Athalie'**

Flower time: July—October
Location: Sun or light shade
Propagation: Divide tubers in May

The Border varieties are the stars, ranging in height from 60 cm (2 ft) to over 1.2 m (4 ft). For rockeries and containers there are the Bedding and Lilliput varieties which are compact with small flowers. Plant rooted cuttings or sprouted tubers after the danger of frost has passed.

DAHLIA
Annual Dahlia

Half-hardy annual

D. **'Dandy'**

Flower time: July—October
Location: Sun or light shade
Propagation: Sow under glass in March

The knee-high Annual dahlias should not be regarded as poor relations of the Garden dahlias in the border. They are bright and long-lasting with single, double or collarette flowers (*D.* 'Dandy'). Heights range from 30 cm (1 ft) to 60 cm (2 ft). Dig in organic matter before planting.

DELPHINIUM
Delphinium

Half-hardy perennial

D. elatum (Elatum Group)

Flower time: June—July
Location: Best in full sun
Propagation: Divide clumps in spring

One of the most impressive plants in the border, but not the easiest to grow. Well-drained soil, staking and watering in dry weather are all necessary. The Elatum group have the classical-shaped blooms on 90 cm-1.8 m (3-6 ft) stems. The Belladonna group have widely-spaced cupped blooms.

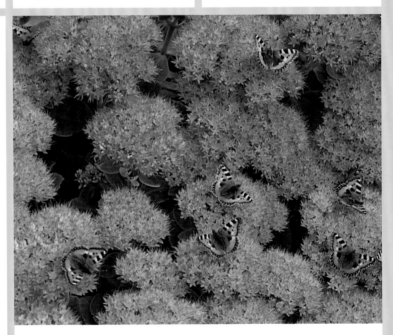

Some bedding plants and border perennials are particularly sought after by butterflies which are attracted by the nectar of the flowers. In the photograph small Tortoiseshells flutter over the blooms of Sedum spectabile — other 'butterfly flowers' include Alyssum saxatile, Aster, Aubretia, Calendula, Centranthus, Dianthus barbatus, Iberis, Muscari, Myosotis, Phlox, Polyanthus and Scabiosa.

DIANTHUS
Sweet William

Hardy biennial

D. barbatus

Flower time: May—July
Location: Best in full sun
Propagation: Sow seeds in June

Sweet william has densely-packed flattened heads of pink-like flowers — it bridges the gap between the spring- and the traditional summer-flowering bedding plants. *D. barbatus* — height 15-45 cm (6 in.-1½ ft) is the basic species. Choose 'Auricula-eyed Mixed' for tall plants with bicoloured flowers.

DIANTHUS
Annual Carnation, Indian Pink

Half-hardy annual

D. caryophyllus Hybrid
(Border Carnation)

Flower time: July—October
Location: Best in full sun
Propagation: Sow under glass in Feb

There are two groups of annuals grown from seed. Annual carnations are hybrids of *D. caryophyllus* — height 30-45 cm (1-1½ ft). The flowers are double. For single flowers with shorter stems grow Indian pinks. These plants are hybrids of *D. chinensis* with 4 cm (1½ in.) wide flowers.

DIANTHUS
Perennial Carnation, Pink

Border perennial
•
Rockery perennial

D. caryophyllus Hybrid
(Border Carnation)

Flower time: Depends on variety
Location: Best in full sun
Propagation: Cuttings under glass in July

A large and varied group. Border carnations — height 60-90 cm (2-3 ft) are July-August flowering hybrids of *D. caryophyllus*. Old-fashioned pinks (June) have smaller flowers and more delicate stems, Modern pinks flower in summer and in autumn, and finally there are the Rockery carnations.

DICENTRA
Bleeding Heart

Border perennial

D. spectabilis

Flower time: May—June
Location: Best in partial shade
Propagation: Divide clumps in spring

Arching stems above ferny leaves bear locket-shaped flowers. *Dicentra* needs a sheltered spot as the young leaves can be damaged by cold winds — it will grow quite happily under trees. The popular choice is *D. spectabilis* — height 60 cm (2 ft), but the hybrids of *D. eximia* are a better choice.

DIGITALIS
Foxglove

Hardy biennial
•
Border perennial

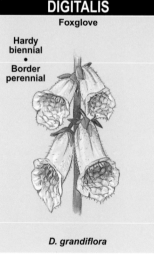

D. grandiflora

Flower time: June—July
Location: Best in partial shade
Propagation: Sow seeds or divide clumps

The tall spikes of flowers will brighten shady borders or woodland areas — not many tall bedding plants can be used in this way. *D. purpurea* — height 1.2-1.5 m (4-5 ft) is the basic species grown as a biennial — choose one of the named hybrids. *D. grandiflora* is the most popular perennial species.

DORONICUM
Leopard's Bane

Border perennial

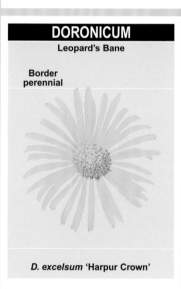

D. excelsum 'Harpur Crown'

Flower time: April—June
Location: Sun or partial shade
Propagation: Divide clumps in autumn

There are many yellow daisy-like flowers for the border — pick this one if you want blooms in spring. In many borders Doronicum provides the first splash of colour of the year. *D. excelsum* 'Harpur Crown' — height 90 cm (3 ft) with 8 cm (3 in.) wide flowers is a popular choice.

ECHINACEA
Coneflower

Border
perennial

E. purpurea 'The King'

Flower time: July—October
Location: Best in full sun
Propagation: Divide clumps in spring

The outstanding feature of this late-flowering border perennial is the prominent cone-like disc at the centre of each bloom with a ring of bent-back petals below it. The popular species is *E. purpurea* — height 90 cm-1.5 m (3-5 ft). The variety 'White Swan' has a yellow cone and white petals.

ECHINOPS
Globe Thistle

Border
perennial

E. ritro

Flower time: July—September
Location: Best in full sun
Propagation: Divide clumps in autumn

An erect plant for the middle or back of the border. The flower heads are globular and the stout stems have deeply-lobed leaves. Wear gloves when handling. Does not do well in shade or shallow soil. The usual choice is *E. ritro* — height 1.5 m (5 ft). There are pale- and dark-blue varieties.

ERANTHIS
Winter Aconite

Bulb

E. hyemalis

Flower time: February—March
Location: Sun or partial shade
Propagation: Divide clumps in June

Glossy yellow flowers begin to appear in late winter — each bloom bears a frilly green collar. The leaves appear later. The most popular species is *E. hyemalis* — height 10 cm (4 in.), self-sown plants can be a nuisance. *E. tubergenii* may be a better choice — it is more robust and is less invasive.

ERIGERON
Fleabane

Border perennial
•
Rockery perennial

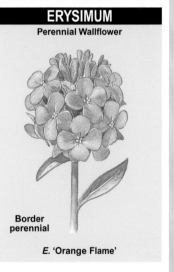

E. 'Foerster's Liebling'

Flower time: June—August
Location: Best in full sun
Propagation: Divide clumps in spring

This cottage garden plant looks like a small Michaelmas daisy, but the petals are more numerous and it blooms earlier. There are tall ones for the border, such as the pink *E.* 'Foerster's Liebling' — height 60 cm (2 ft), and dwarfs for the rockery such as the yellow-flowered *E. aureus*.

ERYNGIUM
Sea Holly

Border
perennial

E. oliverianum

Flower time: July—September
Location: Best in full sun
Propagation: Divide clumps in spring

Easy to recognise — thistle-like leaves form a rosette and thimble-shaped flower heads with an intricately-spined ruff are borne on branching stems. Flowers last for months. The evergreen *E. planum* — height 90 cm (3 ft) is popular and so is *E. varifolium* which has white-veined leaves.

ERYSIMUM
Perennial Wallflower

Border
perennial

E. 'Orange Flame'

Flower time: Depends on variety
Location: Best in full sun
Propagation: Cuttings under glass in May

Unlike its better known relative this plant stays in bloom for many months. An easy plant for the border but unfortunately it is not long-lived. The most popular variety is *E.* 'Bowles Mauve' — height 75 cm (2½ ft), bushy and evergreen with flowers nearly all year round. *E.* 'Orange Flame' is a dwarf variety.

ESCHSCHOLZIA
Californian Poppy

Hardy annual

E. californica

Flower time: June—September
Location: Best in full sun
Propagation: Sow seeds in April

A sprinkling of seed over bare ground in spring produces a summer-long show of silky-petalled flowers. It dislikes transplanting and rich soil. The basic species is *E. californica* — height 30 cm (1 ft). This yellow-flowered species is the parent of many colourful varieties such as 'Alba', 'Dalli' (red/yellow) etc.

EUPHORBIA
Spurge

Border perennial
•
Rockery perennial

E. marginata

Flower time: April—May
Location: Sun or partial shade
Propagation: Divide clumps in autumn

The true flowers are insignificant — the floral display comes from the petal-like bracts. There is a wide range of varieties — you can pick colourful leaves, bright flower heads or types with evergreen foliage on plants ranging from 10 cm to 1.5 m (4 in.-5 ft). Some varieties are invasive.

FRITILLARIA
Fritillary

Bulb

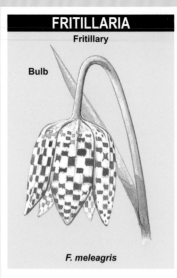

F. meleagris

Flower time: April—May
Location: Best in full sun
Propagation: Divide clumps in summer

Bell-like flowers generally hang down from the top of upright stems. There are two distinct types. *F. meleagris* — height 30 cm (1 ft) is the Snake's head fritillary with 1-2 flowers per stem; the stately *F. imperialis* — height 75 cm (2¹/₂ ft) is the Crown imperial with multi-flowered stems.

FUCHSIA
Bedding Fuchsia

Half-hardy perennial
•
Half-hardy annual

F. 'Swingtime'

Flower time: July—October
Location: Sun or light shade
Propagation: Cuttings under glass in July

Bedding fuchsias are raised from seeds or cuttings and are planted out when the danger of frost has passed — they are lifted and potted up for bringing indoors in October. There are hundreds of varieties of *F. hybrida* — height 30-60 cm (1-2 ft). Trailing types for hanging baskets are available.

FUCHSIA
Border Fuchsia

Border perennial

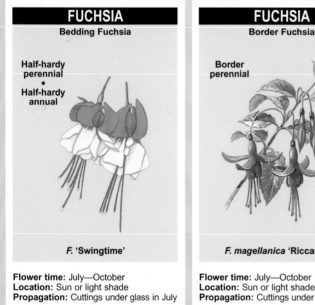

F. magellanica 'Riccartonii'

Flower time: July—October
Location: Sun or light shade
Propagation: Cuttings under glass in July

The plants in this group are hardy, producing graceful branches with pendent flowers year after year. These stems are killed by frost — in the mildest areas the woody stems are permanent so a flowering shrub is produced. The most popular species is *F. magellanica* — height 1.2 m (4 ft).

GAILLARDIA
Blanket Flower

Border perennial

G. 'Wirral Flame'

Flower time: June—September
Location: Best in full sun
Propagation: Divide clumps in spring

The large 5-10 cm (2-4 in.) blooms continue to appear from early summer to autumn. Colourful, but a poor choice if drainage is a problem. The usual type is one of the hybrids of *G. grandiflora* — height 30-90 cm (1-3 ft), producing yellow-tipped red or orange flowers. Divide the clumps every few years.

GALANTHUS
Snowdrop

Bulb

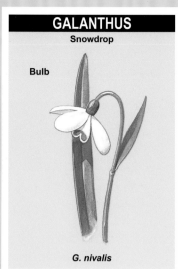

G. nivalis

Flower time: January—March
Location: Sun or light shade
Propagation: Divide clumps in spring

The curtain-raiser of the gardening year — small white flowers hanging on 15 cm (6 in.) stems. *G. nivalis* is the common snowdrop — for double blooms choose the variety 'Flore Pleno' or 'Ophelia'. 'Lutescens' is yellow-marked white and 'S. Arnott' has scented flowers.

GAZANIA
Gazania

Half-hardy annual

G. 'Harlequin'

Flower time: July—October
Location: Full sun
Propagation: Sow under glass in Feb

Each large daisy-like flower bears petals which arch backwards to reveal a central dark ring around the disc. The flowers close in dull weather. *G. hybrida* is usually bought as a multicoloured mixture of varieties — height 20-45 cm (8 in.-1½ ft). 'Sundance' has the largest blooms — 'Mini-Star' is a dwarf variety.

GENTIANA
Gentian

Rockery perennial

G. acaulis

Flower time: Depends on variety
Location: Sun or light shade
Propagation: Divide clumps in summer

A very variable genus. There are spring-, summer- and winter-flowering varieties, easy-to-grow ones and temperamental types, and there are lime-lovers and lime-haters. Beautiful blue trumpets in the rockery, but read the label before purchase. *G. septemfida* is the easiest to grow.

GERANIUM
Crane's Bill

Border perennial
●
Rockery perennial

G. psilostemon

Flower time: July—September
Location: Depends on variety
Propagation: Divide clumps in autumn

Do not confuse it with Pelargonium — the common 'geranium'. This one is an excellent easy-to-grow and drought-tolerant ground cover. Some but not all are evergreen. There are a few tall ones reaching 90 cm (3 ft) but most are in the medium 30-60 cm (1-2 ft) range. *G. cinereum* is a rockery dwarf.

GEUM
Avens

Border perennial

G. 'Lady Stratheden'

Flower time: May—August
Location: Best in full sun
Propagation: Divide clumps in autumn

The popular types form dense clumps at the front of the border — in early summer the yellow, orange or red bowl-shaped flowers appear. *G. chiloense* — height 30-60 cm (1-2 ft) is the basic species and the favourite varieties are 'Mrs J. Bradshaw' (scarlet) and 'Lady Stratheden' (yellow).

GLADIOLUS
Sword Lily

Bulb

G. 'Flower Song'
(Large-flowered Hybrid)

Flower time: July—September
Location: Best in full sun
Propagation: Use cormlets after lifting

There are many types, with heights ranging from 30 cm to 1.2 m (1-4 ft). The Large-flowered hybrids are by far the most popular group — plant corms in spring and lift in October for indoor storage. There are also Primulinus hybrids, Butterfly hybrids and 45-60 cm (1½-2 ft) Miniature hybrids.

GODETIA
Godetia

Hardy annual

G. 'Sybil Sherwood'

Flower time: July—September
Location: Best in full sun
Propagation: Sow seeds in March

Once a favourite bedding plant, but it does not like transplanting and has lost much of its appeal. Large flowers with fluted papery petals are borne freely on upright leafy stalks. The basic species is *G. grandiflora* — height 20-60 cm (8 in.-2 ft). Usually sold as a mixture of varieties.

GYPSOPHILA
Baby's Breath

Border perennial
•
Rockery perennial

G. paniculata 'Bristol Fairy'

Flower time: July—August
Location: Best in full sun
Propagation: Cuttings under glass in June

A welcome relief from the large-flowered plants in the border. A billowy cloud of tiny white or pink flowers appears on thin stems above grey-green grassy leaves. The border species is *G. paniculata* — height 90 cm (3 ft), 'Bristol Fairy' is the usual choice. *G. repens* is a rockery species.

HELENIUM
Sneezewort

Border perennial

H. 'Butterpat'

Flower time: July—September
Location: Sun or light shade
Propagation: Divide clumps in spring

An important source of reds and yellows in the late summer herbaceous border. The daisy-like flowers have a prominent central disc — unlike *Rudbeckia* the petals are notched. There are many varieties of *H. autumnale*. The copper-red 'Moerheim Beauty' — height 90 cm (3 ft) is the popular one.

HELIANTHEMUM
Rock Rose

Rockery perennial

H. 'Ben Hope'

Flower time: May—July
Location: Best in full sun
Propagation: Cuttings under glass in June

One of the best perennials for providing a low-growing sheet of long-lasting colour in summer. Each bloom lasts for only a day or two, but new ones are borne in profusion. Cut back after the first flush. The popular hybrids of *H. nummularium* reach about 20 cm (8 in.). There are 10 cm (4 in.) dwarfs.

HELIANTHUS
Sunflower

Hardy annual

H. annuus

Flower time: July—October
Location: Best in full sun
Propagation: Sow under glass in March

H. annuus is the basic species — height 30 cm-3 m (1-10 ft) with yellow or orange flowers. Check variety height before you buy. The giants may be spectacular, but the compact ones are usually more colourful and are more easily seen. The 1.2 m (4 ft) 'Autumn Beauty' is a good example.

HELICHRYSUM
Straw Flower

Hardy annual

H. bracteatum

Flower time: July—September
Location: Best in full sun
Propagation: Sow under glass in March

The most popular of the group of 'everlasting' flowers which look like double daisies with shiny petals. For drying cut the stems just before the flowers are fully open. Several varieties of *H. bracteatum* — height 30-90 cm (1-3 ft) are available. Seeds are usually sold as a mixture of varieties.

HELLEBORUS
Hellebore

Border perennial

H. orientalis

Flower time: Depends on species
Location: Best in partial shade
Propagation: Buy young plants

The deeply-lobed leaves provide good ground cover and the flower time ranges from mid winter to late spring. *H. niger* 30 cm (1 ft) is the Christmas rose — white blooms in January-March. *H. orientalis* 45 cm (1½ ft) is the Lenten rose — various colours — blooms in March.

HEMEROCALLIS
Day Lily

Border perennial

H. 'Stafford'

Flower time: June—August
Location: Sun or light shade
Propagation: Divide clumps in autumn

Branching flower stalks rise above clumps of strap-like leaves in summer. Each bloom lasts for only a day or two, but new ones continue to appear for many weeks. There are many hybrids in a wide range of colours — height 60-90 cm (2-3 ft). Double and spidery-petalled varieties are available.

HEUCHERA
Coral Flower

Border perennial

H. sanguinea

Flower time: June—August
Location: Sun or light shade
Propagation: Divide clumps in autumn

Heuchera, Tellima and Tiarella are ground covers which may be confused at the all-leaf stage, but not when they are in flower. Heuchera blooms are bells borne in loose sprays. *H. sanguinea* is a typical species — height 60 cm (2 ft) with silver-marbled green leaves. Lift every few years.

HOSTA
Plantain Lily

Border perennial

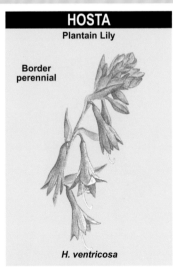

H. ventricosa

Flower time: June—August
Location: Best in partial shade
Propagation: Divide clumps in spring

A dual-purpose plant which is grown for its spikes of trumpet-shaped flowers and its attractive leaves, which are often variegated or distinctly coloured — ideal for growing under trees. There are scores of varieties — height 15-90 cm (6 in.-3 ft). For deep shade choose an all-green variety.

A small clump of daffodils made up of a few bulbs can look attractive, especially if they are grown on their own in a container or if they are a dwarf variety grown in the rockery. In the open garden, however, they are seen at their best when planted as a drift of naturalised bulbs, which means growing them in a way and in a situation which make them look like wild flowers. In the photograph a large drift in grassland is illustrated, but informal planting under a single deciduous tree can create a wholly natural look.

HYACINTHUS
Hyacinth

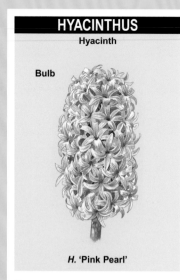

Bulb

H. 'Pink Pearl'

Flower time: April—May
Location: Sun or light shade
Propagation: Use offsets after lifting

An excellent garden bulb, but it has never achieved the popularity of daffodils and tulips. *H. orientalis* — 25-30 cm (10 in.-1 ft) has produced hundreds of varieties, the Dutch hybrids have colours ranging from white to deep purple. Bulbs will overwinter in most soils. Plant medium-sized bulbs.

IBERIS
Annual Candytuft

Hardy annual

I. umbellata

Flower time: May—July
Location: Best in full sun
Propagation: Sow seeds in April

Few annuals are easier to grow — just sprinkle the seed in spring over the ground where it is to flower. Use it as an edging or front-of-the-border plant. The basic species is *I. umbellata* — height 15-30 cm (6 in.-1 ft). The varieties include the dwarf 'Fairy Mixed' and the tall 'White Pinnacle'.

IBERIS
Perennial Candytuft

Rockery perennial

I. sempervirens

Flower time: May—June
Location: Best in full sun
Propagation: Cuttings under glass in July

An evergreen, hardy and easy plant for the rock garden. The flowers cover the foliage — each bloom has two long petals and two short ones. *I. sempervirens* — height 20 cm (8 in.) is the basic species. Look for the varieties 'Snowflake' — 25 cm (10 in.) and the dwarf 'Little Gem' — 10 cm (4 in.).

IMPATIENS
Busy Lizzie

Half-hardy annual

I. walleriana **Hybrids**

Flower time: June—October
Location: Sun or partial shade
Propagation: Buy seedlings

Only *Begonia semperflorens* can rival the ability of Busy lizzie to provide sheets of colour in shade. A large range of *I. walleriana* hybrids are available, growing 20-25 cm (8-10 in.) high in a variety of colours. The blooms may be single or double. The New Guinea hybrids have multi-coloured foliage.

INCARVILLEA
Chinese Trumpet Flower

Border perennial

I. delavayi

Flower time: May—June
Location: Best in full sun
Propagation: Sow seeds in spring

An unusual plant with an exotic appearance. The flower stalks bearing gloxinia-like blooms appear in spring before the leaves. All growth disappears in winter so mark the site with a stick — mulch crowns. *I. delavayi* is the popular species — height 60 cm (2 ft) with pink flowers and ferny foliage.

IPOMOEA
Morning Glory

Half-hardy annual

I. tricolor 'Heavenly Blue'

Flower time: July—September
Location: Best in full sun
Propagation: Sow under glass in March

The wiry stems twine around upright supports and the flowers appear all summer long. Each bloom lasts for only a day but they continue to appear for months. Choose a sheltered site. *I. tricolor* — height 3 m (10 ft) has numerous varieties. The white-throated blooms are blue, blue-striped or red.

IRIS
Bearded Iris

Border perennial

I. 'Jane Phillips'

Flower time: Depends on variety
Location: Best in full sun
Propagation: Divide rhizomes

Most irises spread by rhizomes — the most popular ones are the bearded irises which have fleshy hairs on the outer petals. Sizes vary from the tall group which flower in June — height 75 cm (2½ ft) to miniatures such as the June-flowering *I. pumila* — height 20 cm (8 in.).

IRIS
Bulb Iris

Bulb

I. 'Lemon Queen'

Flower time: Depends on variety
Location: Best in full sun
Propagation: Divide clumps in autumn

The bulb irises are generally smaller than the rhizome ones — the usual home is the rockery. For flowers in Feb-March choose one of the Reticulata group — height 8-15 cm (3-6 in.). For June-July blooms plant one of the Xiphium group such as *I.* 'Lemon Queen' — height 45 cm (1½ ft).

KNIPHOFIA
Red Hot Poker

Border perennial

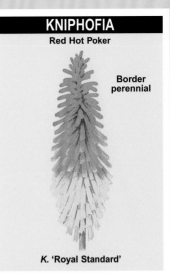

K. 'Royal Standard'

Flower time: July—September
Location: Best in full sun
Propagation: Divide clumps in spring

An easy one to recognise — grassy leaves and spikes of long tubular flowers. Some but not all have the traditional red hot appearance — red at the top and yellow at the base, e.g 'Royal Standard'. *K. uvaria* — height 75 cm-1.5 m (2½ ft-5 ft) has produced many hybrids.

LATHYRUS
Sweet Pea

Hardy annual

L. odoratus 'Leamington'

Flower time: June—September
Location: Best in full sun
Propagation: Sow seeds in April

Modern varieties of sweet peas generally have larger flowers than the old favourites, but some have lost their fragrance. *L. odoratus* is the basic species and the tall group — height 1.5-2.4 m (5-8 ft) dominate the catalogues. There are also intermediate ones and dwarfs.

LAVATERA
Annual Mallow

Hardy annual

L. 'Silver Cup'

Flower time: July—September
Location: Sun or light shade
Propagation: Sow seeds in March

A bushy plant which is covered with trumpet-shaped flowers in summer. *L. trimestris* has produced numerous varieties. The older ones are tall, reaching 90 cm-1.2 m (3-4 ft) and are suitable for screening. These days the more compact modern varieties such as 'Silver Cup' are preferred.

LEUCANTHEMUM
Shasta Daisy

Border perennial

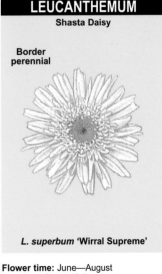

L. superbum 'Wirral Supreme'

Flower time: June—August
Location: Best in full sun
Propagation: Divide clumps in spring

An old favourite which used to be listed as Chrysanthemum. The single or double flowers are white and the centres of the singles are yellow. *L. superbum* is the basic species — height 1 m (3 ft). It has several varieties — the semi-double 'Wirral Supreme' is popular and so is 'Esther Read'.

LEUCOJUM
Snowflake

Bulb

L. vernum

Flower time: Depends on species
Location: Sun or partial shade
Propagation: Divide clumps in spring

At first glance it is a large snowdrop — both have flowers with six petals. But snowflake petals are all the same size and all are green- or yellow-spotted at the tips. There are several species such as *L. autumnale* — height 15 cm (6 in.) which flowers in September, and *L. vernum* which blooms in April-May.

LIATRIS
Gayfeather

Border perennial

L. spicata

Flower time: July—September
Location: Sun or light shade
Propagation: Divide clumps in autumn

Erect spikes are densely clothed with small, fluffy flowers in white, pink or pale purple. An unusual feature is that the blooms open from the top downwards. *L. spicata* — height 1.2 m (4 ft) is pale purple and has a number of more compact varieties such as 'Floristan Weiss' and 'Kobold'.

LIGULARIA
Golden Rays

Border perennial
•
Bog plant

L. dentata

Flower time: July—September
Location: Needs partial shade
Propagation: Divide clumps in autumn

This plant needs space, water-retentive soil and some shade. The large leaves cover the ground and suppress weeds, and in summer the yellow or orange flowers appear. *L. dentata* is the garden species — height 90 cm (3 ft). The variety 'Desdemona' is popular. The giant is 'The Rocket' — 1.5 m (5 ft).

LILY
Hybrid Lily

Bulb

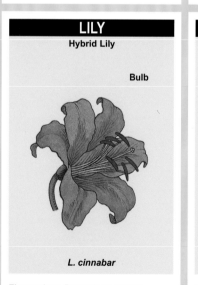

L. cinnabar

Flower time: Depends on variety
Location: Sun or light shade
Propagation: Divide clumps in autumn

The Hybrid lilies set new standards for size and vigour. Most grow to 1-1.5 m (3-5 ft), but the dwarf Pixie strain has become popular. Basic shapes are turk's cap (bent-back petals), trumpet and bowl — flower times fall between June and October. Favourites include 'Enchantment' and 'Stargazer'.

LILY
Species Lily

Bulb

L. candidum

Flower time: July—August
Location: Sun or light shade
Propagation: Divide clumps in autumn

Far fewer types are available compared with the Hybrid lilies, but there are many beautiful old ones here. Favourites include *L. regale* (white) 1.2 m (4 ft), *L. martagon* (pink-purple) 90 cm (3 ft), *L. tigrinum* (black-spotted orange) 90 cm (3 ft) and *L. candidum* (white) 90 cm (3 ft).

LIMONIUM
Statice

Half-hardy annual

L. sinuatum

Flower time: July—September
Location: Best in full sun
Propagation: Sow under glass in Feb

A popular 'everlasting' flower — winged stems bear clusters of tiny papery-petalled blooms. For drying cut stems just before flowers open and hang upside-down in a dry place. *L. sinuatum* — height 45 cm (1¹/₂ ft) has produced a number of varieties in a wide range of colours.

LOBELIA
Lobelia

Half-hardy annual

L. erinus

Flower time: June—September
Location: Sun or light shade
Propagation: Sow under glass in Feb

Lobelias have been a basic feature of the edges of beds and containers for generations, but it is more demanding than many less popular annuals. The soil needs humus, tips must be pinched out and soaking is needed in dry weather. *L. erinus* — height 10 cm (4 in.) is the basic species.

LUPINUS
Lupin

Border perennial

L. 'Russell Hybrids'

Flower time: June—July
Location: Sun or light shade
Propagation: Plant cuttings in March

Large spires of pea-like flowers provide bright splashes of colour. Quick-growing and inexpensive, but they are short-lived. *L. polyphyllus* — height 90 cm-1.2 m (3-4 ft) has produced many hybrids. The 'Russell Hybrids' are the most popular — there are many bicoloured varieties.

LYCHNIS
Campion

Border perennial
•
Rockery perennial

L. chalcedonica

Flower time: Depends on species
Location: Best in full sun
Propagation: Divide clumps in autumn

This sun-loving plant has deeply cut or notched flowers which are generally pink or red. The favourite species is *L. chalcedonica* — height 90 cm (3 ft) with tight flower heads on stiff stems in June-August. *L. coronaria* (July-August) has loose sprays of pink flowers. The dwarf is *L. alpina*.

LYSIMACHIA
Lysimachia

Border perennial
•
Rockery perennial

L. punctata

Flower time: Depends on species
Location: Sun or partial shade
Propagation: Divide clumps in autumn

The popular border species is *L. punctata* (Yellow loosestrife) — height 75 cm (2½ ft) with yellow flowers borne in whorls in June-August. In the rockery you will find *L. nummularia* (Creeping jenny) — height 5 cm (2 in.) with trailing stems studded with yellow flowers in May-August.

MATTHIOLA
Ten Week Stock

Half-hardy annual

M. incana 'Ten Week Mixed'

Flower time: June—August
Location: Sun or light shade
Propagation: Sow under glass in Feb

Stocks have lost much of their popularity but their charm remains — densely-clustered flowering spikes above soft grey-green leaves. *M. incana* — height 20-75 cm (8 in.-2½ ft) is the Ten week stock. Varieties include the dwarf 'Cinderella' and the tall 'Giant Excelsior'.

MATTHIOLA
Brompton Stock

Hardy biennial

M. incana 'Brompton Mixed'

Flower time: April—May
Location: Sun or light shade
Propagation: Buy seedlings

Still very popular with flower arrangers but no longer a favourite bedding plant — raising all-double plants from seed is a tricky business. 'Brompton Mixed' — height 45 cm (1½ ft) are bushy plants with clusters of fragrant flowers. Plant out in February. 'East Lothian Mixed' will grow to 30 cm (1 ft).

MECONOPSIS
Meconopsis

Border perennial

M. betonicifolia

Flower time: Depends on species
Location: Best in light shade
Propagation: Sow under glass in spring

There are just two species you are likely to find — both require humus-rich and moist soil. *M. betonicifolia* — height 90 cm (3 ft) is the Himalayan poppy which produces sky-blue flowers in June-July. The Welsh poppy *M. cambrica* — height 30 cm (1 ft) bears yellow flowers in June-Sept.

MESEMBRYANTHEMUM
Livingstone Daisy

Half-hardy annual

M. crinoflorum

Flower time: July—September
Location: Best in full sun
Propagation: Sow under glass in March

The ground-hugging stems bear glistening succulent leaves and daisy-like flowers in a wide array of colours. Unfortunately the blooms open only when the sun is shining. *M. crinoflorum* — height 10-15 cm (4-6 in.) is the basic species which is usually sold as a mixture of varieties.

MIMULUS
Monkey Flower

Half-hardy annual

M. hybridus

Flower time: June—September
Location: Light or partial shade
Propagation: Sow under glass in March

There are varieties for the border, rockery and bog garden but the bedding plant types are the most popular. There are many varieties of *M. hybridus* — height 15-25 cm (6-10 in.) which can grow in the shade with begonias and busy lizzies. 'Malibu' and 'Magic' are compact — 'Viva' is the tallest.

MONARDA
Bergamot

Border perennial

M. 'Croftway Pink'

Flower time: June—September
Location: Best in light shade
Propagation: Divide clumps in spring

The flower heads, made up of whorls of flowers, are borne on top of stiff stems. Lift and divide the plants every three years. There are many hybrids of *M. didyma* available — height 60-90 cm (2-3 ft). Examples include 'Snow White' (white), 'Cambridge Scarlet' (red) and 'Prairie Night' (lilac).

MUSCARI
Grape Hyacinth

Bulb

M. armeniacum

Flower time: April—May
Location: Best in full sun
Propagation: Divide clumps in autumn

Muscari has none of the glamour of the showier spring bulbs, but it is a popular clump-forming plant for the rockery, edges of beds and between taller bulbs in the border. *M. armeniacum* — height 15-25 cm (6-10 in.) is the popular species with blue and white varieties. 'Blue Spike' has double flowers.

MYOSOTIS
Forget-me-not

Hardy biennial

M. sylvatica 'Ultramarine'

Flower time: April—May
Location: Best in light shade
Propagation: Sow seeds in June

A popular choice for carpeting the ground between tulips or wallflowers — clusters of flowers appear above the grey-green downy leaves. The usual ones are varieties of *M. sylvatica* — height 15-30 cm (6 in.-1 ft). Blue is the usual colour, but white and pink are available.

NARCISSUS
Daffodil

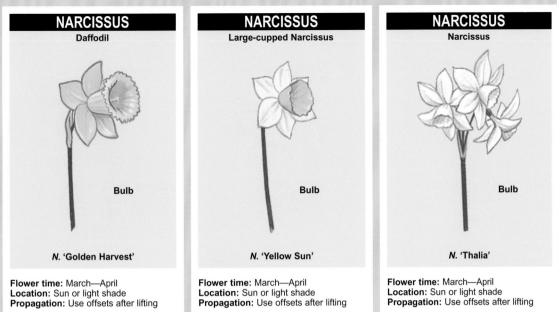

Bulb

N. 'Golden Harvest'

Flower time: March—April
Location: Sun or light shade
Propagation: Use offsets after lifting

The common name 'daffodil' is usually restricted to those varieties with a trumpet which is as long or longer than the petals — height 15-45 cm (6 in.-1$\frac{1}{2}$ ft). 'King Alfred' was once dominant, but the name is now used for other yellows. Let the foliage die down naturally — do not tie in knots.

NARCISSUS
Large-cupped Narcissus

Bulb

N. 'Yellow Sun'

Flower time: March—April
Location: Sun or light shade
Propagation: Use offsets after lifting

Varieties with a cup more than one-third of petal length are included here — height 30-60 cm (1-2 ft). 'Carlton' is a popular large yellow, 'Yellow Sun' is a very early variety. All-whites such as 'Easter Moon' and 'Desdemona' are available — so are bicolours such as 'Salome' (white/pink).

NARCISSUS
Narcissus

Bulb

N. 'Thalia'

Flower time: March—April
Location: Sun or light shade
Propagation: Use offsets after lifting

Included here are all the varieties not belonging in the types described previously. There are hundreds to choose from — Triandrus varieties with more than one drooping flower per stem, Cyclamineus varieties with just one drooping head, Poeticus narcissi with red-edged cups, etc.

NEMESIA
Nemesia

Half-hardy annual

N. strumosa

Flower time: June—September
Location: Sun or light shade
Propagation: Sow under glass in March

A mixture will provide self-colours, bicolours and tricolours. Unfortunately flowering quickly comes to an end in hot and dry weather. For bushy plants pinch out tips after bedding out. *N. strumosa* — height 20-30 cm (8 in.-1 ft) has given rise to many garden varieties.

Most herbaceous borders are multicoloured features with flowers ranging from white to deep red. The monochrome border is seen much less often, although examples can be found at numerous famous gardens such as Wisley and Sissinghurst. The white and the blue border are the two most popular types — the white one illustrated here is either colourless or stylish depending on your personal taste.

NEPETA
Catmint

Border perennial

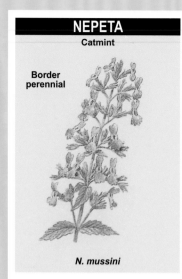

N. mussini

Flower time: May—September
Location: Best in full sun
Propagation: Divide clumps in spring

A great favourite with cats who love to roll in its aromatic grey-green foliage. The flowers are borne in upright spikes — dead-heading will encourage further flushes. The popular species is *N. mussini* — height 30 cm (1 ft). The usual colour is lavender or blue, but 'Snowflake' is a white variety.

NICOTIANA
Tobacco Plant

Half-hardy annual

N. 'Lime Green'

Flower time: June—October
Location: Sun or light shade
Propagation: Sow under glass in March

The old-fashioned *N. alata* has a strong fragrance, but it needs staking and flowers close during the day. Nowadays the usual choice is one of the dwarf varieties — height 20-45 cm (8 in.-1½ ft) or the taller hybrids — height 60-90 cm (2-3 ft) such as 'Lime Green' and the 'Domino' series.

NIGELLA
Love-in-a-mist

Hardy annual

N. damascena 'Miss Jekyll'

Flower time: June—August
Location: Sun or light shade
Propagation: Sow seeds in autumn

The blue ones have been grown for generations, but multicoloured mixtures are now more popular. An easy-to-grow bedding plant, but the flowering season is short. *N. damascena* — height 45 cm (1½ ft) is the basic species and 'Miss Jekyll' is the favourite blue. 'Persian Jewels' is a mixture.

OENOTHERA
Evening Primrose

Border perennial

O. macrocarpa

Flower time: July—September
Location: Best in full sun
Propagation: Divide clumps in spring

The blooms are large, saucer-shaped and silky — somewhat similar to poppies but nothing like primroses. The largest blooms are borne by the dwarf *O. macrocarpa* — height 15 cm (6 in.). For taller yellow-flowered plants choose *O. fruticosa* — for pink blooms grow *O. speciosa* 'Siskiyou'.

OSTEOSPERMUM
Osteospermum

Half-hardy annual

O. 'Starshine'

Flower time: June—October
Location: Best in full sun
Propagation: Sow under glass in March

Once a rarity — now you will find plants at your local garden centre for bedding out in spring. These hybrids reach 60-90 cm (2-3 ft) and are available in various colours. Some (e.g 'Starshine') have daisy-like flowers, but the eye-catching ones (e.g 'Whirligig') have spoon-shaped petals.

PAEONIA
Peony

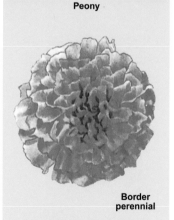

Border perennial

P. officinalis 'Rosea Plena'

Flower time: Depends on species
Location: Best in full sun
Propagation: Buy new plants

Large-headed beauties for the border. Have patience — new plants may take several years to establish. The common peony — height 60 cm (2 ft) is *P. officinalis* which blooms in May-June. For June-July flowers choose the Chinese peony *P. lactifolia* which grows to 75-90 cm (2½-3 ft).

PAPAVER
Oriental Poppy

Border perennial

P. orientale 'Mrs Perry'

Flower time: May—June
Location: Sun or light shade
Propagation: Divide clumps in autumn

A fine sight when in full bloom, but the flowers are short-lived and the foliage looks untidy when flowering is over. The basic species is *P. orientale* — height 45-90 cm (1½-3 ft). The bowl-shaped blooms have black-based petals in a variety of colours. Divide every three years.

PAPAVER
Annual Poppy

Hardy annual

P. somniferum

Flower time: June—September
Location: Sun or light shade
Propagation: Sow seeds in April

Much daintier than their border cousins — buds bow their heads, petals flutter in the breeze and the flowers are short-lived. Despite appearances they are tough and do not need staking. *P. rhoeas* — height 60-90 cm (2-3 ft) is the popular one. *P. somniferum* produces double blooms.

PELARGONIUM
Bedding Geranium

Half-hardy perennial

P. hortorum

Flower time: June—October
Location: Sun or light shade
Propagation: Cuttings under glass in July

The geranium which is seen everywhere. *P. hortorum* — height 15-60 cm (6 in.-2 ft) has hundreds of varieties. Standard blooms, small blooms, semi-doubles, narrow petals — you will find them all in the catalogues. *P. peltatum* is the species with trailing stems which are 60-90 cm (2-3 ft) long.

PELARGONIUM
Regal Pelargonium

Half-hardy perennial

P. domesticum 'Elsie Hickman'

Flower time: June—October
Location: Sun or light shade
Propagation: Cuttings under glass in July

This showy but tender relative of the Bedding geranium bears large flowers which are ruffled and are usually marked with a darker colour — the leaves are saw-edged. *P. domesticum* — height 30-60 cm (1-2 ft) is the basic species and many hybrids are available. Not suitable for cold sites.

PENSTEMON
Penstemon

Border perennial
●
Rockery perennial

P. 'Scarlet Queen'

Flower time: July—October
Location: Best in full sun
Propagation: Cuttings under glass in July

Once considered quite tender, but the popular types can be left in the garden over winter if the soil is free-draining. The basic species *P. barbatus* is 90 cm (3 ft) high — much more popular are the 30-60 cm (2-3 ft) hybrids. There are also 15-20 cm (6-8 in.) dwarfs for the rockery.

PETUNIA
Petunia

Half-hardy annual

P. hybrida Grandiflora Group

Flower time: June—October
Location: Best in full sun
Propagation: Buy new plants

One of the most popular bedding plants — there are upright, spreading and trailing ones, singles and doubles, self-coloured and multicoloured varieties, and each year new types appear. *P. hybrida* and its varieties grow to 15-45 cm (6 in.-1½ ft) — pinch out the tips when 8-10 cm (3-4 in.) high.

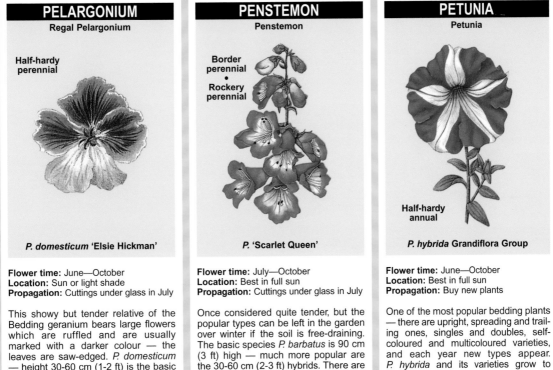

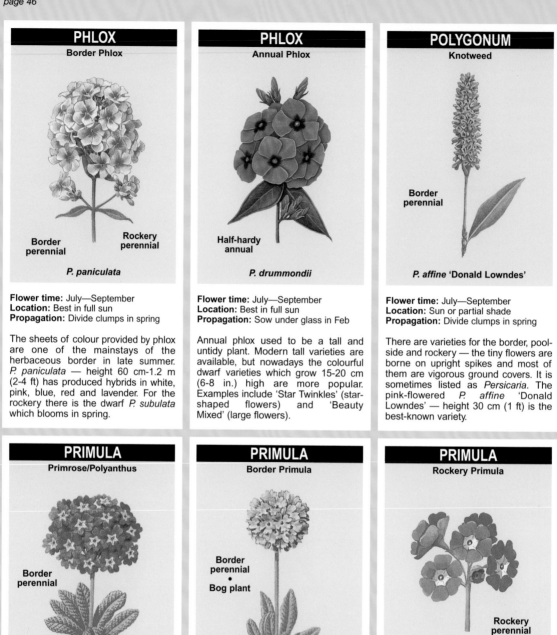

PHLOX
Border Phlox

P. paniculata

Border perennial

Rockery perennial

Flower time: July—September
Location: Best in full sun
Propagation: Divide clumps in spring

The sheets of colour provided by phlox are one of the mainstays of the herbaceous border in late summer. *P. paniculata* — height 60 cm-1.2 m (2-4 ft) has produced hybrids in white, pink, blue, red and lavender. For the rockery there is the dwarf *P. subulata* which blooms in spring.

PHLOX
Annual Phlox

Half-hardy annual

P. drummondii

Flower time: July—September
Location: Best in full sun
Propagation: Sow under glass in Feb

Annual phlox used to be a tall and untidy plant. Modern tall varieties are available, but nowadays the colourful dwarf varieties which grow 15-20 cm (6-8 in.) high are more popular. Examples include 'Star Twinkles' (star-shaped flowers) and 'Beauty Mixed' (large flowers).

POLYGONUM
Knotweed

Border perennial

P. affine 'Donald Lowndes'

Flower time: July—September
Location: Sun or partial shade
Propagation: Divide clumps in spring

There are varieties for the border, poolside and rockery — the tiny flowers are borne on upright spikes and most of them are vigorous ground covers. It is sometimes listed as *Persicaria*. The pink-flowered *P. affine* 'Donald Lowndes' — height 30 cm (1 ft) is the best-known variety.

PRIMULA
Primrose/Polyanthus

Border perennial

P. variabilis

Flower time: March—May
Location: Best in light shade
Propagation: Divide clumps in spring

The common primrose *P. vulgaris* — height 10 cm (4 in.) has its place in the garden, and so do its many hybrids. Polyanthus (*P. variabilis*) — height 20-30 cm (8 in.-1 ft) is a hybrid of primrose and cowslip. There are many colourful varieties, such as 'Pacific Giants'.

PRIMULA
Border Primula

Border perennial
• Bog plant

P. denticulata

Flower time: Depends on species
Location: Best in light shade
Propagation: Divide clumps in spring

The stems are 30-90 cm (1-3 ft) high and these primulas are divided into various groups. There are the Candelabra primroses such as *P. japonica*, the Drumstick primroses (e.g *P. denticulata*) which bear globular heads, and the giant yellow cowslip *P. florindae*.

PRIMULA
Rockery Primula

Rockery perennial

P. marginata

Flower time: April—May
Location: Best in light shade
Propagation: Divide clumps in spring

These dwarf primulas bear upright or pendent flowers above leafy rosettes. They grow 5-10 cm (2-4 in.) high and bloom in spring. *P. marginata* is fragrant and *P. minima* is the baby of the group. *P. pubescens* has produced numerous varieties such as 'Harlow Carr', 'Mrs Wilson' and 'Faldonside'.

PULMONARIA
Lungwort

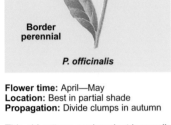

Border
perennial

P. officinalis

Flower time: April—May
Location: Best in partial shade
Propagation: Divide clumps in autumn

This old cottage garden plant is usually grown for its white-spotted leaves, and flowers which change from pink to blue. The species is *P. officinalis* — height 30 cm (1 ft). Blue is not the only colour — white and pink varieties are available. There are also all-green species — all lungworts are invasive.

PULSATILLA
Pasque Flower

Rockery
perennial

P. vernalis

Flower time: April—May
Location: Best in full sun
Propagation: Sow under glass in June

In spring the flower stems emerge, crowned with silky buds. These buds open into starry flowers. The ferny leaves then appear, after which silky seed heads provide an attractive feature. The usual species is *P. vulgaris* — height 20 cm (8 in.) but *P. vernalis* is even more eye-catching.

RANUNCULUS
Persian Buttercup

Bulb

R. asiaticus

Flower time: July—August
Location: Best in full sun
Propagation: Plant bulbs in March

The showiest Ranunculus — bright semi-double or ball-shaped double flowers appear in summer. *R. asiaticus* is the garden species — height 25-30 cm (10 in.-1 ft). Many varieties are listed, but the usual choice is a mixture. Plant with claws pointed downward — lift and store over winter.

RANUNCULUS
Border Buttercup

Border
perennial

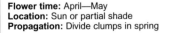

R. acris

Flower time: April—May
Location: Sun or partial shade
Propagation: Divide clumps in spring

These plants are taller than the Persian ones, but the flowers are smaller and less colourful. *R. aconitifolius* is the basic species, reaching 60-90 cm (2-3 ft) and producing masses of small white 'bachelor's buttons'. For yellow flowers, choose the summer-flowering *R. acris*.

RUDBECKIA
Cone Flower

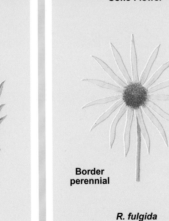

Border
perennial

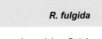

R. fulgida

Flower time: July—October
Location: Sun or light shade
Propagation: Divide clumps in spring

A popular provider of large yellow blooms in the border in late summer and autumn. The prominent cone-shaped disc at the centre of each flower is usually brown or black. The favourite species is *R. fulgida* — height 60-90 cm (2-3 ft). 'Goldsturm' is a good choice — it does not need staking.

RUDBECKIA
Annual Cone Flower

Half-hardy
annual

R. hirta

Flower time: July—October
Location: Sun or light shade
Propagation: Sow under glass in Feb

Daisy-like flowers in yellow, orange or mahogany are carried on stout stems. These annuals are varieties or hybrids of *R. hirta* — height 30-90 cm (1-3 ft). The dwarfs include 'Becky' and 'Toto' — the giants are 'Gloriosa Daisy' and 'Marmalade'. Watch out for slugs. The tall varieties require support.

SALPIGLOSSIS
Painted Tongue

Half-hardy annual

S. sinuata

Flower time: July—September
Location: Best in full sun
Propagation: Sow under glass in Feb

An exotic annual — the velvety trumpet-shaped flowers are prominently veined. A demanding plant which requires sun, shelter and good soil. The garden types are *S. sinuata* and its varieties — height 30-75 cm (1-2¹/₂ ft). 'Casino' is a good choice — compact and more weather resistant than most.

SALVIA
Annual Sage

Half-hardy annual

S. splendens 'Blaze of Fire'

Flower time: June—October
Location: Sun or light shade
Propagation: Sow under glass in March

There are several types of salvia for the garden — herbs, border plants, annuals and biennials. The ones described here are the bedding plant salvias, a group dominated by *S. splendens* — height 30 cm (1 ft). Once 'Blaze of Fire' was the only variety, but now they come in many colours and sizes.

SAXIFRAGA
Saxifrage

Rockery perennial
•
Border perennial

S. urbium

Flower time: Depends on variety
Location: Depends on variety
Propagation: Plant rooted sections

A typical saxifrage is a mossy mat or a group of leafy rosettes from which arise stalks bearing loose clusters of starry flowers in spring or early summer. Most are compact rockery plants such as *S. cochlearis*, but there are border types such as *S. urbium* (London pride) — height 30 cm (1 ft).

SCABIOSA
Scabious

Border perennial

S. caucasica

Flower time: July—August
Location: Best in full sun
Propagation: Divide clumps in spring

A popular border plant which has a long flowering period. The frilly-edged 8 cm (3 in.) wide blooms are attractive but there is never an abundance of flowers at one time. The lavender-coloured *S. caucasica* — height 60 cm (2 ft) is the garden species. There are varieties in white, blue or violet.

SCHIZANTHUS
Poor Man's Orchid

Half-hardy annual

S. pinnatus 'Hit Parade'

Flower time: July—August
Location: Best in full sun
Propagation: Sow under glass in March

Each flower looks like a miniature orchid, streaked or spotted in various colours. These blooms are borne in large numbers above the ferny foliage. The garden species is *S. pinnatus* — height 25-90 cm (10 in.-3 ft). Avoid the tall ones — choose a compact variety such as 'Hit Parade' or 'Bouquet'.

SCILLA
Bluebell, Squill

Bulb

S. siberica

Flower time: Depends on species
Location: Sun or light shade
Propagation: Divide clumps in Sept

A familiar sight in spring — strap-like leaves, bell- or star-shaped drooping flowers on top of upright stems. The favourite species is *S. siberica* — height 15 cm (6 in.). There are some unusual species — the dwarf *S. tubergeniana* has striped flowers, *S. peruviana* blooms in June.

SEDUM
Ice Plant/Stonecrop

Rockery perennial
•
Border perennial

S. spectabile

Flower time: Depends on species
Location: Best in full sun
Propagation: Divide clumps in autumn

The large ones for the border are the ice plants, with plates of tiny flowers in late summer. *S. spectabile* — height 30-60 cm (1-2 ft) is the garden species. The rockery ones are the stonecrops, which sprawl or form mats over soil or rocks and bear starry flowers in early summer.

SOLIDAGO
Golden Rod

Border perennial

S. canadensis

Flower time: July—September
Location: Sun or light shade
Propagation: Divide clumps in spring

The bright yellow heads of golden rod are a common sight in borders in late summer. This is usually *S. canadensis* which is a tall and weedy plant. It is better to grow one of its hybrids — heights range from *S.* 'Queenie' 30 cm (1 ft) to *S.* 'Golden Wings' which reaches 1.8 m (6 ft).

STACHYS
Stachys

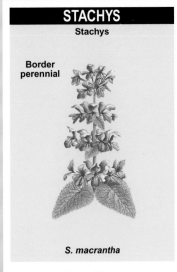

Border perennial

S. macrantha

Flower time: May—July
Location: Sun or partial shade
Propagation: Divide clumps in autumn

The popular one is *S. byzantina* (Lamb's ears) which is grown for its grey woolly leaves rather than its insignificant flowers. For a floral display it is better to grow *S. macrantha* (Big betony) — height 60 cm (2 ft). This species produces 4 cm (1½ in.) long tubular flowers — the foliage is green.

TAGETES
Tagetes

Half-hardy annual

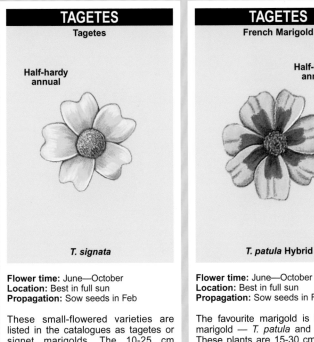

T. signata

Flower time: June—October
Location: Best in full sun
Propagation: Sow seeds in Feb

These small-flowered varieties are listed in the catalogues as tagetes or signet marigolds. The 10-25 cm (4-10 in.) high plants bear masses of 1-3 cm (½-1 in.) wide single flowers above the ferny leaves. They are all hybrids of *T. signata* — the most popular ones are the 'Gem' series.

TAGETES
French Marigold

Half-hardy annual

T. patula Hybrid

Flower time: June—October
Location: Best in full sun
Propagation: Sow seeds in Feb

The favourite marigold is the French marigold — *T. patula* and its hybrids. These plants are 15-30 cm (6 in.-1 ft) high and add yellow, orange or red to bedding schemes everywhere. The old favourite is 'Naughty Marietta' but these days doubles (e.g 'Sophia') are preferred.

TAGETES
African Marigold

Half-hardy annual

T. erecta 'Doubloon'

Flower time: June—October
Location: Sun or partial shade
Propagation: Sow seeds in Feb

African marigolds are taller, more upright and with fewer but larger flowers than French marigolds. All bear double ball-like flowers on 30-90 cm (1-3 ft) stems. Giants include 'Doubloon' and the 'Jubilee' series — at the other end of the scale there are 'Discovery' and 'Inca'.

TANACETUM
Pyrethrum, Tansy

Border perennial

T. coccineum

Flower time: Depends on species
Location: Best in full sun
Propagation: Divide clumps in spring

Once listed as Pyrethrum. There are two types for the border. *T. coccineum* is the common pyrethrum which grows to 45-75 cm (1½-2½ ft) and bears 5 cm (2 in.) wide flowers in early summer. *T. vulgare* is the common tansy which produces masses of tiny yellow flowers on 90 cm (3 ft) high stems in autumn.

TANACETUM
Feverfew

Half-hardy annual

T. parthenium 'Golden Ball'

Flower time: July—September
Location: Best in full sun
Propagation: Sow under glass in Feb

Once listed as Matricaria. The basic species is *T. parthenium* (*Matricaria eximia*) which has 3 cm (1 in.) wide blooms on 10-30 cm (4 in.-1 ft) stems. This single form is no longer popular. The choice these days is either double flowers (e.g 'Snow Puffs') or ball-like heads of tiny flowers (e.g 'Golden Ball').

THALICTRUM
Meadow Rue

Border perennial

T. delavayi

Flower time: Depends on species
Location: Best in full sun
Propagation: Divide clumps in autumn

Tiny flowers are borne in large heads in summer on tall stems above ferny foliage. The popular species is *T. delavayi* which grows to 1.5 m (5 ft). A plant for the back of the border. A shorter type is *T. aquilegifolium* — height 90 cm (3 ft) which produces fluffy blooms in late spring.

THUNBERGIA
Black-eyed Susan

Half-hardy annual

T. alata 'Susie'

Flower time: July—September
Location: Full sun
Propagation: Sow under glass in March

A few species of this conservatory plant can be grown as annuals in the garden. The showy flowers stand out above the arrow-shaped leaves. The only one you are likely to find is *T. alata* 'Susie' — height 1.2 m (4 ft) with white, yellow or orange flowers. A sheltered site is essential.

TRADESCANTIA
Spiderwort

Border perennial

T. andersoniana

Flower time: June—September
Location: Sun or partial shade
Propagation: Divide clumps in autumn

Three-petalled flowers appear from early summer to early autumn, although each bloom lasts for only a day. A grow-anywhere plant, in sun or shade and in damp or dry soil. The garden species is *T. andersoniana* — height 45-60 cm (1½-2 ft). Varieties in white, red, lilac or purple are available.

TROPAEOLUM
Nasturtium

Hardy annual

T. 'Tom Thumb'

Flower time: June—October
Location: Best in full sun
Propagation: Sow seeds in April

The familiar nasturtium with its spurred flowers has many uses in the garden — there are climbers for walls, semi-trailers for window boxes and bushy dwarfs for bedding. Many hybrids of *T. majus* are available, ranging from 'Tom Thumb' — 15 cm (6 in.) to 'Tall Mixed' — 1.8 m (6 ft).

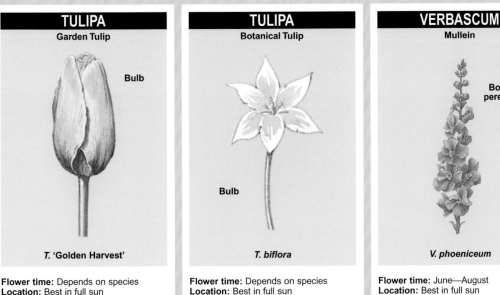

TULIPA
Garden Tulip

Bulb

T. 'Golden Harvest'

Flower time: Depends on species
Location: Best in full sun
Propagation: Use bulblets after lifting

Garden tulips are the types which do not have known specific parents and which are planted in Nov-Dec and then lifted when the foliage has turned yellow. Nearly all the bulbs in the catalogues belong here. There are four basic groups — early, late, large-flowered and fancy-flowered varieties.

TULIPA
Botanical Tulip

Bulb

T. biflora

Flower time: Depends on species
Location: Best in full sun
Propagation: Divide clumps in autumn

Species tulips and hybrids of known species are listed here. Unlike the garden tulips they are generally left in the ground. There is a wide range of shapes and heights. Well known types include the dwarfs *T. biflora* and *T. kaufmanniana* and the taller *T. fosteriana* and *T. greigii*.

VERBASCUM
Mullein

Border perennial

V. phoeniceum

Flower time: June—August
Location: Best in full sun
Propagation: Divide clumps in spring

The border varieties are tall plants with spikes of showy saucer-shaped blooms. Many colours are available with heights ranging from 1.8 m (6 ft) giants to the more popular 1 m (3 ft) ones. *V. olympicum* is a typical giant with 3 cm (1 in.) wide yellow flowers. *V. phoeniceum* is in the short group.

VERBENA
Verbena

Half-hardy annual

V. hybrida

Flower time: July—October
Location: Best in full sun
Propagation: Plant plugs or seedlings

This colourful bedding plant with white-eyed small flowers is *V. hybrida* — height 15-30 cm (6 in.-1 ft) with 5-8 cm (2-3 in.) wide flower heads. There are bushy upright varieties such as 'Novalis' and 'Romance', spreading ones like 'Imagination' and trailers such as 'Tapien'.

The wisdom of underplanting rose beds is a matter of opinion. Some purists feel that roses should always be grown on their own, and others believe that only prostrate leafy ground cover should be used. The problem is that a bed of non-repeat flowering roses can look dull for most of the season and so many gardeners plant flowering ground cover round the shrubs to provide extended interest. The flowers should be neither bold nor bright — Alchemilla mollis has been used here.

VERONICA
Speedwell

Border perennial
•
Rockery perennial

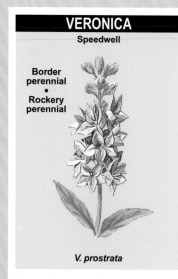

V. prostrata

Flower time: Depends on species
Location: Sun or light shade
Propagation: Divide clumps in autumn

The flat-faced flowers in white, pink or blue are usually borne on tall and narrow spikes on plants ranging from 8 cm (3 in.) to 1.2 m (4 ft). *V. spicata* is a good example of a 45 cm (1½ ft) plant which blooms in June-July. *V. exaltata* is a giant, *V. prostrata* is a lilac dwarf which spreads rapidly.

VIOLA
Pansy

Hardy annual
•
Hardy biennial

V. 'Rippling Waters'

Flower time: Depends on sowing time
Location: Sun or light shade
Propagation: See below

Low-growing flat-faced flowers familiar to everyone. Winter/spring flowering varieties are grown as biennials (sow under glass in June) — summer/autumn varieties are grown as annuals (sow under glass in March). Height variation is small, but the assortment of colours is large.

VIOLA
Viola

Hardy annual
•
Hardy biennial

V. 'Johnny Jump-up'

Flower time: Depends on sowing time
Location: Sun or light shade
Propagation: See pansy box

Similar in appearance to pansies, but violas are generally longer-living, more compact, not as easy to grow and with flowers which are smaller. Can be grown as annuals or biennials — see pansies. Novelties include the cat-faced 'Bambini' and the colour-changing 'Yesterday, Today and Tomorrow'.

VIOLA
Violet

Border perennial
•
Rockery perennial

V. cornuta

Flower time: Depends on species
Location: Sun or light shade
Propagation: Divide clumps in autumn

The violets are the babies of the Viola species, but they have the advantage of being perennials. The two popular border violets are *V. odorata* (Sweet violet) and the taller *V. cornuta* which reaches 15-25 cm (6-10 in.). The easiest rockery species is *V. lutea* — the smallest is *V. jooi*.

ZANTEDESCHIA
Arum Lily

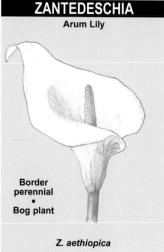

Border perennial
•
Bog plant

Z. aethiopica

Flower time: April—June
Location: Best in full sun
Propagation: Divide clumps in autumn

Only one species of these eye-catching plants is hardy enough to survive outdoors, where moist or wet ground is essential. *Z. aethiopica* — height 90 cm (3 ft) produces white 15-25 cm (6-10 in.) long flowers. The long leaves are arrow-shaped. The one to choose is 'Crowborough' — the hardiest variety.

ZINNIA
Zinnia

Half-hardy annual

Z. elegans 'Ruffles'

Flower time: July—October
Location: Best in full sun
Propagation: Sow under glass in March

Few annuals look as appealing in the seed catalogue, but you will need fertile soil and a warm, dry summer to get similar results. Staking is not necessary. All colours except blue are available, and the daisy-like heads are single, semi-double or double. Varieties grow to 15-75 cm (6 in.-2½ ft).

CHAPTER 5
GARDEN TASKS

Two features dominate the role you have to play in having plants which people will admire and produce the family will savour. First of all you will have to choose the right plants. Their appearance in the catalogue or at the garden centre is of course important but is not enough. You must also ensure that each plant is suitable for the site you have in mind — this may mean looking further than the seed packet or plant label.

It is the second feature which concerns us here — you will have to care for the plant and the soil in which it grows. This is blindingly obvious, but for many people garden care is a rather simple activity apart from the chores of weeding and mowing. Planting is a matter of digging a hole, popping in the plant from the garden centre and then pushing the soil back. Pruning is a matter of cutting off unwanted bits, and avoiding dry weather problems begins with a hose pipe when the leaves wilt.

The garden makeover programmes did more harm than good by showing how quick and easy it could be. In the 48 hours before the family came back from Eastbourne, lawns were laid, walls were built and mature shrubs in full flower were planted. Meant purely for entertainment they say, but some people took it seriously.

There's much more to it than that, but it is equally wrong to turn garden care into a never-ending round of jobs which rob you of gardening's most important task — sitting and enjoying your garden. Things have got simpler in recent years — digging is now regarded as an optional extra in many situations, and the endless round of hand-pulling, spraying and hoeing to keep down the weeds can be much reduced by growing ground cover plants or mulching between the plants.

Proper garden care is simply a matter of doing the right things at the right time. But how do you find out what is the right thing? It isn't obvious if or when the trees and shrubs should be pruned, staking isn't just a matter of a pole and a piece of string, effective watering isn't a matter of reaching for the watering can when everything starts to droop, and so on. There are many things to learn.

A practical course is a good idea if gardening is to be a serious hobby, but for the rest of us there are many other sources of information as outlined on page 3. All are useful, but the main source of information remains the words and illustrations in practical gardening books — in this chapter an A-Z guide to garden tasks is provided.

Do not let it frighten you — it covers all aspects of gardening, not just the jobs you may have to do. Use it to get the maximum amount of enjoyment from the king of all hobbies — gardening.

Blanching

A vegetable-growing technique used for hundreds of years. Light is excluded from some or all of the growing parts of certain types — as a result the natural green colour does not develop. There are several other possible effects — lower fibre content, improved flavour, reduced bitterness and enhanced appearance. The role of blanching is to produce one or more of these responses.

Some vegetables (e.g leek and celery) are earthed up — others are covered with a light-proof pot.

Cutting

Cutting blooms and attractive foliage from flower and shrub borders for arranging indoors is, of course, a basic part of the gardening scene. In this way the fruits of your labours can be enjoyed at any time and in any weather, but there are pitfalls to avoid. Obviously the full beauty of the flower bed or border is diminished, and in the case of newly-planted perennials the loss of stems and green leaves can harm next year's growth. If you have the space and are a keen flower arranger it is a good idea to have a separate bed where plants for cutting can be grown.

In the shrub border this form of spring and summer pruning generally does no harm, but take care during the first year. A newly-planted shrub needs all the stems and green leaves it can muster, so only cut a few flowers and do not remove many leaves. Roses are perhaps the most widely used of all cut flowers — do not remove more than one-third of the flowering stem and always cut just above an outward-facing bud.

Damping down   see page 240

Buying

Successful buying involves more than just choosing the right varieties. It means going to the right supplier at the right time of year and buying plants in the right condition and in the right container to suit your needs and pocket.

As a general rule you get what you pay for. There are times when you may be sold rubbish by a garden centre and many gardeners have obtained excellent plants as a mail order bargain offer — but the general rule still applies. There are numerous sources — garden centres, nurseries, bargain offer and mail order nurseries, market stalls, High St. shops, DIY stores etc. Seeing before you buy is wise, but may not be practical for unusual varieties — the RHS *Plant Finder* will list a supplier.

POTS

Good signs

Clear labelling

Healthy and firm top-growth

Bad signs

Wilted leaves

Dry soil

Long roots growing through drainage holes

PRE-PACKS

Good sign

Plant completely dormant

Bad signs

Leaf buds beginning to open

Shrivelled or diseased stems

Small white roots growing into the damp packing material

BULBS

Good signs

Stem growth absent or only just apparent

Neck firm

Tunic entire, although gaps in tulip skin are acceptable

Base firm

Root growth not apparent

Bad signs

Stem growth clearly present

Neck soft or diseased

Tunic missing. Tissue below diseased, damaged or shrivelled

Base soft

Root growth clearly active

Compost making

The need for a plentiful supply of organic matter to improve soil structure was stressed in Chapter 2. Shop-bought material is too expensive, animal manure is too difficult to find — the answer is to make compost from unwanted plant material.

The instructions in many books are based on the use of a lot of woody matter such as straw, dead leaves etc as well as some greenstuff, and so lime and a nitrogen activator are called for, as well as turning the material during the composting process. In most gardens, however, the main material available is the contents of the grass box on the mower, and here a different technique is required. The method below was tested many years ago by horticultural societies all over the country.

WHAT GOES IN

You must aim for a mixture of carbon-rich and nitrogen-rich materials. As a rough guide, waste plant material which is brown or black is rich in carbon — soft and green material is nitrogen-rich. If you just use grass, weeds and a scatter of prunings, then you will have a mixture which is too rich in nitrogen for active bacterial growth. The result is that no heat is built up and so no humus is produced.

Nitrogen-rich material: grass clippings, vegetable and flower stalks, green leaves, annual weeds and household vegetable waste.

Carbon-rich material: shredded prunings, straw, shredded paper, dry leaves and sawdust.

WHAT COMES OUT

Compost made from grass clippings without some form of insulation and without a rainproof cover is a slimy green mess. Compost made by the method below is quite different. The initial mixture is changed by heat and intense bacterial activity into a brown, crumbly material in which the ingredients are no longer easy to recognise. Compost started in the spring or summer should be ready in late autumn or the following spring. Autumn compost is for forking into the soil — spring compost is excellent for mulching. Compost made with clippings from a weedkiller-treated lawn should be tested. Mix some with seed compost and sow radish seed. Normal germination means it is safe.

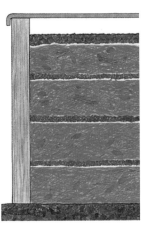

STEP 1   **Use a suitable container** It should be large and the walls should be thick — wood, bricks and breeze blocks are suitable. Heat has to be kept in. A waterproof lid is essential.

STEP 2   **Put down a layer of greenstuff** This should be flat on top and about 25 cm (10 in.) deep, but the exact depth is not critical. See above for suitable materials.

STEP 3   **Sprinkle a layer of carbon-rich material** This stage is essential if the Step 2 layer is just grass and weeds. It should be about 1 cm (½ in.) thick — fork in. See above for suitable materials.

STEP 4   **Cover with a thin layer of soil** This provides a multitude of bacteria, mops up undesirable gases and absorbs water.

STEP 5   **Repeat Steps 2 - 4** Continue until all the clippings etc have been used up.

STEP 6   **Cover the top** Replace the lid to keep out rain. Repeat Steps 2 - 5 next week when you have another load of grass clippings.

Dead-heading

The removal of dead flowers has several advantages — it helps to keep the bed or border tidy, it prolongs the flowering season and in a few cases (e.g lupin and delphinium) it induces a second flush later in the season.

Use garden shears, secateurs, a sharp knife or finger tips depending on the type of plant. Be careful not to remove too much stem. You must not dead-head flowers grown for their seed pods.

It is quite impractical to remove the dead blooms from some annuals and perennials and from most trees and shrubs. There are a few large-flowering woody plants, however, which must be dead-headed. The faded trusses of hybrid tea and floribunda roses should be cut off and the dead flowers of rhododendrons should be carefully broken off with finger and thumb. Cut off the flower heads of lilac once the blooms have faded, but not the large heads of hydrangeas — remove in March.

Disbudding

In general flower buds in the garden are allowed to develop and open naturally to provide the maximum display. For exhibitors, however, and others interested in the size of individual blooms, the flower stems are disbudded. This calls for pinching out side buds as soon as they can be handled, leaving the central bud to develop.

Chrysanthemums, dahlias and carnations are frequently treated in this way for Show purposes. Many hybrid tea roses produce more than one flower bud at the end of each shoot. With this flower it is nearly always desirable to seek maximum size, so disbudding of side shoots is recommended. Delay removing the side buds if you want to hold back flowering for the day of the Show. If the rose variety produces very full blooms which spoil badly in wet weather, reverse the process and pinch out the terminal bud so that the side buds develop.

Dibbing in

Dibbing in is a simple and quicker planting technique than using a trowel. The standard dibber is a stout wooden or metal spike, bought from a garden shop or made at home from an old spade handle. These dibbers are for large seedlings. For pot culture and for small seedlings outdoors use a pencil or dowel. The tip of the dibber should be rounded rather than sharply pointed.

Dibbing in (or dibbling) involves inserting the dibber sufficiently deep into the soil so that the roots will fit comfortably. Place the plant into the hole and then firm the earth by re-inserting the dibber point about 2-5 cm (1-2 in.) away from the stem. Move the dibber towards the plant in order to press the soil around the roots.

This is a good technique for planting vegetables which have been raised in a seed bed. Brassicas, such as cabbages, Brussels sprouts etc, are well-known examples. It is also widely used for planting cuttings, but in all cases you must make sure that the hole is no deeper than necessary. The role of dibbing in is limited — use a trowel and not a dibber for large-size planting material such as bulbs or tubers, and do not use a dibber in heavy, wet soil.

Earthing up

There are several reasons for earthing up — the drawing of soil towards and around the stems. Potatoes are earthed up to avoid the tubers being exposed to light. When the haulm is about 22 cm (9 in.) high a draw hoe is used to pile loose soil against the stems to form a flat-topped ridge.

The greens (broccoli, kale, Brussels sprouts etc) are earthed up by drawing soil around the stems to improve anchorage against high winds.

The stems of leeks and some varieties of celery are earthed up. This begins with celery when it is about 30 cm (1 ft) high — with leeks this is done in stages, the height being increased a little at a time by drawing dry soil around the stems.

Earthing up also has a place in the herbaceous border. Shoots may appear prematurely during a mild spell in early spring — it is advisable to draw loose soil over them with a hoe so as to prevent damage by severe frosts which may come later.

Digging   see page 13

Feeding

There are two basic reasons why soil may fail to support satisfactory growth. Firstly the structure may be poor — too much sand or clay with too little organic matter for proper crumb formation. The answer is to add a bulky humus maker — see page 14. The other reason for poor performance is the shortage of vital nutrients. The addition of compost etc will help a little, but the real answer is to use a fertilizer. A fertilizer is a material which provides appreciable quantities of one or more plant nutrients without adding a significant amount of humus.

WHAT TO USE

Quick-acting fertilizers

These types go to work almost at once, providing plants with a boost. Unfortunately most are not long-lasting. Nearly all the top-selling types belong here, the liquid and soluble powder ones, the proprietary powders and granules for roses, tomatoes etc, the general-purpose granular ones like Growmore and the 'straight' inorganic ones such as sulphate of ammonia.

Slow-acting fertilizers

These types have to break down before going to work, so speed of nutrient release depends on soil conditions. They go on working for longer than the quick-acting ones and are less likely to cause scorch, but do not expect a quick greening-up of the foliage. They are usually organic (hoof & horn, fish meal, bone meal etc) but may be mineral (for example rock phosphate).

Organic or Chemical?

At the plant root level the form of the nitrogen, phosphates and potash which enters is identical. However, some users of plant- and animal-based fertilizers such as dried poultry manure feel that these products have special virtues over chemical ones. Unfortunately the range of these organics is limited and they are generally more expensive than the popular chemical or 'artificial' fertilizers.

Steady-release fertilizers

A post-war development which is widely used by nurserymen for their container-grown plants and is also available to gardeners. A granular fertilizer is coated with a resin and this outer covering breaks down steadily in the soil. The nutrients are thus made available over a prolonged period — usually for 6 months. Spread around trees, shrubs or perennials in the spring.

WHAT TO FEED

You can have a soil analysis carried out, but it is more usual to take action on the basis of plant type, soil type, season of the year and the appearance of the plants. In order of fertilizer needs, vigorous container plants in unfed compost come top of the list followed by heavy-cropping vegetables, bedding plants, lawns and large-flowered perennials. Bottom of the list are well-established trees and shrubs. Soil type is important — sandy soils are hungry, especially in rainy areas. The best nutrient balance depends on the type of plant — see below.

THE FEEDING PROGRAMME

There are a few basic principles but there is no standard feeding programme. The traditional routine is to use a granular balanced fertilizer to enrich the soil before planting (base feeding) or to apply it around growing established shrubs and perennials at the start of the growing season. In late spring and summer a quick-acting liquid fertilizer is used — you will find a range of brands at your local garden centre. There are areas of the garden which are usually fed with a specific rather than a general fertilizer — examples are the lawn and the rose bed.

BALANCED N P_2O_5 K_2O	Nitrogen (N) content similar to Potash (K_2O)	Use as a general-purpose fertilizer for base feeding or as an in-season top dressing
HIGH N N P_2O_5 K_2O	Nitrogen (N) content higher than Potash (K_2O)	Use on grass, leaf vegetables and root-bound plants to boost growth and improve leaf colour
HIGH K_2O N P_2O_5 K_2O	Nitrogen (N) content lower than Potash (K_2O)	Use on fruit, flowers and potatoes to help flower quality and to increase crop yields

Fallowing

In the old days farmers used to fallow fields occasionally — leaving them bare for a whole season to allow bacteria to build up fertility and to allow the weather to improve the soil structure. This practice has practically no place in gardening, although the vegetable plot is mainly bare in winter and so it can be considered a short-term fallow.

Despite the absence of true fallowing, a special form of fallow is widely used in the vegetable garden. Some forms of soil-borne troubles such as eelworm, club root and white rot can live in the ground for several years. Following an attack, the land must be part-fallowed — that is, no susceptible plant must be grown on it for the period specified in the textbooks.

Forcing

Forcing is the process which induces growth, flowering or fruiting earlier than normal — gentle heat is the usual stimulant. There are no general rules — factors which will force one plant may fail miserably with another.

Spring bulbs are forced by keeping the planted bowls cool (5ºC/40ºF) and in darkness for about 8 weeks before moving to warmer conditions — 10ºC (50ºF) at first then 15ºC (60ºF) to 21ºC (70ºF). Daffodil bulbs for extra-early flowering are prepared by keeping in cold storage for several weeks in late summer.

Rhubarb is forced by being kept in the dark at 10ºC (50ºF) rising to 15ºC (60ºF). Many other plants in pots can be forced at a similar temperature, but require light conditions in a greenhouse or cold frame. Examples include potatoes, strawberries, French beans, roses, spiraeas and azaleas.

Forking

A garden fork is not really a digging tool, although it can sometimes be easier to dig a heavy soil with a fork rather than a spade. Forking is really a method of cultivation — lumps are broken down by hitting them with the tines and the surface roughly levelled by dragging the tines across the surface. Forking is sometimes used around growing plants to break up surface crust, and also for moving compost, lifting potatoes and aerating lawns.

Grafting & Budding

A graft is a union between two plants, the roots and lower stem (the stock or rootstock) of one plant uniting with the shoot of another plant (the scion), so that they grow together as one. The main role of grafting is the propagation of trees and shrubs where one or more of the following difficulties prevent easier means of producing planting material:

- Varieties which do not root from cuttings.
- Varieties which do not set or breed true from seed.
- Varieties which fail when grown on their own roots.

A mystique has grown up about grafting, but the principle is very simple. The stock and the scion must be related and there must be physical close contact — it is the thin living layer below the bark which has to knit together. Timing is important — the plants should be just starting to grow after their winter rest, and the union must be protected. This calls for binding with raffia, plastic tape or an elastic tie and then covering the area with grafting wax.

Although the principle is simple, a large number of systems have evolved over the centuries. The most popular method is whip and tongue grafting — see below. The stock and scion should be approximately the same thickness — remove the binding material once new growth has appeared.

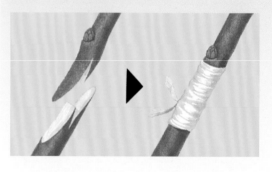

Commercial roses are generally propagated by budding which is carried out in midsummer rather than early spring. A bud or 'eye' of the selected variety is inserted into a T-shaped cut made in the stem of the rootstock — close to the ground for a bush or further up the stem for a standard.

Hardening Off

Plants raised indoors or in a greenhouse have tender tissues — suddenly moving them outdoors in spring means a transition to colder conditions and drying winds for which they are not prepared. The result of this shock is either a severe check or death of the specimen.

To avoid this problem there must be a gradual acclimatisation to the harsher conditions to be faced outdoors — a process known as hardening off. Begin by increasing the ventilation during the day in the greenhouse, after which the plants should be moved to a cold frame. Keep the lights closed at night for several days — then steadily increase the ventilation until the plants are continuously exposed to the outside air for a few days before planting out.

Watch the plants during hardening off. If the leaves turn blue or blotchy and growth stops you will have to slow down the process.

Harvesting

Many gardeners aim to produce giant vegetables to match the ones they see on the show bench, and you may therefore be surprised at some of the harvesting sizes recommended in this book. Turnips the size of a golf ball and carrots no longer than your finger — not economical for the farmer but these are the sizes for top flavour and tenderness. Not all vegetables need to be picked at an early stage — the flavour of swedes, parsnips and celery does not decline with age.

With some crops such as marrows, cucumbers, peas and beans it is essential to pick regularly as just a few ripe fruits or pods left on the plant can bring cropping to an end.

Before you begin, read what to do in the vegetable chapter. Carelessly tearing off pods can damage the stems of pea plants — pulling out roots by their foliage can leave part of the crop in the ground.

Heeling in

Occasionally you will find that trees, shrubs, roses or border perennials arrive before you are ready to plant them. The ground may be frozen or water-logged, the site may not be ready or you may be just too busy. If this delay is to be more than 10 days, heel in the plants by digging a shallow V-shaped trench and then spreading them as a single row against one side of the trench. Cover the roots and lower parts of the stems with soil and tread down. Label with some form of permanent tag — paper labels attached by the supplier may rot away. The plants can be left for several weeks — lift and plant in the ordinary way as soon as you are able to do so.

Hoeing

The hoe has two important functions. Its main task is to keep weeds under control — hoeing must be carried out at regular intervals to keep annual weeds in check and to starve out the underground parts of perennial weeds.

Weeds should be severed just below ground level rather than being dragged to the surface. The second important function of hoeing is to break up the surface pan (see page 9) which can be a problem in some soils after rain.

The proper way to use a hoe depends upon the type (see page 108). With a Dutch hoe you push the blade forward as you walk backwards — the blade is held just below the soil surface. The advantages are the avoidance of walking on the hoed area and the superior weed-cutting action. The draw hoe is used with a chopping rather than a slicing motion — the blade is brought down in short chopping strokes as you walk slowly backwards. There are advantages — it is more effective than a Dutch hoe on hard ground and it is safer for use when working near to plants. Draw hoes have other uses, such as earthing up potatoes and celery, and the corner of the blade is often used for drawing seed drills.

Hoe with care. Roots of some plants lie close to the surface, and much damage is done by hoeing too deeply. Don't hoe if weeds are absent and the surface is not caked — the 'dust mulch' has now been found to be of no value as a way of cutting down water loss.

Lifting

You must use the right technique when lifting plants or you will damage the roots. If the plants or other items to be moved in the garden are bulky and heavy, you can damage yourself.

Use a fork to lift root vegetables and flower tubers — donít try to harvest fully-grown carrots, turnips etc by pulling the foliage. Dig down deeply and prise up gently. Do not store any roots which you accidentally damage. Lifting large shrubs and trees is a skilled job — it is a good idea to cut through the outer roots several months before you plan to lift, and on moving day dig round the root ball and place sacking or wire-netting round it before lifting. Allowing the soil ball to shatter is one of the commonest mistakes at planting time.

Liming   see page 16
Manuring   see page 14

Mowing

START

Begin in **March** or **early April**, depending on the locality and the weather. It is time for the first cut when the soil is reasonably dry and the grass is starting to grow actively. With this first cut set the blades high so that the grass is merely tipped, not shorn.

MARCH

MOW REGULARLY

As a general rule the cutting height should be 2.5 cm (1 in.) and mowing should take place at weekly intervals. However, there are several exceptions to this standard procedure:

- Set the blades at 3-4 cm (1¼-1½ in.) for the first couple of cuts in spring and for the last few cuts in autumn.

- Set the blades at 4 cm (1½ in.) during periods of prolonged drought if the lawn is not being regularly watered. The longer grass will help to cut down water loss.

- Cut at fortnightly rather than weekly intervals if the grass is growing very slowly — for example under trees or during prolonged drought.

- If you have had to be away for a couple of weeks or more in summer then merely tip it at the first cut following your return. Reduce the height at the next cut and then continue with 2.5 cm (1 in.) high cuts.

APRIL

MAY

JUNE

JU

**Cut once
a week
•
Set blades
2.5 cm (1 in.)
high**

AUGU

FINISH

Stop in **October** when the growth of the grass has slowed right down and the soil has become very moist. Put the mower away, but rake off fallen leaves on the surface of the lawn. Keen gardeners lightly tip the grass occasionally in winter when the weather is mild, but it is not essential. Avoid walking on the lawn when it is frozen or covered in snow.

OCTOBER

CHOOSING A MOWER

Size of lawn		Recommended minimum cutting width
Small lawn:	less than 45 sq.m (less than 500 sq.ft)	25–30 cm (10–12 in.)
Average lawn:	45–180 sq.m (500-2000 sq.ft)	30–35 cm (12–14 in.)
Large lawn:	over 180 sq.m (over 2000 sq.ft)	35–45 cm (14–18 in.)

Rotary

Wheels or wheels plus a roller support the machine — under the cover the horizontal blade or blades rotate at high speed. Choose an electric one for a small lawn — for a larger area you will need a self-propelled model where both wheels and blades are motor-driven.

Ride-on

Worth considering if you have an acre or more to care for. Most popular version is the 4-wheeled tractor with a rotary mower fitted between the wheels. Enjoyable, but such mowers are expensive, difficult to use in awkward corners and can cause compaction on heavy land in wet weather.

Hover

A fan creates the air cushion on which the machine floats — the rotating horizontal blade cuts the grass. The hover is easier than the other types to move over the lawn. The 30 cm (12 in.) model is very popular. The petrol version is heavier and noisier — moving in straight lines is difficult.

Cylinder

Rollers or a combination of wheels and rollers support the machine — a series of spiral blades rotate against a bottom fixed blade. Gives the finest cut of all. There are usually 5 blades — 8-12 for a bowling green effect. Generally more expensive than rotary models.

Mulching

Mulching is one of the most important ways of improving both the quality and appearance of your soil. It need cost you nothing and it is simple to do, and yet is usually neglected. Basically a humus mulch is a layer of bulky organic matter placed around plants in order to suppress weeds and to improve both soil structure and plant growth. As noted below it is important to choose the right time for this task. The weed control mulch (see page 171) plays a different role — its purpose is to prevent rather than suppress weed growth without improving the structure of the soil.

WHAT IT DOES

The soil below is kept moist in summer, reducing the need to water. It is also kept cooler than soil without a mulch, and this moist and cool root zone promotes more active growth than in unmulched areas.

The soil is kept warmer than uncovered ground in winter — a definite benefit for many plants.

Some pests and diseases are kept in check. Obviously root flies are deterred and so are moles. U.S research indicates that eelworm numbers are reduced.

Some mulches such as well-rotted manure and garden compost do provide a small amount of plant food, but this is not enough to meet the needs of most plants, so some extra feeding may be needed.

Soil structure is improved for a number of reasons. Humus is added, earthworm activity is increased and soil capping by rain or watering is eliminated.

Leaves are protected from rain splashes bouncing off the soil — a much ignored problem.

Annual weed growth is suppressed — those which break through are easily removed by hand pulling and so there is no need to hoe. Vigorous perennial weeds will be able to break through — consider a weed control mulch (page 171) if they are a serious problem.

HOW, WHEN AND WHAT TO MULCH

Humus mulches are insulators which help to retain the conditions occurring at the time they are put down. This means that the soil should be just right for active growth — warm and moist and not cold and dry. The plants which are recommended for mulching are trees, shrubs, roses and hardy perennials. Vegetables are not often given a humus mulch and annuals are either unmulched or surrounded by a thin layer of grass clippings during the summer months. With young trees and shrubs weeds around the stems can be a serious problem, and so a circle or square of weed-proof material (page 171) is placed around the stem and then covered with gravel or bark chippings. Squares of bituminous felt ('tree spats') can be bought for this purpose.

The standard time for applying a humus mulch is May. Before you begin putting down organic matter it is necessary to prepare the soil surface. Remove debris and hand pull or hoe annual weeds. If these weeds are abundant it is easier to spray with a quick-acting contact weedkiller — see page 170. It is also important to get rid of perennial weeds. Dig

out if only a few are present, otherwise spray with glyphosate. The final job is to apply a general fertilizer and rake in lightly.

The soil is moist, warm and free from weeds — it is now time to spread a 5-7.5 cm (2-3 in.) layer of the chosen mulching material over the ground around the stems. This covered area should extend for about 45 cm (1½ ft) around the centre of a shrub and for 75 cm (2½ ft) around the trunk of a moderate-sized tree. If mulching material is plentiful you can cover the whole bed or border, but with both partial and all-over cover you must make sure that the mulch does not come right up to the stems. A build-up of moist organic matter against the shoots can lead to rotting. Do not disturb this layer during the summer months. If weeds do appear pull out by hand or paint with glyphosate gel.

Some people fork in the mulch during October and then allow the soil to warm up in the spring before applying a new mulch. This is a lot of work, however, and so it is more usual to leave the mulch in place and top up as necessary in May.

Planting

The instructions here may be a little more complex than you expected, but following the rules will avoid problems in the long run.

Do not regard container-grown specimens as a fool-proof way to plant trees and shrubs. If the environment around the soil ball is not right then the roots may not grow properly or indeed may not grow at all. It is not enough to dig a hole, take the plant out of the container, drop it into the hole and replace the earth. First of all, the soil must be neither frozen nor water-logged. Secondly, the space for the soil ball must be wide enough — for a large container the hole should be about 20 cm (8 in.) wider than the soil ball. Finally, the space around the soil ball should be filled with planting mixture — see page 63. Prepare the plant for the move. Keep the soil ball intact — always water before lifting, or dry soil may fall away from the roots.

The planting time for bare-rooted plants is between autumn and spring. If the stems are shrivelled plunge the roots in a bucket of water for two hours before planting.

LIFTED PLANTS • ROOTED CUTTINGS

① Dig the hole to fit the roots. The hole should be much wider than it is deep — the roots at the base and at the side should never have to be bent to fit into the hole.

② Use the right tool. A trowel is the right implement for small plants.

③ Plant at the right depth. Set all bedding plants so that the top of the soil ball is just below ground level.

④ Plant properly. For small plants, fill around the soil ball with loose soil and firm with the fingers or the trowel handle. With larger plants, fine soil should be added, each layer being gently compressed with the fists until the hole is full. Handle plants by the soil ball or the leaves — never by the stem. Water in after planting.

BARE-ROOTED PLANTS
•
LIFTED PLANTS WITH LARGE ROOTS BEYOND THE SOIL BALL

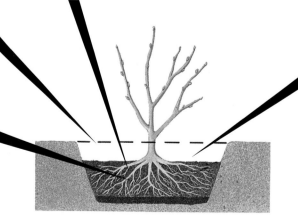

③ Work a couple of trowelfuls of the planting mixture around the roots. Shake the plant gently up and down — add a little more planting mixture. Firm this around the roots with the fists — do not press too hard. Half-fill the hole with more planting mixture and firm it down.

② The old soil mark should be level with the soil surface — set a board across the top of the hole as a guide.

① The hole should be wide enough to allow the roots to be spread evenly. Put a layer of planting mixture (page 63) at the bottom of the hole — important if soil condition is poor.

④ Add more planting mixture until the hole is full. Firm by pressing with the fists or gentle treading — on no account tread heavily. Loosen the surface once the hole has been filled — there should be a shallow water-holding basin after planting. Water in after planting.

CONTAINER PLANTS

•

LIFTED PLANTS WITH COMPACT SOIL BALL

Planting mixture

It is difficult for roots to spread from the humus-rich home they enjoyed in the container to the humus-starved soil present in most gardens. A planting mixture of compost and soil provides a transition zone which reduces the abruptness of this change. Make the mixture in a wheelbarrow — 1 part moist garden compost, 1 part topsoil and 3 handfuls of bone meal per barrowload. Keep in a shed until ready for use.

② Water the pot or container thoroughly at least an hour before planting. Remove the plant very carefully — do not disturb the soil ball. With a pot-grown plant place your hand around the crown of the plant and turn the pot over. Gently remove — tap the sides with a trowel if necessary.

③ Examine the exposed surface — cut away circling or tangled roots but do not break up the soil ball. Fill the space between the soil ball and the sides of the hole with planting mixture. Firm down the planting mixture with your hands.

① The hole should be deep enough to ensure that the top of the soil ball will be about 3 cm (1 in.) below the soil surface after planting. The hole should be wide enough for the soil ball to be surrounded by a layer of planting mixture (see above). Put a 3 cm (1 in.) layer of the planting mixture at the bottom of the hole.

④ After planting there should be a shallow water-holding basin. Water in after planting.

BULBS

② The width of the hole should be about twice the diameter of the bulb. The depth will depend upon the variety you are planting — as a general rule, the common large bulbs such as tulip, narcissus and hyacinth will need to be covered by twice their own height. Most small bulbs are covered to about their own height. The bottom should be reasonably flat and the sides reasonably vertical — avoid making 'ice cream cone' holes.

③ It is vital that there should not be an air space between the bottom of the bulb and the soil at the base of the hole. If the soil is heavy it is useful to put in a shallow layer of grit.

④ Push the bulb down to the base of the hole and twist gently. Make sure the bulb is the right way up.

⑤ Put the earth back and press it down gently. Use the dug-out soil for this job, but it is a good idea to mix it with coarse sand, well-rotted compost or leaf mould if the ground is heavy. Rake over the surface if a large area has been planted and water in if the weather is dry.

① Nearly all bulbs require free-draining soil. Dig about a week before the planting date if the soil is compacted — adding coarse sand or grit will help if the ground is heavy. Free drainage is equally or even more important when planting up containers — make sure that the drainage holes are large enough and not blocked.

⑥ Bulbs leave no above-ground indication of their presence after planting. It is therefore sometimes necessary to put in a label to remind you that there are bulbs below.

Potting

Potting is carried out when a single plant is put into a container — potting-on involves the transfer of a potted plant into a larger container when the roots have filled the compost in the pot and the plant is starting to become pot-bound. Tell-tale signs of this condition are the growth of roots through the drainage hole, compost which dries out very quickly, and slow growth despite favourable conditions.

A suitable sequence of pot sizes is an increase of 5–7.5 cm (2–3 in.) in diameter at each potting on stage. Stop when the desired plant size is reached. Scrub out old pots thoroughly — soak clay ones overnight.

Water the plant. One hour later remove it from the pot as shown above. If difficult to dislodge, knock the pot on the edge of a hard surface and run a knife around the rootball. Remove old crocks.

Cover drainage hole of a clay pot with crocks. Add a layer of potting compost. Place the plant on top of this layer — gradually fill surrounding space with damp potting compost. Firm down with your thumbs.

Tap the pot several times on a hard surface — leave a 3 cm (1 in.) watering space. Water thoroughly using a fine rose. In hot and dry weather keep the pot in a shady spot if possible for about a week.

Puddling

A technique much loved by Victorian gardeners — the roots of herbaceous and woody plants are dipped in a slurry of clay and water before planting. Puddling was supposed to produce a water-holding layer around the roots and to keep pests at bay. Unfortunately there seems to be no scientific evidence for these benefits and it is better to water the planting hole before planting if the weather is dry.

Pinching out

Pinching out is the removal of the growing point and a small amount of stem by nipping between finger and thumb. The purpose of this technique is to induce bushiness — the removal of the tip of the main stem stimulates the development of side shoots. Many annuals (antirrhinum, salvia, lobelia etc) are pinched out at an early stage to produce well-branched plants. This technique is also used to control the flowering time of chrysanthemums and carnations for Show purposes — a technique known as 'stopping'.

Plunging

Plunging describes the burying of pot plants up to their rims outdoors. Pots or bowls can be plunged in ordinary soil but it is more usual to construct a special plunge bed filled with peat or sand. Many indoor plants can spend their summers in the fresh air, their roots protected from sudden rises and falls in temperature by the insulating effect of the plunge bed. One of the main uses is for spring-flowering bulbs — the bowls are placed in a plunge bed and covered with ash or coarse sand in winter. Root formation is stimulated in the cool moist conditions — the ideal preparation for the forcing which takes place later.

Raking

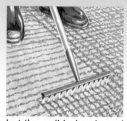

Raking is often described as one of the skilled techniques of gardening — it takes practice to do it properly. Its role is to create a seed bed after the large lumps have been broken down by forking. Choose a day when the surface is dry but the soil below is moist. Work in long sweeps, drawing stones and rubbish towards you and breaking down lumps as you push away. After the plot has been raked in this way, repeat the process at right angles. Obviously the lumps must be broken down, air pockets removed and the surface left smooth, but you must know when to stop. Over-raking leads to excessively fine tilth which caps with the first downpour. Spring-tine rakes are excellent for removing leaves and other debris on lawns but cannot take the place of a rigid rake for seed bed preparation.

Propagating

There are three basic reasons for raising new plants in your own garden. First of all, there is the satisfaction of having plants which are actually home-grown and not raised by somebody else. Next, it is the only way to reproduce a much-admired variety which is not available from a nursery and lastly, but certainly not least, there is a purely practical reason — saving money.

Not all garden plants can be raised at home and the ease with which new stock can be produced varies from child's play to near impossible. There are several techniques — the one most likely to succeed for each plant is given in the appropriate A-Z guide. Everyone who grows a wide range of vegetables is already accustomed to sowing seeds, but not every gardener practises layering or taking cuttings. Do try the techniques on these three pages — there is nothing to lose and much to gain.

DIVIDING HARDY PERENNIALS

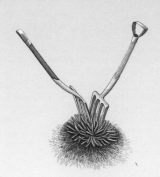

Division is a form of propagation which is often forced upon you — spreading hardy perennials will often deteriorate after a few years if not lifted and divided.

Choose a mild day in spring or autumn when the soil is moist. Dig up the clump with a fork, taking care not to damage the roots more than necessary. Shake off the excess soil and study where the basic divisions should be. You might be able to break the clump with your hands — if the clump is too tough for this technique then use two hand forks or garden forks. Push the forks back-to-back into the centre and prise gently apart. Treat the resulting divisions in a similar fashion or tear apart with your fingers.

DIVIDING SHRUBS

Some small shrubs form clumps which can be lifted and then split up like hardy perennials into several rooted sections. Each section should be planted firmly and then watered in thoroughly.

Best time: Early winter

Examples: Ceratostigma   Lavandula

Many shrubs spread by means of suckers, which are shoots arising from an underground shoot or root. Removing and planting suckers is one of the easiest of all methods of propagation.

Best time: Early winter for deciduous plants; April or September for evergreens

Examples: Corylus   Kerria
Cotinus   Mahonia

LAYERING SHRUBS

Shrubs with flexible stems can be raised very easily by layering — some plants (e.g rhododendron, magnolia) produce new plants naturally by this method. To layer a shrub or climber, a stem is pegged into the ground and left attached to the parent plant until roots have formed at the base of the layered shoot. This takes about 6 to 12 months.

Best time: Spring or autumn

Examples: Berberis   Forsythia
Camellia   Lonicera
Chaenomeles   Magnolia
Clematis   Syringa

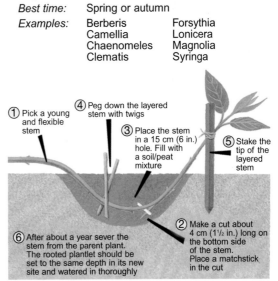

② Lift the sucker with as much root as possible. Replant it to the same depth — water in thoroughly

① Cut all round this sucker with a spade

① Pick a young and flexible stem

④ Peg down the layered stem with twigs

③ Place the stem in a 15 cm (6 in.) hole. Fill with a soil/peat mixture

⑤ Stake the tip of the layered stem

② Make a cut about 4 cm (1½ in.) long on the bottom side of the stem. Place a matchstick in the cut

⑥ After about a year sever the stem from the parent plant. The rooted plantlet should be set to the same depth in its new site and watered in thoroughly

SOWING SEEDS

Indoor sowing

Tender plants are grown from seed in March or April and are set out in late May or early June. Sowing indoors is not restricted to half-hardy subjects — it is useful for hardy types which are to grow in a wet and/or cold area.

Fill container with compost

Use a seed tray, pan or pot. Drainage holes are necessary. Wash used containers before filling — soak clay pots overnight.

Fill with seed or general-purpose compost. Firm lightly with a piece of board. Sprinkle with water the day before seed sowing. It should be moist (not wet) when you scatter the seeds thinly over the surface. Cover with a thin layer of compost — do not cover small seeds. Firm lightly.

Use Under-glass method

Place a sheet of glass on top and cover with brown paper. Keep at 16°–21°C (60°–70°F) — wipe and turn the glass every day. Remove the paper and prop up the glass when seedlings first appear. Remove the glass after a few days and move the container close to the light. Keep the compost moist, but not wet.

or Windowsill method

Place a transparent plastic bag over the pot as shown. Secure with a rubber band and keep at 16°–21°C (60°–70°F) in a shady spot. Remove the bag when seedlings first appear and move the pot to a bright windowsill which is away from direct sunlight. Keep the compost moist but not wet.

Prick out and harden off

Fill a tray or pot with potting compost. Prick out seedlings into this as soon as the first set of true leaves has opened. Handle by the seed leaves, not the stems. Set them about 5 cm (2 in.) apart and keep in the shade for a few days.

The seedlings must be hardened off once they have recovered from pricking out. Move to a cool room and then move outdoors during daylight hours. Finally, leave outdoors for about 7 days before planting out.

Outdoor sowing

March-April is the usual time to sow hardy annuals, but wait if the weather is cold and wet, even though it may mean being a couple of weeks late. Half-hardy annuals should be sown once the danger of frost has passed.

Prepare seed areas

Choose a day when the soil is moist below, dry on top. Tread over and rake until soil is crumbly. Mark out zones with a pointed stick and then scatter seed over each area.

or Seed drills

small seeds   medium seeds   large seeds

Choose a day when the soil is moist below, dry on top. Tread over and rake until soil is crumbly. Do not overdo this raking process — the crumb structure should be retained. Water gently before sowing if the soil is dry.

Sow seed & thin out

Place some seed in your palm and gently sprinkle with thumb and forefinger. Carefully rake the soil back into the drill — firm with the back of the rake. Thin out when the seedlings reach the stage shown above. Reduce to one seedling every 2–5 cm (1–2 in.). Repeat about 10 days later to the distance recommended on the seed packet.

TAKING CUTTINGS

Stem-tip and Heel cuttings

Stem-tip (softwood) cuttings are green at the top and base. Basal cuttings are shoots around the base of the stem which are pulled away and used as cuttings. The recommended time is between early spring and midsummer. Some small shrubs and many border perennials are propagated in this way. **Heel (semi-ripe) cuttings** are green at the top but partly woody at the base. The recommended time is midsummer to early autumn.

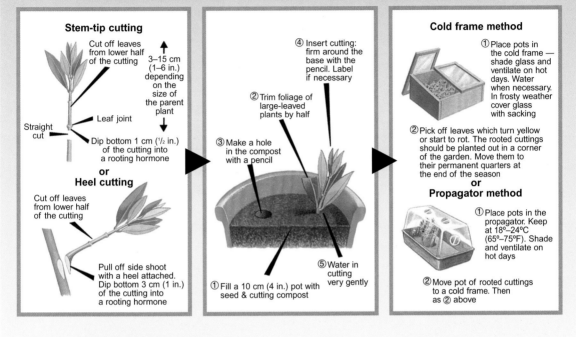

Hardwood cuttings

Hardwood cuttings are taken from a well-ripened shoot of this year's growth. The usual time is late autumn. Can be used for a number of shrubs — see Chapter 8.

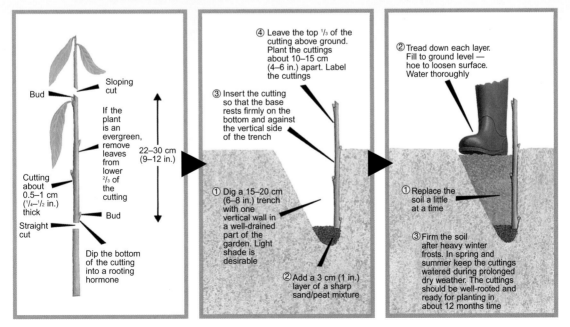

Pruning

It is generally necessary to prune most shrubs and some trees every year. There are three reasons for this task. Firstly, there is the need to remove poor quality wood, such as weak twigs, dead or diseased branches and damaged stems. Next, there is the need to shape the tree or bush — this calls for the removal of good quality but unwanted wood so that the vigour of the plant is directed as required. Finally, trees and shrubs are pruned to regulate the quality and quantity of flower production. Gardeners list pruning as the task they find most puzzling, and it is indeed the most difficult lesson that has to be learnt.

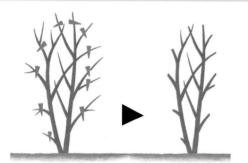

HEADING BACK

The ends of the branches are removed

This may be the removal of just tips or all the stems when a shrub is coppiced or all the branches when a tree is pollarded. The immediate effect is to produce a shrub which is smaller than before. But the buds below the cut are then stimulated and will burst into growth so the long-term effect is to produce a tree or shrub which is bushier and leafier than one left unpruned.

THINNING

Entire branches are cut right back to the main stem

This may be the removal of just one or two branches or the removal of all the branches from the main stem below the crown to produce a standard tree. The immediate effect is to direct extra energy to the remaining branches. Their growth will be accelerated, so the long-term effect is to produce a tree or shrub which is bigger and more open than one left unpruned.

SHEARING

All the growing points with only a small amount of stem attached are removed by cutting with shears or a hedge trimmer. This technique is used to maintain the shape of hedges and topiary.

CROWN LIFTING

The lower branches are removed by lopping to allow free access and to let in more light under the tree. Use with care if the tree has a weeping growth habit.

LOPPING

The removal of a large branch from the trunk of a tree

Make a smooth sloping cut beyond the raised ridge (branch collar) at the base of the branch — leaving the collar on the tree will speed up healing. Begin by making a shallow cut on the underside, then saw downwards to sever the branch. Consider using a tree surgeon if the branch is heavy or out of reach.

ANNUAL PRUNING

As a general rule most trees and shrubs grown for their foliage require little regular pruning — all that is necessary is the removal of dead and badly damaged wood together with the pruning back of over-long branches. Flowering shrubs are different — some will soon become leggy and unproductive if not cut back regularly. Do not guess what to do — some shrubs are damaged by hard pruning. Follow the rules below, but if in doubt remember that too little pruning is safer than too much.

STEP 1

Pick the right time. It is essential that pruning takes place at the correct growth stage of the tree or shrub — cutting back severely at the wrong time often leads to the loss of a whole season's flowers and occasionally it leads to the death of the plant.

The best plan is to look up the particular tree or shrub in the A - Z guide in Chapter 8 — the following timing rules are only a general guide and there are exceptions.

Foliage deciduous trees & shrubs	Between January and March
Deciduous trees & shrubs which bloom before the end of May	As soon as flowering has finished — do not delay
Deciduous trees & shrubs which bloom after the end of May	Between January and March — do not wait until growth starts
Flowering cherries	Late summer
Broad-leaved evergreens	May
Conifers	Autumn

STEP 2

Cut out dead wood. It is quite natural for the lower branches of some shrubs and trees to die under the dense canopy of the upper leaves. Prune back to where the dead branch joins the stem from which it arose.

STEP 3

Cut out damaged and diseased wood. All branches which have been broken by wind or snow should be removed and all badly diseased or cankered wood should be cut out. The pruned surface should not bear tell-tale brown staining.

STEP 4

Cut out weak and overcrowded wood. Prune all very thin and weak stems — then stand back and look at the network of branches. If there is a tightly-packed arrangement of criss-crossed stems at the centre of the bush, some thinning of the old wood will help to open up the shrub and improve its vigour and appearance.

STEP 5

Remove suckers. With grafted plants the suckering growth produced from the rootstock will weaken the plant and may allow these unwanted stems to take over if left unchecked. Some shrubs which grow on their own roots may also produce suckers, and these too should be removed if you want to keep the plant within bounds. Failure to remove the suckers can lead to a dense thicket of stems within a few years.

STEP 6

Cut back overgrowth. Once again stand back and look at the plant. Are some of the branches awkwardly placed? Is it becoming too invasive? Are the stems overhanging the path? Remember that overgrowth should be tackled every year and not left until major surgery is required.

STEP 7

Prune (if necessary) for floral display. Many but not all flowering shrubs and trees require pruning each year to ensure a regular and abundant supply of flowering stems. Look up the plant in the A - Z guide in Chapter 8 — the following rules are only a general guide and there are exceptions:

Deciduous trees and shrubs which bloom before the end of May. Examples: Ribes, Forsythia, Philadelphus, Exochorda, Weigela and Deutzia	Flowers are produced on old wood. Cut back the branches which have flowered — remove about one third of the length. With vigorous shrubs a few of the oldest stems can be cut down to ground level. New, vigorous growth will develop and this will bear flowers next season.
Deciduous trees and shrubs which bloom after the end of May. Examples: Fuchsia, Potentilla, Tamarix, Buddleia davidii	Flowers are produced on new wood. The old stems should be cut back — the amount of wood to remove depends on the tree or shrub concerned. New, vigorous growth will develop and this will bear flowers this season.
Flowering cherries	No further pruning needed.

Spacing trees & shrubs

It is easy to see why people plant too closely. The plants from the garden centre or nursery are usually small, and it is hard to imagine at this stage what they will look like when they are mature. But they will reach maturity, and if you have planted them too closely there are only two alternatives — you can either dig out some of the cramped shrubs (which is the more sensible but the less popular choice) or you can hack them back each year, which destroys so much of their beauty.

Of course, the better plan is to start correctly:

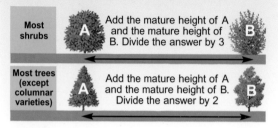

Most shrubs — Add the mature height of A and the mature height of B. Divide the answer by 3

Most trees (except columnar varieties) — Add the mature height of A and the mature height of B. Divide the answer by 2

Use the rule of thumb guide below if you do not know the expected mature height of the plants:

Trees — 5-8 m (16-26 ft) apart, depending on whether they are small, medium or large types.

Shrubs — 0.5 m-1.5 m (1½-5 ft) apart, depending on whether they are small, medium or large types.

Staking trees & shrubs

A tree or tall spindly shrub can be rocked by strong winds if its roots are not able to anchor it firmly in the ground. A newly-planted specimen does not have this anchorage, so it can be dislodged or blown over. Staking is the answer — it is a job to do at planting time and not after the damage has been done.

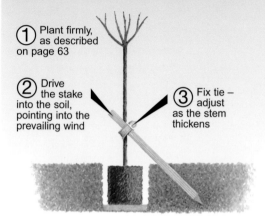

① Plant firmly, as described on page 63

② Drive the stake into the soil, pointing into the prevailing wind

③ Fix tie — adjust as the stem thickens

Storing

Nearly all vegetables can be kept for a few days or even a week or two in the refrigerator, but there will be times when long-term storage will be necessary. With beans there is always a sudden glut, and it is far better to pick them at the tender stage for storage rather than trying to extend the harvest period to the time when they will be tough and stringy.

In the pre-deep freeze era storage methods had to be devised so that a winter supply of vegetables could be provided. Peas and beans were dried and then shelled. Onions and cabbages were hung up in bags or laid out on open trays. Runner beans were salted, onions and beetroots were pickled in vinegar.

Nowadays long-term storage has been transformed by the advent of the home freezer. This is the ideal storage method for many vegetables. The routine is to blanch, cool, drain and then freeze. See *The Garden to Kitchen Expert* for full instructions.

Maincrop roots are generally lifted in autumn for storage indoors as layers between sand (e.g carrots, beetroots) or in sacks (potatoes) in a frost-free shed. Harvest after a few days of dry weather. You can let the vegetable plot act as a vegetable store for some roots — swedes, parsnips and turnips can be lifted as required.

Thinning

Thinning is carried out at several stages in the life cycle of some plants — from the time when they are seedlings to the fruiting period of large trees. Despite the often-repeated recommendation to sow thinly you will usually find that the seedlings emerging in the vegetable plot or in seed trays are too close together. Thinning is necessary, and this is a job to be tackled as soon as the plants are large enough to handle. Delay means spindly plants which never fully recover. The soil should be moist — water if necessary. Hold down the soil around the unwanted seedling with one hand and pull it up with the other. If the seedlings are too close together to allow this technique, nip off the top growth of the unwanted ones and leave the roots in the soil. After thinning, firm the soil around the remaining seedlings and water gently.

Thinning out of stems may be necessary in the herbaceous border, and it is often required with ornamental and fruit trees when branches become overcrowded. Following the pruning of roses two or more shoots may develop from a single bud behind the cut. Rub out the weaker shoot.

Several kinds of fruit trees and bushes sometimes set a heavier crop than is required. Crowded fruits do not develop properly, and so thinning is required to allow the remaining ones to develop fully. Recommended distances between fruits are peaches 22 cm (9 in.), apples 15 cm (6 in.), plums 8 cm (3 in.), gooseberries 3 cm (1 in.). Grapes are thinned by removing some of the fruit with vine scissors from each bunch.

Training & Supporting

Training and supporting are not quite the same thing. Supporting involves the provision of a post, stake or framework to which weak stems can be attached. Staking at planting time is a vital task for some plants — see details on page 70. In this section supporting at various stages in the growth of the plants is described.

Training involves the fixing of branches into desired positions so that an unnatural but desirable growth habit is produced. Training may be an essential feature in the cultivation of the plant — climbing roses, cordon fruit trees and wall shrubs are examples.

TRAINING

Many trees, especially weeping ones, require training from an early stage if a mass of untidy branches is to be avoided. To train a standard, select the branch which will form the trunk and attach it to an upright stake — trim away all low-growing side branches. At the desired height (waist-high for a short standard, shoulder-high for a half standard and head-high for a full standard) let the main stem branch out to produce the head. With some plants (e.g roses) these branches can be trained downwards over a wire frame to form a weeping standard. Wisteria can be trained as a weeping standard in this way.

Climbers must be trained against a support from the outset to ensure that they remain attached to it and grow in the desired direction. Use trellis work, posts, pillars, pergolas, fences etc. Make sure that all fence posts are well-anchored. For covering walls use plastic-covered straining wire stretched horizontally at 45 cm (1½ ft) intervals — there should be at least 7cm (3 in.) between the wire and the wall. Many plants can be grown against walls in this way, including weak-stemmed non-climbers such as winter jasmine and Forsythia suspensa. The wire ties used to attach the main stems to the supports should not be tied too tightly. When training climbers up a pole or pillar, wind the stems in an ascending spiral (see illustration) rather than attaching with ties to one side of the support.

The main stems need not all be trained vertically — spreading them horizontally to form a fan can dramatically increase the display.

SUPPORTING

A tall plant can be rocked by strong winds if its roots are not able to anchor it firmly in the ground. A newly-planted specimen does not have this anchorage, so it can be dislodged or blown over. Staking is the answer — it is a job to do at planting time and not after the damage has been done. Inspect ties regularly — adjust as stem thickens.

Some herbaceous plants, such as chrysanthemums or dahlias, are also staked at planting time. Stout bamboo canes or wooden stakes are used. Tie the stems to the support as growth proceeds — use soft twine or raffia. This single-pole method is suitable for plants with spire-like heads, such as delphiniums. In these cases the stake must be tall enough to support the columnar head.

In most cases, however, tying to a single stake should be avoided. With bushy plants an ugly 'drumstick' effect is produced and is the sign of a poor gardener — the all-too-familiar sight of a tight group of stems attached to a cane and a splayed-out spray of flowers above.

Unfortunately weak-stemmed plants, tall varieties on exposed sites, large-headed flowers and climbers all need support, and stakes, wires, canes etc are not things of beauty in themselves. The answer is to choose the type of support with care and try to put it in position when the plant is quite small so that the stems can grow through to hide it.

For many plants all you will need is brushwood or pea sticks pushed into the soil around the young plants when the stems are about 30 cm (1 ft) high. For more robust and bushy herbaceous plants insert 3 or 4 canes around the stems and enclose the shoots with twine tied round the canes at 25 cm (10 in.) intervals. You can buy circular wire frames which are inserted into the soil and produce the same effect. In all cases follow the golden rule — never leave staking until the plant has collapsed.

The only plants which regularly require staking in the vegetable garden are beans and peas. Peas can be supported with twigs when young but may require plastic netting when fully grown — runner beans are best grown against stout canes.

When a tree has outgrown its stake it may still need support. This can be provided by fixing a collar to the middle of the trunk and then securing it to the ground by means of 3 strong wires.

Some shrubs with lax spreading stems may require support after a few years. Use 3 or 4 stakes with a band joining the top of each stake — never rely on a single pole and twine.

Watering

The way that most people treat their plants during a prolonged dry spell is wrong. Not only does it involve a lot of effort but it can also do more harm than good in some cases. When the drought arrives the usual sequence of events is as follows. At first we do nothing, hoping that rain will fall in a day or two. It doesn't, and drought symptoms begin to appear on a few of the plants. The foliage turns dull and wilting takes place. Brown patches appear on the lawn. So we spring into action — the lawn sprinkler is used for a short time each day and we go around the garden with a watering can or hose to dampen the surface on a daily basis.

There are two basic errors — we try to water everything instead of the high-risk areas and we apply too little water too frequently. Soil with an average cover of plants loses about 25 litres of water per sq.m (4½ gallons per sq. yard) every week during the summer months. In the case of a prolonged drought the roots of a plant must be able to tap the soil reserves of water if rain has not fallen and the ground has not been watered. The ability of a plant to tap these reserves depends on a number of things — soil type, plant type, how long the specimen has been planted etc. The golden rule is not to try to water everything unless the garden is really small. To replace the soil reserves about 2.5 cm (1 in.) of rain or tap water has to fall on the surface. When watering it is essential that this water should not be applied in dribbles on a daily basis. This would result in rapid water loss by evaporation, development of surface roots which are damaged in hot weather, and germination of weed seeds.

Do not wait until the dry days of summer before you begin your battle against drought. Follow the plan on the next page. For lawns (page 243) there are special sets of rules.

THE HIGH-RISK PLANTS & AREAS

Risk higher than average. Water promptly and properly in times of drought — see the next page.

- **Bedding plants** for at least 6 weeks after planting
- **Hardy perennials** for the first year after planting
- **Shrubs** and **trees** for the first 1-2 years after planting
- Numerous **vegetables** such as tomatoes, cucumbers, sweet corn, beans, peas, onions, marrows and celery
- Several **soft fruits** such as strawberries and currants

- **Containers** — tubs, hanging baskets, window boxes, growing bags etc
- **Sandy** and **low-humus soils**
- **Shallow-rooted plants**. Not all of these plants are small — some (e.g hydrangea, silver birch, rhododendron etc) are large shrubs or trees
- **Plants in a rain shadow** — specimens growing within 60 cm (2 ft) of the house wall

THE LOW-RISK PLANTS

Risk lower than average. No need to water during ordinary dry periods. If you decide to water, do it properly.

Achillea	Cistus	Euonymus	Iberis	Sedum
Alyssum	Convolvulus	Genista	Lavandula	Spiraea
Armeria	Cotoneaster	Grasses	Mahonia	Stachys
Buddleia	Cytisus	Helianthemum	Pyracantha	Thymus
Ceanothus	Dianthus	Hypericum	Rosmarinus	Yucca

THE 6-STEP WATERING PLAN

STEP ONE

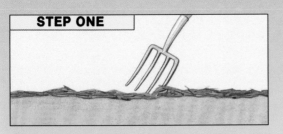

Plants look lovely at the garden centre in summer, but wait until autumn if you can when the dry season will be over. Before planting build up the water-holding capacity by forking in plenty of humus-making material such as compost or manure — see Chapter 2 for details.

STEP TWO

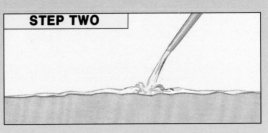

The water reservoir in the soil should be reasonably full before you begin sowing or planting. This calls for watering thoroughly if the soil is dry — the ground should be moist to a depth of about 22 cm (9 in.). Now you are ready to start planting — follow the rules on pages 62-63.

STEP THREE

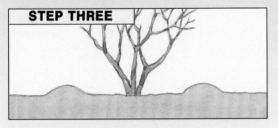

Water gently but thoroughly to settle the soil around the roots. With large plants it is a good idea to create a water catchment area for any future water-ing which may be necessary. With shrubs and trees build a ridge of soil around the base to create a watering basin. With large herbaceous plants such as dahlias or tomatoes you should bury a pot at planting time near to the base of the stem.

STEP FOUR

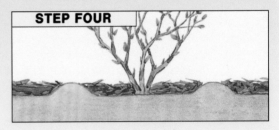

Now comes mulching — a vital but underused tech-nique. The basic principle is to apply an organic layer of compost, well-rotted manure, bark chippings etc around the base of the plant when the soil is moist and reasonably warm. May is the best time, and this layer should be topped up if necessary each year. The ability of the plant to withstand drought is markedly increased — see page 61.

STEP FIVE

As noted in the list of high-risk plants on page 72 it is sometimes necessary to water newly-planted specimens. Look for the tell-tale signs of drought — dull foliage, wilting etc and then fill the watering basin or the pot (see Step 3 above) using 5–18 litres (1-4 gallons) depending on the size of plant, soil type and air temperature. With smaller plants or shrubs etc without a water catchment area apply the water overall at the rate of 10-20 litres per sq.m (2–4 gallons per sq. yard). Hold the watering can spout or hose nozzle close to the ground and water slowly — do not use a rose or spray nozzle unless you are watering bedding plants.

STEP SIX

It may be necessary to repeat the watering if rain does not fall — do not assume that a light summer shower will top up the water reserves in the soil. There is no easy way to determine the right time for this repeat watering — dig down with a trowel and examine the soil at 8-10 cm (3-4 in.) below the sur-face. It is time to water if it is dry. As a general rule watering is required every 5-7 days during a period of drought in summer — on no account should you water every couple of days because the plants con-tinue to droop or are not growing. Only newly-planted ornamentals and some vegetables should need watering if you have followed Steps 1-4.

CHAPTER 6

VEGETABLES

Rich and poor, north and south, mansion and cottage — millions of people grow vegetables, and interest is continuing to expand.

There are a number of reasons why Grow-your-own is so popular. If your plot, home freezer and garden shed storage space are large enough you can aim to be almost self-sufficient, but this is only rarely the gardener's goal. An important motive is that you can harvest at the peak of tenderness and flavour instead of having to wait for maximum yields like the professional grower. In addition you can cook and serve these vegetables within an hour or two of picking or cutting — with sweet corn, beans and asparagus this provides a new flavour experience.

Another reason for growing your own at home is that you can produce vegetables which are not in the shops. You are not involved in maximum financial returns so you can grow high flavour/low yielding varieties and also vegetables types which are not grown commercially.

There are calculations to show that you can save money by growing your own, but this and the reasons given above are not the main motive for most people — above all else is the sheer joy in turning a packet of seed or a shop-bought small seedling into a fully-grown vegetable for the kitchen. There is the satisfaction in the work involved and the sight of the growing crop, and then the pride of providing food for the table. It is not any ordinary cabbage — it's MY cabbage!

Most of the principles of vegetable growing have been with us for hundreds of years — some of the basics are as old as civilisation itself. But the subject doesn't stand still. Baby vegetable varieties are now listed in the seed catalogues, and new varieties of standard vegetables appear every year. It is fun to try something different, but do not be too experimentally-minded — make sure that all or nearly all of the area is devoted to those vegetables which the family like to eat.

A word or two for beginners. Before you decide on growing a particular vegetable, make sure it is suitable for your site. It is often possible to avoid a glut by sowing short rows at intervals.

A wonderful and active hobby, then, but unfortunately not for everyone. Growing vegetables by the traditional allotment method is laborious and may be out of the question for the elderly or physically handicapped. For these people the raised bed method should be considered — for details see the *Vegetable & Herb Expert*. Then there are the potato tubs for Christmas and the pots of herbs for the windowsill. Grow-your-own is indeed for everyone!

Using this A-Z guide

Listed on the following pages are the popular vegetables that dominate the Grow-your-own scene — on each page you will find scores of facts to help you with your plants. Check up each time you decide to buy or have a new job to do. The calendar sets out the right time for each task, but do remember that the weather has the final say — you may have to delay sowing seed or planting out if the soil is too wet. A final word on timing. Remember to deal with serious pests and problems as soon as they are seen. For unusual vegetables such as salsify and kohl rabi and for perennials like Welsh onion or cardoon see the *Vegetable & Herb Expert*.

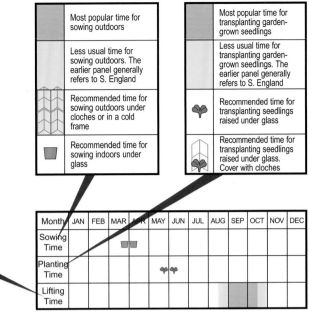

	Most popular time for sowing outdoors
	Less usual time for sowing outdoors. The earlier panel generally refers to S. England
	Recommended time for sowing outdoors under cloches or in a cold frame
	Recommended time for sowing indoors under glass

	Most popular time for transplanting garden-grown seedlings
	Less usual time for transplanting garden-grown seedlings. The earlier panel generally refers to S. England
	Recommended time for transplanting seedlings raised under glass
	Recommended time for transplanting seedlings raised under glass. Cover with cloches

	Most popular time for harvesting
	Less usual time for harvesting

Month	JAN	FEB	MAR	APR	MAY	JUN	JUL	AUG	SEP	OCT	NOV	DEC
Sowing Time												
Planting Time												
Lifting Time												

Crop rotation

Do not grow a vegetable in the same spot year after year. If you do then soil pests and diseases will increase and soil nutrient levels will become unbalanced. Crop rotation is the answer and the standard 3 year plan is shown below. If this seems like too much trouble follow a very simple routine — roots this year, an above-ground vegetable on that ground next year and then back to a root crop.

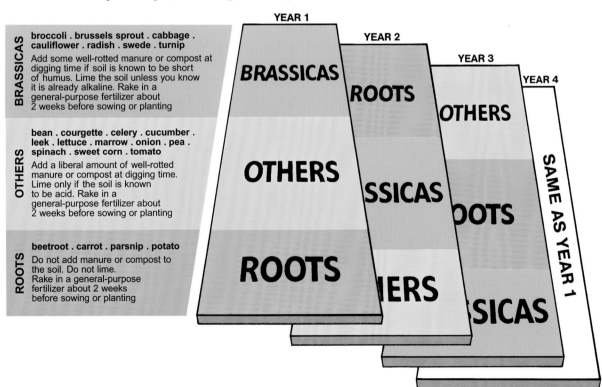

BRASSICAS

broccoli . brussels sprout . cabbage . cauliflower . radish . swede . turnip

Add some well-rotted manure or compost at digging time if soil is known to be short of humus. Lime the soil unless you know it is already alkaline. Rake in a general-purpose fertilizer about 2 weeks before sowing or planting

OTHERS

bean . courgette . celery . cucumber . leek . lettuce . marrow . onion . pea . spinach . sweet corn . tomato

Add a liberal amount of well-rotted manure or compost at digging time. Lime only if the soil is known to be acid. Rake in a general-purpose fertilizer about 2 weeks before sowing or planting

ROOTS

beetroot . carrot . parsnip . potato

Do not add manure or compost to the soil. Do not lime. Rake in a general-purpose fertilizer about 2 weeks before sowing or planting

YEAR 1 — BRASSICAS / OTHERS / ROOTS

YEAR 2 — ROOTS / BRASSICAS / OTHERS

YEAR 3 — OTHERS / ROOTS / BRASSICAS

YEAR 4 — SAME AS YEAR 1

Asparagus

Succulent young shoots appear in spring and are cut for the kitchen. Attractive ferny foliage develops later but this should never be cut for flower arranging. Not an easy crop — it needs thorough soil preparation, space and regular hand weeding. Well worth growing, however, if you have free-draining soil, adequate land which can be tied up for a decade or more and also patience — you will have to wait two years for your first hearty meal. Use 1-year-old crowns — you can buy 2- or 3-year-old crowns but they are temperamental. Asparagus can also be raised from seed but it will be 3 years before regular cropping can begin and it really isn't worth losing a year.

In a nutshell

Productive life	8 - 20 years
Expected yield per mature plant	20 - 25 spears
Time between planting 1-year crowns and cutting	2 years
Ease of cultivation	Not easy

Varieties

CONNOVERS COLOSSAL Still the most popular variety, available as seed and crowns. Crops early.

MARTHA WASHINGTON The best known American variety. Long spears — rust resistant.

FRANKLIM An all-male variety with thick spears. Can be lightly cropped in the year after planting.

STEWART'S PURPLE Purple does not fade when cooked. Unusually low in stringy fibre.

GEYNLIM An all-male modern hybrid — can be cut earlier than most other varieties.

Connovers Colossal

Franklim

Sowing & Planting

- Seed can be sown in 3 cm (1 in.) deep drills 30 cm (1 ft) apart for transplanting later, but it is better to buy 1-year-old crowns.

- The site should be sunny, sheltered and free-draining. Dig thoroughly in the autumn before planting, incorporating garden compost. Fork over in March and rake in a general-purpose fertilizer.

- Plant in trenches 1 m (3 ft) apart — see below.

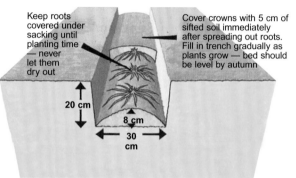

Keep roots covered under sacking until planting time — never let them dry out

Cover crowns with 5 cm of sifted soil immediately after spreading out roots. Fill in trench gradually as plants grow — bed should be level by autumn

20 cm

8 cm

30 cm

Calendar

Month	JAN	FEB	MAR	APR	MAY	JUN	JUL	AUG	SEP	OCT	NOV	DEC
Sowing Time			▓	▓								
Planting Time			▓	▓								
Cutting Time				▓	▓	▓						

see key — page 75

Plant care & Harvesting

- Do not cut any of the spears which appear after planting — little or no cutting should take place in the year after planting. Cutting in earnest can begin in the second year after planting.

- Keep the beds clean by hand weeding.

- In spring make a ridge of soil over each row with a draw hoe before the spears appear. Sever spears about 8 cm (3 in.) below the surface using a serrated knife when spears reach 10-15 cm (4-6 in.). Cut every day if necessary — never let the spears grow too tall before cutting.

- Stop cutting in mid June. All spears must now be allowed to develop into fern in order to build up reserves for next year's crop.

- Provide support for the stems if necessary and water during dry weather. Remove any berries from female varieties before they fall to the ground.

- In autumn cut down the ferny stems when they turn yellow. Leave stumps 2-5 cm (1-2 in.) above the surface.

Bean, Broad

This crop produces the first beans of the season and is one of the easiest vegetables to grow. Standard-sized varieties grow about 1.2 m (4 ft) high and the dwarf ones reach 30-45 cm (1-1½ ft). There are three types. The Longpods have long, narrow pods — noted for hardiness, early cropping and high yields. The Windsors have shorter and broader pods — noted for flavour but you cannot sow in autumn. The Dwarfs have pods with 3-5 beans — the best choice for exposed sites and mini-gardens.

In a nutshell

Expected germination time	7 - 14 days
Expected yield from a 3m (10 ft) double row	9 kg (20 lb)
Approximate time between auumn sowing and picking	26 weeks
Approximate time between spring sowing and picking	14 weeks
Ease of cultivation	Easy

Varieties

AQUADULCE CLAUDIA (Longpod) The standard variety for autumn sowing — hardy and prolific.

BUNYARD'S EXHIBITION (Longpod) Not the biggest, tastiest or heaviest cropper, but very reliable.

HYLON (Longpod) The longest-podded variety recommended for showing and freezing.

MASTERPIECE LONGPOD (Longpod) A popular early cropper with a fine flavour. Good for freezing.

STEREO (Longpod) Small pods with miniature white beans which are cooked like mangetout peas.

GREEN WINDSOR (Windsor) A heavy cropper with perhaps the best-tasting broad beans.

THE SUTTON (Dwarf) The most popular dwarf variety — bears short pods with plump beans.

Hylon

The Sutton

Sowing

- Choose a reasonably sunny spot which did not grow beans last year.

- Attempt autumn sowing in the open only if your plot is sheltered, free-draining and in a mild area — for an early crop it is better to sow under cloches in February.

- Prior to spring sowing dig the soil in autumn, adding compost if it was not enriched for the previous crop. Apply a general-purpose fertilizer about a week before sowing — discard all seeds with small, round holes.

- Begin sowing in March and then at monthly intervals until May to provide beans throughout the summer.

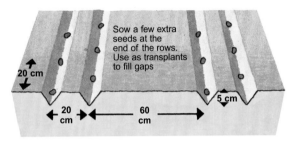

Sow a few extra seeds at the end of the rows. Use as transplants to fill gaps

20 cm

20 cm   60 cm   5 cm

Calendar

Month	JAN	FEB	MAR	APR	MAY	JUN	JUL	AUG	SEP	OCT	NOV	DEC
Sowing Time												
Picking Time												

see key — page 75

Plant care & Harvesting

- Regular hoeing will probably be necessary when the plants are small, but watering should not be needed.

- Support is likely to be necessary — place a stout stake at the corner of each double row and then string between the posts at 30 cm (1 ft) intervals.

- Pinch out the top 10 cm (4 in.) of stem as soon as the first pods appear — this will ensure an earlier harvest and help to keep down blackfly. Spray if this pest persists. Water copiously if the weather turns dry when the pods are swelling.

- Begin picking when the first pods are 5-8 cm (2-3 in.) long — cook them whole. The time to pick pods for shelling is when the beans can be seen through the pod — don't wait until the bean scars are black.

- Apply a sharp downward twist to remove each pod. Dig in the plants after cropping has finished.

Bean, French

A half-hardy annual which likes warm conditions. The blooms are white, pink or red and it is decorative enough to be grown in the flower garden. Standard varieties are bushy plants with 10-15 cm (4-6 in.) green pods, but there are variations. You can buy purple- or yellow-podded types as well as climbing varieties which can grow as tall as runner beans. There are two types of pods. Flat-pods — flat, rather wide and liable to be stringy when mature, and Pencil-pods which are round and stringless.

In a nutshell

Expected germination time	7 - 14 days
Expected yield from a 3m (10 ft) row	3.5 kg (8 lb) (bush vars.)
Expected yield from a 3m (10 ft) row	5.5 kg (12 lb) (climbing vars.)
Approximate time between sowing and picking	8 - 12 weeks
Ease of cultivation	Easy

Varieties

THE PRINCE (Flat-pod) Long, slender pods on dwarf bushes. Very popular.

MASTERPIECE (Flat-pod) Good for early sowing and growing under cloches. An old favourite.

BORLOTTO (Flat-pod) Both young pods and beans are green with bright red blotches. Good for drying.

KINGHORN WAX (Pencil-pod) A yellow stringless bean which is renowned for its flavour.

SAFARI (Pencil-pod) Low growing with pods held above the foliage. Good disease resistance.

BLUE LAKE (Pencil-pod) A popular climbing variety, producing an abundant supply of pods.

TENDERGREEN (Pencil-pod) Early cropping and prolific — suitable for growing in a pot.

The Prince

Safari

Kinghorn Wax

Sowing

- Choose a reasonably sunny spot which was not used for beans last year. Any soil will do provided it is neither very heavy nor acid. Lime, if necessary, in winter.

- Dig in autumn and add garden compost. Prepare the seed bed about 2 weeks before sowing — apply a general-purpose fertilizer at this time. Do not sow before the recommended date — seed will rot in cold and wet soil.

- Beans planted under glass in April are planted out once the danger of frost has passed. Sow the first maincrop in May. For beans up to early October sow successively until the end of June.

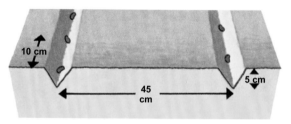

Calendar

Month	JAN	FEB	MAR	APR	MAY	JUN	JUL	AUG	SEP	OCT	NOV	DEC
Sowing Time												
Picking Time												

see key — page 75

Plant care & Harvesting

- Hoe the young plants regularly to keep the weeds down — protect seedlings against slugs. Support the stems with short twigs to prevent them from toppling over. Use plastic netting to support climbing varieties.

- Moisture around the roots is essential to ensure good root development and a long cropping period, so water copiously in dry weather during and after flowering. Spraying the flowers with water is not necessary.

- Begin picking when the pods are about 10 cm (4 in.) long. A pod is ready when it snaps easily when bent but before bulges appear along its length. Pick several times a week — cropping should continue for 5-7 weeks. Take care not to loosen the plants when picking — hold the stems as you tug the pods, or use scissors.

- For dried beans (haricots) wait until the pods are straw-coloured and then hang to dry. Shell and dry on paper for several days, then store the beans in an air-tight container.

Bean, Runner

Britain's favourite home-grown bean — decorative in flower and highly productive. There are several basic needs — thorough soil preparation in winter, strong supports, weekly watering in dry weather once the pods have formed and finally picking every other day in late summer. Let a few pods reach maturity and the flower-producing mechanism will switch off. Standard varieties can grow up to 2.5-3 m (8-10 ft), but there are also a few true dwarfs.

In a nutshell

Expected germination time	7 - 14 days
Expected yield from a 3m (10 ft) row	25 kg (55 lb)
Approximate time between sowing and picking	12 - 14 weeks
Ease of cultivation	Not really easy

Varieties

ENORMA Long and slender pods — a popular choice for the garden show. Above average flavour.

SCARLET EMPEROR An all-round performer. Similar to the old favourite Kelvedon Marvel but the pods are longer.

LADY DI Slender stringless pods up to 30 cm (1 ft) long. There is a long cropping season.

KELVEDON MARVEL Can be grown as a bushy plant — pinch out growing points when plants are 30 cm (1 ft) high.

POLESTAR A scarlet-flowered runner — provides heavy crops of stringless pods. Cropping starts early.

DESIREE White-flowered variety — produces well even in dry weather.

WHITE LADY A white-flowered stringless variety which sets well in hot weather.

PICKWICK A dwarf variety for tub or flower garden — little or no support is needed.

Enorma

White Lady

Pickwick

Sowing

- Choose a sheltered site. Dig in autumn and add garden compost. Lime, if necessary, in late winter. Rake in a general-purpose fertilizer about 2 weeks before sowing or planting.

- Sow once the danger of frost has passed. Alternatively plant out seedlings when there is no longer a risk of frosty nights (late May-early June). These seedlings are shop-bought or raised under glass from a late April sowing.

- Support with poles, as shown below — tie a horizontal holding bar across the ridge. Alternatively erect a wigwam of poles.

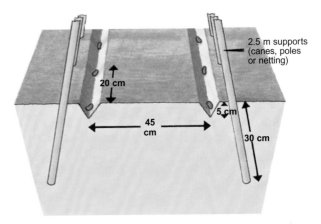

2.5 m supports (canes, poles or netting)

20 cm

5 cm

45 cm

30 cm

Calendar

Month	JAN	FEB	MAR	APR	MAY	JUN	JUL	AUG	SEP	OCT	NOV	DEC
Sowing Time (outdoors)												
Sowing Time (indoors)												
Picking Time												

see key — page 75

Plant care & Harvesting

- Tie young plants to supports, then leave to climb naturally. Protect from slugs.

- Hoe regularly — water in dry weather once pods have formed. Misting is not necessary. Liquid feed occasionally during the cropping season. Remove tips when stems reach the top of the supports, and dig in stems at the end of the season.

- Pick regularly when the pods reach 15-20 cm (6-8 in.) but before beans have started to swell. Pick every 2 days — leaving only a small number of pods to ripen will stop production. Cropping should continue for about 8 weeks.

Beetroot

Two secrets of success — avoid any check to growth and lift the roots before they become large and woody. This calls for sowing short rows at monthly intervals and watering in dry weather. There are three types — the popular Globe, the less common Cylindrical and the exhibitor-only Long. Most, but not all, are red-fleshed and some, but not all, are bolt-resistant.

In a nutshell

Expected germination time	10 - 14 days
Expected yield from a 3m (10 ft) row	4 kg (9 lb) (globe vars.)
Approximate time between sowing and lifting	11 weeks (globe vars.)
Ease of cultivation	Easy

Varieties

BOLTARDY (Globe) The usual choice for early sowing — bolt-resistant. Deep red flesh.

GOLDEN (Globe) A yellow-fleshed beetroot which retains its colour when cooked.

PABLO (Globe) Smooth-skinned roots which are bolt-resistant. Sweet flavour — can be grown for baby beets.

MONETA (Globe) A monogerm variety which produces a single seedling from the seed cluster.

RED ACE (Globe) A kitchen/exhibition variety. Better than most for dry conditions.

PRONTO (Globe) An excellent baby beet. Suitable for late sowing up to early July.

CYLINDRA (Cylindrical) The most popular intermediate-sized beetroot — excellent keeping qualities.

FORONO (Cylindrical) Ideal family size — 15-20 cm (6-8 in.) long and 5 cm (2 in.) wide.

CHELTENHAM GREEN TOP (Long) The most popular tapered variety — it is grown for the garden show.

Red Ace

Forono

Cheltenham Green Top

Sowing

- Choose a sunny spot — dig in late autumn and add garden compost if the organic content is low. Apply lime if the soil is acid.

- Prepare the seed bed in spring — rake in a general-purpose fertilizer 2-3 weeks before sowing.

- A bolt-resistant variety can be sown under cloches for a late May-early June crop. The main sowing period begins in mid April — a second sowing in mid May will provide a regular supply of tender roots. Sow in June for an October crop which can be stored in dry sand for winter use.

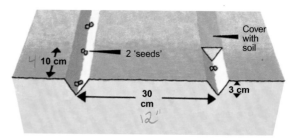

Calendar

Month	JAN	FEB	MAR	APR	MAY	JUN	JUL	AUG	SEP	OCT	NOV	DEC
Sowing Time												
Lifting Time												

see key — page 75

Plant care & Harvesting

- Thin out seedlings when they are about 3 cm (1 in.) high — leave a single plant at each station. Do not use the thinnings as transplants. Protection from birds may be necessary.

- Hoe to keep down weeds — be careful not to touch the plants. Dryness leads to woodiness, and a subsequent downpour can lead to splitting — water every fortnight during dry spells to avoid these problems.

- Lift alternate Globe beetroots as needed — they should be no larger than golf-ball size. Leave the remainder to develop — these should be lifted when they are about the size of a cricket ball.

- Cylindrical and Long varieties should be carefully prised out of the soil with a fork — shake off the soil and discard damaged roots.

- The next step with lifted roots is to twist off the foliage to leave a 5 cm (2 in.) crown of stalk bases. Cutting off the leaves with scissors or a knife will result in bleeding. Roots can be stored between layers of sand in boxes in the garden shed.

Broccoli

Seeds are sown in spring and the seedlings are planted out in summer. The Green calabrese varieties are harvested in autumn — with both Purple Sprouting and White Sprouting broccoli you will have to wait until the following spring. Purple Sprouting is the hardiest and most popular broccoli — White Sprouting has small cauliflower-like spears, and some Green calabrese varieties produce a large central head followed by secondary spears.

In a nutshell

Expected germination time	7 - 12 days
Expected yield per plant	700 gm (1½ lb)
Approximate time between sowing and cutting	12 weeks (calabrese vars.)
Approximate time between sowing and cutting	44 weeks (purple and white vars.)
Ease of cultivation	Easier than cauliflower

Varieties

EARLY WHITE SPROUTING The white variety to grow if you want to cut spears in March.

LATE WHITE SPROUTING Spears appear in April and May.

EARLY PURPLE SPROUTING The favourite variety — spears are ready for cutting in March.

RED ARROW (Early Purple) Award-winning variety, providing February/March spears.

RUDOLPH (Early Purple) Large spears appear from February onwards.

LATE PURPLE SPROUTING Tall and robust plants — spears are not ready for cutting until April.

EXPRESS CORONA (Calabrese) Cropping starts in August — delicate flavour.

MARATHON (Calabrese) Large, bluish-green heads for October-November picking.

Early Purple Sprouting

Express Corona

Sowing & Planting

- In the seed bed thin seedlings to about 8 cm (3 in.) apart — transplant when 8-10 cm (3-4 in.) high. Water the rows the day before transplanting.

- Pick a sheltered and reasonably sunny spot for the place where the plants will grow. Broccoli likes firm ground which is rich in organic matter. Dig in autumn. Lime, if necessary, in autumn. In spring apply a general-purpose fertilizer. Before planting seedlings tread down gently and rake lightly — do not fork over.

- Plant firmly, setting the plants about 3 cm (1 in.) deeper than they were in the seed bed. Leave 45 cm (1½ ft) between Purple or White Sprouting varieties — 30 cm (1 ft) between Green varieties. Water after planting.

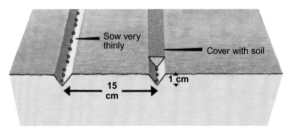

Calendar

Month	JAN	FEB	MAR	APR	MAY	JUN	JUL	AUG	SEP	OCT	NOV	DEC
Sowing Time												
Planting Time												
Cutting Time		EARLY vars.		LATE vars.					GREEN vars.			

see key — page 75

Plant care & Harvesting

- Hoe regularly and protect the young plants against birds. Summer care consists of watering in dry weather and watching for pests.

- As winter approaches draw up soil around the stems and stake the plants if necessary. Firm the plants if they have been loosened by wind or frost. Pigeons can be a menace at this time of year — netting may be necessary.

- Cut the flower shoots ('spears') when they are well formed but before the small flower buds have opened. When in flower the spears are woody and tasteless.

- Cut or snap off the central spear or cauliflower-like head first. Side shoots will be produced and these should be picked regularly.

- Spears are suitable for kitchen use when they are about 10-15 cm (4-6 in.) long, and cropping should continue for about 6 weeks.

Brussels Sprout

You can begin picking in September and finish in March if you grow both early and late varieties — each plant should remain productive for about 8 weeks. The old favourite varieties have been overtaken by the F_1 hybrids which usually have a compact growth habit and produce large crops of uniform-sized and long-lasting sprouts. Unfortunately they do tend to mature all at the same time.

In a nutshell

Expected germination time	7 - 12 days
Expected yield per plant	1 kg (2 lb)
Approximate time between sowing and picking	28 weeks (early vars.)
Approximate time between sowing and picking	36 weeks (late vars.)
Ease of cultivation	Not difficult

Varieties

BRILLIANT (F_1) An early variety with good bolt-resistance. September-October.

MAXIMUS (F_1) Listed in the catalogues as the replacement for the mid-season Peer Gynt.

SILVERLINE (F_1) Grown for its fine flavour. Medium-sized sprouts November-January.

TRAFALGAR (F_1) Light-coloured buttons make it a good choice for exhibiting.

PEER GYNT (F_1) One of the first F_1 hybrids and once a favourite variety but it has been replaced in the catalogues.

WELLINGTON (F_1) Noted for its resistance to disease and frost damage. December-March.

FILLBASKET Heavy-cropping old favourite. Large sprouts October-January.

RUBINE The red one with poor yields and good flavour. October-January.

Peer Gynt

Trafalgar

Fillbasket

Sowing & Planting

- In the seed bed thin seedlings to about 8 cm (3 in.) apart — transplant when about 15 cm (6 in.) high. Water the rows the day before transplanting.

- Pick a sheltered and reasonably sunny spot for the place where the plants will grow. Dig in autumn only if necessary — work in garden compost or well-rotted manure if the soil is poor. Lime, if necessary, in winter. In spring apply a general-purpose fertilizer. Do not fork over the surface before planting — just tread down gently and lightly rake over the surface.

- Plant firmly, setting the plants with their lowest leaves just above the surface. Leave about 75 cm (2½ ft) between standard varieties, 45 cm (1½ ft) between compact F_1 varieties. Water after planting.

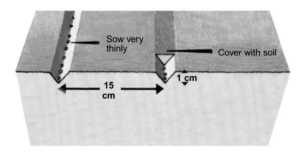

Calendar

Month	JAN	FEB	MAR	APR	MAY	JUN	JUL	AUG	SEP	OCT	NOV	DEC
Sowing Time												
Planting Time												
Picking Time												

see key — page 75

Plant care & Harvesting

- Hoe regularly and protect the young plants from birds. Feed in early summer. Watch out for caterpillars and aphids — spray if necessary.

- As autumn approaches earth up around the stems and stake tall varieties. The old practice of removing the tops to hasten maturity is no longer recommended.

- Begin harvesting when the lowest sprouts are about the size of a walnut and are still tightly closed. Snap them off with a sharp downward tug or cut them off with a sharp knife.

- Work steadily up the stem at each picking session, removing yellowed leaves and open ('blown') sprouts as you go. Pick only a few sprouts at any one time from each stem to extend the cropping period. The sprouts should be hard and they should be boiled briskly for a short time.

Cabbage

If you have the space and inclination you can have cabbages from the garden all year round. By choosing the proper varieties, having enough land to spare and then sowing and transplanting at the right time you can have a non-stop supply. This quest for year-round cabbage is not for everyone, but even if you grow just one variety you should avoid sowing too many at one time — just a small row every few weeks is the proper way. Nearly all of the varieties fall neatly into one of the three major groups — Spring, Summer or Winter cabbage. You can cut-and-come-again with Spring and Summer cabbages. The season refers to the time of harvesting and not planting. Savoys are less popular than the basic three types and may be listed separately in the catalogue. For something quite different you can try one of the Chinese varieties — details in the *Vegetable & Herb Expert*.

Types

SPRING CABBAGE
These cabbages are planted in the autumn to provide tender spring greens (collards) in early spring and larger mature heads later in the season. They are generally conical in shape and smaller than the Summer and Winter varieties.

SUMMER CABBAGE
These cabbages are generally ball-shaped with a few conical exceptions. The normal pattern is to sow outdoors in April, transplant in May and cut in August or September. For June cabbages sow an early variety under cloches in early March.

WINTER CABBAGE
These cabbages are generally ball-headed or drum-headed. They are green or white and suitable for immediate cooking. The white varieties are also used for coleslaw and can be stored for months. Sow in May and transplant in July.

SAVOY
These cabbages are easily recognised by their crisp and puckered dark green leaves. They are grown as Winter cabbages but the varieties have a wider range of harvesting times — from September to March.

In a nutshell

Expected germination time	7 - 12 days
Expected yield per plant	300 gm - 1.5 kg (½ - 3 lb)
Approximate time between sowing and cutting	35 weeks (spring vars.)
Approximate time between sowing and cutting	20 - 35 weeks (summer, winter, savoy vars.)
Ease of cultivation	Not difficult

Sowing & Planting

- In the seed bed thin seedlings to about 8 cm (3 in.) apart — transplant when they have 5 or 6 leaves. Water the rows the day before transplanting.

- Pick a reasonably sunny spot for the place where the plants will grow. Dig in autumn only if necessary — work in garden compost. Lime, if necessary, in winter. In spring apply a general-purpose fertilizer about a week before planting all types except Spring cabbage. Do not fork over the surface before planting — just tread down gently and lightly rake over the surface.

- Plant firmly. With large-headed varieties leave 45 cm (1½ ft) between plants — reduce to 30 cm (1 ft) for compact types. Water after planting. With Spring cabbage you can plant at 10 cm (4 in.) intervals along the rows and thin in March, using the thinnings as spring greens.

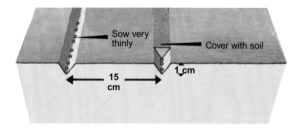

Plant care & Harvesting

- Hoe regularly and protect the young plants from birds. Feed as the heads begin to mature. In autumn earth up the stems of Spring cabbage. In winter firm down any plants loosened by frost.

- Cut stems with a sharp knife close to ground level. With Spring and Summer varieties cut 1 cm (½ in.) deep cross cuts into the stumps — a secondary crop of small cabbages will then be produced.

- Cabbages are usually cut for immediate use. Winter white cabbages can be cut in November and stored for winter use. Remove outer leaves and place in straw-lined boxes. The heads should keep until March.

Cabbage varieties

SPRING cabbage

APRIL Compact small- to medium-sized heads. Dark green — matures early.

OFFENHAM 2 — FLOWER OF SPRING The one to grow if you want large solid heads in April-May.

DURHAM EARLY Popular as a source of spring greens — forms conical poor-quality hearts.

WHEELERS IMPERIAL Noted for its flavour. The dark green heads are small and pointed.

SPRING HERO Something different — a ball-headed Spring cabbage. Sow in August.

Month	JAN	FEB	MAR	APR	MAY	JUN	JUL	AUG	SEP	OCT	NOV	DEC
Sowing Time							▓	▓				
Planting Time									▓	▓		
Cutting Time			▓	▓	▓							

April

SUMMER cabbage

GREYHOUND An old favourite — compact, pointed heads which mature quickly.

HISPI An F_1 hybrid which is even earlier than the look-alike Greyhound.

PRIMO Compact and firm, an old-established ball-headed variety for July-August cropping.

MINICOLE Small oval heads are produced in early autumn by this popular F_1 hybrid.

RED DRUMHEAD The most popular red cabbage. Solid in September for cooking or pickling.

STONEHEAD An F_1 hybrid which produces heavy round heads — stands well without splitting.

CARDISA A modern F_1 hybrid which is claimed to be the sweetest-tasting of all. Can be grown as a mini-sized 'baby' vegetable.

Month	JAN	FEB	MAR	APR	MAY	JUN	JUL	AUG	SEP	OCT	NOV	DEC
Sowing Time		▓	▓									
Planting Time				▓	▓							
Cutting Time					▓	▓	▓	▓				

see key — page 75

WINTER cabbage

CELTIC Blue-green and ball-headed — an F_1 hybrid with savoy-like leaves. Ready in December.

CHRISTMAS DRUMHEAD Earlier than Celtic. Reliable variety renowned for hardiness.

JANUARY KING Savoy-type but without crinkled leaves. A drumhead variety for December-January.

HOLLY An award-winning cabbage similar to January King apart from its purple colour.

HOLLAND LATE STORAGE A November-December white cabbage for coleslaw and storage.

TUNDRA Extremely frost hardy — cropping stretches from November to April.

Month	JAN	FEB	MAR	APR	MAY	JUN	JUL	AUG	SEP	OCT	NOV	DEC
Sowing Time				▓	▓							
Planting Time					▓	▓	▓					
Cutting Time	▓									▓	▓	▓

Celtic

SAVOY

TAVOY Large heads of crinkled leaves for cutting between late autumn and early spring.

BEST OF ALL The one to grow for an early crop — large drumhead-type cabbages.

ORMSKIRK A popular late variety for cutting after Christmas. Large, dark green heads.

Month	JAN	FEB	MAR	APR	MAY	JUN	JUL	AUG	SEP	OCT	NOV	DEC
Sowing Time				▓	▓							
Planting Time						▓	▓					
Cutting Time	▓	▓								▓	▓	▓

see key — page 75

Ormskirk

Carrot

Carrots are not difficult if the soil is good and the dreaded carrot fly is kept away. Short-rooted varieties are golf-ball round or finger-long carrots which are the first to be sown and mature quickly. Intermediate-rooted varieties are the best all-rounders for the average garden — some are pulled for immediate use and the rest are left for winter storage. Long-rooted varieties are the tapered giants of the show bench.

In a nutshell

Expected germination time	17 days
Expected yield from a 3m (10 ft) row	3.5 kg (8 lb) (early vars.)
Expected yield from a 3m (10 ft) row	4.5 kg (10 lb) (maincrop vars.)
Approximate time between sowing and lifting	12 weeks (early vars.)
Approximate time between sowing and lifting	16 weeks (maincrop vars.)
Ease of cultivation	Not difficult

Varieties

AMSTERDAM FORCING (Short) Blunt-ended — one of the earliest which needs little care.

PARMEX (Short) The most popular round variety, suitable for growing in tubs or stony soil.

EARLY NANTES (Short) Blunt-ended — renowned for its flavour. Good for freezing.

CHANTENEY RED CORED (Intermediate) An old favourite — smooth-skinned and deep orange.

AUTUMN KING (Intermediate) Unusually long for an Intermediate. Extremely hardy.

FLYAWAY (Intermediate) Main claim to fame is good resistance to carrot fly.

ST. VALERY (Long) Very long and pointed — a popular choice for exhibition.

NEW RED INTERMEDIATE (Long) One of the longest, despite its name.

Amsterdam Forcing

Flyaway

New Red Intermediate

Sowing

- For an early crop which will be ready in June, sow a Short-rooted variety in a sheltered spot in late March or April. For summer carrots continue sowing every 2-3 weeks. For maincrop carrots sow an Intermediate- or Long-rooted variety between mid April and early June for lifting in September and October. Delay the sowing of maincrop carrots until June if carrot fly is known to be a nuisance.

- Pick a sunny spot which has not been manured during the past year. You will need soil which is deep, fertile and rather sandy if you want to grow a Long-rooted variety.

- Dig in autumn — do not add manure or garden compost. Prepare the seed bed 1 or 2 weeks before sowing — rake a general-purpose fertilizer into the surface. Mixing the seed with sand will help you to avoid sowing too thickly.

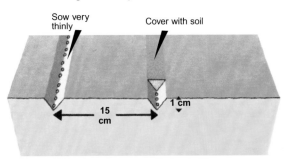

Sow very thinly   Cover with soil   1 cm   15 cm

Calendar

Month	JAN	FEB	MAR	APR	MAY	JUN	JUL	AUG	SEP	OCT	NOV	DEC
Sowing Time												
Lifting Time												

see key — page 75

Plant care & Harvesting

- Thin out the seedlings to 5-8 cm (2-3 in.) apart when they are large enough to handle. Care is needed at this stage in order not to attract carrot fly — water if the soil is dry, work in the evening, firm the soil around the remaining plants and bury the thinnings.

- Keep down weeds by hoeing near seedlings, but by hand pulling around established plants. Water in dry weather to keep the soil damp — a downpour on dry soil can lead to splitting of the roots.

- Pull out small carrots as required from June onwards — ease out with a fork if the soil is hard. Harvest maincrop carrots in October for storage.

- Only sound roots should be stored. Cut off leaves at 1 cm (½ in.) above the crowns and place the roots between layers of sand in a box. Store in a shed.

Cauliflower

Cauliflower is not an easy vegetable to grow. It needs rich and deep soil, and during the growing season there must not be any check to growth — failure to satisfy these conditions usually leads to the production of tiny 'button' heads. Proper soil preparation, careful planting and regular watering are essential, and so is the choice of a suitable variety. There are types to produce heads at almost any time of the year. Compact Summer varieties, large-headed Autumn varieties and the Winter ones which mature in spring and are really heading broccoli, not true cauliflowers.

In a nutshell

Expected germination time	7 - 12 days
Expected yield per plant	500 gm - 1 kg (1 - 2 lb)
Approximate time between sowing and cutting	18 - 24 weeks (summer and autumn vars.)
Approximate time between sowing and cutting	40 - 50 weeks (winter vars.)
Ease of cultivation	Quite difficult

Varieties

ALL THE YEAR ROUND (Summer) An old favourite. With successional sowing heads can be available all summer and autumn.

SNOWBALL (Summer) An early variety — the heads are tight but not large.

SNOW CROWN (Summer) A Snowball-like variety with much bigger heads. The large leaves provide protection.

CANDID CHARM (Autumn) Large, pure white heads ready in early October.

GRAFFITI (Autumn) Purple curd — leave the heads uncovered. Cutting can start in August.

WALCHEREN WINTER (Winter) A Dutch variety which has taken over from English Winter.

Snowball

Walcheren Winter

Sowing & Planting

- For a June crop sow seeds of a Summer variety under glass in January and transplant in early April. Outdoors Summer varieties are sown in early April, Autumn ones in late April and Winter varieties in May.

- In the seed bed thin seedlings to about 8 cm (3 in.) apart — transplant when they have 5-6 leaves. Water the rows the day before transplanting.

- Pick a reasonably sunny spot for the place where the plants will grow. Avoid a frost pocket for Winter varieties. Cauliflowers need firm soil — dig if necessary in autumn but not in spring. Lime in winter. In spring apply a general-purpose fertilizer. Do not fork over the surface before planting — just tread down gently, and lightly rake over the surface.

- Plant firmly, setting the seedlings at the same level as in the seed bed. Leave 60 cm (2 ft) between Summer and Autumn varieties, 75 cm (2½ ft) between Winter types. Water after planting.

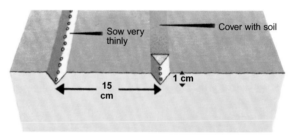

Calendar

Month	JAN	FEB	MAR	APR	MAY	JUN	JUL	AUG	SEP	OCT	NOV	DEC
Sowing Time												
Planting Time												
Cutting Time			WINTER Vars.				SUMMER Vars.			AUTUMN Vars.		

see key — page 75

Plant care & Harvesting

- Hoe regularly and protect the young plants from birds. Cauliflower is a hungry crop, so feed occasionally. Water in dry weather — never keep the crop short of water. With Summer varieties bend a few leaves over the developing curd — protect the winter crop from frost by breaking a few leaves over each curd.

- Begin cutting while some cauliflowers are still quite small so as to avoid a glut of mature ones. You have waited too long if the florets in the curd have started to separate.

- Cut in the morning — leave until midday if the weather is frosty.

Celery

Celery is a lot of effort. Trenches must be prepared and the stems must be earthed up at intervals so that only the green tips are showing. The main purpose of this 'blanching' process is to lengthen and improve the stems and not to whiten them. You can now sow self-blanching varieties so that neither trenching nor blanching is required, but these varieties are less crisp and cannot be left in the ground once the frosts arrive. Self-blanching varieties do make celery growing easier, but not easy.

In a nutshell

Expected germination time	12 - 18 days
Expected yield from a 3m (10 ft) row	5 kg (11 lb)
Approximate time between sowing and lifting	40 weeks (trench vars.)
Approximate time between sowing and lifting	25 weeks (self-blanching vars.)
Ease of cultivation	Difficult

Varieties

GIANT WHITE The standard white-stalked celery. Needs good growing conditions. Trench var.

GIANT PINK Ready in January. Trench var.

GIANT RED Very hardy. Trench var.

AMERICAN GREEN (green) Basic green variety — now hard to find. Trench var.

VICTORIA (green) The most popular self-blanching variety. Less demanding than older varieties.

GOLDEN SELF-BLANCHING (yellow) The standard yellow self-blanching variety — ready in August.

LATHOM SELF-BLANCHING (yellow) A better choice than Golden Self-blanching.

CELEBRITY Similar to Lathom Self-blanching, but with longer stalks.

Giant White   *American Green*

Sowing & Planting

- A sunny site and well-prepared soil are necessary. For trench varieties prepare a trench (see below) in April.

- For self-blanching types dig a bed in April — incorporate a dressing of manure or compost.

- Sow seed under glass and harden off the seedlings before planting. Seedlings are ready for transplanting when they are 5 or 6 leaves.

- Self-blanching varieties are planted 25 cm (10 in.) apart in a square block (not in rows) so that crowded plants will shade each other. Trench varieties are planted as shown below.

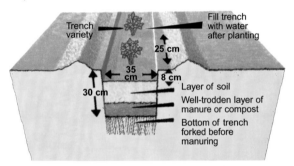

Calendar

Month	JAN	FEB	MAR	APR	MAY	JUN	JUL	AUG	SEP	OCT	NOV	DEC
Sowing Time			▣	▣								
Planting Time					🌱	🌱						
Lifting Time												

see key — page 75

Plant care & Harvesting

- Water copiously in dry weather — feed in summer.

- Begin blanching trench varieties in early August by covering stems with newspaper or cardboard and then filling the trench with soil. In late August mound moist soil against the stems. In September heap up again so that only the green tops are showing. Do not let soil fall into the hearts.

- With self-blanching varieties tuck straw between the plants which form the outside lines of the bed.

- Lift trenching varieties according to type — white varieties up to Christmas and coloured ones in January. Start at one end of the row and replace soil after lifting to protect the remaining plants.

- Lift self-blanching varieties as required — finish lifting before the frosts arrive. Remove outer plants first — use a trowel to avoid disturbing neighbouring plants.

Cucumber, Greenhouse

The greenhouse cucumber is straight, long, cylindrical and smooth-skinned, but its cultivation involves a lot of work and so perhaps it is best left to the keen gardener and exhibitor. Growing outdoor cucumbers is much less work. The traditional greenhouse cucumbers are the Ordinary varieties, which have now been largely replaced by the All-female ones. These newer ones are more disease-resistant, more prolific and spare you the tiresome job of removing male flowers. There are two drawbacks — the fruits tend to be shorter and a higher temperature is required.

In a nutshell

Expected germination time	3 - 5 days
Expected yield per plant	25 cucumbers
Approximate time between sowing and cutting	12 weeks
Ease of cultivation	Difficult

Varieties

TELEGRAPH (Ordinary) An old variety with several improved strains. The only popular Ordinary type.

CONQUEROR (Ordinary) Once a favourite for growing in a cold house — now hard to find.

PEPINEX (All-female) The first of the All-female varieties. Smooth fruit — good flavour.

BRUNEX (All-female) A high-yielding variety. Male flowers occasionally appear.

PETITA (All-female) Small fruits — more tolerant of less ideal conditions than most varieties.

BELLA (All-female) Excellent disease resistance is its main selling point.

FUTURA (All-female) Suitable for growing in a cold house. Good powdery mildew resistance.

Pepinex

Brunex

Petita

Sowing & Planting

- In a heated house sow in late February/early March — plant out in April for June cropping. Most gardeners, however, grow cucumbers in a cold (unheated) house — sow in late April, plant out in late May for fruits from July onwards.

- Seedlings are raised under glass — a temperature of 20°-25°C (68°-78°F) is essential. Place a single seed edgeways 1 cm (½ in.) deep in compost in a 7 cm (3 in.) pot. When the first leaves have expanded transfer to a 12 cm (5 in.) pot. Keep the compost moist.

- Plant out when there are 5-6 leaves. Do not grow in the border — plant in 25 cm (10 in.) pots of compost (1 per pot) or in growing bags (2 per bag). Water in after planting.

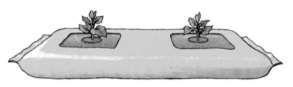

Calendar

Month	JAN	FEB	MAR	APR	MAY	JUN	JUL	AUG	SEP	OCT	NOV	DEC
Sowing & Planting Time		▣	▣ ❀	❀ ▣	❀							
Cutting Time												

see key — page 75

Plant care & Harvesting

- The minimum temperature should be 15°-20°C (58°-68°F). Keep the compost moist but not water-logged — make slits in the bottom of growing bags. The air should be kept moist and well-ventilated — spray the floor with water.

- Train each stem up a vertical wire or cane. Pinch out the growing point when the leader reaches the roof — pinch out the tip of each side shoot at 2 leaves beyond a female flower. Pinch out any male flowers — they have a thin stalk, not miniature fruit, behind them. Pinch out the tip of flowerless side shoots when they are about 60 cm (2 ft) long.

- After 4-6 weeks growing bags should be fed every 2 weeks with tomato fertilizer.

- Cut (do not pull) when the fruit sides are parallel — this is usually at about 30 cm (1 ft). Cropping will cease if you allow cucumbers to mature and turn yellow on the plant.

Cucumber, Outdoor

Things have changed. Outdoor or ridge cucumbers were all short, dumpy and warty. Now there are some which bear 30 cm (1 ft) long smooth-skinned cucumbers. Once they were grown on raised beds or ridges — now they are grown on the flat or are supported by nets or poles. Various types are available. The old Standard varieties are small, thick and knobbly, and the Gherkins are even shorter. The newer F_1 hybrids are larger, smoother and more disease-resistant, and the Japanese types have the length and smoothness of greenhouse cucumbers. The All-female types do not need pollinating and do not contain seeds. The Ball varieties are round and yellow.

In a nutshell

Expected germination time	6 - 9 days
Expected yield per plant	10 cucumbers
Approximate time between sowing and cutting	12 - 14 weeks
Ease of cultivation	Not easy

Varieties

LONG GREEN RIDGE An improved form of the old favourite Bedfordshire Prize. Crops heavily.

BUSH CHAMPION A bushy F_1 hybrid for pots or growing bags. Matures quickly.

BURPLESS TASTY GREEN A good one to choose — short fruits devoid of bitterness.

MARKETMORE Does better than most when the conditions are not ideal.

SWING An All-female variety which provides a heavy crop of 20 cm (8 in.) dark green cucumbers.

CRYSTAL APPLE Apple-shaped, now replaced in some catalogues by Crystal Lemon. Eat fresh or pickle.

Bush Champion   *Burpless Tasty Green*   *Crystal Apple*

Sowing & Planting

- Sow in late May or early June for cropping in August. For an earlier crop sow seed under glass (see page 88 for instructions) in late April, harden off and plant out in early June.

- Choose a sunny spot protected from strong winds — the soil must be well drained and rich in humus. Pre-pare planting pockets as shown below about 2 weeks before sowing seed or planting seedlings.

- Sow 3 seeds 2 cm (1 in.) deep and 5 cm (2 in.) apart at the centre of each pocket. Cover with a large jar or cloche to hasten germination. When the true leaves have appeared thin out to leave the strongest seedling.

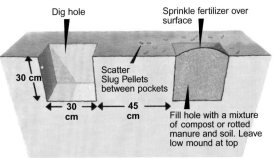

Dig hole

Sprinkle fertilizer over surface

30 cm

Scatter Slug Pellets between pockets

30 cm   45 cm

Fill hole with a mixture of compost or rotted manure and soil. Leave low mound at top

Calendar

Month	JAN	FEB	MAR	APR	MAY	JUN	JUL	AUG	SEP	OCT	NOV	DEC
Sowing Time (outdoors)												
Sowing Time (indoors)												
Cutting Time												

see key — page 75

Plant care & Harvesting

- Pinch out the tip when the plant has developed 6 or 7 leaves. Side shoots will develop — let them trail over the ground or train them up stout netting. Shoots not bearing flowers should be pinched out at the 7th leaf.

- Keep the soil moist — water around and not over the plants. Place black plastic sheeting over the soil in summer before the fruits develop.

- Do not remove the male flowers. Use a liquid tomato fertilizer once the first fruits appear.

- Cut the cucumbers before they reach their maximum size — 15-20 cm (6-8 in.) for most varieties. Use a sharp knife — don't tug the fruits away from the stem.

Leek

Leeks will withstand the hardest winter and are generally untroubled by pests and diseases. But they are not an 'easy' crop — transplanting and earthing-up are required. Early varieties are popular with exhibitors for sowing under glass at the start of the year for the September show. The most popular leeks for the kitchen gardener are the Mid-season varieties which mature during the winter months. The Late varieties mature between January and early April when home-grown vegetables are scarce.

In a nutshell

Expected germination time	14 - 18 days
Expected yield from a 3m (10 ft) row	5 kg (11 lb)
Approximate time between sowing and lifting	30 weeks (early vars.)
Approximate time between sowing and lifting	45 weeks (late vars.)
Ease of cultivation	Not difficult

Varieties

JOLANT (Early) A vigorous grower which is chosen when extra-long stems are required.

LYON PRIZETAKER (Early) A favourite variety for the show bench — long, thick stems with dark green leaves.

MUSSELBURGH (Mid-season) This old favourite remains the No. 1 choice. Reliable and fine flavoured, but the stems are not long.

OARSMAN (Mid-season) A dark-leaved leek which shows good resistance to bolting and rust.

KING EDWARD (Mid-season) The stems are longer than most other Mid-season varieties.

WINTER CROP (Late) This variety is often recommended for northern exposed sites as it is the hardiest of all.

Lyon Prizetaker

Winter Crop

Musselburgh

Sowing & Planting

- Sow seeds outdoors in spring when the soil is workable and warm enough for germination. In the seed bed thin the seedlings to 5 cm (2 in.) apart.

- Pick a sunny site for where the plants will grow to maturity. Any reasonable soil will do provided it is neither highly compacted nor badly drained. Add garden compost with the winter digging if this was not done for the previous crop. Leave the surface rough — level the surface in spring by raking and treading. Incorporate a general-purpose fertilizer into the surface about 1 week before planting.

- The young leeks are ready for transplanting when they are pencil-thick and about 20 cm (8 in.) high. Water the bed the day before lifting. Trim off root ends and leaf tips, then set in rows 30 cm (1 ft) apart, leaving 15 cm (6 in.) between the transplants. Make a 15 cm (6 in.) deep hole with a dibber, drop in transplant and gently fill the hole with water — do not fill with soil.

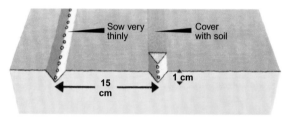

Calendar

Month	JAN	FEB	MAR	APR	MAY	JUN	JUL	AUG	SEP	OCT	NOV	DEC
Sowing Time												
Planting Time												
Sowing Time (under glass)												
Lifting Time												

see key — page 75

Plant care & Harvesting

- Hoe carefully and make sure the plants are not short of water — do not deliberately fill the holes. Gently draw soil around the stems when the plants are well developed. Increase the height a little at a time — be careful not to allow soil to fall between the leaves. Finish earthing-up in late October. Feeding will increase the thickness of the stems — stop in late August.

- Do not aim to produce giants for the kitchen — flavour reduces as size increases. Begin lifting when the leeks are still quite small — in this way there will be a long harvesting period. Never try to wrench the plant out of the soil — lift gently with a fork. Leeks can remain in the ground during the winter months — lift as required.

Lettuce

In the average garden the cultivation of lettuce is a simple matter. A row or two is sown in spring and again in early summer — the seedlings are thinned when they are obviously overcrowded and they are cut when the heads are mature. Unfortunately pests and diseases take their toll and the survivors all mature at the same time. You should buy a packet of mixed seed containing varieties which mature at different times or preferably sow in short rows at fortnightly intervals. Another cause of disappointment is bolting (running to seed) before maturity — the usual reason is transplanting at the wrong time or in the wrong way. So lettuce is not truly 'easy', but with care, the right varieties and some cloches you can enjoy them nearly all year round.

Types

CRISPHEAD LETTUCE
The Crispheads produce large hearts of curled and crisp leaves. In general they are more resistant to bolting than Butterheads, and their popularity has increased in Britain. They have always been the popular group in the U.S where the Iceberg type (Crispheads with a solid heart and few outer leaves) are dominant.

BUTTERHEAD LETTUCE
The Butterheads are still the most popular lettuce group. They are quick-maturing and will generally tolerate poorer conditions than the other types. The leaves are soft and smooth-edged — most are summer varieties but a few are hardy lettuces which are used to produce a spring crop and several others are forcing varieties for growing under glass.

LOOSE-LEAF LETTUCE
These varieties do not produce a heart. The leaves are curled and are picked like spinach — a few at a time without cutting the whole plant. Sow seed in April or May.

COS LETTUCE
The Cos or Romaine lettuce is easy to recognise by its upright growth habit and oblong head. The leaves are crisp and the flavour is good. They are generally a little more difficult to grow than the cabbage-shaped types.

In a nutshell

Expected germination time	6 - 12 days
Expected yield from a 3m (10 ft) row	10 - 20 heads
Approximate time between sowing and cutting	8 - 14 weeks (cabbage and cos vars.)
Approximate time between sowing and cutting	6 - 8 weeks (loose-leaf vars.)
Ease of cultivation	Not difficult

Sowing

- Lettuce needs non-acid soil containing adequate organic matter which requires to be kept moist throughout the life of the crop. For summer lettuce choose a sunny or lightly shaded site. Dig and incorporate garden compost in autumn or early winter. Rake to produce a fine tilth shortly before sowing time and apply a general-purpose fertilizer.

- You can grow seedlings in a pot for transplanting but lettuce hates to be moved — sow seed whenever you can where the crop is to grow.

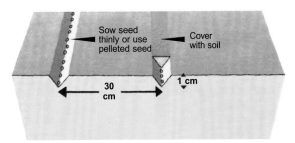

Plant care & Harvesting

- Thin the seedlings as soon as the first true leaves appear. Water the day before thinning. Continue thinning at intervals until the plants are 30 cm (1 ft) apart — Tom Thumb, Little Gem 20 cm (8 in.), Salad Bowl 15 cm (6 in.).

- Protect against slugs and birds. Hoe regularly. Keep the plants watered — avoid watering in the evening as this would increase the chance of disease. Keep watch for greenfly and grey mould — see Chapter 9.

- Lettuce is ready for cutting as soon as a firm heart has formed. Test by pressing the top of the plant with the back of your hand — squeezing the heart will damage the tissues.

- The heart will begin to grow upwards if not cut at this stage — a sign that it is getting ready to bolt. You must cut immediately for kitchen use.

- Harvest in the morning when the heads have dew on them. Pull up the plant and cut off the roots and lower leaves. Put the unwanted material on the compost heap.

Lettuce varieties

BUTTERHEAD lettuce

ALL THE YEAR ROUND A popular medium-sized variety — it can be sown in spring, summer or autumn.

AVONDEFIANCE A dark green and mildew-resistant variety for June-August sowing.

ARCTIC KING A good one to choose for sowing in winter for an early spring crop.

KWIEK A forcing variety for growing under glass for an early winter crop.

TOM THUMB The favourite variety for small plots — the heads are tennis-ball size.

COS lettuce

LOBJOIT'S GREEN An old favourite with large, dark green leaves.

WINTER DENSITY The No. 1 winter-hardy Cos — sow in August or September.

LITTLE GEM Compact and regarded by many as the sweetest lettuce. Tie loosely with wool.

FRECKLES More open and more decorative than the other Cos — red-spotted green leaves.

CRISPHEAD lettuce

WEBB'S WONDERFUL Reliable, large-hearted with frilly leaves — found in most catalogues.

ICEBERG The best known Crisphead but not the best choice for growing in the garden.

SALADIN An Iceberg type with large heads of crisp leaves. Sow in April-July.

LAKELAND Bred to be more reliable in Britain than the original Iceberg variety.

LOOSE-LEAF lettuce

SALAD BOWL The leaves are intricately cut and curled. Pick regularly. A reddish-brown variety is available.

DELICATO The cut-and-come-again variety with oak-shaped leaves and a dark red colour.

LOLLO ROSSA The most popular of the red Loose-leaf varieties. Frilly, purple-edged foliage.

All The Year Round

Winter Density

Iceberg

Calendar

For a Summer/Autumn Crop

Sow outdoors in late March - late July for cutting in June - October. For a mid May - mid June crop sow under glass in early February and plant out in early March under cloches.

Month	JAN	FEB	MAR	APR	MAY	JUN	JUL	AUG	SEP	OCT	NOV	DEC
Sowing Time		▣	✿									
Cutting Time												

O

For an Early Winter Crop

Sow a mildew-resistant variety such as Avondefiance outdoors in early August. Cover with cloches in late September — close ends with glass. Harvest period November - December.

Month	JAN	FEB	MAR	APR	MAY	JUN	JUL	AUG	SEP	OCT	NOV	DEC
Sowing Time								▮				
Cutting Time												

O

For a Midwinter Crop

Grow a forcing variety such as Kwiek. Sow seed under heated glass in September or October — plant out as soon as the seedlings are large enough to handle. Harvest period January - early March.

Month	JAN	FEB	MAR	APR	MAY	JUN	JUL	AUG	SEP	OCT	NOV	DEC
Sowing Time									▣▣	✿✿✿		
Cutting Time												

O

For a Spring Crop

In mild areas sow a winter-hardy variety such as Winter Density in late August - early September. Thin to 8 cm (3 in.). Complete thinning to 30 cm (1 ft) spacing in early spring — cutting period May. For other areas sow a winter-hardy or forcing variety in mid October under cloches. Harvest period April.

Month	JAN	FEB	MAR	APR	MAY	JUN	JUL	AUG	SEP	OCT	NOV	DEC
Sowing Time								▮		⇕		
Cutting Time												

see key — page 75

Marrow, Courgette & Squash

There are no exact dividing lines between these members of the cucumber family. Until quite recently the Marrow varieties dominated, producing large vegetable marrows. Now the Courgette varieties have taken over, and they are nothing more than selected varieties of marrows which are cut at the immature stage. Summer squashes are non-standard shaped marrows — winter squashes differ by having a hard rind and fibrous flesh. Finally the Pumpkin varieties are the giants, grown mainly for show.

In a nutshell

Expected germination time	5 - 8 days
Expected yield per plant	4 (marrows)
Expected yield per plant	4 (courgettes)
Approximate time between sowing and cutting	10 - 14 weeks
Ease of cultivation	Not difficult

Varieties

GREEN BUSH (Marrow) The favourite all-rounder — cut the small fruits as courgettes and let a few mature to become marrows.

LONG GREEN TRAILING (Marrow) Large and cylindrical for kitchen and exhibition.

TIGER CROSS (Marrow) An F_1 hybrid similar to Green Bush, but more productive.

GOLD RUSH (Courgette) One of the yellow varieties — creamy white flesh and good flavour.

DEFENDER (Courgette) The popular choice — a green variety which crops heavily.

CUSTARD SQUASH (Squash) A scalloped-edged flat summer variety — cook like courgettes.

VEGETABLE SPAGHETTI (Squash) A winter variety which produces spaghetti-like strands.

ATLANTIC GIANT (Pumpkin) The variety to grow for the Largest Pumpkin competition.

Gold Rush

Vegetable Spaghetti

Sowing & Planting

- Sow in late May or early June — the first courgettes will be ready in late July or August.

- Choose a sunny site protected from strong winds. The soil must be well drained. It is better to prepare planting pockets rather than sowing in rows.

- Soak the seeds overnight and sow 3 seeds 3 cm (1 in.) deep and about 6 cm (2 in.) apart at the centre of each pocket. Cover with a cloche to speed up germination. When the first true leaves appear thin out to leave the strongest seedling.

- Seedlings can be raised indoors for an earlier crop, but the results are usually less satisfactory. Sow a single seed edgeways 1 cm (½ in.) deep in compost — keep at a minimum of 18°C (65°F) until germination. Harden off and transplant in early June.

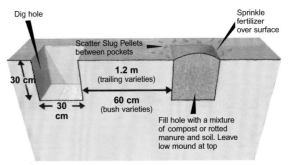

Dig hole
Sprinkle fertilizer over surface
Scatter Slug Pellets between pockets
30 cm
30 cm
1.2 m (trailing varieties)
60 cm (bush varieties)
Fill hole with a mixture of compost or rotted manure and soil. Leave low mound at top

Calendar

Month	JAN	FEB	MAR	APR	MAY	JUN	JUL	AUG	SEP	OCT	NOV	DEC
Sowing Time (outdoors)					▮							
Sowing Time (indoors)				▮	❀							
Cutting Time												

see key — page 75

Plant care & Harvesting

- Pinch out the tips of trailing varieties when the shoots are 60 cm (2 ft) long. Water round and not over the plants. Syringe lightly in dry weather.

- If the weather is cold remove a mature male flower (thin stalk behind petals) on a dry day, fold back petals and push gently into each female flower.

- Feed every 14 days with a tomato fertilizer once the fruits start to swell. Limit pumpkins to 2 per plant. Keep marrows on a tile to prevent rotting.

- Cut when the fruits are still quite small. Continual cropping is essential to prolong the fruiting period. Allow pumpkins and winter squashes to mature on the plant — remove before frosts arrive.

Onion, from sets

Sets (small onions) have several advantages over seeds. They mature more quickly, are hardier and are less prone to onion fly and mildew. In addition high soil fertility is not required and less work is involved. The drawbacks are the extra cost involved and the extra risk of bolting. Shallots are milder in flavour than onions and the ones you buy are already full-sized — they quickly start to grow after planting and in summer produce a cluster of 8-12 similar-sized bulbs.

In a nutshell

Expected sprouting time	11 - 14 days
Expected yield from a 3m (10 ft) row	3 kg (7 lb)
Approximate time between planting and lifting	20 weeks
Ease of cultivation	Easy

Varieties

AILSA CRAIG (Onion) An old favourite — round, large and straw-coloured with mild-flavoured flesh.

STUTTGARTER GIANT (Onion) Flat, mild-flavoured onions with good keeping qualities.

STURON (Onion) Large, round bulbs with excellent resistance to bolting.

SETTON (Onion) Bred from Sturon — it is claimed to be higher yielding.

NEW FEN GLOBE (Onion) A large, pale yellow onion which matures early. Good keeping qualities.

GOLDEN GOURMET (Shallot) Smooth yellow-skinned bulbs which have taken over from Dutch Yellow. Stores well.

RED SUN (Shallot) Shiny red-tinged bulbs which have taken over from Dutch Red.

HATIVE DE NIORT (Shallot) The usual choice by exhibitors — dark brown, perfectly shaped.

Ailsa Craig

Red Sun

Planting

- All onions require reasonable soil and good drainage, but sets do not need the fine tilth and the high humus content which are necessary for seed-sown ones. Dig in early spring and incorporate some compost if available. Lime if necessary. Firm the surface before planting and rake in a general-purpose fertilizer.

- If planting is delayed, spread out the sets in a cool, well-lit place to prevent premature sprouting.

- Plant onion sets 10 cm (4 in.) apart in mid March - mid April. Shallots require wider (15 cm/6 in.) and earlier (mid February - mid March) planting.

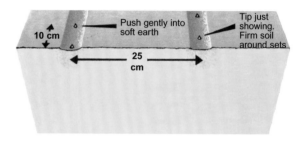

Calendar

Month	JAN	FEB	MAR	APR	MAY	JUN	JUL	AUG	SEP	OCT	NOV	DEC
Planting Time												
Lifting Time												

see key — page 75

Plant care & Harvesting

- If birds are a nuisance in your area protect the sets with netting. Keep weeds down by hoeing and hand pulling. Push back any sets which have been lifted by frost or birds.

- Water if the soil is dry and feed occasionally. Break off any flower stems which appear. Mulching will reduce the need for watering and weeding. Stop watering once the bulbs have swollen — pull back the covering mulch or earth to expose the bulbs to the sun.

- Shallots: The leaves will turn yellow in July. Lift and separate the bulbs, remove dirt and brittle stems, and store in net bags in a cool, dry place for up to 8 months.

- Onions: Bulbs are mature when the foliage is yellow and topples over. Leave for 2 weeks and then lift with a fork on a dry day. Spread out on sacking or in trays for drying — move indoors if it starts to rain. Drying takes 7-21 days — store in trays or nets in a cool and well-lit place. Do not store bulbs which are soft, spotted or have abnormally thick necks.

Onion, from seed

The Standard varieties are grown for their large bulbs which can be stored throughout the winter — most of them are suitable for spring sowing. The Japanese varieties make late summer sowing a more reliable routine, but their midsummer crop cannot be stored. Apart from these large bulb onions there are the Salad varieties (scallions or spring onions) and the Pickling varieties — small silverskin onions which are sown in April and lifted in July.

In a nutshell

Expected germination time	21 days
Expected yield from a 3m (10 ft) row	4 kg (9 lb)
Approximate time between sowing and lifting	46 weeks (August-sown vars.)
Approximate time between sowing and lifting	22 weeks (spring-sown vars.)
Ease of cultivation	Easy

Varieties

AILSA CRAIG (Standard) Very large — a popular choice for the kitchen and show bench.

BEDFORDSHIRE CHAMPION (Standard) Stores better than Ailsa Craig but is very susceptible to mildew.

RED BARON (Standard) The most popular red-skinned variety. Flattish bulbs which store well.

KEEPWELL (Standard) Pale brown skin. The one to choose if you plan to sow in August.

SENSHYU (Japanese) Flattish bulbs which are ready for lifting in July.

WHITE LISBON (Salad) By far the most popular Salad variety. Can provide spring onions for 6 months of the year.

PARIS SILVERSKIN (Pickling) The most popular Pickling variety. Pull when the bulbs are marble-sized.

Ailsa Craig

White Lisbon

Paris Silverskin

Sowing & Planting

- For an August/September crop sow as soon as the land is workable in the spring. For a July crop sow in mid August. In cold areas and for exhibition sow under glass in January, harden off in March and transplant in April. Sow Salad onions in March - July for a June - October crop and again in August for onions in March - May.

- Choose an open sunny site with good drainage. Dig in autumn, incorporating garden compost. Lime in late winter if necessary. Before sowing or planting apply a general-purpose fertilizer and rake when the soil is reasonably dry. Tread over the area and rake again to produce a fine tilth.

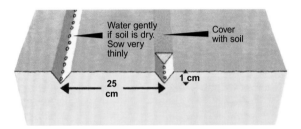

Water gently if soil is dry. Sow very thinly — Cover with soil — 25 cm — 1 cm

Calendar

Month	JAN	FEB	MAR	APR	MAY	JUN	JUL	AUG	SEP	OCT	NOV	DEC
Sowing Time (outdoors)			▨					▨				
Sowing Time (indoors)	▨			🌱								
Lifting Time							▨	▨	▨			

see key — page 75

Plant care & Harvesting

- Thin the spring-sown crop to 3-5 cm (1-2 in.) when the seedlings have straightened, and later to 10 cm (4 in.) at the small 'spring onion' stage. Seedlings grown under glass should be set 10 cm (4 in.) apart in 20 cm (8 in.) wide rows. Let the roots fall vertically in the planting hole. Plant firmly.

- Sow Japanese varieties in rows 20 cm (8 in.) apart. Thin seedlings to 3 cm (1 in.) and then to 10 cm (4 in.) intervals in spring. Rows of Salad onions should be 10 cm (4 in.) apart.

- Hoe carefully or weed by hand. Water if the soil is dry and feed occasionally. Break off any flower stems which appear. Mulching will reduce the need for watering and weeding. Stop watering once the bulbs have swollen — pull back the covering mulch or earth to expose the bulbs to the sun.

- Bulbs are mature when the foliage is yellow and topples over. Leave for 2 weeks and then lift with a fork. See page 94 for drying instructions.

Parsnip

The parsnip is generally regarded as too sweet and too strong-flavoured to serve as a potato substitute, and they are not popular. This is a pity, as there are recipes which can turn this Cinderella into a number of tasty dishes — see the *Garden to Kitchen Expert*. Parsnips need very little attention, and radish or lettuce can be grown between the rows. The roots can be left in the ground in winter to be dug up as required. The usual choice is a short- or medium-rooted variety — a deep and stone-free soil is required for long roots.

In a nutshell

Expected germination time	10 - 28 years
Expected yield from a 3m (10 ft) row	4 kg (9 lb)
Approximate time between sowing and lifting	34 weeks
Ease of cultivation	Easy

Varieties

AVONRESISTER One of the shortest — 12 cm (5 in.) roots with canker resistance.

THE STUDENT Thick and tapered — the one to choose for top flavour.

TENDER AND TRUE Long-rooted variety for kitchen and exhibition. Very little core — high resistance to canker.

HOLLOW CROWN Another long one for kitchen and show bench. High yields.

COUNTESS A smooth-skinned variety noted for its yields and flavour. Canker resistant.

GLADIATOR The first F$_1$ hybrid parsnip. Matures very early — good canker resistance.

JAVELIN Long, slender and canker resistant — one to choose for the show bench.

Avonresister   Tender and True

Sowing

- February is the traditional month for sowing parsnips, but it is better to wait until March. Sow short-rooted varieties in April.

- Any soil in sun or light shade can grow a good crop of parsnips — do not choose a long variety if the soil is heavy or stony. Dig in autumn or winter — do not add garden compost or manure, but lime if necessary. Rake in a general-purpose fertilizer when preparing the seed bed.

- Seed is very light — sow on a dry day. Germination is slow in cold weather. Throw thinnings away — parsnips seldom produce satisfactory roots after transplanting.

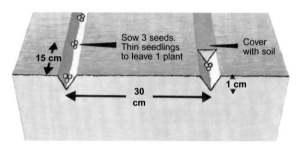

Calendar

Month	JAN	FEB	MAR	APR	MAY	JUN	JUL	AUG	SEP	OCT	NOV	DEC
Sowing Time												
Lifting Time												

see key — page 75

Plant care & Harvesting

- Hoe regularly to keep down weeds — do not touch the crowns of the plants. Very few pests attack parsnips — squash between your fingers the leaf blisters which contain celery fly grubs. Little attention is needed, but it will be necessary to water if there is a prolonged dry spell.

- The roots are ready for lifting when the leaves begin to die down in autumn. Lift the crop as required, using a fork to loosen the soil. Leave the remainder in the soil for harvesting later — the cropping season can extend until early March.

- It is a good idea to lift some of the roots in November for storage before the season of hard frosts and snow arrives. Lift the remaining roots in February or early March.

- Only sound roots should be stored. Cut off leaves at 1 cm (½ in.) above the crowns and place the roots between layers of sand in a stout box. Store in a dry shed or garage.

Pea

Quite often peas are disappointing as a garden crop. The yield can be quite small for the area occupied, and if the soil is poor or the weather is hot it can seem that the amount obtained is not worth all the trouble. But if you want to discover how good peas can taste then pick the pods when they are quite small and within an hour boil the shelled peas for about 4 minutes in a small amount of water. There are many types of peas and their classification is complex. There are garden peas and also Mangetout, which are sown in April or May and cooked whole. There are Round and Wrinkled peas, tall and dwarf plants, and first early, second early and maincrop varieties. Never sow peas in cold and wet soil, make sure that the soil is fertile, keep the birds away and spray when necessary.

In a nutshell

Expected germination time	7 - 10 days
Expected yield from a 3m (10 ft) row	5 kg (11 lb)
Approximate time between autumn sowing and picking	32 weeks
Approximate time between spring sowing and picking	12 - 16 weeks
Ease of cultivation	Not easy

Sowing

- Choose an open site which has not grown peas for at least two seasons. The soil should be non-acid and have a crumbly structure and adequate humus. Dig the soil in autumn or early winter, incorporating a bucket or two of garden compost or well-rotted manure to each sq. metre (10 sq.ft). Apply a light dressing of a general-purpose fertilizer shortly before sowing time — do not over-feed.

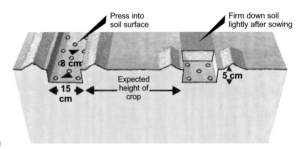

Plant care & Harvesting

- Protection from birds immediately after sowing is vital. Do not rely on a chemical deterrent — place twiggy branches along the rows or use plastic netting. Wire-mesh guards are best of all.

- Hoe regularly to keep the weeds under control. Insert twigs along the rows to provide support when the seedlings are about 8 cm (3 in.) high. Do not delay this operation — leaving the stems to straggle over the ground will encourage slugs. Medium- or tall-growing varieties will require extra support— erect a sturdy screen of plastic netting along each row.

- Water during dry periods in summer. Mulch between the rows to conserve moisture. Maggoty peas are a familiar problem — the best way to avoid an attack by pea moth is to sow a quick-maturing crop early or late in the season.

- A pod is ready for picking when it is well-filled but there is still a little space between each pea. Start harvesting at this stage, beginning at the bottom of the stem and working upwards. Use both hands, one to hold the stem and the other to pick off the pods. Pick regularly.

Types

ROUND PEA
The seeds remain smooth and round when dried. They are all First Earlies — hardier and quicker-maturing than other types and more able to withstand poor growing conditions than the Wrinkled types. Round varieties are used for late autumn and early spring sowing.

WRINKLED PEA
The seeds are distinctly wrinkled when dried. These 'marrowfat' peas are sweeter, larger and heavier cropping than the Round ones, and are therefore much more widely grown. They are, however, less hardy and should not be sown before March. These Wrinkled varieties are classified by the time taken from sowing to first picking. First Earlies take 11-12 weeks, Second Earlies 13-14 weeks and Maincrop 15-16 weeks.

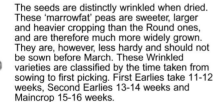

MANGETOUT
Rather easier to grow than garden peas. Begin sowing in April — you can continue sowing until the end of May. Crop in August - early September. Pick before the peas swell and cook the pods whole.

PETIT POIS
Petit pois are not immature peas gathered from small pods of any garden pea variety — they are a small number of dwarf varieties which produce tiny peas which are uniquely sweet. Begin sowing in April — you can continue sowing until the end of May.

Pea varieties

ROUND PEA varieties

FELTHAM FIRST (1st Early) An old favourite which needs little support. 45 cm (1½ ft).

METEOR (1st Early) Baby of the group — very hardy. The one to choose for February sowing. 30 cm (1 ft).

WRINKLED PEA varieties

EARLY ONWARD (1st Early) Not as popular as Onward but it matures 10 days earlier. 60 cm (2 ft).

KELVEDON WONDER (1st Early) Popular for successional sowing from March to July. 45 cm (1½ ft).

LITTLE MARVEL (1st Early) Blunt-ended pods are borne in pairs. Good flavour. 45 cm (1½ ft).

ONWARD (2nd Early) The most popular garden pea. Crops heavily, good disease resistance. 75 cm (2½ ft).

HURST GREEN SHAFT (2nd Early) Popular for kitchen and exhibition. Resistant to mildew. 75 cm (2½ ft).

ALDERMAN (Maincrop) Height, yield and pod length are all large. Prolonged cropping period. 1.5 m (5 ft).

SENATOR (Maincrop) The Maincrop for the smaller garden — pods borne in pairs. 75 cm (2½ ft).

MANGETOUT varieties

OREGON SUGAR POD Pick the fleshy, curved pods when they are about 8 cm (3 in.) long. 1 m (3 ft).

DELIKATA Similar to Oregon Sugar Pod, but earlier. Mildew resistant. 1 m (3 ft).

SUGAR SNAP Thick fleshy pods — leave some to mature and shell as garden peas. 1½ m (5 ft).

PETIT POIS varieties

WAVEREX The only Petit pois variety you are likely to find. Yields are high. 60 cm (2 ft).

Feltham First

Waverex

Calendar

For a May/June Crop
Pick a sheltered site — expect some losses if the site is cold and wet. Grow a Round variety — Feltham First is widely available and reliable for both early spring and late sowings. Cover seedlings and plants with cloches.

Month	JAN	FEB	MAR	APR	MAY	JUN	JUL	AUG	SEP	OCT	NOV	DEC
Sowing Time		↓	↓							↓	↓	
Picking Time					▓	▓						

○

For a June/July Crop
For sowing in mid March choose a Round variety or a first early Wrinkled variety such as Kelvedon Wonder or Early Onward. For sowing in late March or April pick a second early Wrinkled type — Onward is a popular choice.

Month	JAN	FEB	MAR	APR	MAY	JUN	JUL	AUG	SEP	OCT	NOV	DEC
Sowing Time			▓	▓								
Picking Time						▓	▓					

○

For an August Crop
Sow a maincrop Wrinkled variety in April or May. Height is one of the most important points to consider — tall-growing ones like Alderman need nearly 2 m (6 ft) between the rows. If space is limited choose Senator.

Month	JAN	FEB	MAR	APR	MAY	JUN	JUL	AUG	SEP	OCT	NOV	DEC
Sowing Time				▓	▓							
Picking Time								▓	▓			

○

For a September/October Crop
Sow in June or July for a September - October crop. It is necessary to choose the right variety — a first early Wrinkled variety.

Month	JAN	FEB	MAR	APR	MAY	JUN	JUL	AUG	SEP	OCT	NOV	DEC
Sowing Time						▓	▓					
Picking Time									▓	▓		

see key — page 75

Potato

Earlies give you 'new' potatoes in summer — Maincrops provide tubers for storage over winter. If space is limited then an Early variety should be your only choice. Yields will be lower than from a Maincrop but will take up less space, miss the damaging effect of blight, and provide new potatoes when shop prices are high.

In a nutshell

Expected yield from a 3m (10 ft) row	5 kg (11 lb) (early vars.)
Expected yield from a 3m (10 ft) row	9 kg (20 lb) (maincrop vars.)
Approximate time between planting and lifting	13 weeks (early vars.)
Approximate time between planting and lifting	22 weeks (maincrop vars.)
Ease of cultivation	Not difficult

Varieties

FIRST EARLY varieties

ARRAN PILOT White flesh. An old favourite which tolerates dry weather better than most.

ROCKET White, waxy flesh, perhaps the earliest of all. Lift when mature — do not leave in the ground.

FOREMOST White flesh. A high-yielding variety — stays firm when boiled.

PENTLAND JAVELIN White, waxy flesh. The crop is heavy — matures later than most First Earlies.

MARIS BARD White, waxy flesh. The one to grow for a very early and heavy crop.

SECOND EARLY varieties

ESTIMA Pale yellow, waxy flesh. Good chip variety — popular for exhibiting.

MARIS PEER White, waxy flesh. Good disease resistance, but disappointing in dry soil.

CHARLOTTE Yellow, waxy flesh — the favourite salad potato. Easy to grow.

KESTREL White flesh, purple-splashed skin. A good choice for chips and the show bench.

ANYA Yellow, waxy flesh. Long tubers with a 'new potato' flavour.

MAINCROP varieties

MARIS PIPER Creamy flesh. Excellent yields, but slug and drought resistance are low.

DESIREE Pale yellow flesh. A good choice — yields are high and drought resistance is good.

KING EDWARD Creamy flesh — grow it if you want quality rather than quantity.

CARA Creamy flesh. Pink-blotched like King Edward, but yields and blight resistance are higher.

Planting

- First Early varieties are planted in mid March - early April. Lift in June or July. Second Earlies are planted in early to mid April for lifting in July or August. Maincrop varieties are planted in mid to late April. Tubers can be lifted in August for immediate use or in September - early October for storage.

- Do not grow on land which has been used for this crop within the past 2 seasons. Choose a sunny spot and avoid frost pockets. Dig the soil in autumn and add compost if the soil was not manured for the previous crop. Break down any clods and sprinkle a general-purpose fertilizer over the surface.

- Chit the seed potatoes when you obtain them in February. Set them out rose end (where most of the eyes are) uppermost in egg boxes or wooden trays. Keep them in a light (not sunny) frost-free place — in about 6 weeks there will be several 1-3 cm (½-1 in.) long shoots.

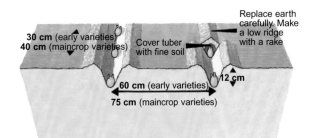

30 cm (early varieties)
40 cm (maincrop varieties)
Cover tuber with fine soil
Replace earth carefully. Make a low ridge with a rake
60 cm (early varieties)
75 cm (maincrop varieties)
12 cm

Calendar

Month	JAN	FEB	MAR	APR	MAY	JUN	JUL	AUG	SEP	OCT	NOV	DEC
Planting Time												
Lifting Time												

see key — page 75

Plant care & Harvesting

- Draw a little soil over emerging shoots if there is a danger of frosts. Earth-up when the stems are about 25 cm (10 in.) high — see page 56. Water liberally in dry weather.

- Harvesting Earlies can start when the flowers open or the buds drop. Carefully remove soil from a small part of the ridge and examine the tubers — they are ready for lifting as new potatoes when they are the size of hens' eggs. Push a flat-tined fork into the ridge and well away from the stems and lift the roots forward into the trench between the ridges.

- With Maincrops for storage cut off and remove stems when the leaves have turned brown. Wait 10 days before lifting — see 'Storing' on page 70.

Radish

Summer radishes are practically trouble-free and the round or thumb-long roots are ready about a month after sowing. It is a pity that so many gardeners stop there, when there are unusual ones to try — pink or all-white ones, Japanese varieties which can reach 30 cm (1 ft) etc. In addition there are the large Winter radishes which can weigh up to 1 kilo (2¼ lb) or more. They have white, black or pink skins and a stronger flavour than the Summer varieties.

In a nutshell

Expected germination time	4 - 7 days
Expected yield from a 3m (10 ft) row	2 kg (4 lb) (summer vars.)
Expected yield from a 3m (10 ft) row	5 kg (11 lb) (winter vars.)
Approximate time between sowing and lifting	3 - 6 weeks (summer vars.)
Approximate time between sowing and lifting	10 - 12 weeks (winter vars.)
Ease of cultivation	Easy

Varieties

CHERRY BELLE (Summer) An all-red popular globular variety. Mild flavour — slow to go woody.

SCARLET GLOBE (Summer) An all-red popular globular variety. Good choice for poor soil.

FRENCH BREAKFAST (Summer) A popular red and white medium-length variety — quick-growing.

LONG WHITE ICICLE (Summer) All-white, long and crisp. Pick when 8-15 cm (3-6 in.) long.

MINOWASE SUMMER (Summer) A Japanese variety which can reach 30 cm (1 ft). Harvest at 15 cm (6 in.).

CHINA ROSE (Winter) The baby of the Winter radishes — oval roots weighing up to 500 g (1 lb).

BLACK SPANISH ROUND (Winter) Large, black-skinned and globular — very hot when eaten raw.

Scarlet Globe

French Breakfast

China Rose

Sowing

- Sow Summer varieties under cloches in January or February — sow outdoors in March. For a prolonged supply sow every few weeks or buy 'Mixed Radish' seed. Sowing after early June can be unreliable.

- Sow Winter varieties in July or early August — begin lifting roots in late October.

- For maximum tenderness and flavour the crop must be grown quickly. This calls for some soil preparation. Choose a sunny spot for early sowing, but later crops need some shade. Dig compost into the soil if it was not manured for the previous crop. Apply a general-purpose fertilizer before sowing and rake the surface to a fine tilth.

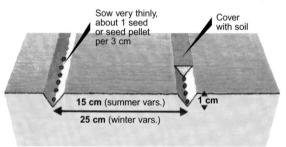

Sow very thinly, about 1 seed or seed pellet per 3 cm

Cover with soil

15 cm (summer vars.)
25 cm (winter vars.)
1 cm

Calendar

Month	JAN	FEB	MAR	APR	MAY	JUN	JUL	AUG	SEP	OCT	NOV	DEC
Sowing Time												
Lifting Time												

see key — page 75

Plant care & Harvesting

- Thin Summer varieties if overcrowded — leave 3 cm (1 in.) between small types — 5-10 cm (2-4 in.) between larger ones. With Winter radishes thin to leave 15 cm (6 in.) between the plants.

- Protect against birds. Quick and uninterrupted growth is essential for good results, so hoe to keep down weeds and water when the weather is dry. Summer radishes sown in July or August are often disappointing because of hot and dry weather.

- Pull the Summer varieties when the round ones are about 3 cm (1 in.) across and the medium-length roots are no longer than your thumb — overgrown ones are woody and hollow. Japanese varieties are not pulled until they are 15 cm (6 in.) long — they can be left to grow longer if required for cooking rather than salads.

- Winter varieties are left in the ground and lifted as required — cover the crowns with fleece or straw. However, it is a better idea to lift in November and store — see page 70.

Spinach

Grow this vegetable only if the family likes it, and that calls for learning to cook it properly — see the *Garden to Kitchen Expert*. There are two types of true spinach — Summer varieties are round-seeded and are harvested between late May and the end of September. These are the ones to grow for maximum flavour and tenderness. The Winter varieties are prickly-seeded and are picked between October and April. The New Zealand variety is not a true spinach — it is a half-hardy annual for sowing in late May and picking between June and September. Perpetual spinach is a type of leaf beet.

In a nutshell

Expected germination time	12 - 20 days
Expected yield from a 3m (10 ft) row	2 - 5 kg (4 - 11 lb)
Approximate time between sowing and picking	8 - 14 weeks
Ease of cultivation	Not easy

Varieties

BLOOMSDALE (Summer) A dark green variety with reasonable resistance to bolting.

BORDEAUX (Summer) A popular variety with dark green leaves and red stems.

MEDANIA (Summer) A modern variety — vigorous growth, slow to bolt and good mildew resistance.

NORVAK (Summer) One of the early modern varieties — with reduced risk of bolting.

SCENIC (Winter) Excellent resistance to mildew — use young leaves in salads.

GIANT WINTER (Winter) Noted for its hardiness and length of its cropping season.

MONNOPA (Winter) A fine-flavoured variety with a low oxalic acid content — the one for baby food.

Norvak

New Zealand Spinach

Sowing

- Summer varieties should be sown every few weeks between mid March and late May — Winter varieties are sown in August and again in September.

- The soil must be fertile and humus-rich in order to avoid a bitter-tasting crop. The ideal place for Summer spinach is between rows of tall-growing vegetables — the dappled shade reduces the risk of the plants running to seed. Sow Winter and New Zealand spinach in a sunny spot. Dig in winter and apply lime if necessary. Rake in a general-purpose fertilizer about 2 weeks before sowing. New Zealand spinach needs more space than the true spinach varieties. Sow 3 seeds about 3 cm (1 in.) below the surface, spacing the groups 60 cm (2 ft) apart. Thin each group to a single plant.

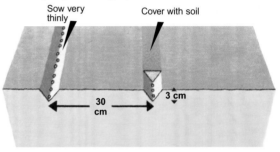

Sow very thinly — Cover with soil — 30 cm — 3 cm

Calendar

Month	JAN	FEB	MAR	APR	MAY	JUN	JUL	AUG	SEP	OCT	NOV	DEC
Sowing Time			▩		▩	▩		▩	▩			
Picking Time	▩	▩	▩	▩		▩	▩	▩	▩	▩	▩	▩

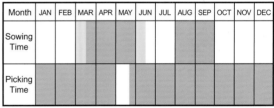

see key — page 75

Plant care & Harvesting

- Thin the seedlings of Summer and Winter varieties to 8 cm (3 in.) apart as soon as they are large enough to handle. Remove alternate plants a few weeks later for kitchen use.

- Hoe to keep down weeds. Water copiously during dry spells in summer. Use cloches or fleece to cover Winter varieties from October onwards.

- Start picking when the leaves have reached a reasonable size. Take the outer leaves, which should still be at the young and tender stage. Pick continually so that fresh growth is encouraged. With a Summer variety you can take up to half the leaves — with Winter spinach you must pick more sparingly. Pick the leaves with your fingernails. With New Zealand spinach pull off a few young shoots from the base of the plant at each harvesting session.

Swede

Swedes are closely related to turnips but the flesh is usually yellow and the flavour is both milder and sweeter. In addition the plants are hardier and the yields are greater. The introduction of disease-resistant varieties has made this winter vegetable even easier to grow. All you have to do is sprinkle some seed along the rows in late spring or early summer, thin a few weeks later and then lift the large globular roots either as you need them from autumn to spring or in autumn to store for use later.

In a nutshell

Expected germination time	6 - 10 days
Expected yield from a 3m (10 ft) row	13 kg (29 lb)
Approximate time between sowing and lifting	20 - 24 weeks
Ease of cultivation	Easy

Varieties

BEST OF ALL A purple-skinned and mild-flavoured variety — very hardy and noted for reliability.

MARIAN A popular choice — high yields, good flavour and some resistance to club root and mildew.

INVITATION A breakthrough — a swede which is resistant to club root as well as mildew.

BRORA Reputed to be the sweetest swede. Purple shiny skin. Lift before Christmas.

ACME Purple-topped roots which are ready for lifting from early October. Orange flesh.

ANGELA A rival to Acme. Cropping may start in September — purple skin, yellow flesh, outstanding flavour.

RUBY A fully winter hardy and easy-to-grow variety. Good mildew resistance.

Marian

Ruby

Sowing

- In order to avoid mildew it is usual to delay sowing until May or early June. Water the drills before sowing if the weather is dry.

- As with other members of the cabbage family, this crop needs a firm, non-acid soil which drains reasonably freely. Pick a sunny spot and dig in autumn — lime if necessary. In spring apply a general-purpose fertilizer to the surface — prepare the seed bed about a week later.

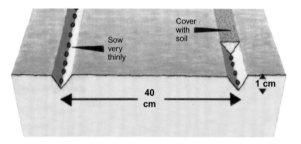

Calendar

Month	JAN	FEB	MAR	APR	MAY	JUN	JUL	AUG	SEP	OCT	NOV	DEC
Sowing Time					░	▓						
Lifting Time	░								░	▓	▓	▓

see key — page 75

Plant care & Harvesting

- Thin out as soon as the seedlings are large enough to handle. Do this in stages until the plants are 25 cm (10 in.) apart. Hoe the soil to keep down weeds. It is necessary to water copiously in periods of dry weather — failure to do so will result in small and woody roots. Another problem with failing to water is that rain following a prolonged dry spell will cause the roots to split.

- Pests can be a nuisance. A heavy attack by flea beetle can seriously weaken the plants — an insecticidal spray is the answer here. Cabbage root fly is an important pest of leafy brassicas, but swedes are much less likely to be seriously affected.

- Begin harvesting in autumn when the roots are large enough to use. You can leave them in the soil and lift with a fork as required until spring.

- Frozen soil in the new year can make lifting a problem, so it is usually more convenient to lift them in December and store them indoors for later use. This involves twisting off the leaves before placing the roots between layers of sand in a stout wooden box which is kept in a dry, cool place.

Sweet Corn

The flavour of home-grown sweet corn cooked within an hour of picking is so much better than shop-bought corn. There is still a widespread view that sweet corn cannot be grown in northern counties, but this is no longer true. Choose one of the F_1 hybrids listed below which have revolutionised the reliability of sweet corn in this country — the older open-pollinated varieties produce heavy crops but require a better climate than ours. The 1-2 m (3-7 ft) stems bear 15-25 cm (6-10 in.) long cobs. The tassels at the top of the plant are the male flowers — the female flowers ('silks') are at the top of the immature cobs.

In a nutshell

Expected germination time	10 - 12 days
Expected yield from a 3m (10 ft) row	10 cobs
Approximate time between sowing and picking	14 weeks
Ease of cultivation	Not difficult

Varieties

SUNDANCE A large-cobbed variety which matures early — a good choice for cooler areas.

KELVEDON GLORY A popular mid-season variety — the cobs are large and well-filled.

HONEY BANTAM A bicoloured, early variety — the only open-pollinated one you are likely to find.

SWEET 77 A mid-season supersweet variety. Very large cobs, but vigour and yields are only moderate.

EARLY XTRA SWEET Another of the supersweets — early and tasty, but the cobs are not well-filled.

LARK A mid-season supersweet variety — the cobs are large and the corn is thin skinned.

SWIFT The first of the thin-skinned supersweets — dwarf growth habit with early-maturing cobs.

Kelvedon Glory

Sweet 77

Honey Bantam

Sowing & Planting

- In southern counties sow in May for late August - September picking. For extra reliability and an earlier crop sow under glass. In other areas sow under cloches in mid May. Alternatively sow under glass in mid April - early May and plant out in late May - early June.

- Good drainage and adequate humus are necessary. Choose a sheltered spot in full sun. Dig in winter, incorporating old compost if the previous crop was not manured. Rake in a general-purpose fertilizer about 2 weeks before sowing or planting.

- Sow or plant in rectangular blocks. Sowing in pots indoors is the most reliable way of growing sweet corn. Use fibre pots — sow 2 seeds about 3 cm (1 in.) deep — remove the weaker seedling. Set transplants 45 cm (1½ ft) apart.

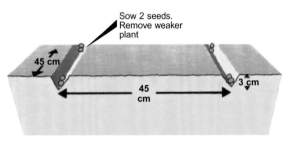

Calendar

Month	JAN	FEB	MAR	APR	MAY	JUN	JUL	AUG	SEP	OCT	NOV	DEC
Sowing Time (Outdoors)					▮							
Sowing Time (Indoors)				▮	▮							
Picking Time								▮	▮			

see key — page 75

Plant care & Harvesting

- Remove cloches when the foliage touches the glass. Protect from birds — hoe around plants if necessary. Cover surface roots with soil — do not remove side shoots. Water in dry weather. Stake if the plants are tall and the site is exposed.

- Tap the tassels at the top of each stem in late June or July to help pollination. Apply a liquid fertilizer when the cobs begin to swell.

- Test for ripeness when the silks at the top of each cob have turned brown. Pull back part of the outer sheath and squeeze a couple of grains between thumbnail and fingernail. The cob is unripe if a watery liquid squirts out, it is just right for picking if the liquid is creamy, and it is overripe if the contents are thick and doughy.

Tomato, Greenhouse

The Ordinary varieties are red salad tomatoes grown for their reliability (Moneymaker), flavour (Ailsa Craig) or earliness (Harbinger). The F₁ Hybrids are similar to the Ordinary ones but have important advantages — the yields and disease resistance are higher. The Beefsteak varieties have large and meaty fruits — they are stopped at the fourth truss. Finally there are the Novelty ones, which are either non-round or non-red. A few of the F₁ Hybrids and Novelty varieties are cherry tomatoes — bite-sized and full of flavour.

In a nutshell

Expected germination time	8 - 11 days
Expected yield per plant	4 kg (9 lb)
Approximate time between sowing and picking	16 weeks
Ease of cultivation	Not easy

Varieties

MONEYMAKER (Ordinary) One of the old favourites. Large trusses of heavy fruit, but the flavour is bland.

ALICANTE (Ordinary) Early cropping variety. Noted for reliability and heavy cropping. Good flavour.

HARBINGER (Ordinary) Early, but there are no other outstanding virtues.

AILSA CRAIG (Ordinary) Popular variety which produces medium-sized tomatoes. Good flavour.

SHIRLEY (F₁ Hybrid) Few rivals — early cropping, fine flavour and good disease resistance.

SWEET MILLION (F₁ Hybrid) The thin-skinned cherry tomatoes are super sweet.

NIMBUS (F₁ Hybrid) An early variety — high yields coupled with outstanding disease resistance.

VANDOS (F₁ Hybrid) Excellent flavour, but yields are modest and so is disease resistance.

BRANDYWINE (Beefsteak) Not the prettiest Beefsteak, but its flavour is unequalled.

BEEFEATER (Beefsteak) Its plus points are heavy yields and long picking season.

FERLINE (Beefsteak) Smaller than others in the group, but it has the best resistance to blight.

GOLDEN CHERRY (Novelty) Golden yellow cherry tomatoes on long trusses. Excellent flavour.

TIGERELLA (Novelty) The fruits bear tiger stripes of red and yellow when mature.

Sowing & Planting

- Seed can be sown in compost-filled trays, lightly covered with sifted compost and then kept moist at about 18°C (65°F) — the seedlings are pricked out into 8 cm (3 in.) compost-filled fibre pots when a pair of true leaves has been produced.

- If only a few plants are required it is better to sow a couple of seeds in each 8 cm (3 in.) fibre pot, removing the weaker seedling before planting out. Alternatively, you can buy seedlings.

- Planting in border soil is not a good idea. When the seedlings are 15-20 cm (6-8 in.) high and the flowers of the first truss are beginning to open, plant them in pots or growing bags.

Calendar

Month	JAN	FEB	MAR	APR	MAY	JUN	JUL	AUG	SEP	OCT	NOV	DEC
Sowing & Planting (Heated greenhouse)	🪴	🌱🌱										🪴
Sowing & Planting (Cold greenhouse)			🪴🪴		🌱🌱							
Picking Time												

see key — page 75

Plant care & Harvesting

- Tie the main stem loosely to a cane — pinch out side shoots when they are about 3 cm (1 in.) long. Remove leaves below the first truss when the plants are about 1.2 m (4 ft) tall. Take off yellowing leaves below the trusses as the season develops.

- Water regularly to keep the compost moist — feed with a soluble tomato fertilizer. Mist the plants occasionally to aid pollination. Ventilate and shade the glass in summer. Remove the tip at 2 leaves above the top truss when the plants have reached the top of the house or the 7th truss has set.

- Pick the fruit when they are ripe and fully coloured. Hold the tomato in your palm, and with your thumb break off the fruit at the knuckle (swelling on the stalk).

- At the end of the season remove the green fruits and place them in a tray. Put them in a drawer and next to the tray set a couple of ripe apples which will generate the ripening gas ethylene.

Tomato, Outdoor

Outdoor varieties are classified by their growth habit. Cordon varieties with single stems have to be supported, trimmed and stopped — a number of greenhouse varieties such as Ailsa Craig, Shirley and Moneymaker can be grown as Cordons outdoors. Next come the Bush varieties — multi-stemmed bushes growing 30-75 cm (1-2½ ft) high which do not need supporting, trimming nor stopping. Finally the Trailing varieties — treated like the Bush ones. They grow to less than 25 cm (10 in.).

In a nutshell

Expected germination time	8 - 11 days
Expected yield per plant	2 kg (4 lb)
Approximate time between sowing and picking	20 weeks
Ease of cultivation	Not easy

Varieties

GARDENER'S DELIGHT (Cordon) Cherry tomatoes with a superb flavour. Can be grown under glass.

SUMMER SWEET (Cordon) Small plum variety. Long cropping season — yields are high.

MARMANDE (Cordon) The irregular-shaped 'Beefsteak' fruit are large and fleshy with few seeds.

OUTDOOR GIRL (Cordon) A reliable variety with slightly ribbed fruit. Very early.

SUNGOLD (Cordon) Orange-red cherry tomatoes. Very sweet — can be grown under glass.

THE AMATEUR (Bush) The most popular but not the best of the Bush tomatoes. Medium-sized fruit.

RED ALERT (Bush) Compact growth habit — a good choice where space is limited. Very early.

GLACIER (Bush) Nothing special apart from its outstanding tolerance of cold conditions.

TORNADO (Bush) Compact, very early and better than most in poor weather.

TINY TIM (Bush) A good choice for pots or a window box. Bright red cherry tomatoes.

TOTEM (Bush) Dwarf and compact — another one for growing in pots or growing bags.

TUMBLER (Trailer) Not a true trailer, but its weak stems will trail down from a hanging basket.

TUMBLING TOM RED (Trailer) The first true trailer. Grow it in baskets, window boxes etc.

Sowing & Planting

- Most people buy pot-grown seedlings — they should be dark green, sturdy and about 20 cm (8 in.) high. Seedlings can be raised at home — sow seed under glass in late March - early April and plant out when the danger of frost has passed.

- You can grow tomatoes outdoors in 15 litre (4 gal.) pots, compost-filled growing bags or the vegetable plot. Remember that container growing calls for regular feeding and much more regular watering than tomatoes in a bed or border.

- Plant out when the flowers of the first truss are beginning to open. The top of the soil ball should be set just below the soil surface.

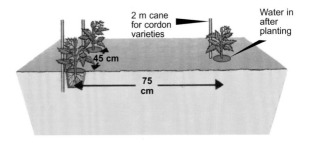

Calendar

Month	JAN	FEB	MAR	APR	MAY	JUN	JUL	AUG	SEP	OCT	NOV	DEC
Sowing & Planting Time			▧	▧	♣							
Picking Time									▨	▨		

see key — page 75

Plant care & Harvesting

- With a Cordon variety tie the stem loosely to the cane. Make the ties at 30 cm (1 ft) intervals as the plant grows. Pinch out side shoots when they are about 3 cm (1 in.) long. Remove yellowing leaves below fruit trusses as the season progresses, but never overdo this deleafing process. When small tomatoes have developed in the 4th truss remove the tip at 2 leaves above this truss. This trimming and stopping is not needed with Bush and Trailing varieties.

- With all varieties water regularly during dry weather to keep the soil moist — alternate drying and flooding will cause blossom end rot or fruit splitting.

- Follow the harvesting rules on page 104.

Turnip

Turnips are best known as an ingredient for casseroles and stews, but that is not their only use. The Early varieties are sown in spring and then pulled when they are the size of golf balls for salads or boiled whole for the dinner plate. Maincrop varieties can be sown in autumn to provide spring greens in March - April, as well as being sown in July - August for roots to lift in mid October onwards. An easy-to-grow and quick-maturing crop, but remember that Early varieties are more demanding than Maincrop ones.

In a nutshell

Expected germination time	6 - 10 days
Expected yield from a 3m (10 ft) row	3 kg (7 lb) (early vars.)
Expected yield from a 3m (10 ft) row	5 kg (11 lb) (maincrop vars.)
Approximate time between sowing and lifting	6 - 12 weeks
Ease of cultivation	Easy

Varieties

ATLANTIC (Early) Fast growing — useful for intercropping as a catch crop. Good flavour.

PURPLE-TOP MILAN (Early) A popular variety — flat and reddish on top. Matures very quickly.

SNOWBALL (Early) The favourite globular variety. Good for growing under cloches.

TOKYO CROSS (Early) Sow in May - August for small, white globes 6 weeks later.

MILAN WHITE FORCING (Early) Choose this one for growing under cloches or in frames.

GOLDEN BALL (Maincrop) The most popular and best of the Maincrops. Yellow-fleshed.

GREEN-TOP STONE (Maincrop) The variety recommended for use as spring greens.

Snowball

Green-top Stone

Sowing

- Turnips belong to the cabbage family and like the other members require a firm, non-acid soil which has reasonable drainage. Early varieties require the soil to be fertile and are not suitable for sandy or shallow ground.

- Choose a non-shady site and dig in autumn — lime if necessary. In spring apply a general-purpose fertilizer and prepare the seed bed about a week later.

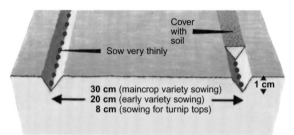

Sow very thinly

Cover with soil

30 cm (maincrop variety sowing)
20 cm (early variety sowing)
8 cm (sowing for turnip tops)

1 cm

Calendar

Month	JAN	FEB	MAR	APR	MAY	JUN	JUL	AUG	SEP	OCT	NOV	DEC
Sowing Time												
Lifting Time			TOPS ONLY									

see key — page 75

Plant care & Harvesting

- Thin out turnips which are being grown for roots as soon as the seedlings are large enough to handle. Do this in stages until the plants are 25 cm (10 in.) apart for Maincrop varieties or 15 cm (6 in.) for Early ones. Do not thin turnips which are being grown for their tops. Hoe around the plants — water during dry weather.

- The roots of Early varieties should be pulled out of the ground rather than being levered out of the soil with a fork. Pull while the roots are still small — golf-ball sized if they are to be eaten raw or between golf-ball and tennis-ball sized if they are to be cooked.

- Begin lifting Maincrop turnips as soon as they are large enough to use. Harvesting usually begins in October and in most areas you can leave them in the ground and lift as required. In cold and wet areas it is preferable to lift in early November for storage — twist off the leaves and place the roots between layers of sand in a stout box. Keep in a cool shed.

- In March or April cut off the tops of turnips grown for spring greens when about 15 cm (6 in.) high. Leave the roots to resprout — several cuts can be obtained.

CHAPTER 7
GARDEN TOOLS

For many gardeners who have the time, energy and inclination to enjoy gardening to the full there may be little to learn from this chapter. They will already have a collection of well-loved and well-used tools.

For most people with a garden, however, there could be something to learn from the next few pages. More than three in every four gardeners own six of the seven basic tools — a spade, fork, rake, trowel, mower, watering can and secateurs. But what other tools which line the walls of the garden centre would be useful?

Your first job is to decide which piece of equipment you should buy, and then look up the appropriate section to discover what you should look for before making your purchase. With a number of items there are versions which can make work easier for the elderly or physically challenged — this can sometimes mean the difference between being able to do a task or not.

Now you know what tool you want and the features to look for, it is time to go to the garden centre or DIY store. There you will find a bewildering display, and perhaps you will envy the old days when there was a much smaller choice of gardening equipment ... and you would be wrong. In a textbook written over 300 years ago there is a list of well over 100 tools, and Victorian catalogues offered hundreds of different sorts of hoes, spades, forks, knives etc. So, as always, the gardener has to make a choice from a wide variety of items.

By all means be guided by the maker's name, any in-store advice or the manufacturer's advertisement, but for many tools it is essential for you to ensure that the item suits you. With spades, forks, hoes, secateurs, shears and so on you must see that both the weight and balance are suitable. A spade which may be right for a strong youth might be quite wrong for a frail, elderly person.

A well-known name on the handle may be a safeguard, but it can mean a higher price. With tools you usually (but not always) get what you pay for, so it is best to avoid an unusually low-priced 'bargain' if it is something you plan to use regularly. Ordinary steel is much cheaper than the stainless variety and is quite satisfactory if cared for properly.

Finally, a few words on caring for your tools and equipment. After use clear off all mud, grass etc and then wipe down with an oily rag before storing away. Keep hand tools off the floor of the garage or shed — hang them on the wall if possible. Keep sharp tools out of harm's way. Turn the lawnmower so that the blades are away from the line of traffic. Check during winter if sharpening is required.

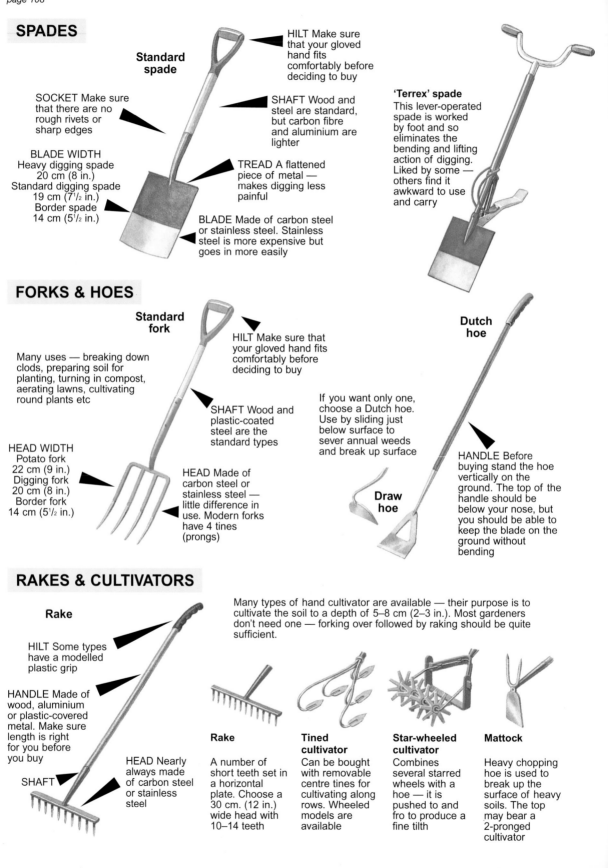

SPADES

Standard spade

HILT Make sure that your gloved hand fits comfortably before deciding to buy

SOCKET Make sure that there are no rough rivets or sharp edges

SHAFT Wood and steel are standard, but carbon fibre and aluminium are lighter

BLADE WIDTH
Heavy digging spade
20 cm (8 in.)
Standard digging spade
19 cm (7½ in.)
Border spade
14 cm (5½ in.)

TREAD A flattened piece of metal — makes digging less painful

BLADE Made of carbon steel or stainless steel. Stainless steel is more expensive but goes in more easily

'Terrex' spade
This lever-operated spade is worked by foot and so eliminates the bending and lifting action of digging. Liked by some — others find it awkward to use and carry

FORKS & HOES

Standard fork

HILT Make sure that your gloved hand fits comfortably before deciding to buy

Many uses — breaking down clods, preparing soil for planting, turning in compost, aerating lawns, cultivating round plants etc

SHAFT Wood and plastic-coated steel are the standard types

HEAD WIDTH
Potato fork
22 cm (9 in.)
Digging fork
20 cm (8 in.)
Border fork
14 cm (5½ in.)

HEAD Made of carbon steel or stainless steel — little difference in use. Modern forks have 4 tines (prongs)

Dutch hoe

If you want only one, choose a Dutch hoe. Use by sliding just below surface to sever annual weeds and break up surface

Draw hoe

HANDLE Before buying stand the hoe vertically on the ground. The top of the handle should be below your nose, but you should be able to keep the blade on the ground without bending

RAKES & CULTIVATORS

Rake

HILT Some types have a modelled plastic grip

HANDLE Made of wood, aluminium or plastic-covered metal. Make sure length is right for you before you buy

SHAFT

HEAD Nearly always made of carbon steel or stainless steel

Many types of hand cultivator are available — their purpose is to cultivate the soil to a depth of 5–8 cm (2–3 in.). Most gardeners don't need one — forking over followed by raking should be quite sufficient.

Rake
A number of short teeth set in a horizontal plate. Choose a 30 cm. (12 in.) wide head with 10–14 teeth

Tined cultivator
Can be bought with removable centre tines for cultivating along rows. Wheeled models are available

Star-wheeled cultivator
Combines several starred wheels with a hoe — it is pushed to and fro to produce a fine tilth

Mattock
Heavy chopping hoe is used to break up the surface of heavy soils. The top may bear a 2-pronged cultivator

CUTTING TOOLS

There always seems to be a cutting job to do in the garden — dead-heading, trimming hedges, pruning, lopping off branches etc. This can be hard work, but you can make it much easier if you have the right tools. There are four rules. Firstly you must choose the right type of cutting tool for the thickness of wood to be severed and you must then choose the most suitable example of this type — for instance you will find that some secateurs are quite wrong for your hands and needs. Lastly, having decided which tools you want to buy make sure you pick the best quality you can afford and keep them sharp and clean after use.

Garden knife

It is a joy to watch a skilled gardener using a knife for pruning, budding etc, but in the hands of the inexperienced it can be a dangerous weapon. If you have not been trained in its use carry a folding pocket knife for cutting twine and so on, but use secateurs for cutting stems

BLADES Keep cleaned and oiled after use

SAFETY CATCH Make sure that you can reach it easily

SPRING May be exposed or hidden. The handles should open quickly after cutting

HANDLES Check weight and comfort before purchase. Make sure that they are not too big — handles should not push hard against your palm when open

Secateurs vary in size from delicate flower gatherers to large heavy-duty types. You should need only one pair of secateurs — a general-purpose model about 20 cm (8 in.) long. Use them for stems up to 1 cm ($\frac{1}{2}$ in.) in diameter.

Anvil secateurs

One sharpened blade cuts on to a flat platform (anvil). Always cut down on to the anvil. Cuts with less effort than the curved type, but the cut may be a little more ragged

Curved secateurs

One sharpened blade cuts against a broad blade — side anvil secateurs is an alternative name. Generally last longer than anvil type. The most popular type

Ratchet secateurs

These are the secateurs to buy if you have a weak or painful grip. Only a light squeeze is needed — the stem is partly cut and the ratchet moves the blade forward. Another light squeeze deepens the cut — up to 4 squeezes may be necessary

Long-handled pruner

Ordinary secateurs should not be used on branches which are more than 1 cm ($\frac{1}{2}$ in.) across as the tool may be damaged. For cutting 1-4 cm ($\frac{1}{2}$-$1\frac{1}{2}$ in.) wide stems use a pair of long-handled pruners. The 45-60 cm ($1\frac{1}{2}$-2 ft) handles give extra leverage — telescopic-handled pruners are available

Garden shears

The main use is the trimming of hedges, although shears are also used for cutting long grass, dead-heading annuals, trimming perennials etc. Choose a pair with comfortable handles and light-weight blades — holding heavy shears becomes a chore when cutting a long hedge

Hedge trimmer

A wise investment if you have a long hedge to cut. A mains model is suitable if the hedge is near a power point — otherwise buy a battery-operated one. For heavy duty a petrol-driven model may be necessary, but it is heavy to carry. A 45 cm ($1\frac{1}{2}$ ft) blade is recommended

Pruning saw

When branches are thicker than a broom handle it is necessary to use a saw rather than an instrument with blades. For the occasional branch you can use an ordinary saw, but many prefer the curved Grecian saw which cuts only on the pull stroke

WATERING EQUIPMENT

The need to water can be reduced by good soil preparation and mulching — see Chapter 2. There are times, however, when the application of water is necessary. A wide range of watering equipment is available — the best choice depends on the size of your garden and the depth of your pocket. The best (and most expensive) system for beds and borders is an underground drip or leaky-pipe arrangement with an electronic on-off tap linked to a soil moisture sensor. Easy-care, but at a price. The tap connecting an underground system to the mains must be fitted with a non-return valve.

Watering can

Impractical for overall watering in anything larger than a tiny garden. Vital, however, for point watering a few plants. Choose the right size and sort of can — 10 litre (2 gallon) with metal rose for garden use and 5 litre (1 gallon) with long spout for the greenhouse

HOSE PIPES

Flat tubing

Lay-flat tubing is lighter than round tubing. It is wound into a cassette-like case for easy storage. A flat hose pipe is worth considering if you are short of space, but it is expensive and must be unwound before use

Round tubing

The basic type which will last for many years if treated properly. A long length should be stored on a wheeled or wall-attached reel. Leaving the hose crushed on the floor can lead to kinks and punctures. Empty and store indoors in winter

Single wall   **Double wall**   **Reinforced**

The usual type of hose pipe is made of PVC and is available in 15 m and 30 m (50 ft and 100 ft) lengths. Single wall tubing is inexpensive, but it is not suitable for regions with high water pressure. Double wall tubing is more suitable for general garden use, but reinforced tubing is the best (and most expensive) type you can buy — there is a layer of fibre or braided nylon between the inner and outer tubes. Ribbed tubing is easier to hold than smooth tubing when wet. In recent years Quick Release fittings have largely replaced screw fittings for securing attachments

OVERALL WATERING EQUIPMENT

Sprinkler hose

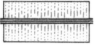

Basically a flattened hose pipe bearing a series of fine holes on the upper surface. A long rectangular spray pattern is obtained — excellent for grass paths and rows of vegetables

Seep hose

Basically a plastic hose pipe bearing a series of pinholes along the sides. These holes are situated close to plants — the water seeps through these holes to water the ground around the roots. Useful in the shrub or mixed border, but planting areas are limited to the locations of the holes in the pipe

Sprinkler

The simplest type of sprinkler system. The pattern is quite even but the area covered is relatively small, so a series of these fixed watering points is necessary to water a bed or border. For lawns underground sprinklers are available which pop up when switched on — popular in the U.S but not in Britain

Leaky pipe

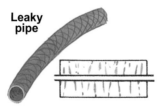

This watering system is an advance on the seep hose. The hose pipe is porous so that water seeps out along its whole length — plants do not have to be set at any particular point along the pipe. Buy in kit form — connect to the water supply with a standard hose and bury the porous hose several centimetres below the soil surface

Drip system

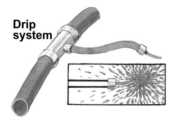

The most sophisticated system of all, especially when linked with an electronic tap to control the water supply. Drip valves are sited close to plants in the border and connected by small-bore flexible tubes to the main supply hose which is buried below ground level. Efficient — water goes only where it is needed

SPRAYERS

The popular choice was once between a metal syringe and a metal flit gun — now it is between a trigger-operated sprayer and a compression sprayer. It is essential to wash out the sprayer immediately after use.

Aerosol

Ready-to-use trigger sprayer

Refillable trigger sprayer

Compression sprayer

A convenient way to treat house plants for insects. Weed-killing aerosols are available for spot-treating lawns. Aerosols are expensive for large-scale treatment. Keep the recommended distance away from plant foliage

Several brands have been available for many years, but only recently has the ready-to-use sprayer become popular. You can buy spray guns containing insecticides, weedkillers or moss-killers

This sprayer is operated by the pump action of the trigger. There are many brands available — the usual capacity is 500 ml or 1 pint. Make sure that there is a filter at the bottom of the diptube

The best type to buy for general garden use — choose a 5 litre (1 gallon) model. Air is hand pumped into the container and pressure built up to about 40 psi. The nozzle is adjustable

POWER CULTIVATORS

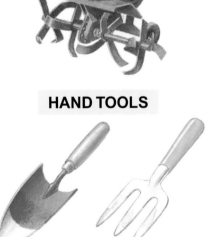

A motorised cultivator seems like a good idea — a petrol-driven jack-of-all-trades to take the hard work out of gardening. Unfortunately it will not be of much help in the established ornamental garden. The main value of a motor-driven cultivator to the average gardener is the ability to dig over a large area when creating a new garden. If you are going to make a large vegetable garden as well as other features, then it is worth considering purchasing one of the many models available. If, however, the area is not large and most of the cultivated ground is lawn and ornamental areas, it is a much better idea to hire one if you plan to create a new bed or border in uncultivated ground. This will mean less work than digging, but it will also be less thorough. If you buy one there should be an adequate range of attachments — hoes, picks, ridgers, soil aerators etc.

HAND TOOLS

A **trowel** is essential for planting specimens too small for a spade. It is also used for digging out perennial weeds. Buy stainless steel if you can afford it and make sure the handle is comfortable. Buy two — a standard size one and a small narrow type with a blade about 5 cm (2 in.) across. Look for a strong neck and don't buy a long-handled one unless you find bending difficult.

Hand forks are about the same width as trowels, but bear 3-5 short tines instead of a scoop-like blade. They are used for weeding and cultivating soil around plants — buy a long-handled version to reach to the back of the border. The tines are available in various forms — flat, curved and twisted. Choose a fork with flat tines — the other shapes have drawbacks. The hand fork, unlike the trowel, is not essential.

WHEELBARROWS

The traditional **wheelbarrow** is illustrated above — a 0.06-0.12 cu.m (2-4 cu.ft) container carried on a tubular metal frame and bearing a single narrow wheel. Galvanised metal is the usual material. Plastic wheelbarrows are available — attractive but liable to break if subject to very heavy treatment. Always test a barrow before buying.

The traditional type is highly manoeuvrable and a good choice for heavy, uneven ground. However, to make pushing easier buy one with a wide pneumatic tyre or buy a **ball wheelbarrow** with an inflated, ball-like wheel. If you are not strong or if you are disabled, consider a **two-wheel cart** instead of a wheelbarrow. You will find it easier to push and less liable to tip over.

MISCELLANEOUS AIDS

Grabber

Picking up piles of leaves or cuttings from the ground usually involves bending over to gather them up between two boards. The grabber is operated from one or both long handles and the need to bend is removed. The grabber edges may be smooth or toothed. Check that the weight and height are suitable before buying

Shredder

Thick woody prunings can pose a disposal problem. Building a bonfire may not be practical and taking them to a dump is time-wasting. An electric shredder turns 2.5 cm (1 in.) wide stems into wood meal which is a good ingredient for making compost — see page 55. Read and follow all the safety instructions

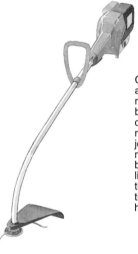

Strimmer

Cutting long grass in areas inaccessible to the mower can be a back-breaking job with a pair of shears. The strimmer makes it quite a simple job — the motor drives a nylon cord rather than a blade. Buy an electric lightweight model unless the area is very large — the petrol version is heavy and very noisy

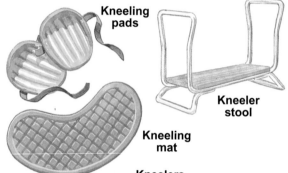

Kneeling pads

Kneeler stool

Kneeling mat

Kneelers

Kneeling on hard ground can be painful for all and damaging for the elderly. Strap-on plastic foam kneeling pads can be used for knee protection, or you can use a kneeling mat. A kneeler stool is useful if getting up and down is a problem. One way up it is a kneeler with arm supports — turn it over and it is a seat

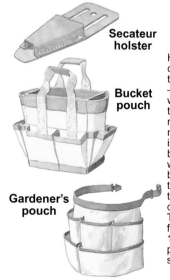

Secateur holster

Bucket pouch

Gardener's pouch

Tool tidy — outdoors

Having to keep on bending down to pick up secateurs, twine, a trowel etc can be tiring — it is much more efficient to wear a gardener's belt or pouch to carry small tools as you move round the garden. The minimum tidy you should have is a secateur holster to keep both hands free at pruning time when you are not cutting branches. Some people prefer to use a bucket pouch rather than a body one, especially during the hot days of summer. This pouch or bag is made from canvas and fits around a 10 litre (2 gallon) bucket — pockets hold gloves, seeds, secateurs, string, hand fork etc

Tool tidy — indoors

All too often tools are left leaning against the wall or on the floor of the garage or shed when not in use. Time is wasted in having to hunt for a particular tool when there is a job to do and there is also the danger of treading on rakes, hoes etc. It is much better to attach a series of galvanised or plastic-coated wire tool racks to the wall

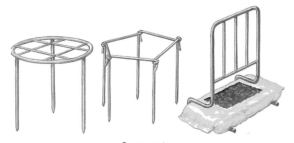

Supports

Supports for weak-stemmed plants should always be inserted before they flop and look unsightly. You can stick to the traditional cane or stake plus string method, but these days there is a range of wire supports which do not need string — they are 30-120 cm (1-4 ft) tall and are useful for lilies, paeonies, delphiniums etc. Several proprietary types of growing bag support are available — buy a stout one for cucumbers and tomatoes

Tip bag

It is not always easy to take your wheelbarrow to all parts of the garden when collecting prunings, leaves, grass clippings etc. A tip bag made from plastic fabric, such as the Bosbag, can be carried about very easily and when full carried to the compost heap, bonfire etc. The bag can be folded and stored flat when not in use

One-handed scissors

One-handed grabber

One-handed tools

A number of one-handed tools are available — shears which are operated by squeezing the handles together and grabbers for pruning etc which are operated by squeezing the trigger. A boon for people who have limited or no use of one hand, but more tiring to use than the two-handed versions of these tools

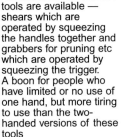

Long-handled tools

A good deal of gardening work involves using short-handled tools and working on your hands and knees. For many people this is not possible because of age or infirmity, and for them there are several ranges of long-handled trowels, forks, weeders etc. The usual plan is to buy a handle with a set of interchangeable heads

Bulb planter

The trowel is the most popular planting tool and is the best one to use if the bulbs have widely different diameters. A bulb planter is often recommended, but it is the preferred alternative only if a number of conditions apply. The soil is moist and not sandy, the bulbs are to be set at approximately the same depth and the long-handled model is chosen to save bending. The planter is pushed in by foot and the plug is removed from the corer by a hand-operated lever

Gloves

Leather gloves are used to protect the hands from prickles, sharp objects and caustic materials such as lime. But they are heavy, somewhat inflexible and uncomfortable in hot weather. Cotton gloves are much more comfortable, but are no protection against rose thorns. A good compromise is to buy a pair of fabric gloves with leather palms or a pair of the popular fabric gloves impregnated with green plastic to give a protective suede-like finish.

CHAPTER 8
TREES & SHRUBS

In most gardens shrubs (and to a lesser extent trees, conifers and climbers) have a vital role to play. Bulbs, roses, bedding plants, border perennials etc provide colour from spring to autumn, but in the depths of winter we must rely on evergreen or winter-flowering trees and shrubs to provide most of the interest in the garden. Even more important is the fact that the woody plants give the living part of the garden its shape — they provide the skeleton which rises above the other plants.

The list of virtues does not end there. Shrubs and trees bring an air of maturity and they can also be used to increase privacy, act as wind breaks, cut down the weed problem and screen out unsightly objects. It is no wonder that the popularity of these plants has greatly increased in recent years.

For the gardener who wants to save work there is an additional virtue — trees and shrubs are much less trouble than annuals, vegetables, lawns, fruit and the herbaceous border. Once fully established there is little work to be done — no constant feeding or spraying, no regular dead-heading and staking, no annual replanting or sowing ritual and no rushing out with the watering can or hosepipe every time the weather turns dry.

This labour-saving aspect of woody plants is well-known and you will find it mentioned in the textbooks, but there is a drawback which is not often raised. Trees, conifers and large shrubs are expensive compared with border perennials, bedding plants and packets of seed, so you should follow the rules for siting, planting, pruning etc — you will find them in this book. The basic rule to remember is that various shrubs, conifers, climbers and so on laid out for you at the garden centre differ widely in their requirements, reliability, ease of cultivation and height at maturity. The first step therefore is to choose wisely. Some shrubs can be quite a lot of work and can be a challenge to grow — others are trouble-free and as tough as weeds. Having made your choice it is essential that the specimens you have bought should be planted properly. You will probably have selected container-grown plants rather than bare-rooted ones which have to be put in during the cold months of the year, but do not regard container planting as 'easy'. Follow the rules laid down on page 63.

Equally important is the need to leave enough space between the plants — see page 70. The final point concerns pruning. For specific rules for each plant see the *Tree & Shrub Expert*.

The stated height on the following pages is the anticipated height after 10 years

ABELIA
Abelia

Deciduous or evergreen shrub

A. grandiflora

Flower time: June—October
Location: Best in full sun
Propagation: Cuttings under glass/summer

The prolonged flowering period makes this shrub worth growing — the tubular flowers are borne in clusters. The semi-evergreen *A. grandiflora* is the usual garden species and the yellow-leaved 'Francis Mason' — height 1.5 m (5 ft) is the popular variety. The tender *A.schumannii* loses its leaves in winter.

ABIES
Silver Fir

Conifer

A. alba

Flower time: —
Location: Best in full sun
Propagation: Buy a new plant

The strap-shaped leaves have a small sucker-like base and are usually white or grey underneath. Most species are Xmas-tree like and grow too tall for the ordinary garden. Exceptions include the blue-grey *A. arizonica* 'Compacta' — 2 m (7 ft) and the dwarf *A. balsamea* 'Hudsonia' — 30 cm (1 ft).

ACER
Maple

Deciduous tree

A. platanoides 'Goldsworth Purple'

Flower time: —
Location: Best in full sun
Propagation: Buy a new plant

The ordinary sycamore is an Acer, but so are many excellent medium-sized garden trees with colourful foliage or attractive bark. Tolerant of most soils and conditions. *A. negundo* 'Variegatum' — 5 m (16 ft) bears white-edged leaflets, and *A. platanoides* 'Goldsworth Purple' — 6 m (20 ft) has purple leaves.

ACER
Japanese Maple

Deciduous shrub

A. palmatum 'Dissectum'

Flower time: —
Location: Best in light shade
Propagation: Buy a new plant

Most Acers are trees — see above. The Japanese maples, however, are slow-growing shrubs — height 1-2 m (3-7 ft) with attractive leaves which colour in the autumn. Protect from morning sun and cold winds. Varieties include *A. palmatum* 'Dissectum' (green leaves turning orange).

AESCULUS
Horse Chestnut

Deciduous tree or shrub

A. hippocastanum

Flower time: Depends on species
Location: Best in full sun
Propagation: Buy a new plant

The Common horse chestnut is a fine sight when in full flower in May, but it is far too large for most gardens. Choose instead one of the shrubby horse chestnuts. There are *A. parviflora* — 3 m (10 ft) with white flowers in July-August, and the similar-sized *A. pavia* which bears red candles in July.

ALNUS
Alder

Deciduous tree

A. incana

Flower time: March—April
Location: Sun or partial shade
Propagation: Hardwood cuttings/autumn

This conical tree grows to 10-12 m (33-40 ft) with attractive catkins in spring. Alder is a good choice if you need a fast-growing hedge in a boggy part of the garden — most species will not tolerate chalky soil. The Common alder (*A. glutinosa*) has glossy leaves — *A. incana* leaves are grey below.

AMELANCHIER
Snowy Mespilus

Deciduous tree or shrub

A. canadensis

Flower time: April—May
Location: Sun or partial shade
Propagation: Rooted suckers/autumn

A tree or large shrub grown for its changing display. Coppery foliage and white flowers in spring, red berries in summer and orange-red leaves in autumn. The most popular species is *A. canadensis* — height 6 m (20 ft). Its starry flowers are borne in erect clusters, and its berries ripen to black.

ARALIA
Japanese Angelica

Deciduous shrub

A. elata 'Aureovariegata'

Flower time: August—September
Location: Best in full sun
Propagation: Buy a new plant

A large shrub which suckers freely — give it the space it needs. Each leaf is about 1 m (3 ft) long, neatly divided into leaflets. Choose a sheltered site. The garden species is *A. elata* which grows to 3 m (10 ft) — it bears large heads of tiny flowers. *A. e.* 'Aureovariegata' has cream-edged leaves in spring.

ARBUTUS
Strawberry Tree

Evergreen shrub

A. unedo 'Rubra'

Flower time: October—December
Location: Sun or partial shade
Propagation: Buy a new plant

Something out of the ordinary — a slow-growing bush which bears pendent flowers and strawberry-like fruits at the same time in late autumn — these fruits are flavourless. The popular one is *A. unedo* — height 2 m (7 ft). The flowers are white — *A. u.* 'Rubra' bears pink-flushed flowers.

ARUNDINARIA
Bamboo

Evergreen shrub

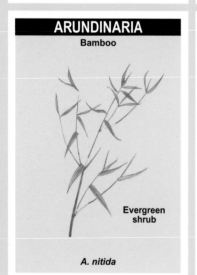

A. nitida

Flower time: —
Location: Best in partial shade
Propagation: Divide clumps in autumn

Bamboos are becoming increasingly popular as focal points and for screening. Many have an exotic look but they are quite easy to grow. Provide some shelter. *A. nitida* — 3 m (10 ft) has purple stems. You will also find *A. murieliae* — 3 m (10 ft) yellow stems, and the giant 6 m (20 ft) *A. fastuosa*.

AUCUBA
Aucuba

Evergreen shrub

A. japonica 'Variegata'

Berry time: September—January
Location: Sun or partial shade
Propagation: Hardwood cuttings/autumn

A popular choice when looking for an evergreen with large colourful leaves for a shady spot. A 'grow anywhere' plant, but icy winds can scorch new growth. The all-green *A. japonica* — height 2 m (7 ft) has many varieties, such as 'Longifolia' (narrow leaves) and 'Picturata' (yellow-centred leaves).

BERBERIS
Barberry

Deciduous or evergreen shrub

B. darwinii

Flower time: April—May
Location: Sun or partial shade
Propagation: Cuttings under glass/summer

All sorts of shapes and sizes, but the species have a few features in common — yellow or orange flowers, spiny stems and/or leaves, and all are easy to grow. Evergreens include *B. darwinii* — 2.5 m (8 ft) and *B. linearifolia*. Typical deciduous types are *B. thunbergii* — 1.5 m (5 ft) and *B. t.* 'Atropurpurea'.

BETULA
Birch

Deciduous tree

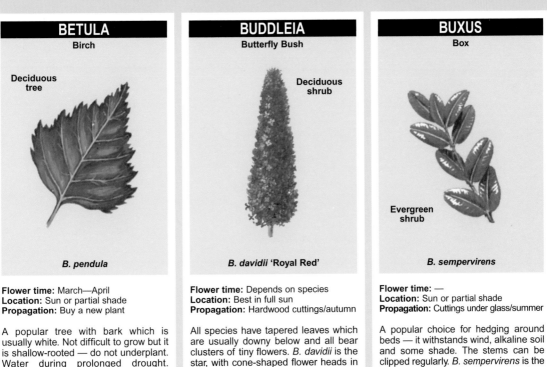

B. pendula

Flower time: March—April
Location: Sun or partial shade
Propagation: Buy a new plant

A popular tree with bark which is usually white. Not difficult to grow but it is shallow-rooted — do not underplant. Water during prolonged drought. *B. pendula* 9 m (30 ft) is the popular one — yellowish catkins, white bark, pendulous branches. 'Purpurea' has purple leaves and branches.

BUDDLEIA
Butterfly Bush

Deciduous shrub

B. davidii 'Royal Red'

Flower time: Depends on species
Location: Best in full sun
Propagation: Hardwood cuttings/autumn

All species have tapered leaves which are usually downy below and all bear clusters of tiny flowers. *B. davidii* is the star, with cone-shaped flower heads in August–mid September — annual pruning is essential. Other species include *B. globosa* (orange ball-like heads in June) and the arching *B. alternifolia*.

BUXUS
Box

Evergreen shrub

B. sempervirens

Flower time: —
Location: Sun or partial shade
Propagation: Cuttings under glass/summer

A popular choice for hedging around beds — it withstands wind, alkaline soil and some shade. The stems can be clipped regularly. *B. sempervirens* is the basic species — it will grow to 3 m (10 ft) if left unpruned. 'Aureovariegata' has yellow-blotched leaves — 'Suffruticosa' is a dwarf.

CALLISTEMON
Bottle Brush

Evergreen shrub

C. citrinus 'Splendens'

Flower time: June—July
Location: Best in full sun
Propagation: Cuttings under glass/summer

Small flowers with prominent stamens are tightly packed along a cylindrical spike. The popular species are reasonably hardy, but grow the plant against a sunny wall. *C. citrinus* 'Splendens' 2 m (7 ft) has deep pink flowers and long leaves — *C. rigidus* 1.5 m (5 ft) is a hardier type.

Mowing right up to the base of trees is a tricky and sometimes damaging operation. A band of evergreen ground cover such as Pachysandra instead of grass around the trunk saves both time and trouble, but do not cover this area until the tree is well established. Growing turf or an evergreen right up to the base of a young tree will slow down its development.

CALLUNA
Heather

Evergreen shrub

C. vulgaris 'H.E. Beale'

Flower time: Depends on variety
Location: Best in full sun
Propagation: Cuttings under glass/summer

All relish starved soil and sunshine, and none can tolerate lime. Foliage is often coloured and there are no winter- or spring-flowering ones — see the other heather (Erica) for contrast. *C. vulgaris* — height 25-50 cm (10 in.-1½ ft) is the only species, but there are many varieties with white, pink or lilac blooms.

CAMELLIA
Camellia

Evergreen shrub

C. japonica 'Adolphe Audusson'

Flower time: Depends on species
Location: Sun or light shade
Propagation: Cuttings under glass/summer

The showy blooms 5-15 cm (2-6 in.) across are single or double and available in white, pink or red. Non-alkaline soil is necessary, and so is protection from cold winds. There are two species — *C. japonica* 2 m (7 ft) with February-April blooms and *C. williamsii* 2 m (7 ft) with February-May flowers.

CAMPSIS
Trumpet Vine

Deciduous climber

C. radicans

Flower time: August—September
Location: Full sun necessary
Propagation: Cuttings under glass/summer

This self-clinging climber is grown for its tubular flowers which are borne in clusters. Both support and shelter are necessary. Red or red-orange is the usual flower colour — *C. radicans* 5 m (16 ft) is an example with 8 cm (3 in.) long blooms. The yellow Trumpet vine is *C. r.* 'Flava' 5 m (16 ft).

CARPENTERIA
Tree Anemone

Evergreen shrub

C. californica

Flower time: June—July
Location: Full sun necessary
Propagation: Cuttings under glass/summer

An unusual shrub which needs the protection of a south- or west-facing wall. Some shoots may be killed if winter frosts are prolonged. *C. californica* 2 m (7 ft) bears white flowers with a central boss of golden stamens. Leaves woolly white below. The variety 'Ladham's Variety' is freer-flowering.

CARPINUS
Hornbeam

Deciduous tree

C. betulus

Flower time: —
Location: Best in full sun
Propagation: Buy a new plant

A stately tree, but it has none of the popularity of its taller relative, the Common beech. Like beech it keeps its leaves when used as a hedge. *C. betulus* 8 m (26 ft) has grey, fluted bark and hop-like fruit. The variety 'Fastigiata' 7 m (23 ft) has an upright growth habit.

CARYOPTERIS
Blue Spiraea

Deciduous shrub

C. clandonensis

Flower time: September—October
Location: Full sun necessary
Propagation: Cuttings under glass/summer

A rounded shrub for the front of the border — it will thrive in all sorts of soils including chalky ones. The basic garden species is *C. clandonensis* — height 1 m (3 ft). The leaves are grey-green and the terminal clusters of lavender flowers are 10 cm (4 in.) long. 'Kew Blue' has dark blue flowers.

CATALPA
Indian Bean Tree

Deciduous tree or shrub

C. bignonioides

Flower time: August
Location: Sun or partial shade
Propagation: Buy a new plant

This summer-flowering tree or shrub is easily recognised by its unusually large heart-shaped leaves. Quick-growing and wide-spreading — well-suited to town gardens if space allows. *C. bignonioides* — height 9 m (30 ft) is the basic species with flowers which are horse-chestnut like.

CEANOTHUS
Californian Lilac

Deciduous or evergreen shrub

C. 'Gloire de Versailles'

Flower time: Depends on species
Location: Full sun necessary
Propagation: Cuttings under glass/summer

Most varieties are evergreen — grow against a wall. Leaves are small and glossy, the flowers are in thimble-like clusters. *C.* 'Burkwoodii' 2 m (7 ft) is a May- or September-blooming example. The deciduous group are hardier and have larger leaves and flowers. *C.* 'Gloire de Versailles' is popular.

CEDRUS
Cedar

Conifer

C. libani

Flower time: —
Location: Best in full sun
Propagation: Buy a new plant

C. libani (Cedar of Lebanon) is too large for the ordinary garden, but there are dwarf and weeping varieties such as 'Nana' and 'Sargentii'. *C. atlantica* 'Glauca' 3 m (10 ft) has blue-green leaves and *C. deodara* 3 m (10 ft) has a drooping growth habit — smaller varieties include 'Golden Horizon'.

CERATOSTIGMA
Hardy Plumbago

Deciduous shrub

C. willmottianum

Flower time: July—October
Location: Best in full sun
Propagation: Divide clumps in autumn

The stems of this shrub may be killed by frost, but hard pruning in spring will ensure new stems which will bear clusters of phlox-like blue flowers in summer and autumn. The hardiest species is *C. willmottianum* — height 1 m (3 ft). Others include *C. griffithii* and the dwarf *C. plumbaginoides*.

CERCIS
Cercis

Deciduous tree or shrub

C. siliquastrum

Flower time: May—June
Location: Full sun necessary
Propagation: Buy a new plant

A tall and spreading shrub which in time reaches tree-like proportions. It is not a plant for cold or clayey soils, but it grows quite happily in mild areas. *C. siliquastrum* — height 3 m (10 ft) is the Judas tree which bears pink blooms. *C. canadensis* 'Forest Pansy' has red leaves and insignificant flowers.

CHAENOMELES
Japonica, Ornamental Quince

Deciduous shrub

C. speciosa

Flower time: March—May
Location: Sun or partial shade
Propagation: Cuttings under glass/summer

It thrives in sun or shade in all types of soil and the bright spring flowers are followed by large golden fruits. One of the garden species is *C. speciosa* — height 2-3 m (7-10 ft). It is grown as a wall plant. The foliage is rather sparse — for the border grow *C. superba* 1 m (3 ft) which is a dense, rounded bush.

CHAMAECYPARIS
Lawson Cypress

Conifer

C. lawsoniana

Flower time: —
Location: Best in full sun
Propagation: Buy a new plant

Very popular — even a modest nursery will have a range of varieties. There are dwarfs for the rockery and tall trees for the large garden. *C. lawsoniana* is the most popular species — varieties include 'Elwoodii' (blue in winter), 'Minima Aurea' (yellow, dwarf) and 'Lane' (gold, columnar).

CHIMONANTHUS
Winter Sweet

Deciduous shrub

C. praecox 'Luteus'

Flower time: December—March
Location: Best in full sun
Propagation: Buy a new plant

The flowers on the bare stems are not particularly eye-catching, but they do appear very early in the season and have a spicy aroma. *C. praecox* — height 2 m (7 ft) is the garden species — the pendent, purple-centred yellow flowers have waxy petals. The variety 'Luteus' is showier than the species.

CHOISYA
Mexican Orange Blossom

Evergreen shrub

C. ternata

Flower time: April—May
Location: Sun or light shade
Propagation: Cuttings under glass/summer

This neat and rounded shrub provides year-round dense leaf cover. Flat heads of waxy flowers appear in spring — both leaves and flowers are fragrant. The garden species is *C. ternata* — height 2 m (7 ft). Late summer flowers may appear. 'Sundance' has yellow foliage — 'Aztec Pearl' has narrow leaves.

CISTUS
Rock Rose

Evergreen shrub

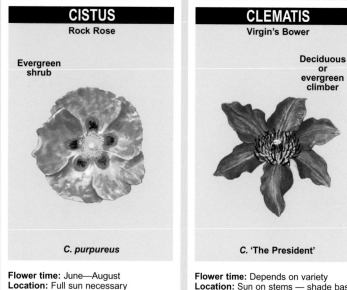

C. purpureus

Flower time: June—August
Location: Full sun necessary
Propagation: Cuttings under glass/summer

The short-lived blooms are often blotched at the base. Buds appear regularly and the shrub is constantly in flower during summer. There are short varieties reaching less than 1 m (3 ft) — examples are *C.* 'Silver Pink' and the white *C. corbariensis*. Example of a tall one is *C. purpureus*.

CLEMATIS
Virgin's Bower

Deciduous or evergreen climber

C. 'The President'

Flower time: Depends on variety
Location: Sun on stems — shade base
Propagation: Rooted suckers/autumn

Our most popular climber but not an easy plant. Two types — the Species group (e.g *C. montana* and the evergreen *C. armandii*) are easier to grow. The Hybrids are larger but more difficult. Examples include *C.* 'Nelly Moser' and *C.* 'The President'. Read the instructions before planting.

CONVOLVULUS
Shrubby Bindweed

C. cneorum

Evergreen shrub

Flower time: May—August
Location: Full sun necessary
Propagation: Cuttings under glass/summer

An attractive but rather tender shrub which provides year-round interest. The leaves are silvery-grey and the white flowers appear all summer long. *C. cneorum* — height 50 cm (1½ ft) bears pink buds which open into trumpet-shaped blooms. Frost may damage the foliage.

CORDYLINE
Cabbage Palm

Evergreen tree

C. australis

Flower time: June
Location: Sun or partial shade
Propagation: Rooted offsets/autumn

This palm-like plant is usually bought as a rosette of arching leaves — in time it grows to become a short tree. Grow it in a large pot or in a border in a mild locality. *C. australis* 2 m (7 ft) bears 30 cm-1 m (1-3 ft) pale green leaves — 'Purpurea' has purple foliage. 'Torbay Dazzler' has white-striped leaves.

CORNUS
Dogwood

Deciduous or evergreen tree or shrub

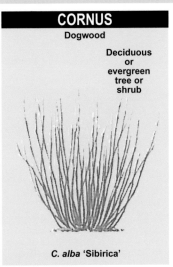

C. alba 'Sibirica'

Flower time: Depends on species
Location: Best in full sun
Propagation: Buy a new plant

There are two types. The popular one (*C. alba*) is the deciduous coloured-bark dogwood grown for its bright winter stems. Less common is the flowering dogwood which has brightly-coloured autumn leaves. *C. mas* 3 m (10 ft) is the one you are most likely to see — yellow flowers appear in February.

CORONILLA
Coronilla

Deciduous or evergreen shrub

C. valentina

Flower time: May—October
Location: Full sun necessary
Propagation: Buy a new plant

Its outstanding feature is that it starts to flower in spring and then continues at intervals until the first frosts. Reasonably reliable when grown against a sunny wall. *C. valentina* 1.5 m (5 ft) bears yellow pea-like flowers — 'Glauca Variegata' has yellow-splashed leaves. *C. emerus* is deciduous.

CORYLOPSIS
Winter Hazel

Deciduous shrub

C. spicata

Flower time: March—April
Location: Best in light shade
Propagation: Buy a new plant

Tassels of flowers appear before the leaves. It is not as popular as its relative Witch hazel — the problem is that it is not robust, and frost can damage the blooms. *C. spicata* 2 m (7 ft) bears purple-anthered yellow flowers. *C. glabrescens* 3.5 m (11 ft) is a wide-spreading, free-flowering shrub.

CORYLUS
Hazel

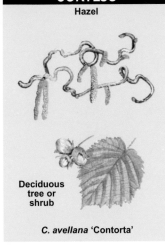

Deciduous tree or shrub

C. avellana 'Contorta'

Flower time: February
Location: Sun or partial shade
Propagation: Rooted suckers/autumn

Green-leaved types are used for hedging, but there are colourful ones to grow as specimen plants. Winter catkins hang from the bare branches. *C. avellana* 3 m (10 ft) is the usual green-leaved one — its variety 'Aurea' has yellow foliage. 'Contorta' has curiously twisted branches.

COTINUS
Smoke Bush

Deciduous tree or shrub

C. coggygria

Flower time: June
Location: Best in full sun
Propagation: Rooted suckers/autumn

An easy plant to recognise. Intricately-branched flower heads appear in summer and after flowering the feathery stalks remain. They give a smoke-like effect, hence the common name. The usual species is *C. coggygria* 3 m (10 ft), was once called *Rhus cotinus*. 'Notcutt's Variety' has red leaves.

COTONEASTER
Cotoneaster

Deciduous or evergreen shrub

C. horizontalis

Berry time: October—November
Location: Sun or partial shade
Propagation: Cuttings under glass/summer

An important berrying shrub. Unlike Pyracantha the leaves are smooth-edged and the branches are thornless. The evergreen group vary from the ground-hugging *C. dammeri* to the 3 m (10 ft) *C.* 'Cornubia'. The deciduous group contains the popular *C. horizontalis* 50 cm (1½ ft).

CRATAEGUS
Hawthorn

Deciduous tree or shrub

C. laevigata 'Paul's Scarlet'

Flower time: May—June
Location: Sun or shade
Propagation: Buy a new plant

A tree, shrub or hedge in gardens everywhere. The thorny branches bear white, pink or red flowers which are followed by red or orange berries. *C. monogyna* 6 m (20 ft) is the white-flowered Common hawthorn. *C. laevigata* is less vigorous — 'Paul's Scarlet' bears red, double blooms.

CRYPTOMERIA
Japanese Cedar

Conifer

C. japonica

Flower time: —
Location: Best in full sun
Propagation: Buy a new plant

C. japonica has no place in the average garden. There are, however, several small varieties. The green leaves turn reddish brown in winter. *C. japonica* 6 m (20 ft), will reach 25 m (80 ft) when mature. 'Elegans' 3 m (10 ft) bears feathery foliage — 'Vilmoriniana' is a popular rockery dwarf.

CUPRESSOCYPARIS
Leyland Cypress

Conifer

C. leylandii

Flower time: —
Location: Sun or partial shade
Propagation: Cuttings under glass/summer

'Leylandii' has replaced Lawson cypress (page 120) as our most popular conifer hedge. It withstands hard pruning, but this is often neglected and it becomes a menace. *C. leylandii* 10 m (33 ft) if pruned — 20 m (65 ft) if left unpruned. Cut hedges 3 times between late spring and early autumn.

CUPRESSUS
Cypress

Conifer

C. macrocarpa

Flower time: —
Location: Best in full sun
Propagation: Buy a new plant

Differs from Chamaecyparis by having branches which grow in all directions and by having cones which are large and leathery. Stake young trees — do not prune. There is the column-like *C. sempervirens* 3 m (10 ft) and the conical *C. macrocarpa* 3 m (10 ft). Its popular yellow variety is 'Goldcrest'.

CYTISUS
Broom

Deciduous shrub

C. scoparius

Flower time: April—June
Location: Full sun necessary
Propagation: Cuttings under glass/summer

The whippy stems bearing tiny leaves are covered with pea-like blooms during the flowering season — it will grow in starved soil. *C. scoparius* — height 1.5 m (5 ft) and its varieties and hybrids are widely grown. *C. decumbens* is a ground-cover variety. The 5 m (16 ft) giant is *C.battandieri*.

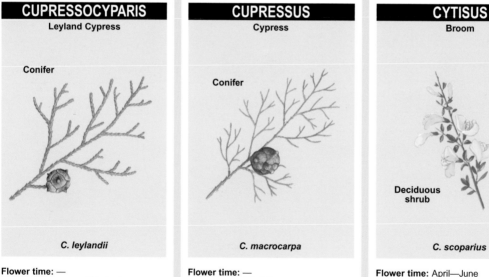

DAPHNE
Daphne

Deciduous or evergreen shrub

D. mezereum

Flower time: Depends on species
Location: Sun or light shade
Propagation: Cuttings under glass/summer

All the popular ones, such as *D. mezereum* 1 m (3 ft), bear fragrant flowers in February-March followed by poisonous berries. The evergreen *D. odora* 'Marginata' has cream-edged leaves. For early summer flowers grow the semi-evergreen *D. burkwoodii* or the evergreen *D. tangutica*.

DESFONTAINIA
Desfontainia

Evergreen shrub

D. spinosa

Flower time: July—October
Location: Best in light shade
Propagation: Cuttings under glass/summer

It may look like holly but it is much more difficult to grow. This shrub needs a mild site with a partially shaded wall nearby. The garden species *D. spinosa* 50 cm (1½ ft) has yellow-edged red flowers. Buy a large specimen if you have space to fill — growth is very slow for about 10 years.

DEUTZIA
Deutzia

Deciduous shrub

D. scabra 'Plena'

Flower time: Depends on species
Location: Sun or light shade
Propagation: Hardwood cuttings/autumn

The blooms cover the whole bush, so give this plant plenty of space. Late frosts can damage flower buds, but it is easy to grow. *D. rosea* — height 1 m (3 ft) bears pink flowers on arching branches in May. *D. scabra* and its double-flowering variety 'Plena' 2 m (7 ft) produce their blooms in May-June.

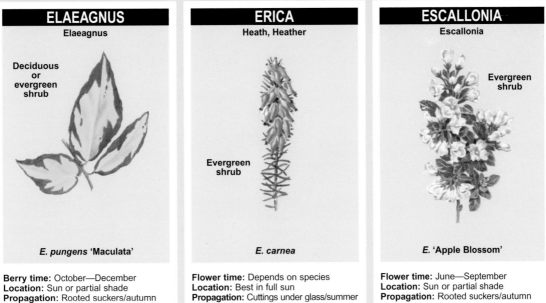

ELAEAGNUS
Elaeagnus

Deciduous or evergreen shrub

E. pungens 'Maculata'

Berry time: October—December
Location: Sun or partial shade
Propagation: Rooted suckers/autumn

Elaeagnus is grown for its foliage — berries appear in late autumn. The young leaves and shoots have a metallic sheen. *E. pungens* 'Maculata' — height 2 m (7 ft) is the popular one — *E. ebbingei* is grown for its leathery grey-green leaves. *E. commutata* is the deciduous species.

ERICA
Heath, Heather

Evergreen shrub

E. carnea

Flower time: Depends on species
Location: Best in full sun
Propagation: Cuttings under glass/summer

More versatile than Calluna (page 118). There are varieties for blooming in any month, and colours from white to near black. There are lime-tolerant species such as *E. carnea* 20 cm (8 in.) with January-April flowers, and lime-hating ones such as *E. cinerea* 25 cm (10 in.) with July-September flowers.

ESCALLONIA
Escallonia

Evergreen shrub

E. 'Apple Blossom'

Flower time: June—September
Location: Sun or partial shade
Propagation: Rooted suckers/autumn

Small, bell-shaped flowers cover the bush in summer. Growth is upright at first, then arching, with the stems clothed with small, shiny leaves. The popular *E.* 'Apple Blossom' 1.5 m (5 ft) is slow growing — *E.* 'Donard Seedling' has pink blooms and is hardier — *E. rubra* 'Macrantha' is more vigorous.

EUCALYPTUS
Gum Tree

Evergreen tree or shrub

E. gunnii

Flower time: —
Location: Best in full sun
Propagation: Buy a new plant

E. gunnii — height 6 m (20 ft) is the only popular species. It grows quickly, reaching 15 m (50 ft) when mature. You can prune it each year to maintain the blue juvenile leaves or you can let it grow as a tree with adult sickle-shaped foliage. *E. pauciflora* 'Niphophila' 7 m (23 ft) is the grey-green Snow gum.

EUCRYPHIA
Eucryphia

Deciduous or evergreen shrub

E. glutinosa

Flower time: June—September
Location: Best in light shade
Propagation: Cuttings under glass/summer

Showy but not often seen — Eucryphia needs space and is not easy to grow. There are two to choose from. *E. glutinosa* 3 m (10 ft) is deciduous with white flowers and good autumn colour. *E. nymansensis* 'Nymansay' 3 m (10 ft) is evergreen with masses of 8 cm (3 in.) white flowers in late summer.

EUONYMUS
Spindleberry

Deciduous shrub

E. europaeus 'Red Cascade'

Fruiting time: October—December
Location: Sun or partial shade
Propagation: Cuttings under glass/summer

The deciduous Euonymus species are tall shrubs with colourful autumn foliage and fruits — if possible grow several to ensure cross-pollination. The Common spindle is *E. europaeus* — height 4 m (13 ft) with red fruits and orange seeds. *E. alatus* 1.5 m (5 ft) has winged stems and red autumn leaves.

EUONYMUS
Euonymus

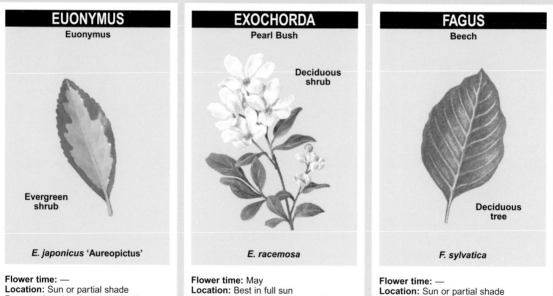

Evergreen shrub

E. japonicus 'Aureopictus'

Flower time: —
Location: Sun or partial shade
Propagation: Hardwood cuttings/autumn

The evergreen Euonymus species are more popular than the deciduous types. A must for every shrub border. The variegated forms provide winter colour, and there are bushy forms for hedging. *E. fortunei* 1 m (3 ft) is the ground cover species — *E. japonicus* is the taller one for hedging.

EXOCHORDA
Pearl Bush

Deciduous shrub

E. racemosa

Flower time: May
Location: Best in full sun
Propagation: Rooted suckers/autumn

An attractive shrub in late spring when the white flowers are borne on short spikes. There is a drawback — the flowering period lasts for only 7-10 days. *E. giraldii* 3 m (10 ft) has the largest flowers, *E. racemosa* is taller but has smaller flowers, and *E. macrantha* 'The Bride' is the favourite one.

FAGUS
Beech

Deciduous tree

F. sylvatica

Flower time: —
Location: Sun or partial shade
Propagation: Sow nuts in autumn

Stately beech trees are found in parks and in grand gardens — beech hedges are found around countless houses. *F. sylvatica* 8 m (26 ft) is the Common beech with green leaves, but there are colourful varieties such as 'Purpurea Pendula' (Weeping copper beech) and 'Zlatia' (Golden beech).

FATSIA
Castor Oil Plant

Evergreen shrub

F. japonica

Flower time: October—November
Location: Best in partial shade
Propagation: Cuttings under glass/summer

A plant which provides large decorative leaves in a sunless spot. *F. japonica* 3m (10 ft) produces tiny cream blooms in globular heads in autumn, which are followed by black berries. The deeply-lobed shiny leaves are hardy. 'Variegata' has white-edged leaves — it is less hardy than the species.

FORSYTHIA
Golden Bells

Deciduous shrub

F. 'Lynwood'

Flower time: March—April
Location: Sun or partial shade
Propagation: Hardwood cuttings/autumn

The blooms are widely-flared shallow bells — there are varieties to clothe walls, cover bare ground, to provide hedges and to stand alone as specimen bushes. *F. intermedia* 3 m (10 ft) is the usual upright bush choice — *F.* 'Lynwood' has broader petals. *F. suspensa* is used for screening.

FOTHERGILLA
Fothergilla

Deciduous shrub

F. gardenii

Flower time: April—May
Location: Best in light shade
Propagation: Buy a new plant

There are bottlebrush flower heads in spring before the leaves appear, but the main display is in autumn when the foliage turns bright yellow, orange or red. *F. gardenii* 1 m (3 ft) has small flowers and growth which is not robust. The taller *F. major* is the better choice — 'Monticola' turns red in autumn.

FRAXINUS
Ash

Deciduous tree

F. excelsior

Flower time: —
Location: Sun or partial shade
Propagation: Buy a new plant

The Common ash *F. excelsior* 10 m (33 ft) is not suitable for the average garden — it is late coming into leaf and it is too tall. Choose a compact variety — *F. e.* 'Jaspidea' (Golden ash) has yellow leaves and bark, 'Pendula' is a weeping tree, and 'Ornus' has white flowers and purple autumn leaves.

FUCHSIA
Fuchsia

Deciduous shrub

F. magellanica 'Gracilis'

Flower time: July—October
Location: Sun or light shade
Propagation: Cuttings under glass/summer

Colourful, bell-like flowers hang from the branches. Stems may be killed by frost, but the garden varieties will sprout new shoots in spring. The hardiest ones are varieties of *F. magellanica* — 'Gracilis' bears slender flowers. There are also many hybrids, such as 'Mrs Popple' and 'Tom Thumb'.

GARRYA
Silk Tassel Bush

Evergreen shrub

G. elliptica

Flower time: January—February
Location: Sun or partial shade
Propagation: Cuttings under glass/summer

This tall shrub 3 m (10 ft) is grown against a wall for its winter interest — long and slender tassels hang from the branches. *G. elliptica* bears 20 cm (8 in.) long tassel-like catkins which are grey-green at first. The variety 'James Roof' has thicker tassels which are nearly twice as long.

GENISTA
Broom

Deciduous shrub

G. lydia

Flower time: Depends on species
Location: Full sun necessary
Propagation: Sow seeds in spring

This group of brooms generally have wiry stems, tiny leaves and pea-like flowers in summer. All bloom freely if given a sunny spot and no fertilizer. *G. lydia* 60 cm (2 ft) blooms in May-June on arching stems — flowers appear on the spiny branches of *G. hispanica* 30 cm (1 ft) in June-July.

GLEDITSIA
Honey Locust

Deciduous tree

G. triacanthos 'Sunburst'

Flower time: —
Location: Sun or light shade
Propagation: Sow seeds in spring

A graceful tree grown for its attractive leaves, which appear late in the season, and its long seed pods. Most have thorns on the trunk. *G. triacanthos* 8 m (26 ft) is a quick-growing tree with yellow leaves in autumn. The young leaves of the variety 'Sunburst' are yellow — later greenish-yellow.

HAMAMELIS
Witch Hazel

Deciduous shrub

H. mollis 'Brevipetala'

Flower time: December—February
Location: Best in full sun
Propagation: Buy a new plant

Spidery flowers appear on the leafless stems for many weeks in winter, after which there are hazel-like leaves. Autumn foliage takes on attractive tints. The usual species is *H. mollis* 3 m (10 ft) which bears large fragrant flowers. 'Pallida' is yellow, 'Brevipetala' bronzy-yellow.

HEBE
Shrubby Veronica

Evergreen shrub

H. 'Great Orme'

Flower time: Depends on variety
Location: Best in full sun
Propagation: Cuttings under glass/summer

The Whipcord hebes have scale-like leaves — e.g *H. armstrongii* 1 m (3 ft). The Low-growing hebes reach less than 50 cm (1½ ft) — e.g *H.* 'Carl Teschner', and the Tall-growing hebes grow to more than 50 cm (1½ ft) — e.g 'Great Orme'. Not all are hardy — hardiness decreases with leaf size.

HEDERA
Ivy

Evergreen climber

H. canariensis 'Variegata'

Flower time: —
Location: Best in shade
Propagation: Rooted runners/autumn

Ivy is a reliable and colourful climber if you choose wisely and prune properly. Neither trees nor brickwork is damaged, but you must keep it in check. Smooth-edged types are available (e.g *H. colchica*) and so are variegated ones (e.g *H. helix* 'Goldheart' and *H. canariensis* 'Variegata').

HELIANTHEMUM
Sun Rose

H. 'Fire Dragon'

Evergreen shrub

Flower time: May—July
Location: Full sun necessary
Propagation: Cuttings under glass/summer

The papery blooms of this low-growing shrub form a sheet of colour for many weeks in summer, but each bloom lasts for only a day or two. Annual pruning is important. The Wisley series 20 cm (8 in.) have silvery-grey leaves — the Ben series (e.g *H.* 'Ben Hope') are neat and hardy.

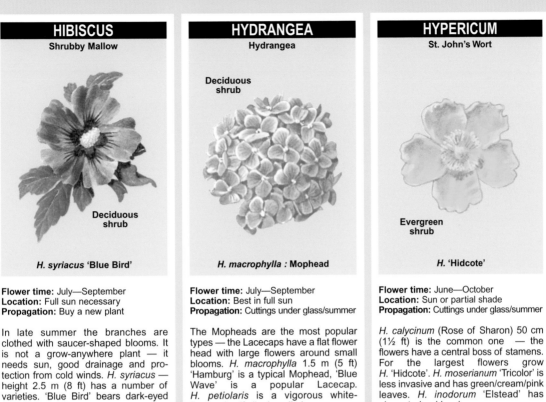

HIBISCUS
Shrubby Mallow

Deciduous shrub

H. syriacus 'Blue Bird'

Flower time: July—September
Location: Full sun necessary
Propagation: Buy a new plant

In late summer the branches are clothed with saucer-shaped blooms. It is not a grow-anywhere plant — it needs sun, good drainage and protection from cold winds. *H. syriacus* — height 2.5 m (8 ft) has a number of varieties. 'Blue Bird' bears dark-eyed violet flowers — 'Woodbridge' is pink.

HYDRANGEA
Hydrangea

Deciduous shrub

H. macrophylla : Mophead

Flower time: July—September
Location: Best in full sun
Propagation: Cuttings under glass/summer

The Mopheads are the most popular types — the Lacecaps have a flat flower head with large flowers around small blooms. *H. macrophylla* 1.5 m (5 ft) 'Hamburg' is a typical Mophead, 'Blue Wave' is a popular Lacecap. *H. petiolaris* is a vigorous white-flowered self-clinging climber.

HYPERICUM
St. John's Wort

Evergreen shrub

H. 'Hidcote'

Flower time: June—October
Location: Sun or partial shade
Propagation: Cuttings under glass/summer

H. calycinum (Rose of Sharon) 50 cm (1½ ft) is the common one — the flowers have a central boss of stamens. For the largest flowers grow *H.* 'Hidcote'. *H. moserianum* 'Tricolor' is less invasive and has green/cream/pink leaves. *H. inodorum* 'Elstead' has elongated red berries.

ILEX
Holly

Evergreen tree or shrub

I. altaclarensis 'Golden King'

Berry time: October—December
Location: Sun or partial shade
Propagation: Hardwood cuttings/autumn

The Common holly is the symbol of Christmas, but there are varieties which differ from the spiky, all-green leaves of *I. aquifolium* — height 3 m (10 ft). The variety 'Golden King' has yellow-edged leaves — grow 'Argentea Marginata' for white edges. I. *crenata* 'Golden Gem' has box-like leaves.

Evergreens can offer more than a display of attractive green leaves during the winter months. Many bear flowers and some produce an eye-catching display of berries — a few possess all three features. The example in the photograph is Skimmia japonica 'Bowles Dwarf' with white flowers and over-wintered red berries showing among the dark green foliage in spring. Other foliage/flower/fruiting types include varieties of Berberis, Pieris, Cotoneaster and Pyracantha.

ITEA
Sweetspire

Deciduous or evergreen shrub

I. ilicifolia

Flower time: Depends on species
Location: Sun or partial shade
Propagation: Cuttings under glass/summer

There are two quite different species. *I. ilicifolia* 2.5 m (8 ft) bears evergreen holly-like leaves and in August-September 30 cm (1 ft) long catkin-like tassels of white flowers appear. *I. virginica* 1 m (3 ft) has deciduous, oval leaves and upright cylindrical heads of white flowers in July.

JASMINUM
Jasmine

Deciduous or evergreen shrub or climber

J. nudiflorum

Flower time: Depends on species
Location: Best in full sun
Propagation: Cuttings under glass/summer

The Bushy jasmines are evergreen — e.g *J. nudiflorum* 3 m (10 ft) which flowers in November-February — *J. humile* bears yellow flowers in midsummer. The Climbing jasmines are deciduous — e.g *J. officinale* 'Grandiflorum' 8 m (26 ft) white, July-September.

JUNIPERUS
Juniper

Conifer

J. virginiana 'Skyrocket'

Flower time: —
Location: Sun or partial shade
Propagation: Buy a new plant

Juvenile leaves are needles — adult leaves are scale-like. There are many types — ground huggers such as *J. horizontalis*, medium-sized shrubs like *J. media* 'Pfitzerana' and tall trees such as *J. virginiana* 'Skyrocket'. You can find ones with green, grey, blue or yellow foliage.

KERRIA
Jew's Mallow

Deciduous shrub

K. japonica 'Pleniflora'

Flower time: April—May
Location: Sun or shade
Propagation: Hardwood cuttings/autumn

This shrub will grow almost anywhere, but it does need annual pruning. Flowers are produced in spring, and occasionally in summer and autumn. *K. japonica* — height 2 m (7 ft) is the garden species, with yellow single flowers on arching stems. For double blooms grow the variety 'Pleniflora'.

LABURNUM
Golden Rain

Deciduous tree

L. anagyroides

Flower time: May—June
Location: Sun or partial shade
Propagation: Buy a new plant

A graceful tree which casts dappled shade. The yellow-flowered, long sprays are followed by brown pods. All parts are poisonous. *L. anagyroides* is the Common laburnum — height 5 m (16 ft). 'Vossii' is the popular variety with larger flowers and sprays up to 50 m (1½ ft) long.

LARIX
Larch

Conifer

L. decidua

Flower time: —
Location: Best in full sun
Propagation: Buy a new plant

This tree belongs in the grounds around a country house — not one for the average garden. It is one of the few deciduous conifers. There are bare branches in winter — in spring tufts of needle-like leaves appear. The Common larch (*L. decidua*) reaches 25 m (80 ft) or more when mature.

LAURUS
Bay Laurel

Evergreen tree or shrub

L. nobilis

Flower time: —
Location: Sun or partial shade
Propagation: Buy a new plant

This plant is grown in the herb garden to supply bay leaves for the kitchen, or in a container as a neatly-trimmed shrub. *L. nobilis* is the Sweet bay — height 2.5 m (8 ft). It needs a sheltered site — the leaves may be damaged by frosts. Yellow flowers — black berries may appear on female trees.

LAVANDULA
Lavender

Evergreen shrub

L. angustifolia 'Hidcote'

Flower time: July—September
Location: Best in full sun
Propagation: Cuttings under glass/summer

A low-growing bush for the front of the border or for dwarf hedging. *L. angustifolia* 75 cm (2½ ft) is Old English lavender. Its flowers are pale blue — for purple blooms choose 'Hidcote'. *L. stoechas* (French lavender) bears purple flowers. The green-leaved, white-flowered species is *L. viridis*.

LAVATERA
Tree Mallow

Evergreen shrub

L. 'Rosea'

Flower time: June—October
Location: Best in full sun
Propagation: Hardwood cuttings/autumn

A good choice if you want a quick-growing shrub which will produce large flowers all summer long. Easy to grow, but you must hard prune it every year. *L.* 'Rosea' 2 m (7 ft) bears pink flowers — for red-eyed pinkish-white ones choose *L.* 'Barnsley'. *L. maritima* is not fully hardy.

LEPTOSPERMUM
New Zealand Tea Tree

Evergreen shrub

L. scoparium 'Nichollsii'

Flower time: May—June
Location: Best in full sun
Propagation: Cuttings under glass/summer

The saucer-shaped blooms are long-lasting and cover the foliage — a good choice if the conditions are right. It needs a mild climate or the shelter of a south-facing wall and free-draining soil. *L. scoparium* 2.5 m (8 ft) has white flowers — a variety with coloured flowers (e.g 'Kiwi') is the usual choice.

LEUCOTHOE
Leucothoe

Evergreen shrub

Evergreen shrub

L. fontanesiana

Flower time: May
Location: Best in light shade
Propagation: Cuttings under glass/summer

A ground cover with year-round interest — it needs acid soil and a shady situation. All varieties are attractively coloured in winter and some bear flowers in late spring. *L. fontanesiana* 1 m (3 ft) has green leaves which turn bronzy-purple — 'Rainbow' has green/yellow/pink/cream leaves.

LIGUSTRUM
Privet

Evergreen shrub

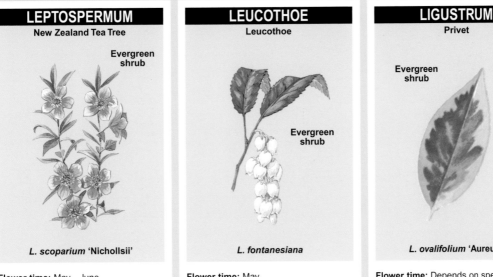

L. ovalifolium 'Aureum'

Flower time: Depends on species
Location: Sun or partial shade
Propagation: Hardwood cuttings/autumn

Privet is no longer the first choice for urban hedging — the Common privet (*L. vulgare*) has plain all-green leaves, but colourful varieties are available. *L. ovalifolium* 'Aureum' 2 m (7 ft) has green-centred yellow leaves — 'Argenteum' is yellow-edged. Several species bear flower heads in summer.

LIQUIDAMBAR
Sweet Gum

Deciduous tree

L. styraciflua

Flower time: —
Location: Sun or light shade
Propagation: Buy a new plant

The maple-like leaves are arranged alternately on the branches — the main feature is the highly-coloured autumn foliage — orange, red or purple. *L. styraciflua* 5 m (16 ft) is the garden species — leaves are lobed and the corky bark is attractive. The variety 'Variegata' bears white-edged leaves.

LIRIODENDRON
Tulip Tree

Deciduous tree

L. tulipifera

Flower time: June—July
Location: Best in full sun
Propagation: Buy a new plant

The leaves are unique — 4-lobed with a flattened tip. At the end of the season the foliage turns bright gold. *L. tulipifera* bears green/yellow/pink tulip-like flowers — unfortunately they do not appear for about 25 years. 'Fastigiatum' is pillar-like. 'Aureomarginatum' has yellow-edged foliage.

LONICERA
Honeysuckle

Deciduous or evergreen shrub or climber

L. periclymenum

Flower time: Depends on species
Location: Sun or light shade
Propagation: Cuttings under glass/summer

The climbers are less demanding than clematis. *L. periclymenum* 6 m (20 ft) produces cream-coloured flowers in July-August — the yellow/rose blooms of *L. americana* open in June-September. There are bushy ones for hedging, e.g *L. nitida*, and for floral display, e.g *L. fragrantissima*.

LUPINUS
Tree Lupin

Evergreen shrub

L. arboreus

Flower time: June—August
Location: Full sun necessary
Propagation: Sow seeds in autumn

The Tree lupin is a rarity, unlike its herbaceous border cousin. It is short-lived, and the floral spikes are shorter than on the hardy perennial hybrids. *L. arboreus* 1.5 m (5 ft) bears yellow, fragrant flowers and greyish-green leaflets — 'Mauve Queen' is a purple variety. Not for heavy soil.

MAGNOLIA
Magnolia

Deciduous or evergreen shrub

M. soulangiana

Flower time: Depends on species
Location: Best in full sun
Propagation: Buy a new plant

A fine sight in full bloom. Plant in April and add compost to the soil. Provide protection from cold winds and mulch in May. *M. stellata* 1.5 m (5 ft) bears white starry flowers in March-April, *M. soulangiana* produces its goblet-shaped blooms in April, and *M. grandiflora* blooms in late summer.

MAHONIA
Mahonia

Evergreen shrub

M. 'Charity'

Flower time: Depends on species
Location: Best in partial shade
Propagation: Cuttings under glass/summer

Hardy and easy to grow — not fussy about soil type nor shade. Fragrant flowers in winter or spring are followed by purple or black berries. *M. aquifolium* 1 m (3 ft) bears its flowers in clusters — *M. japonica* 2 m (7 ft) produces flower spikes which radiate from stem tips in winter. *M. 'Charity'* is a specimen shrub.

MALUS
Ornamental Crab

Deciduous tree

M. 'John Downie'

Flower time: April—May
Location: Best in full sun
Propagation: Buy a new plant

Prunus is our favourite spring-flowering tree, but Malus has some extra points. There are red as well as white and pink varieties, showy fruits are produced, and heavy soil is tolerated. *M.* 'John Downie' 6 m (20 ft) is a popular variety — grow *M.* 'Golden Hornet' for yellow fruit and 'Profusion' for red ones.

MYRTUS
Myrtle

Evergreen shrub

M. communis

Flower time: July—September
Location: Best in full sun
Propagation: Cuttings under glass/summer

Myrtle has been one of our garden shrubs for hundreds of years, but it is not popular. The problem is that it is damaged by hard frosts and icy winds. *M. communis* — height 3 m (10 ft) is the basic species. The small white flowers have a central boss of fluffy stamens. 'Variegata' has cream-edged leaves.

NANDINA
Heavenly Bamboo

Evergreen shrub

N. domestica

Flower time: June—July
Location: Best in full sun
Propagation: Divide clumps in autumn

Colours change as the year progresses. Spring foliage is tinged with red and in autumn the leaves are flushed with purple. *N. domestica* 1 m (3 ft) is the basic species — the white starry blooms are borne in cone-shaped flower heads — berries appear later. 'Firepower' is even more colourful.

OLEARIA
Daisy Bush

Evergreen shrub

O. scilloniensis

Flower time: Depends on species
Location: Best in full sun
Propagation: Cuttings under glass/summer

The bush is covered with daisy-like flowers in summer, but it will become gaunt when not in flower if it is not pruned annually. *O. macrodonta* 2.5 m (8 ft) bears flowers in June above holly-like leaves — *O. hastii* has box-like leaves. *O. scilloniensis* 1.5 m (5 ft) flowers in May.

OSMANTHUS
Osmanthus

Evergreen shrub

O. burkwoodii

Flower time: Depends on species
Location: Sun or light shade
Propagation: Cuttings under glass/summer

A neat bush covered with evergreen leaves — the flowers have a jasmine-like fragrance. *O. delavayi* 1 m (3 ft) is the most popular species, with tubular flowers in April-May. *O. burkwoodii* is more vigorous — *O. heterophyllus* 'Variegata' blooms in September and has holly-like leaves.

PACHYSANDRA
Japanese Spurge

Evergreen shrub

P. terminalis 'Variegata'

Flower time: March
Location: Best in shade
Propagation: Divide clumps in spring

Pachysandra is a good choice if you need a ground-cover plant which will grow under a leafy tree. The densely-packed leathery leaves suppress weed growth. *P. terminalis* 20 cm (8 in.) is the usual one — the white flowers are insignificant. 'Green Carpet' is more compact.

PAEONIA
Tree Peony

Deciduous shrub

P. suffruticosa

Flower time: May—June
Location: Best in full sun
Propagation: Buy a new plant

Tree peonies are less popular than their herbaceous border relatives. The flowers are large bowls or balls of papery petals. The stems of double-bloomed varieties require staking. *P. delavayi* 1.5 m (5 ft) is a popular single, red variety — for double blooms try a *P. suffruticosa* variety.

PARTHENOCISSUS
Virginia Creeper

Deciduous climber

P. tricuspidata

Flower time: —
Location: Sun or partial shade
Propagation: Cuttings under glass/summer

This spreading vine is generally used to cover house walls. Support is required at first, but unlike some vines it is self-clinging. The leaves turn red in autumn. *P. tricuspidata* 7 m (23 ft) is Boston ivy — the leaves are usually, but not always, 3-lobed. *P. henryana* has white-veined green leaves.

PASSIFLORA
Passion Flower

Deciduous or evergreen climber

P. caerulea

Flower time: July—September
Location: Full sun necessary
Propagation: Cuttings under glass/summer

Very few types can be grown outdoors — the one to choose is *P. caerulea* — stem length 7 m (23 ft). Even this one is quite tender — grow it against a south-facing wall. Frost may kill stems, but new ones appear. The intricate flowers have prominent stamens, styles and stigmas.

PERNETTYA
Prickly Heath

Evergreen shrub

P. mucronata 'Alba'

Berry time: November—February
Location: Sun or partial shade
Propagation: Rooted suckers/autumn

Masses of early summer flowers are followed by large porcelain-like berries on female plants of this low-growing prickly bush. These fruits are left alone by birds. *P. mucronata* 75 cm (2½ ft) is the garden species — 'Cherry Ripe' bears red berries. 'Mascula' is male — 'Bell's Seedling' is male/female.

PEROVSKIA
Russian Sage

Deciduous shrub

P. atriplicifolia

Flower time: August—October
Location: Full sun necessary
Propagation: Cuttings under glass/summer

Tiny blue flowers on long spikes appear above the erect stems and grey leaves. Lavender-like at first glance, but the leaves are deeply cut and have a sage-like smell. *P. atriplicifolia* — height 1 m (3 ft) bears 25 cm (10 in.) long flower-spikes. Hard pruning is necessary, so there is little to see in spring.

PHILADELPHUS
Mock Orange

Deciduous shrub

P. 'Virginal'

Flower time: June—July
Location: Best in full sun
Propagation: Cuttings under glass/summer

A popular shrub. The usual height is 2 m (7 ft) but there are taller ones and dwarfs. The blooms have an orange-blossom fragrance. Tall varieties include the double white *P. 'Virginal'*. *P. coronarius* 'Aureus' is average height with yellow leaves, and *P. 'Sybille'* is a 1 m (3 ft) dwarf.

PHLOMIS
Jerusalem Sage

Evergreen shrub

P. fruticosa

Flower time: June—July
Location: Best in full sun
Propagation: Cuttings under glass/summer

Easy to recognise — whorls of hooded flowers are borne on the top of woolly-leaved stems. Plants become unattractive with age — hard prune every year to ensure new stems. *P. fruticosa* 1 m (3 ft) bears 5 cm (2 in.) wide whorls of yellow flowers. *P. chrysophylla* is similar, but leaves turn yellow in autumn.

PHOTINIA
Photinia

Evergreen shrub

P. fraseri 'Robusta'

Flower time: April
Location: Best in full sun
Propagation: Cuttings under glass/summer

P. fraseri 'Red Robin' has become a firm favourite — height 2.5 m (8 ft). The young foliage in spring is bright red — cut back once this colour has faded and new red leaves will appear. Clusters of small flowers appear after a mild winter. Plant in a sheltered spot. *P. f.* 'Robusta' is similar but new growth is coppery.

PHYGELIUS
Cape Figwort

Evergreen shrub

P. capensis

Flower time: July—October
Location: Sun or light shade
Propagation: Cuttings under glass/summer

The flower heads are eye-catching — worth trying if you live in a mild area. In spring cut back all stems or just trim frost-affected side shoots. *P. capensis* 2.5 m (8 ft) bears yellow-throated red flowers all round the spike — *P. aequalis* 'Yellow Trumpet' is smaller and has one-sided flower heads.

PICEA
Spruce

Conifer

P. omorika

Flower time: —
Location: Best in full sun
Propagation: Buy a new plant

The Norway spruce (*P. abies*) is the traditional Christmas tree, but there are other shapes. *P. omorika* is a narrow cone, *P. abies* 'Nidiformis' is a 30 cm (1 ft) flat-topped dwarf. There are also other colours — *P. pungens* is the Blue spruce and *P. orientalis* 'Aurea' 3.5 m (11 ft) has yellow foliage in spring.

SHRUBS SUITABLE FOR SHADY SITES

Aucuba japonica
Buxus sempervirens
Camellia species
Elaeagnus pungens
Euonymus radicans
Fatsia japonica
Hypericum calycinum
Ligustrum species
Lonicera nitida
Mahonia aquifolium
Osmanthus heterophyllus
Pachysandra terminalis
Prunus laurocerasus
Rubus species
Skimmia japonica
Symphoricarpos species
Vinca species

SHRUBS SUITABLE FOR HEAVY SOILS

Berberis species
Choisya ternata
Forsythia species
Hypericum species
Mahonia species
Philadelphus species
Potentilla species
Ribes sanguineum
Spiraea species
Viburnum species
Weigela species

SHRUBS TO ATTRACT WILDLIFE

Berberis ....Bi
Buddleia ....Bi, Bu
Chaenomeles ....Bi
Cotoneaster ....Bi
Daphne ....Bi
Hebe...................Bi, Bu
Hypericum ....Bi
Ilex ....Bi
Lavandula ....Bu
Ligustrum.................Bu
Mahonia ....Bi
Pyracantha ....Bi
Rhus ....Bi
Skimmia ....Bi
Symphoricarpos ....Bi
Syringa ....Bi, Bu
Viburnum ....Bi

KEY: Bi — Birds Bu — Butterflies

PIERIS
Andromeda

Evergreen shrub

P. formosa forrestii

Flower time: March—May
Location: Best in light shade
Propagation: Buy a new plant

A neat and slow-growing bush. In spring there are long sprays of blooms, and with the more popular varieties there is a bright red display of young foliage. *P. formosa forrestii* 3 m (10 ft) has white flowers and red foliage when it is young. *P. japonica* is a more compact species.

PINUS
Pine

Conifer

P. sylvestris

Flower time: —
Location: Full sun necessary
Propagation: Buy a new plant

Most pines are far too tall for the average garden, but there are slow-growing ones and dwarfs for border and rockery. The Scots pine *P. sylvestris* has a number of varieties suitable for the garden, and *P. nigra* is a good specimen tree. Dwarfs include *P. mugo* 60 cm (2 ft) and *P. strobus* 'Nana'.

PITTOSPORUM
Pittosporum

Evergreen shrub

P. tenuifolium

Flower time: May
Location: Sun or light shade
Propagation: Cuttings under glass/summer

The black twigs with their wavy-edged leaves are popular with flower arrangers, but few types produce a floral display. Part or all of the bush may die in a severe winter. *P. tenuifolium* 3 m (10 ft) is reasonably hardy. *P. tobira* is the best flowering type, but tender.

PLATANUS
Plane

Deciduous tree

P. hispanica

Flower time: —
Location: Sun or partial shade
Propagation: Buy a new plant

For nearly everyone this is a tree to admire and not to grow — it would soon overwhelm the average garden. *P. hispanica* is the London plane — height 10 m (33 ft). It is easily recognised from the creamy patches below the flaking bark. *P. orientalis* is even more spreading than London plane.

POLYGONUM
Russian Vine

Deciduous climber

P. baldschuanicum

Flower time: July—October
Location: Sun or partial shade
Propagation: Cuttings under glass/summer

The quickest way to hide with foliage an unsightly wall, ugly fence or dead tree. Masses of flowers cover the heart-shaped leaves all summer long — it may need hard pruning every year. *P. baldschuanicum* can grow 5 m (16 ft) in a year. It has a twining growth habit and you must provide stout support.

POPULUS
Poplar

Deciduous tree

P. alba

Flower time: —
Location: Sun or partial shade
Propagation: Buy a new plant

Not a tree for small gardens — its roots can damage nearby drains, foundations and paths. The leaves of *P. alba* 10 m (33 ft) are woolly below, and the leaves of *P. candicans* 'Aurea' are blotched with white. The Lombardy poplar *P. nigra* 'Italica' is one of the best columnar trees.

POTENTILLA
Shrubby Cinquefoil

Deciduous shrub

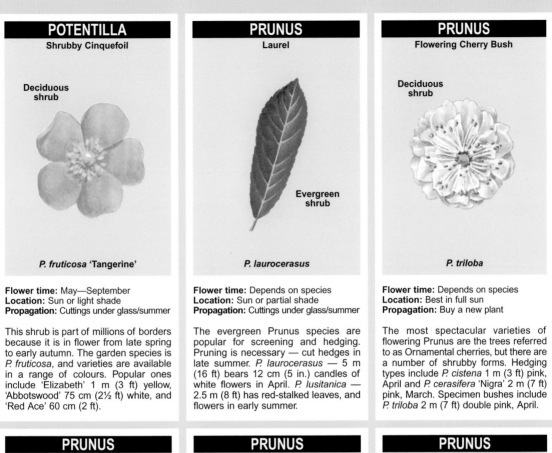

P. fruticosa 'Tangerine'

Flower time: May—September
Location: Sun or light shade
Propagation: Cuttings under glass/summer

This shrub is part of millions of borders because it is in flower from late spring to early autumn. The garden species is *P. fruticosa*, and varieties are available in a range of colours. Popular ones include 'Elizabeth' 1 m (3 ft) yellow, 'Abbotswood' 75 cm (2½ ft) white, and 'Red Ace' 60 cm (2 ft).

PRUNUS
Laurel

Evergreen shrub

P. laurocerasus

Flower time: Depends on species
Location: Sun or partial shade
Propagation: Cuttings under glass/summer

The evergreen Prunus species are popular for screening and hedging. Pruning is necessary — cut hedges in late summer. *P. laurocerasus* — 5 m (16 ft) bears 12 cm (5 in.) candles of white flowers in April. *P. lusitanica* — 2.5 m (8 ft) has red-stalked leaves, and flowers in early summer.

PRUNUS
Flowering Cherry Bush

Deciduous shrub

P. triloba

Flower time: Depends on species
Location: Best in full sun
Propagation: Buy a new plant

The most spectacular varieties of flowering Prunus are the trees referred to as Ornamental cherries, but there are a number of shrubby forms. Hedging types include *P. cistena* 1 m (3 ft) pink, April and *P. cerasifera* 'Nigra' 2 m (7 ft) pink, March. Specimen bushes include *P. triloba* 2 m (7 ft) double pink, April.

PRUNUS
Ornamental Cherry

Deciduous tree

P. 'Cheal's Weeping Cherry'

Flower time: March—May
Location: Best in full sun
Propagation: Buy a new plant

Flowering Prunus trees are one of the brightest sights in the spring garden, and the Ornamental cherries are the largest group. The Ordinary types include *P. padus*, *P. avium* and *P. serrula* — examples of the Japanese ones are *P.* 'Cheal's Weeping Cherry' and *P.* 'Kanzan'.

PRUNUS
Ornamental Almond

Deciduous tree

P. dulcis

Flower time: March
Location: Best in full sun
Propagation: Buy a new plant

The flowers appear before the leaves in early spring — these flowers are almost stalkless. *P. dulcis* (*P. amygdalus*) is the Common almond — height 7 m (23 ft). The flowers are pale pink and the lance-shaped leaves are narrow. *P. amygdalo persica* 'Pollardii' is an almond-peach hybrid.

PRUNUS
Ornamental Peach

Deciduous tree

P. persica 'Klara Meyer'

Flower time: Depends on species
Location: Best in full sun
Propagation: Buy a new plant

These trees are neither long-lived nor robust. The almost stalkless flowers appear before the leaves. *P. persica* is the Common peach — height 4 m (13 ft). The April flowers are pink or red and the leaves are lance-shaped. *P. davidiana* bears pink flowers in January-February.

PRUNUS
Ornamental Plum

Deciduous tree or shrub

P. blireana

Flower time: March—April
Location: Best in full sun
Propagation: Buy a new plant

The flowers are produced on short stalks before or at the same time as the leaves. Foliage is sometimes purple or coppery. *P. blireana* 5 m (16 ft) has pink double blooms and coppery leaves. *P. cerasifera* bears white flowers, and *P. spinosa* 3 m (10 ft) has white flowers and spiny shoots. Useful for hedging.

PYRACANTHA
Firethorn

Evergreen shrub

P. coccinea 'Lalandei'

Berry time: October—January
Location: Sun or partial shade
Propagation: Cuttings under glass/summer

A tough and hardy shrub to grow as a hedge or specimen plant. Late spring white flowers are followed by clusters of berries. The leaves are toothed and the stems are spiny. *P. coccinea* 'Lalandei' 4 m (13 ft) bears orange-red berries — *P.* 'Teton' produces yellow ones. *P. atalantioides* grows upright.

QUERCUS
Oak

Deciduous or evergreen tree

Q. rubra

Flower time: —
Location: Best in full sun
Propagation: Sow acorns in autumn

For nearly all gardeners this is a tree to admire and not to grow — nearly all are too tall and spreading. The Common oak (*Q. robur*) — height 8 m (26 ft) has lobed oblong leaves — the variety 'Fastigiata' is column-like. *Q. rubra* has red leaves in autumn. The Holm oak *Q. ilex* has oval, evergreen leaves.

RHODODENDRON
Rhododendron

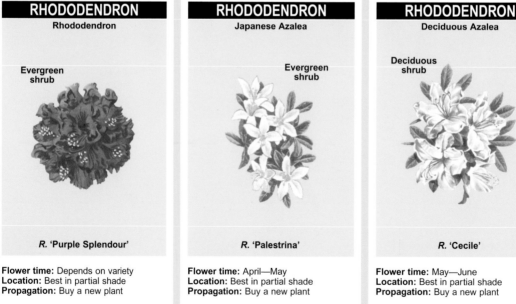

Evergreen shrub

R. 'Purple Splendour'

Flower time: Depends on variety
Location: Best in partial shade
Propagation: Buy a new plant

The average rhododendron is about 1.5 m (5 ft) tall and blooms in May, but there are many variations — heights range from 30 cm (1 ft) to 6 m (20 ft) and flowering times range from February to August. There are Hardy Hybrid types, Dwarf Hybrids and Species (e.g *R. arboreum*).

RHODODENDRON
Japanese Azalea

Evergreen shrub

R. 'Palestrina'

Flower time: April—May
Location: Best in partial shade
Propagation: Buy a new plant

Azaleas are usually daintier plants with smaller leaves than rhododendrons, but not always. The evergreen group are described here. They are low-growing, reaching 60 cm-1.5 m (2-5 ft) and there are several groups, such as the Vuyk Hybrids, Kaempferi Hybrids and the small-flowered Kurume Hybrids.

RHODODENDRON
Deciduous Azalea

Deciduous shrub

R. 'Cecile'

Flower time: May—June
Location: Best in partial shade
Propagation: Buy a new plant

The average height is 1.5-2.5 m (5-8 ft) — taller and later flowering than the Japanese ones. There are a number of types, including the Ghent, Knap Hill, Exbury and Mollis Hybrids. Before they fall the leaves develop rich colours in autumn. Popular ones include *R.* 'Cecile' and *R.* 'Persil'.

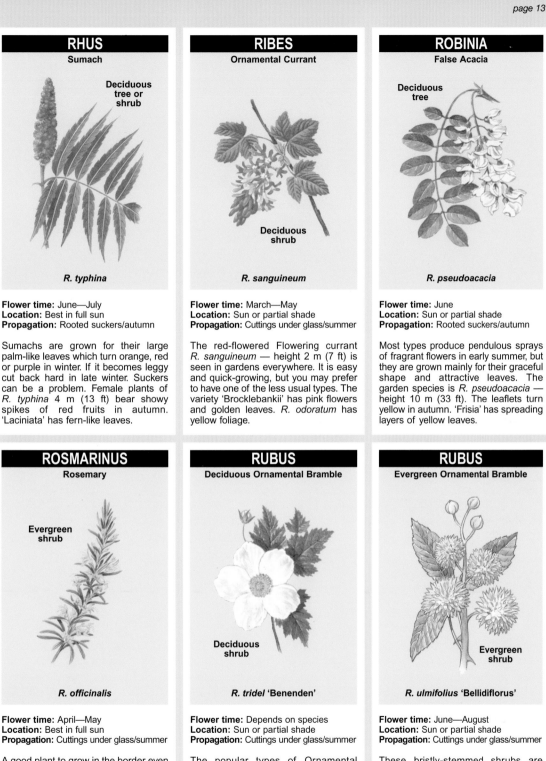

RHUS
Sumach

Deciduous tree or shrub

R. typhina

Flower time: June—July
Location: Best in full sun
Propagation: Rooted suckers/autumn

Sumachs are grown for their large palm-like leaves which turn orange, red or purple in winter. If it becomes leggy cut back hard in late winter. Suckers can be a problem. Female plants of *R. typhina* 4 m (13 ft) bear showy spikes of red fruits in autumn. 'Laciniata' has fern-like leaves.

RIBES
Ornamental Currant

Deciduous shrub

R. sanguineum

Flower time: March—May
Location: Sun or partial shade
Propagation: Cuttings under glass/summer

The red-flowered Flowering currant *R. sanguineum* — height 2 m (7 ft) is seen in gardens everywhere. It is easy and quick-growing, but you may prefer to have one of the less usual types. The variety 'Brocklebankii' has pink flowers and golden leaves. *R. odoratum* has yellow foliage.

ROBINIA
False Acacia

Deciduous tree

R. pseudoacacia

Flower time: June
Location: Sun or partial shade
Propagation: Rooted suckers/autumn

Most types produce pendulous sprays of fragrant flowers in early summer, but they are grown mainly for their graceful shape and attractive leaves. The garden species is *R. pseudoacacia* — height 10 m (33 ft). The leaflets turn yellow in autumn. 'Frisia' has spreading layers of yellow leaves.

ROSMARINUS
Rosemary

Evergreen shrub

R. officinalis

Flower time: April—May
Location: Best in full sun
Propagation: Cuttings under glass/summer

A good plant to grow in the border even if you do not use its leaves in the kitchen. The upright stems are densely clothed with strap-like leaves, and small flowers appear on the stems in spring. *R. officinalis* 1.5 m (5 ft) has grey-green leaves and lavender flowers — 'Albus' has white blooms.

RUBUS
Deciduous Ornamental Bramble

Deciduous shrub

R. tridel 'Benenden'

Flower time: Depends on species
Location: Sun or partial shade
Propagation: Cuttings under glass/summer

The popular types of Ornamental bramble are the ones that lose their leaves in winter and are grown either for their colourful stems or their flower/fruit display. *R. cockburnianus* 3 m (10 ft) has upright stems covered with white bloom — *R. tridel* 'Benenden' bears fragrant flowers in May.

RUBUS
Evergreen Ornamental Bramble

Evergreen shrub

R. ulmifolius 'Bellidiflorus'

Flower time: June—August
Location: Sun or partial shade
Propagation: Cuttings under glass/summer

These bristly-stemmed shrubs are either plants with spreading shoots or are tall climbers. The flowers of most types look like single roses. *R. tricolor* 60 cm (2 ft) bears white flowers and red fruits — *R. ulmifolius* 'Bellidiflorus' has double pink flowers. *R. henryi* 6 m (20 ft) is a climber.

SALIX
Willow

Deciduous tree

S. chrysocoma

Flower time: February—March
Location: Best in full sun
Propagation: Hardwood cuttings/autumn

Willow trees are attractive, but you must be careful to choose a suitable one. S. chrysocoma 10 m (33 ft) needs a lot of space like most other Weeping willows. S. caprea 'Pendula' 3 m (10 ft) is much more compact, and so is S. purpurea. S. matsudana 'Tortuosa' has twisted branches.

SALIX
Shrubby Willow

Deciduous shrub

S. lanata

Flower time: March—April
Location: Sun or partial shade
Propagation: Hardwood cuttings/autumn

Not all willows are trees — there are low-growing ones for the rockery as well as bold coloured-bark types for the border. S. lanata 1m (3 ft) is an example of the compact willows — silvery-green leaves with erect woolly catkins. The coloured-stem willows are varieties of S. alba, such as 'Vitellina'.

SAMBUCUS
Elder

Deciduous tree or shrub

S. racemosa 'Plumosa Aurea'

Flower time: May—June
Location: Sun or partial shade
Propagation: Hardwood cuttings/autumn

The Common elder is S. nigra — height 5 m (16 ft). It is a familiar sight with its white flowers followed by black berries. For the garden there are 'Aurea' (yellow leaves) and 'Marginata' (cream-edged leaves). S. racemosa 'Plumosa Aurea' 2 m (7 ft) bears yellow leaves and cream flowers.

SANTOLINA
Cotton Lavender

Evergreen shrub

S. chamaecyparissus

Flower time: June—August
Location: Full sun necessary
Propagation: Cuttings under glass/summer

A low-growing bush for the front of the border. Colour is provided by the silvery leaves and the yellow button-like flowers. S. chamaecyparissus 60 cm (2 ft) is the basic species — the flower buds are sometimes removed to improve the foliage display. 'Nana' is used for edging.

SARCOCOCCA
Christmas Box

Evergreen shrub

S. hookeriana 'Digyna'

Flower time: January—February
Location: Sun or shade
Propagation: Cuttings under glass/summer

A plant much loved by flower arrangers — the branches are used for late winter displays. S. confusa 75 cm (2½ ft) has oval leaves and black berries — S. hookeriana 'Digyna' 1.5 m (5 ft) bears narrow purple-tinged leaves. The variety 'Humilis' is a 30 cm (1 ft) dwarf and is a useful ground cover.

SENECIO
Shrubby Ragwort

Evergreen shrub or climber

S. 'Sunshine'

Flower time: June—July
Location: Full sun necessary
Propagation: Cuttings under glass/summer

The popular species is S. 'Sunshine' 1 m (3 ft) — may be listed as S. greyi or S. laxifolius. It is a spreading shrub which is grown for its silvery oval leaves as well as its yellow daisy-like flowers. S. monroi has crinkled-edged leaves, and S. scandens is a white-flowered rather tender climber.

SKIMMIA
Skimmia

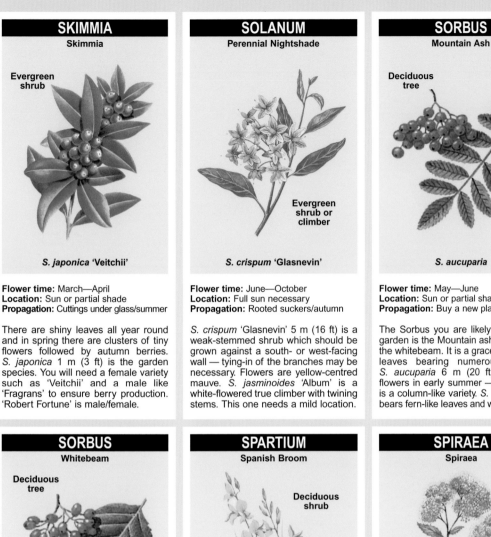

Evergreen shrub

S. japonica 'Veitchii'

Flower time: March—April
Location: Sun or partial shade
Propagation: Cuttings under glass/summer

There are shiny leaves all year round and in spring there are clusters of tiny flowers followed by autumn berries. *S. japonica* 1 m (3 ft) is the garden species. You will need a female variety such as 'Veitchii' and a male like 'Fragrans' to ensure berry production. 'Robert Fortune' is male/female.

SOLANUM
Perennial Nightshade

Evergreen shrub or climber

S. crispum 'Glasnevin'

Flower time: June—October
Location: Full sun necessary
Propagation: Rooted suckers/autumn

S. crispum 'Glasnevin' 5 m (16 ft) is a weak-stemmed shrub which should be grown against a south- or west-facing wall — tying-in of the branches may be necessary. Flowers are yellow-centred mauve. *S. jasminoides* 'Album' is a white-flowered true climber with twining stems. This one needs a mild location.

SORBUS
Mountain Ash

Deciduous tree

S. aucuparia

Flower time: May—June
Location: Sun or partial shade
Propagation: Buy a new plant

The Sorbus you are likely to find in a garden is the Mountain ash rather than the whitebeam. It is a graceful tree with leaves bearing numerous leaflets. *S. aucuparia* 6 m (20 ft) has white flowers in early summer — 'Fastigiata' is a column-like variety. *S. cashmiriana* bears fern-like leaves and white berries.

SORBUS
Whitebeam

Deciduous tree

S. intermedia

Flower time: May—June
Location: Sun or partial shade
Propagation: Buy a new plant

The whitebeams have oval leaves which are green above and grey or white below, turning yellow in autumn. The white flowers are followed by oval berries in autumn. *S. aria* 'Lutescens' 7 m (23 ft) has new leaves which are silvery-white. *S. intermedia* 6 m (20 ft) leaves are yellowish-grey below.

SPARTIUM
Spanish Broom

Deciduous shrub

S. junceum

Flower time: June—September
Location: Full sun necessary
Propagation: Cuttings under glass/summer

The green rush-like stems are clothed with yellow pea-like flowers throughout the summer — foliage is sparse. *S. junceum* 3 m (10 ft) is the only species available. The green stems provide an evergreen effect over winter. Annual pruning is necessary if the site is not in full sun.

SPIRAEA
Spiraea

Deciduous shrub

S. japonica 'Anthony Waterer'

Flower time: Depends on species
Location: Sun or partial shade
Propagation: Cuttings under glass/summer

The spring-flowering types bear tiny white flowers in clusters on arching stems — e.g *S. nipponica* 'Snowmound' 1 m (3 ft). The summer-flowering ones are more compact with flowers in flat heads, domes or spikes — e.g *S. japonica* 'Anthony Waterer' 1 m (3 ft) — pink flowers, July-September.

SYMPHORICARPOS
Snowberry

Deciduous shrub

S. albus

Berry time: October—January
Location: Sun or shade
Propagation: Hardwood cuttings/autumn

A grow-anywhere plant — in full sun or dense shade, in rich or poor soil. Use it to cover large areas of the wilder parts of the garden. *S. albus* 2 m (7 ft) suckers freely — the berries are white. *S. orbicularis* 'Variegata' is an odd one out — needs sun and has yellow-edged leaves and purple berries.

SYRINGA
Lilac

Deciduous shrub

S. vulgaris 'Madame Lemoine'

Flower time: May—June
Location: Best in full sun
Propagation: Buy a new plant

The Common lilac *S. vulgaris* 1.5-3 m (5-10 ft) has a host of varieties — there are single-flowered ones like 'Charles X' and doubles such as 'Charles Joly'. Dead blooms and suckers should be removed. Less well known are the Syringa species such as *S. microphylla* 1.5 m (5 ft).

TAMARIX
Tamarisk

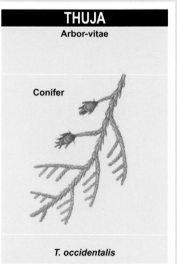

Deciduous shrub

T. ramosissima

Flower time: Depends on species
Location: Best in full sun
Propagation: Hardwood cuttings/autumn

The tiny leaves and tall plumes of small pink flowers combine to give a unique feathery effect. There are two types — *T. tetranda* 2.5 m (8 ft) bears 60 cm (2 ft) high plumes of flowers in May-June. The flowers of *T. ramosissima* appear later in August-September. Prune annually to avoid gaunt growth.

TAXODIUM
Swamp Cypress

Conifer

T. distichum

Flower time: —
Location: Sun or partial shade
Propagation: Buy a new plant

This tree will grow in any lime-free loamy soil, and is the only one to choose for swampy land. *T. distichum* — height 5 m (16 ft) is the garden species. The bark is fibrous and reddish — the leaves turn coppery-yellow in autumn. The variety 'Imbricatum' has a narrow cone shape.

TAXUS
Yew

Conifer

T. baccata

Flower time: —
Location: Sun or partial shade
Propagation: Buy a new plant

A slow-growing conifer which is widely used as a hedge, but there is a range of shapes from prostrate ground covers to tall column-like trees. *T. baccata* 2 m (7 ft) is the popular hedging variety. The variety 'Fastigiata' is a narrow column — 'Repandens' is a 60 cm (2 ft) dwarf. *T. media* 'Hicksii' is a rounded bush.

THUJA
Arbor-vitae

Conifer

T. occidentalis

Flower time: —
Location: Sun or light shade
Propagation: Buy a new plant

There is a wide range of shapes and sizes, ranging from the dwarf *T. occidentalis* 'Hetz Midget' 60 cm (2 ft) to the pyramid-shaped Western red cedar (*T. orientalis* 'Plicata') — height 5 m (16 ft). Green, yellow and coppery varieties are available — nearly all have aromatic foliage.

TILIA
Lime

Deciduous tree

T. platyphyllos

Flower time: May—June
Location: Sun or partial shade
Propagation: Buy a new plant

The heart-shaped leaves unfold in early spring and remain until late autumn — aphids on some species produce a sticky deposit. *T. platyphyllos* 8 m (26 ft) is the Large-leaved lime — 'Rubra' has bright red twigs. *T.* 'Petiolaris' is a better choice — it is aphid-free.

TRACHYCARPUS
Windmill Palm

Evergreen tree

T. fortunei

Flower time: June
Location: Best in full sun
Propagation: Buy a new plant

Only one true palm (the Chusan or Chinese windmill palm) can be considered to be hardy. It withstands winter frosts in most areas but needs protection against icy winds. *T. fortunei* 3 m (10 ft) bears leaves up to 1 m (3 ft) wide on top of a stout trunk. Large heads of tiny flowers appear in summer.

ULEX
Gorse

Evergreen shrub

U. europaeus 'Flore Pleno'

Flower time: Depends on species
Location: Full sun necessary
Propagation: Cuttings under glass/summer

An excellent shrub for hedging or large-scale ground cover provided the soil is sandy or stony in a sunny site. All types are spiny. *U. europaeus* 2 m (7 ft) is the Common gorse — pea-like flowers appear in spring and occasionally later. The semi-double variety 'Flore Pleno' 1.5 m (5 ft) is a better choice.

ULMUS
Elm

Deciduous tree

U. glabra

Flower time: —
Location: Sun or light shade
Propagation: Buy a new plant

Dutch elm disease has swept away countless examples of the popular elms such as *U. glabra* and *U. procera*. Choose carefully — pick a species noted for its disease resistance. The Chinese elm *U. parvifolia* is a good example. 'Geisha' is a small variety bearing white-edged leaves.

Lawson cypress, Leyland cypress and juniper tower above and around the gardener, but he planted them as small specimens from a garden centre only 8 years before. In this estate setting their height is desirable, but in a small plot the result would have been disastrous. The message is clear — always check the expected ultimate height before buying a conifer.

VIBURNUM
Viburnum

Deciduous or evergreen shrub

V. tinus

Flower time: Depends on species
Location: Sun or light shade
Propagation: Cuttings under glass/summer

A wide range of sizes, shapes and colours are available, but there are several features in common — all are easy to grow, hardy and do not need regular pruning. *V. opulus* 'Sterile' 2.5 m (8 ft) bears ball-like white flower heads in May. *V. tinus* produces its white flowers in winter.

VINCA
Periwinkle

Evergreen shrub

V. minor

Flower time: March—May
Location: Sun or partial shade
Propagation: Divide clumps in autumn

The trailing stems of this lowly plant root into the soil as they spread, and the tangled mass of shoots and oval leaves provide an effective ground cover. *V. major* 25 cm (10 in.) bears 3 cm (1 in.) wide flowers and is very invasive. *V. minor* 10 cm (4 in.) has smaller flowers.

VITIS
Ornamental Vine

Deciduous climber

V. coignetiae

Fruiting time: October
Location: Sun or partial shade
Propagation: Cuttings under glass/summer

Vines are generally grown for their fruit, but several are planted for the glowing colours of their autumn foliage. Vitis is not self-clinging — support is necessary. *V. coignetiae* 12 m (40 ft) bears tasteless purple fruit and red leaves in autumn. The leaves of *V. vinifera* 'Purpurea' are red, changing to purple.

WEIGELA
Weigela

Deciduous shrub

W. florida 'Variegata'

Flower time: May—June
Location: Sun or partial shade
Propagation: Hardwood cuttings/autumn

This shrub does best when grown in fertile soil and pruned annually, but it is reliable almost anywhere. *W. florida* 'Variegata' 1.5 m (5 ft) has pale pink flowers and variegated leaves. For brighter blooms choose a hybrid — *W.* 'Bristol Ruby' 2 m (7 ft) is the favourite one, bearing ruby red flowers.

WISTERIA
Wistaria

Deciduous climber

W. sinensis

Flower time: May—June
Location: Best in full sun
Propagation: Buy a new plant

The twining stems covered with hanging trails of pea-like flowers are a familiar sight in late spring. Plant in a sheltered spot. *W. sinensis* 15 m (50 ft) is the Chinese wistaria — the 30 cm (1 ft) long flower heads bear lilac blooms. *W. floribunda* 'Macrobotrys' has 60 cm (2 ft) flower heads.

YUCCA
Yucca

Evergreen shrub

Y. filamentosa

Flower time: July—August
Location: Best in full sun
Propagation: Rooted offsets/autumn

Despite its exotic appearance — sword-like leaves and large flower heads — it is quite hardy. *Y. filamentosa* has 60 cm (2 ft) long stiff leaves with white threads along the edges. Flower stalks are 1.5 m (5 ft) high. *Y. flaccida* bears less rigid leaves, but *Y. gloriosa* leaves are bayonet-pointed.

CHAPTER 9
GARDEN TROUBLES

A variety of troubles are going to occur in your garden. The nature of the plant is important here. Some hardy shrubs and trees may remain trouble-free all their lives, but an old shrub rose may be host to an assortment of pests and diseases. The weather is another basic factor — there will be slugs when it is wet, greenfly when it is dry, frost damage when it is cold and red spider mite damage when it is hot under glass. These problems affect both expert and novice alike — the big difference is that the expert knows what to look for, what steps to take in order to cut down the risk involved and what to do as soon as a serious problem occurs.

In the following pages you will find pictures and descriptions of a large number of problems. Many but not all are pests and diseases — disorders such as frost-damaged fruit blossom, and onions running to seed may not appear in the pest charts but are nevertheless important plant problems. In addition, you will also have to cope with weeds in beds, borders and the lawn.

It is not the intention of this chapter to frighten you — no matter how long you garden you will never see all the troubles on the following pages. On the contrary, the purpose of this chapter is to take away the worry of having problems you cannot identify and to tell you whether a preventive measure or treatment is necessary.

Garden troubles are tackled in two basic ways — culturally and chemically. In recent years there has been a dramatic shift in the relative importance of these two approaches. Until quite late in the 20th century we could rely on a large armoury of sprays to kill pests in the lawn, go inside the plant to tackle blights and mildew, destroy moss in the lawn without affecting the grass, and so on. These products are no longer available, and so we must now rely on good husbandry to a greater extent than we did a quarter of a century ago.

Avoiding trouble in the garden begins before you buy or sow the plant and ends with the proper disposal of the dead material when its life-span is over. It starts when you look at the planting site — you will have to pick plants which can flourish under such conditions. Next look for good stock — you can sometimes avoid future trouble at the buying stage by looking for *resistant* on the label. This means that the effect of the disease in question will be slight if it occurs — *immune* means that it cannot catch the disease.

Prevent trouble before it starts

CULTIVATE THE GROUND THOROUGHLY Pull out the roots of perennial weeds when cultivating soil prior to planting. If the soil is in poor condition you must incorporate organic matter.

CHOOSE THE RIGHT PLANTS Make sure the plant is suited to the site. Avoid sun-lovers if shade is a problem, do not pick tender types if the garden is exposed and prone to frosts, and forget about acid-loving plants if the ground is chalky. Next, buy good quality stock. Reject soft bulbs, lanky bedding plants and disease-ridden or damaged perennials and shrubs.

PLANT PROPERLY You have chosen the right plants and the soil is in a fit state to receive them, but you must also follow the rules for good planting. These rules ensure that there will be no air pockets and that the roots will spread into the garden soil in the minimum possible time. Successful seed sowing calls for sowing at the right time into soil in the right condition.

GUARD AGAINST ANIMALS Use netting to protect seedlings, vegetables and soft fruit from birds. A cylinder of wire netting around the trunk is the easiest way to keep rabbits, squirrels, cats and dogs away from the base of trees.

ROTATE CROPS IN THE VEGETABLE GARDEN It is wise to follow a crop rotation programme in the vegetable plot to avoid a build-up of soil pests and diseases which thrive on specific crops.

FEED PROPERLY Shortage of nutrients can lead to many problems — poor growth, undersized blooms, lowered disease resistance and discoloured leaves. Take care — overfeeding can cause scorch.

REMOVE RUBBISH, WEEDS ETC Rotting plants can be a source of infection — some actually attract pests to the garden. Boxes, old flower pots and so on are a breeding ground for slugs.

PESTS

A pest is an animal which attacks plants. Nearly all are insects (small creatures with six legs at the adult stage) and here are found the flies, caterpillars and beetles. A few small pests such as mites are often referred to as 'insects'. Some pests (e.g eelworms) are smaller than insects — others (e.g birds) are much larger.

DISEASES

A disease is a plant trouble caused by a living organism which is transmitted from one plant to another. Most diseases are caused by fungi, and there is a limited range of chemicals to prevent some of them attacking your plants. The other diseases, caused by bacteria and viruses, can rarely be controlled in this way.

DISORDERS

A disorder is a plant trouble which may have disease-like symptoms, but is not caused by a living organism. Unlike diseases they are caused, not caught. Disorders indicate that something is or has been wrong with the environment — common examples are waterlogging, water shortage, late frosts and shortage of a vital nutrient.

WEEDS

A weed is a plant growing in a place where you don't want it to be. The natural flora of the bed, border or lawn (the true wild flowers of your garden) are 'weeds' only because they are not wanted. Garden plants when they are in the wrong place, such as self-sown annuals in the rose bed, are also weeds.

Tackle trouble without delay

DON'T TRY TO KILL EVERYTHING

Not all insects are pests — many are positive allies in the war against plant troubles. Obviously these should not be harmed and neither should the majority of the insect population — the ones which are neither friends nor foes. There will be times when plant pests and diseases will attack, but even here small infestations of minor pests can be ignored or picked off by hand.

REMOVE BADLY INFECTED PLANTS

Do not leave sources of infection in the garden — remove and destroy incurable plants when this book tells you to do so.

EXAMINE DEAD PLANTS

Look at the soil ball and the ground which held the plant. If roots have not developed from the original soil ball, make sure you follow the rules for good planting next time. If the roots have rotted consider improving the drainage before replanting.

SPRAY IF YOU HAVE TO

Spraying is called for when an important pest is in danger of getting out of hand. Pesticides are safe to use in the way described on the label, but you must follow the instructions and precautions carefully. Look at the label carefully before making your choice. The front will tell you whether it is an insecticide, a fungicide or a herbicide. Make sure that the product is recommended for the plants you wish to spray. If it is to be used on fruit or vegetables check that the harvest interval is acceptable.

The leaves should be dry and the weather should be neither sunny nor windy. Use a fine forceful jet and spray thoroughly until the leaves are covered with liquid which is just beginning to run off. Do not spray open delicate blooms.

After spraying wash out the equipment, and wash hands and face. Do not keep any spray solution you have made up until next time and always store packs in a safe place. Do not keep unlabelled packs.

INSECTICIDES

Insecticides are products which kill insects and/or other small pests

- **NON-SYSTEMIC TYPES**
  The types available these days work by hitting and killing the pests — they do not work as preventives. Examples — insecticidal soap, pyrethrins.

- **SYSTEMIC TYPES**
  These work by going inside the plant and then moving in the sap stream. They have activity against pests which arrive after spraying. Examples — thiacloprid, imidacloprid.

Many of the products on the shelves are **chemical insecticides** which are modern complex materials. The number of active ingredients has been greatly reduced in recent years. These days we must rely much more on **organic insecticides** such as soaps, oils and pyrethrins. **Biological insecticides** are living organisms which are natural enemies of the pest in question — used mainly in greenhouses.

FUNGICIDES

Fungicides are products which are used to control diseases caused by fungi. They have no effect on cankers, leaf spots or diseases caused by bacteria or viruses

- **NON-SYSTEMIC TYPES**
  These work by providing a protective coat which kills fungal spores which arrive after spraying — repeat as instructed. Example — sulphur.

- **SYSTEMIC TYPES**
  These work by going inside the plant and then moving in the sap stream. Protection is better than with a non-systemic fungicide. There may be a minor curative effect. Example — myclobutanil.

Some of the products on the shelves are **chemical fungicides** which are modern complex materials. Many of the favourite ones have been withdrawn and the choice these days is very limited. You will also find 'green' fungicides which are based on simple age-old remedies such as copper salts and sulphur.

Flower troubles

The major problems	Border perennials	Bulbs	Bedding plants	Rockery plants
INSECT PESTS & DISEASES	page	page	page	page
APHID	147		147	
BULB ROT		147		
CAPSID BUG	147			
CATERPILLAR	147			147
CUTWORM	147		147	147
FOOT & ROOT ROT			147	
GREY MOULD	147			147
NARCISSUS FLY		148		
POWDERY MILDEW	148			
SLUGS & SNAILS	148		148	148
STEM & BULB EELWORM		148		
THRIPS		148		
TULIP FIRE		148		
VINE WEEVIL		148		
VIRUS	148	148		
ANIMAL PESTS				
BIRDS				164
CATS			164	
DISORDERS				
DROUGHT			162	162
FROST			162	
WATERLOGGING	163			163

Powdery mildew on Michaelmas daisy

Yellow stripe virus on Narcissus

APHID

There are many species of aphid (greenfly and blackfly) in colours ranging from white to black. Common ones include the black bean aphid and peach-potato aphid. Nearly all flowering plants may be attacked — infestations are worst in warm, settled weather. Young growth is distorted and weakened, the leaves may be twisted and discoloured and both the quality and quantity of the floral display is reduced. Infested buds may fail to open. Some aphids pose an additional threat as carriers of virus diseases. Another damaging effect is caused by the honeydew which these pests deposit on the leaves — this sticky layer becomes covered with light-robbing **sooty mould**. Spray with a greenfly killer when colonies are first seen — repeat as recommended. Sprays include thiacloprid, pyrethrum and horticultural soap.

CATERPILLAR

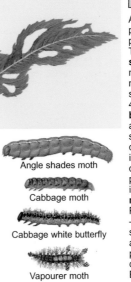

Angle shades moth

Cabbage moth

Cabbage white butterfly

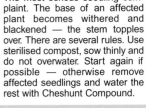
Vapourer moth

A wide variety of leaf-eating caterpillars attack annuals and perennials in the flower garden. The 5 cm velvety smooth **angle shades moth** can be a serious nuisance on dahlia, gladiolus and many border perennials. The 3 cm smooth **cabbage moth** and the 4 cm slightly hairy **cabbage white butterfly** attack several annuals and perennials and may skeletonize the leaves. The 2.5 cm colourful and hairy **vapourer moth** is a tree and shrub pest but may damage the leaves of some border perennials. There are others, including the pink **rosy rustic moth** and the **garden tiger moth**. Pick off the caterpillars if practical — if the damage is widespread spray with an insecticide such as acetamiprid, permethrin or pirimiphos-methyl. For biological control use the bacterium B. thuringiensis.

BULB ROT

Basal rot

Never plant soft or mouldy bulbs and remove rotten bulbs from store. **Smoulder** causes narcissus bulbs to decay — fungal growths appear on the surface. **Basal rot** begins at the base of narcissus and lily bulbs — the brown rot spreads upwards. **Tulip fire** can be serious (see page 148) — fungal growths appear on the skin.

DAMPING OFF

The most serious seedling complaint. The base of an affected plant becomes withered and blackened — the stem topples over. There are several rules. Use sterilised compost, sow thinly and do not overwater. Start again if possible — otherwise remove affected seedlings and water the rest with Cheshunt Compound.

CAPSID BUG

These sap-sucking bugs attack dahlia, chrysanthemum and many other flowers. At first the leaves are spotted — as the foliage expands brown-edged ragged holes appear. Buds may be killed — if they open the flowers are lop-sided. Spray plants and the ground below with a contact insecticide such as pyrethrins.

FOOT & ROOT ROT

Numerous fungi can attack the roots and stem bases. Above ground the leaves turn yellow and wilt — below ground the roots are blackened and rotten. Young and weak plants are the most susceptible. There is no cure — dig up and burn badly diseased plants, improve drainage and do not replant with the same type.

CUTWORM

The 5 cm green, grey or brown caterpillars live just below the soil surface. They can be a serious pest, feeding on the surface at night and severing the stems of young plants at ground level. July-August is the danger period. Hoe around healthy plants in an affected area — pick up and destroy caterpillars brought to the surface.

GREY MOULD

Grey mould (**botrytis**) is a fungal disease which can be destructive in wet weather. Affected areas on leaves, stems and flowers become rotten and a fluffy mould grows over the surface. Avoid poor drainage, overwatering, overcrowding and too much nitrogen. Remove badly diseased plants. Chemical sprays are not available.

NARCISSUS FLY

The flies lay eggs in the bulb necks of narcissus, hyacinth, iris and snowdrop as the foliage dies down. After hatching the grubs burrow into the bulbs and feed on the central core. Affected bulbs are hollow and produce few leaves and no flowers. Do not plant soft bulbs — rake soil up around the necks as leaves wither after flowering.

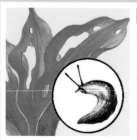

POWDERY MILDEW

A white mealy coating covers the leaf surface. It is encouraged by overcrowding and lack of moisture at the roots. Plants which may be badly affected include michaelmas daisy, delphinium and chrysanthemum. Spray with myclobutanil at the first sign of disease and 7 days later. Repeat if disease reappears.

SLUGS & SNAILS

A menace in the garden, especially if the weather is wet and cool. Irregular holes appear in the leaves and tell-tale slime trails can be seen. Plants attractive to slugs include hosta, delphinium, tulip, iris, annuals and alpines. The pests hide under debris and come out at night, so clear away garden rubbish. For control see page 155.

Phlox

Narcissus

STEM & BULB EELWORM

A number of types of these tiny worms occur and each one attacks a specific group of plants. The phlox eelworm is a pest of phlox, gypsophila, evening primrose, aubretia and solidago. The young leaves of infested plants are strap-like and die off prematurely. Older leaves are distorted and few flowers appear. Several types of stem & bulb eelworm attack bulbous plants. Affected daffodil, tulip and hyacinth bulbs are soft and rotten — when cut open tell-tale dark rings can be seen inside. Foliage and flowers are pale, twisted and distorted — characteristic small yellow swellings appear on the surface of infested narcissus leaves. There are no control chemicals you can use. Dig up and burn infested plants and throw away soft and rotten bulbs. Do not replant with susceptible plants or bulbs for at least 3 years.

THRIPS

Silvery flecking and streaking occur on flowers and leaves. The minute black or yellow flies are just visible and attacks are worst in hot weather. Gladiolus is particularly susceptible. An insecticide such as acetamiprid, horticultural soap etc can be used, but thrips are usually ignored. Water the plants during dry spells.

TULIP FIRE

A serious disease of tulips. Scorched areas occur on the leaves — the flowers are spotted. Young shoots are covered with a grey mould and the bulbs rot (see page 147). Cut off diseased emerging shoots below ground level. Manzoceb which was used to stop the disease spreading is no longer available.

VINE WEEVIL

These wrinkled white grubs are extremely destructive underground both outdoors and under glass. The roots of many plants may be attacked, but the favourite targets are alpines and plants growing in containers. If a plant suddenly dies, look in the soil for this rolled-up grub. Imidacloprid is a long-lasting preventative.

Normal   Infected

VIRUS

Numerous viruses attack flowering plants and all sorts of distortions, discolorations and growth problems may be produced. Affected leaves may be all-yellow or they may be covered with yellow spots or patches (**mosaic**). Stems or leaves may be covered with brown stripes (**streak**) and flowers may show patches or streaks of abnormal colour (**colour break**). Leaves may be crinkled, distorted or white-veined and the plants may be killed, stunted or not noticeably affected. Viruses are carried by insects, tools or fingers and there is no cure. Buy healthy stock — destroy infected plants, but only if you are sure of the diagnosis. Do not handle healthy plants after you have touched diseased ones and do not take cuttings from virus-infected stock. Keep aphids and other sap-sucking pests under control.

Tree, Shrub & Rose troubles

The major problems	Trees & Shrubs	Roses
INSECT PESTS & DISEASES	page	page
APHID	150	150
CANKER	150	150
CATERPILLAR	150	
CORAL SPOT	150	
DIEBACK	150	150
FIREBLIGHT	150	
HONEY FUNGUS	150	150
LEAF MINER	150	
PEACH LEAF CURL	151	
PHYTOPHTHORA ROT	151	
ROSE BLACK SPOT		151
ROSE MILDEW		151
ROSE RUST		151
ROSE SICKNESS		151
SHOT HOLE BORER	151	
SILVER LEAF	151	
ANIMAL PESTS		
DEER	164	
DOGS	164	
RABBITS	164	
DISORDERS		
BALLING		162
DROUGHT	162	162
NUTRIENT SHORTAGE		163
POOR PLANTING DAMAGE	163	163
SPRING SCORCH	163	
WATERLOGGING	163	163
WEEDKILLER DAMAGE		163
WINTER DAMAGE	163	

Silver leaf on Ornamental plum

Coral spot on Judas tree

WHY TREES & SHRUBS DIE

- Old age
- Wind rock
- Poor site preparation
- Fatal pests & diseases
- Frost damage • Spring scorch
- Poor choice
- Poor planting
- Water shortage
- Rabbits and Deer
- Poor-quality planting material

APHID

The commonest and most serious of all rose pests. The first clusters of greenfly feed on the sap of tender young shoots in spring and vigour is seriously reduced. Shoots and leaves are distorted and infested buds may fail to open. Sticky honeydew is secreted and this is soon covered by a black fungus (**sooty mould**). Aphids may be orange, red, green or black and few shrubs or trees are immune. Each species has its own range of host plants — this may be restricted to just one or two (e.g juniper aphid) or there may be a wide variety of susceptible garden plants (e.g peach-potato aphid). Spraying before aphids become serious is recommended for roses — use a systemic insecticide such as thiacloprid or a contact one such as pyrethrins or horticultural soap. Repeat as instructed if aphids return.

CORAL SPOT

Raised pink spots appear on the branches. Dead wood is the breeding ground for the fungus, and the air-borne spores infect living trees and shrubs through wounds. The effect can be fatal, so never leave dead wood laying about. Cut out affected areas, going well beyond the patch of pink pustules on the bark. Burn all prunings.

DIEBACK

Shoots may die back, beginning at the tip and progressing steadily downwards, for a number of reasons. The cause may be a disease, such as canker, rose mildew or rose black spot, or there may be a cultural problem such as drought, waterlogging or nutrient deficiency. Cut off and burn the affected shoot.

CANKER

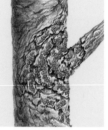

A general term for a diseased area on the bark. The canker is usually cracked and sunken, and will kill the branch if neglected and allowed to encircle it. Some attack a wide range of woody plants — others are specific. Rose canker can be a problem. Take care when hoeing — cut out and burn all of the diseased wood.

FIREBLIGHT

A devastating disease of shrubs and trees of the rose family. The tell-tale sign is the presence of brown wilted leaves which do not fall. Cankers develop on the bark and diseased shoots die back — cut out affected branches to 60 cm (2 ft) below the brown leaves. Trees die when the trunk is infected — remove and burn.

CATERPILLAR

Leaf-eating caterpillars are more serious on trees, shrubs and roses than in the flower garden — some species of these pests form large colonies and all the leaves on a shrub may be stripped with only the veins remaining. The 5 cm **buff-tip moth** attacks numerous trees, some shrubs and roses. The black and yellow 'looper' caterpillar of the **magpie moth** is smaller but is also more damaging — some shrubs may be defoliated. The green 'looper' **winter moth** devours young leaves and may spin them together and the 2.5 cm colourful **vapourer moth** feeds on trees, shrubs and roses from May to August. Pick off caterpillars if practical — if the damage is widespread spray with an insecticide such as thiacloprid, acetamiprid or pyrethrins. Pick off 'tents' of tent-making caterpillars.

Buff-tip moth

Magpie moth

Winter moth

Vapourer moth

HONEY FUNGUS

A common cause of the death of shrubs and trees. A white fan of fungal growth occurs below the bark near ground level. On roots black 'bootlaces' are found. Toadstools appear in autumn at the base. Burn diseased stems and roots and replant with non-woody types. Chemical treatments are no longer available.

LEAF MINER

Blisters or long winding mines are produced by small grubs feeding on the tissues within the leaf. Many trees and shrubs can be affected, including holly, lilac, rose, privet, honeysuckle, azalea and birch. Pick off and destroy damaged leaves, but it is a minor problem so spraying with a systemic insecticide is rarely worthwhile.

PEACH LEAF CURL

This serious disease of ornamental cherries, almonds etc leads to early leaf fall and weakening of the tree. The leaves are infected in spring and large reddish blisters develop. The fungus overwinters between the bud scales and not on fallen leaves, so spray with copper in mid-February, 2 weeks later and again at leaf fall.

PHYTOPHTHORA ROT

The soil fungus first kills the roots around the main stem, later spreading to other roots. The bark and the roots in the affected area are usually blackened. An important disease of ornamental cherries and many other trees — leaves are small and sparse, stems die back. Avoid waterlogged sites. There is no cure — dig out and burn.

ROSE BLACK SPOT

The tell-tale signs are black spots with yellow edges. As the disease develops the yellow areas spread, premature leaf fall takes place and stems may die back. The fungus overwinters on stems and fallen leaves — infection takes place early in the season although the symptoms may not be clearly visible until July. The severity of the attack depends on the variety (shrub roses are usually less resistant than modern hybrids), the location (pure air encourages the disease) and the growing conditions (black spot thrives in warm, wet weather). It is difficult to control. Remove and burn fallen leaves and cut off black-spotted stems when pruning. Spraying is necessary with susceptible varieties. Apply myclobutanil when leaf buds are opening and repeat 7 days later. Spray again when first spots appear — repeat every 2 weeks.

ROSE RUST

Not common, but it is often fatal when it strikes. Orange swellings which turn black in August appear on the underside of the leaves. New shoots turn reddish and shrivel. It is encouraged by a cold spring following a hard winter and by potash shortage in the soil. Apply myclobutanil when first seen — repeat as directed.

ROSE MILDEW

This form of powdery mildew is the most widespread rose disease. A white, powdery mould develops on leaves, buds and shoots. Affected leaves curl and may fall prematurely — diseased buds may not open properly. The disease is encouraged by closed-in conditions, dryness at the roots, poor feeding and by hot days which are followed by cold nights. Climbers growing against walls are especially susceptible — ensure there is adequate air space between the wires and the bricks. Some roses are much more resistant than others — check before buying. Cut off and burn badly infected shoots when pruning, use a balanced and not a nitrogen-rich fertilizer when feeding and mulch in spring. Spray with myclobutanil or triticonazole when the first spots are seen — repeat every 2 weeks.

ROSE SICKNESS

If the site has grown roses for more than 10 years then it is liable to be rose-sick. The old roses on the site may show little or no ill-effects, but planting a new rose in such soil can result in poor growth (**replant disease**). For this reason the topsoil in the planting area should be changed. If it is not practical to provide new soil 60 x 60 x 60 cm (2 x 2 x 2 ft) for each new rose to be planted then you can help matters by adding a liberal amount of compost or well-rotted manure plus a dressing of high-nitrogen fertilizer to the remaining soil before planting. This should reduce but not eliminate the effect of replant disease.

SHOT HOLE BORER

Several types of shot hole borer or **bark beetle** attack ornamental trees — the **elm bark beetle** carrying dutch elm disease is the best known. Small round holes appear in the bark and the layer beneath is usually mined with tunnels. There is no cure. Maintain good growing conditions and remove damaged branches.

SILVER LEAF

The spores enter through wounds and the first sign is a silvery look to the leaves. It is a serious disease of ornamental cherry — other hosts include laburnum, hawthorn, willow and rhododendron (leaves not silvered). Dieback occurs and wood is stained. Cut back to clean wood before July — dig out bracket toadstools if they appear.

Vegetable troubles

The major problems	Beans & Peas	Brassicas	Carrots & Parsnips	Lettuces	Onions & Leeks	Potatoes	Spinach & Beetroot	Tomatoes & Cucumbers
INSECT PESTS & DISEASES	page	page	page	page	page	page	page	page
APHID	153		153	153			153	153
CABBAGE CATERPILLAR		153						
CABBAGE ROOT FLY		153						
CARROT FLY			153					
CLUBROOT		153						
DOWNY MILDEW				153			153	153
EELWORM					153	153		
FLEA BEETLE		154						
GREY MOULD				154				154
LEAF SPOT	154							
MANGOLD FLY							154	
MEALY APHID	154							
NECK ROT					154			
ONION FLY					154			
PARSNIP CANKER			154					
PEA MOTH	155							
POTATO BLIGHT						155		155
SLUGS & SNAILS		155		155		155		
VIRUS						155		155
WHITE ROT					155			
WIREWORM						155		
ANIMAL PESTS								
BIRDS	164	164		164				
DISORDERS								
BLOSSOM END ROT								162
BOLTING				162	162		162	

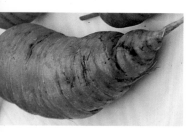

Carrot fly

Pea moth

Blossom end rot

APHID

Broad bean

Potato

You may find greenfly or blackfly on many different vegetables, but the severity of the attack depends on the type of vegetable grown as well as the weather. The black bean aphid is the most serious of all broad bean pests — stunting growth, damaging the flowers and distorting pods. Onions, on the other hand, are avoided by greenfly. Infestations are worst in hot, settled weather — carrot leaves are discoloured, lettuce is puckered and blackened, and potato leaflets turn brown. In some cases aphids do far more harm by spreading virus diseases than by sucking sap from the host plants. The answer is to spray thoroughly with an insecticide as soon as the colonies begin to build up — repeat as instructed if the weather remains warm and dry. Sprays include thiacloprid, horticultural soap and rape oil.

CABBAGE CATERPILLAR

Holes appear in the leaves of brassicas such as cabbage, cauliflower and broccoli. The 2.5 cm **small cabbage white** is velvety — the 4 cm **large cabbage white** is slightly hairy and the **cabbage moth** is smooth. Attacks are worst in hot, dry weather. Pick off if practical or spray with thiacloprid or acetamiprid.

CABBAGE ROOT FLY

The tell-tale sign is blue-tinged foliage which wilts in sunny weather — recent transplants are particularly susceptible. Small maggots eat the roots, leaving a blackened stump. Young plants are killed, older cabbages fail to heart and cauliflowers form tiny heads. Place felt discs around base of the stems.

CARROT FLY

The tell-tale sign is reddish foliage which wilts in sunny weather — at a later stage the leaves turn yellow. The 5 mm maggots are a serious pest of carrot, parsnip and celery — seedlings are killed, mature roots are riddled. Delay sowing maincrop carrots until June — lift as soon as practical. Sow thinly — destroy all thinnings.

CLUBROOT

The tell-tale sign of this brassica disease is discoloured foliage which wilts in sunny weather. Roots become swollen — it can be disastrous in a wet season. Ensure land is free-draining and well limed before planting — no chemicals are available for prevention of the disease. Do not use land for brassicas for several years.

DOWNY MILDEW

Pea

Lettuce

A leaf disease which affects a wide range of vegetables. Discoloured blotches appear on the upper surface and below them on the undersurface are grey or purple mouldy areas — these patches may spread to cover the whole surface. It thrives in cool and wet conditions. On peas and beans the undersurface patches are pale purple and the infected pods are spotted and distorted. On members of the cabbage family the underleaf patches are white and furry — it is usually restricted to young plants. It can be serious on lettuce — large pale patches appear between the veins on the upper leaf surface of older leaves. Onion leaves shrivel from the tips and the bulbs are soft. Practise crop rotation. Avoid overcrowding. Do not overwater seedlings. Chemical sprays are no longer available.

EELWORM

Root-knot eelworm

Potato cyst eelworm

These microscopic worm-like creatures (**nematodes**) live in the soil and can be a menace to a number of vegetables. There are several types with their particular list of hosts. **Root-knot eelworm** causes gall-like growths on the roots of cucumber, lettuce, tomato and french beans. Leaves are discoloured — growth is stunted. **Potato cyst eelworm** produces pinhead-sized cysts on the roots of tomato and potato. Leaves wilt, growth is stunted and potato haulm dies down prematurely. **Stem & bulb eelworm** causes distorted leaves which are often swollen — onion is the main host but peas, beans and carrots may be attacked. There is no cure for eelworm. Lift and burn infested plants — do not grow susceptible varieties in the soil which is infested with eelworm for at least 6 years.

FLEA BEETLE

A pest of seedlings of the cabbage family which can be serious during warm and dry spells in April and May. Small round holes can be seen in the leaves and growth may be checked. The tiny beetles jump when disturbed. Spray or dust with pyrethrins when the first attacks are noticed. Water if the weather is dry.

MANGOLD FLY

Small white grubs of the mangold fly burrow inside the leaves of beetroot, producing blisters which turn brown and shrivel. Attacks occur from May onwards. Growth of young plants is retarded and their yield is reduced, but attacks on older plants have little effect. Remove damaged leaves — spray with pyrethrins.

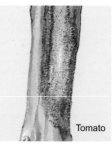

Lettuce

Tomato

GREY MOULD

Grey mould (**botrytis**) attacks plants through damaged areas and can spread to all the above-ground parts. Affected areas are usually brown and soft at first and then are covered with a grey or pale brown fluffy mould. Nearly all types of vegetables may be affected and it is encouraged by cool, wet and badly ventilated situations. On brassica leaves it often follows frost damage — on peas and beans the pods develop a velvety coating in wet weather. Infected lettuce plants turn reddish-brown at the base and may break off at stem level. Infected tomato stems bear grey furry patches and the fruit may show spots (**ghost spotting**) on the surface. The standard treatment is to remove diseased parts or whole plants — chemical sprays are no longer available. Always remove decaying leaves, fruit etc to prevent infection.

MEALY APHID

Large clusters of waxy, greyish greenflies can be found on the underside of leaves and on the stem tips of brassicas from June onwards in hot, dry weather. Affected leaves turn yellow — **sooty mould** may develop and brussels sprouts can be ruined. Not easy to control — spray with pyrethrins.

NECK ROT

A storage disease of onions — greyish mould develops near the neck and the bulbs turn soft and rotten. Follow the rules for proper storage — dry the bulbs thoroughly and store only hard, undamaged ones in a cool place. Don't store bulbs with fleshy, green necks. Remove rotten bulbs. Treated seed is available.

LEAF SPOT

A number of different fungi can cause dark spots to appear on the leaves of vegetables. With beetroot, lettuce and spinach the spots are small and brown — the central area of each spot may drop out. The effect is unsightly but the result is not usually serious. **Leaf & pod spot** attacks peas — brown sunken spots appear on the pods and stems. Several leaf spot diseases attack brassicas — the usual one is **ring spot** which causes brown rings on the older leaves. There are a number of other types — celery leaf spot, chocolate spot (broad beans), anthracnose (beans and cucumbers) etc. As a general rule leaf spots are encouraged by wet weather and overcrowding. Practise crop rotation. Remove diseased parts. Chemical treatment is no longer available. Lift and burn badly diseased plants.

Spinach

Pea

ONION FLY

The tell-tale sign of this onion pest is yellow drooping foliage. The 8 mm white maggots burrow into the base of the bulbs — young plants are frequently killed and older ones fail to develop properly. Attacks are worst in dry weather. Firm the soil around the plants — hoe regularly. Remove all thinnings from the site.

PARSNIP CANKER

The tops of parsnip roots become cracked and blackened — the tissues below may rot. A soil-borne fungus may be responsible, but this disease is usually linked with poor growing conditions, such as acid or starved soil and irregular rainfall. Don't sow too early. Next year choose a resistant variety such as Avonresister.

PEA MOTH

Maggoty peas are a familiar problem. The 8 mm greenish caterpillars burrow through the pods and into the peas, making them unusable. The best way to avoid trouble is to sow a quick-maturing variety either early or late in the season. Spraying with a contact insecticide 7-10 days after the start of flowering is less effective.

POTATO BLIGHT

Potato

Tomato

The first signs are brown patches on potato or tomato leaves — in damp weather each blight spot on the underside has a fringe of white mould. This disease can destroy all the foliage in a wet season. The disease does not travel down the stems to the tubers — the fungal spores are washed off the leaves and on to the soil by rain. If the tubers come into contact with live spores when harvesting then the tubers will develop blight in store. To prevent this from happening earth up the stems to keep the tubers covered and then cut off and remove all diseased growth 10 days before lifting. Infected tomatoes develop brown, sunken areas and soon rot. Spray potato plants with a copper fungicide in July — treat tomatoes as soon as they have been stopped. Repeat every 2 weeks if the weather is damp.

SLUGS & SNAILS

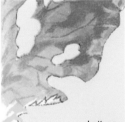

Lettuce

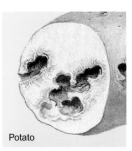

Potato

Generally regarded as enemy No.1 in the garden, especially when the weather is wet and cool. They are not usually seen during the day, so look for the tell-tale slime trails. Young plants are particularly susceptible and may be killed — the leaves of lettuce, brassicas, celery etc are holed and stems are damaged. Potato tubers may be riddled by the underground keeled slug. Keep the surrounding area free from rubbish. The standard method of control is to scatter slug pellets thinly around the plants at the first sign of attack. Non-chemical methods of killing or deterring slugs and snails are using traps filled with beer, placing a ring of gritty sand around individual plants and applying slug-killing nematodes to the soil. On heavy land avoid planting slug-susceptible potato varieties such as Cara and Maris Piper.

VIRUS

Cucumber mosaic virus

Potato leaf roll virus

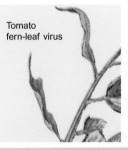

Tomato fern-leaf virus

Virus diseases attack many vegetables and there is no cure. The main carriers are aphids, but there are other pests which take viruses from plant to plant — weevils, whiteflies, beetles etc. Infection may also be due to tools or hands which have touched diseased plants. There are numerous types — the most widespread are the **mosaic virus** diseases and the usual cause is the **cucumber mosaic virus**. Plants susceptible to attack by one or more of the mosaic viruses include marrows, cucumbers, beans, turnips, lettuces, potatoes and tomatoes. Affected leaves are mottled with yellow and dark green patches — the surface becomes puckered and distorted. The plants are severely stunted and may collapse. **Mottle virus** produces more diffuse patches of yellow than the mosaic viruses — carrots can be badly affected. Potatoes are the crop most likely to suffer from disease if virus-free seed is not used, and **leaf roll virus** is the one most likely to occur. **Tomato fern-leaf virus** is a common complaint of tomatoes — leaflets are extremely narrow. Tackling virus diseases involves several steps. Destroy badly infected plants. Buy virus-free seed or plants. Spray to control sap-sucking insects. Wash hands and tools after handling infected plants. Do not touch tomato plants after smoking.

WHITE ROT

A serious disease of onions which is worst in hot, dry summers. A fluffy white mould in which small black fungal bodies are embedded grows on the base of the bulbs. The foliage turns yellow and wilts. There is no chemical treatment — lift and burn the diseased plants. Do not grow onions on infected land for at least 5 years.

WIREWORM

These pests can be a problem in new gardens and in plots adjoining grassland. They are slow moving — not active like the friendly centipede. Wireworms eat the roots of many vegetables and burrow into potato tubers. There is no chemical to use — good soil preparation and regular cultivation are the answer.

Tree Fruit troubles

The major problems	Apples	Pears	Plums	Cherries
INSECT PESTS & DISEASES	page	page	page	page
APHID	157	157		157
APPLE CANKER	157	157		
APPLE SAWFLY	157			
BACTERIAL CANKER			157	157
BLOSSOM WILT	157	157	157	
BROWN ROT	157		157	157
CATERPILLAR	157	157		
CODLING MOTH	157			
FIREBLIGHT	157			
HONEY FUNGUS	158			
PEACH/CHERRY SLUGWORM		158		158
PEAR MIDGE		158		
PEAR STONY PIT		158		
PLUM SAWFLY			158	
POWDERY MILDEW	158			
RED SPIDER MITE	158		158	
SCAB	158	158		
SILVER LEAF			158	158
WASP		158	158	
ANIMAL PESTS				
BIRDS			164	164
DISORDERS				
FRUIT DROP	162	162	162	

Brown rot

Bacterial canker

APHID

Several species of greenfly attack tree fruit — cherry foliage can be severely distorted by blackfly. The usual symptom of aphid infestation is curling of the young foliage — shoot growth is stunted and sticky honeydew coats young stems and leaves. Spray with thiacloprid at green cluster — repeat if necessary.

BROWN ROT

Infected fruit turns brown and concentric rings of yellowish mould appear. Most tree fruit can be affected, but the disease is worst on apples. It is necessary to destroy diseased fruit as soon as it is seen on the tree or on the ground. Store only sound fruit and examine them at regular intervals. Spraying is not effective.

APPLE CANKER

The bark shrinks and cracks in concentric rings. A tell-tale sign is the presence of red growths in winter. A serious disease of apples and pears, especially on badly-drained soil. Cut off damaged twigs — cut out cankers from stems and branches and treat with a wound paint. Copper sprays at leaf fall help to prevent canker.

CATERPILLAR

There are a number of caterpillars which eat the leaves of apples, pears, plums etc. The 2.5 cm colourful **vapourer moth** feeds on the foliage from May to August and the 5 cm black and yellow **buff-tip moth** can defoliate a young tree. The most important group are the 'looper' caterpillars which move with a looping action and may spin young leaves together. New foliage is devoured in spring and they then feed on the petals and flower stalks later in the season. All grow to about 3 cm but there are various colours. **March moth** is green with pale green stripes, **winter moth** is green and yellow, and the **mottled umber moth** is brown and yellow. Trees can be protected by encircling each trunk with a grease band — alternatively you can spray with thiacloprid before or after blossom time when they are seen.

Mottled umber moth

Winter moth

Vapourer moth

APPLE SAWFLY

A ribbon-like scar is produced on the surface of the fruit. Later the grub burrows down to feed on the central core which causes the fruit to drop in June and July. The grubs go into the ground in July. Sticky frass can be seen around the hole. Spray with thiacloprid at petal fall to prevent attack — burn all damaged apples.

BACTERIAL CANKER

A serious disease of plums, cherries and other stone fruit. Pale-edged spots appear on the leaves — at a later stage gum oozes from the bark and affected branches die back. Tackle it promptly to save the tree. Cut out diseased branches and apply a wound paint. Apply a copper spray in August, September and October.

CODLING MOTH

The pale pink grub bores into developing fruit and feeds on the central core — the tell-tale sign of codling moth attack is sawdust-like frass. Apples are the main host but pears and plums may also be attacked. Grubs can be found inside the fruit in July and August. Spray with pyrethrins in mid June — repeat 3 weeks later.

BLOSSOM WILT

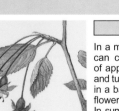

In a mild, wet spring this disease can cause the blossom trusses of apples, pears and plums to wilt and turn brown — shoots are killed in a bad attack. Remove infected flowers and dead twigs in spring. In summer remove all fruit affected by brown rot. A winter tar oil spray was the standard preventative treatment but is no longer available.

FIREBLIGHT

A serious disease of pears which can occur on apples. Affected shoots wilt and die. Old cankers ooze in spring. The tell-tale sign is the presence of brown withered leaves which do not fall. Cut out affected branches to 60 cm (2 ft) below the brown leaves. Trees die when the trunk is infected — lift and burn.

HONEY FUNGUS

Honey fungus is a common cause of the death of apple trees. A white fan of fungal growth occurs below the bark near ground level. On roots black 'bootlaces' are found. Toadstools appear in autumn at the base. Destroy stems and roots of diseased trees. The use of a phenolic drench around the trees is no longer permitted.

POWDERY MILDEW

A major disease of apples which may also attack pears — young leaves, shoots and flower trusses are covered with greyish-white mould in spring. Growth is stunted, leaves may fall and fruit may fail to set. Remove infected twigs. For chemical control use a spray containing myclobutanil — repeat as instructed.

PEAR/CHERRY SLUGWORM

These slimy, slug-like insects are the larval stage of the pear and cherry sawfly — they attack the leaves of pears, cherries, apples and plums between June and October. The slugworm feeds on the upper surface of the leaf, producing irregular shaped papery windows. Spray with a contact insecticide if the attack is severe.

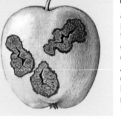

RED SPIDER MITE

The first sign of attack on apples and plums is a faint mottling of the upper leaf surface. In warm, dry weather the infestation may be severe — the leaves turn bronze, become brittle and die. Look for the tiny mites on the underside of the leaves. Spray with pyrethrins in late May and repeat if necessary 3 weeks later.

PEAR MIDGE

A serious pear pest. Fruitlets which have been attacked start to turn black a few weeks after petal fall and usually drop from the tree. Inside the fallen fruit there is a large cavity in which there are numerous 3 mm pale buff grubs. Pick and burn blackened fruit and keep the soil around the trunk well cultivated.

SCAB

A serious disease of apples and pears — leaves are spotted, twigs are blistered and the dark-coloured scabs on young fruit develop into large corky areas. Attacks are worst in warm, damp weather. Mancozeb is no longer available. Spray with myclobutanil and repeat every 14 days.

PEAR STONY PIT

This virus disease of pears is dangerous — affected trees have to be dug up and destroyed. Diseased fruits are small and mis-shapen with the surface covered with dimples and lumps. The flesh is woody and inedible. It usually occurs on old trees and it can spread to surrounding pears. Always buy virus-free stock.

SILVER LEAF

The most serious disease of plums which can also affect apples, cherries and peaches. The spores enter through a wound, and the first sign is silvering of the leaves. Dieback occurs and the wood is stained. Cut out dead branches before July to 15 cm below the infection — dig out bracket toad-stools if they appear on the bark.

PLUM SAWFLY

The tell-tale sign of this serious pest of plums is a hole surrounded by black sticky frass on the surface of the fruit. Inside can be found the 1 cm creamy-white grub of the plum sawfly. Damaged fruits fall to the ground before maturity. Cultivate the soil around the trees. Thiacloprid can be sprayed 7 days before petal fall to prevent attack.

WASP

All types of fruit may be attacked by wasps. Soft-skinned types such as plums are favoured and may be completely devoured. Apples and pears usually escape if the surface is undamaged. Spraying is not effective — the answer is to find the nest and destroy it with a chemical wasp-killer. Do this job at dusk.

Soft Fruit troubles

The major problems	Blackberries	Blackcurrants	Gooseberries	Raspberries	Strawberries
INSECT PESTS & DISEASES	page	page	page	page	page
AMERICAN MILDEW		160			
APHID	160	160	160	160	160
BIG BUD MITE		160			
CANE SPOT	160			160	
CAPSID BUG	160	160	160		
GALL MIDGE		160			
GOOSEBERRY SAWFLY			160		
GREY MOULD	160	160		160	160
LEAF SPOT		160	160		
MAGPIE MOTH			161		
RASPBERRY BEETLE				161	
RASPBERRY MOTH	161			161	
RUST	161	161	161		
SLUGS & SNAILS					161
SPIDER MITE		161			161
SPUR BLIGHT	161			161	
STRAWBERRY MILDEW					161
VIRUS		161		161	161
ANIMAL PESTS					
BIRDS			164	164	164

A fruit cage is the ideal way of protecting canes and bushes against attack by birds, but for the average gardener the answer is to drape netting over the plants.

AMERICAN MILDEW

A crippling disease of gooseberries which appears on the young leaves and later on the fruits as a white mould which changes to brown. It is encouraged by overcrowding. Cut out diseased branches in September — next year spray with myclobutanil when first flowers open and repeat twice at 2 week intervals.

APHID

Blister aphid

Leaf-curling aphid

Numerous types of aphid attack soft fruit and the damage they do can be serious. In some cases there is severe leaf distortion, but the main danger is usually due to the viruses they carry. Currants are attacked by **currant blister aphid** which produces coloured blisters on the leaves. Both **lettuce aphid** and **gooseberry aphid** cause severe leaf curling on goose-berries. Two aphid species attack raspberries — the **rubus aphid** and the stem-coating **raspberry aphid**. Strawberries can be invaded by other species — the **strawberry aphid** and the more serious **shallot aphid** which can cripple the plant. A winter phenolic spray to kill the eggs is no longer permitted. The usual treatment is to apply a contact insecticide such as thiacloprid when the pests appear and then repeat the spray as recommended.

BIG BUD MITE

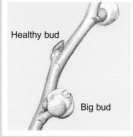

Healthy bud

Big bud

The tell-tale sign is the presence of winter buds which are swollen and less pointed than normal — in spring these infested buds fail to open. The microscopic mites enter the buds in summer — they are carriers of the reversion virus (page 161). Pick off enlarged buds in winter — dig up and burn badly infested plants.

CANE SPOT

In early summer small purple spots appear on raspberry and logan-berry canes — these spots increase in size to form shallow white pits with purple borders. Canes may be killed. Cut out badly diseased canes in autumn. Fungicides which were formerly recommended for this disease are no longer available.

CAPSID BUG

All types are attacked, especially currants and gooseberries. Small bugs puncture the leaf surface, producing brown spots. As the leaves expand these spots turn into ragged brown-edged holes. Not easy to control — if the trouble occurs each year apply a fatty acid spray when first flowers open and again at fruit set.

GALL MIDGE

The gall midge or **leaf midge** is a serious pest of blackcurrants. The small maggots at the shoot tips cause the young foliage to become twisted, distorted and discoloured — these leaves usually turn black as they develop. Affected shoots may die. It is not easy to control — cut out and burn affected shoot tips.

GOOSEBERRY SAWFLY

This 2.5 cm spotted caterpillar is a serious pest of gooseberries and currants — a bush can be com-pletely defoliated in a few days. Keep careful watch from May onwards — the caterpillars feed at the edges of the leaf tissue. Spray with a systemic insecticide such as thiacloprid — a second spray may be necessary.

GREY MOULD

This fluffy mould is destructive to raspberries, strawberries, currants and grapes in a wet summer — the fungus usually enters through wounds caused by pests such as slugs. Remove mouldy plant material immediately. Fungicides which were formerly recommended for this disease are no longer available.

LEAF SPOT

An important disease of black-currants — gooseberries may also be attacked. Brown spots appear and early leaf fall takes place. Remove diseased leaves. Strawberry leaf spot does not warrant spraying, and in addition fungicides which were formerly recommended for this disease are no longer available.

MAGPIE MOTH

This brightly-coloured looper caterpillar can seriously defoliate gooseberries and currants in spring and early summer but it is no longer a common pest. Hand picking will usually give satisfactory control. A heavy infestation calls for spraying with thiacloprid or insecticidal soap when the first flowers are about to open.

RASPBERRY BEETLE

The most serious pest of raspberries, loganberries and blackberries — the adult beetles feed on the flowers and the grubs bore inside the fruits where they feed. Use pyrethrins — spray raspberries when the first fruits turn pink. Spray loganberries when the petals have fallen and blackberries just before the first flowers open.

RASPBERRY MOTH

Dead or dying shoots of raspberries may indicate that the 1 cm red caterpillars of the raspberry moth are present. The young caterpillars live in the soil in winter and move to the shoots in April, where they bore into and feed on the pith. A tar oil spray to kill hibernating caterpillars is no longer permitted. Cut out and burn withered shoots.

RUST

Several rust diseases affect soft fruit — examples are **cluster cup rust** on gooseberries, **raspberry rust**, **blackberry rust** and **white pine rust** on blackcurrant (illustrated). Remove stems which are badly diseased. Fungicides which were formerly recommended for this disease are no longer available.

SLUGS & SNAILS

A large hole eaten in the side of a strawberry is usually due to slugs and snails (look for slime trails) or the strawberry ground beetle. Gooseberries, currants and raspberries are less seriously affected. Keep the area free from dead leaves and rubbish. The standard method of control is to scatter slug pellets thinly around the plants.

Strawberry mite

SPIDER MITE

Several types attack soft fruit — **red spider mite**, **bryobia mite**, **strawberry mite** etc. The general symptoms are bronze-coloured leaves and the presence of minute mites on the undersurface. Some but not all can be kept in check by spraying with pyrethrins every 3 weeks — the strawberry mite is not controlled by spraying.

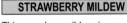

SPUR BLIGHT

Purplish patches appear around the buds on raspberry and loganberry canes in early autumn. These patches turn silvery and the buds are killed. Reduce overcrowding. Cut out diseased canes when purple patches appear. Fungicides which were formerly recommended for this disease are no longer available.

STRAWBERRY MILDEW

This powdery mildew is easy to recognise. Dark patches appear on the upper surface of the leaves — the infected foliage curls upwards to expose greyish mould patches. Diseased fruits are dull and shrivelled. Spray with sulphur at the start of flowering and again 2 weeks later. Cut off and burn leaves after harvesting.

Mosaic

Yellow edge

VIRUS

Virus diseases are a major problem of raspberries and strawberries. Other soft fruit types are less affected although the **reversion** virus is a serious complaint of blackcurrants. Aphids are the major carriers. **Mosaic** is the most damaging virus disease of raspberries — yellow patches appear on the distorted leaves and yields are reduced. Do not confuse with the yellow patches caused by the leaf and bud mite which is harmless. Strawberries are susceptible to several viruses — **crinkle** occurs in late spring, **yellow edge** in autumn and **arabis mosaic** in spring or autumn. Always buy plants which are certified as virus-free and look for aphid-resistant varieties. Remove and burn infected plants — grow replacement stock on a fresh site. Do not propagate from infected plants.

Disorders

BALLING

Rose buds develop normally, but the petals fail to open properly and then turn brown. It is usually due to the effect of wet weather on varieties with large, thin-petalled blooms. Balling is always worst in a shady area where the buds are shielded from the drying rays of the sun. It can also be caused by a heavy aphid attack.

BLOSSOM END ROT

A leathery dark-coloured patch occurs at the bottom of tomatoes — it is nearly always restricted to greenhouse crops and to the first few trusses at the start of the season. The cause is poor calcium uptake because of irregular watering — never let the compost dry out in growing bags. Small-fruited varieties are rarely affected.

BOLTING

Several vegetables may flower and run to seed before they have reached the harvesting stage — onions, beetroot, celery, lettuce and spinach are the usual ones. Common causes are sowing or planting too early, shortage of water and abnormally cold spring weather. Look for varieties which are bolt-resistant when buying seed.

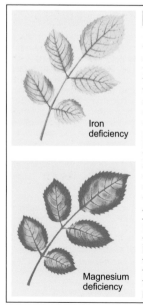

Iron deficiency

Magnesium deficiency

CHLOROSIS

Chlorosis is the yellowing of leaf tissues. It is natural for an occasional tree or shrub leaf to turn yellow, but when most or all of the foliage changes in this way during the active growing season then something is wrong. The most common reason is **lime-induced chlorosis** — many shrubs such as rhododendron, camellia and hydrangea develop pale green or yellow leaves when grown in alkaline soil. The cause is **iron deficiency** (young leaves worst affected) or **manganese deficiency** (old leaves worst affected). Add peat to the soil when planting — apply a chelated compound. **Magnesium deficiency** causes yellowing at the centre and early leaf fall. Red tints develop between the veins — apply a fertilizer containing magnesium. Chlorosis of the lower leaves is often due to poor drainage.

COLD DAMAGE

A sudden cold snap in spring can affect developing leaves and buds of many herbaceous perennials, annuals and bulbs by destroying chlorophyll. The affected leaf, when it expands, may be yellow-edged (anemone, sweet pea etc), almost white (many bedding plants) or white-banded (narcissus). Pick off badly affected leaves.

DROUGHT

Dryness at the roots is the commonest cause of plant death. With woody plants the first sign is wilting of the foliage and in the early stage the effect is reversible. The next stage is browning of the foliage and then leaf drop which is extremely serious or fatal. Water before symptoms appear — mulch around plants.

FRUIT DROP

Fruitlets may drop after insect damage — look for grubs in fallen apples, pears and plums. Healthy fruitlets may also drop — this may be beneficial if there has been a heavy set. The first drop of apples takes place when the fruitlets are pea-sized but the major shedding of fruit is the **June drop**. It is normal for newly-planted trees to shed most of their fruit at this time and some varieties (e.g Cox's Orange Pippin) have a notoriously heavy June drop. If the number of fallen fruit is abnormally high for the variety and age of tree you should suspect starvation, irregular watering, frost damage or overcrowding.

Rose

Apple

FROST

With non-hardy plants frost threatens life itself — it is essential to wait until the danger of frost is over before sowing or transplanting. A hard frost can damage the tender new growth of hardy plants such as potatoes, roses, apples etc. The affected leaves may be bleached, blistered, cracked or scorched along the margins. The stems of early potatoes may be blackened — the crop can be protected by covering with newspaper if frosts are expected. The worst effects of frost are seen in the fruit garden. Frost at blossom time can cause the blossom of tree fruit to turn brown and drop off. With cane fruit some or all the buds may fail to open in the spring. The damage usually occurs when frost follows an unusually mild spell at the time when the buds are about to burst. To protect shrubs etc use horticultural fleece over the stems.

NUTRIENT SHORTAGE

Nitrogen deficiency · Potash deficiency

Some minerals are required by the plant in quite large quantities — these major nutrients include nitrogen, phosphorus, potassium, calcium and magnesium. Others are needed in only small amounts — these trace elements include iron, boron, manganese, copper, zinc and molybdenum. Trees and shrubs growing in the open garden are unlikely to show symptoms of nutrient shortage unless you are growing a lime-hating variety in alkaline soil. On the other hand fruit, vegetables, roses and flowers may show deficiency symptoms.

LEAF SYMPTOMS

Nitrogen deficiency produces young leaves which are pale and undersized — with some plants such as roses the mature foliage develops red spots or all-over red or yellow tints. **Potash deficiency** results in brown brittle margins and downward-turning tips. With **manganese deficiency** there is browning between the veins — it is often associated with the use of high-potash fertilizers.

Heart rot

NON-LEAF SYMPTOMS

A number of vegetable disorders are due to nutrient shortage:
Marsh spot — peas. Brown-lined cavity in the centre of each pea due to manganese deficiency. **Heart rot** — beetroot. Blackened area within the flesh due to boron deficiency. **Speckled yellows** — beetroot. Rolled leaves, yellow patches between the veins due to manganese deficiency. **Whiptail** — cauliflower. Thin, strap-like leaves due to molybdenum deficiency. **Brown curd** — cauliflower. Discoloured heads due to boron deficiency. **Blossom end rot** — tomatoes. Leathery patch at base due to calcium deficiency.

Whiptail

Prevention and treatment measures include feeding with a compound fertilizer and mulching with compost or old manure each spring — use a product which contains the deficient element.

Brown curd

SHADE & SUN DAMAGE

Always check the light requirement before buying a plant. Few plants will thrive in dense shade but a number will flourish in semi-shade. Most plants, however, thrive best in sunny situations — this is especially true for annuals. There are three basic types of shade damage. Stems of affected plants become leggy and the leaves are pale. In addition the number and size of blooms are reduced. The third problem is that the leaves of variegated plants lose their yellow or white colouring. In the greenhouse there is an opposite problem — the need for shading against the rays of the midday summer sun.

SPRING SCORCH

The least understood of early spring problems. Cold-induced drought leads to the browning or death of evergreens — sunshine and drying winds stimulate water loss but the roots are not yet active enough to satisfy the demand. Protect from east winds if you can — spray newly-planted evergreens with water in spring.

WATERLOGGING

The plant is affected in two ways. Root development is crippled by the shortage of air in the soil. The root system becomes shallow and the root hairs die. Leaves often turn pale and growth is stunted. The second serious effect is the stimulation of root-rotting diseases. There is no cure once the roots have been seriously damaged — the answer is to prevent waterlogging. This is not easy if the soil is very heavy and the water table is high — you can raise the bed by bringing in top soil or you can dig in humus before planting. This must be done over a large area — merely putting peat into the planting hole is of little help.

WEEDKILLER DAMAGE

Traces of lawn weedkiller can cause distortion of many flowers, vegetables, roses etc — leaves become fern-like and twisted. Equipment such as sprayers and watering cans which have been used for applying weedkillers should not be employed for any other purpose. Never spray on a windy day.

POOR PLANTING DAMAGE

Poor planting is one of the commonest causes of poor growth or death of trees and shrubs which have been grown in containers. Matted roots on the surface of the soil ball must be teased out, the planting hole must be wide enough for a good supply of planting mixture (see page 63) and this mixture must be properly firmed down around the plant. Soak the roots of bare-rooted plants before planting if they are dry and make sure to spread out these roots in the planting hole. In the vegetable garden failure to firm the soil around brassica transplants results in blown brussels sprouts and heartless cabbages.

WINTER DAMAGE

Many trees and shrubs are at risk in a severe winter, especially if they are slightly tender or newly planted. They can be damaged in several ways — waterlogging in an abnormally wet season can lead to root rot, heavy frost can cause brown blotches at the tips of leaves and deep snow can break the branches of evergreens.

Animal Pests

BIRDS

The flower garden is least affected — only crocus, polyanthus and Primula wanda are stripped of buds and flowers. Vegetables can suffer badly, especially peas and brassicas. Seed and seedlings are eaten, sparrows tear flowers and pigeons strip away the soft portion of leaves (illustrated). Flowers of forsythia and some other shrubs may be stripped but it is the fruit garden which suffers most of all. Bullfinches (illustrated) and sparrows devour buds of cherries, gooseberries etc — ripening fruit is also attacked. Small areas can be protected with soft plastic netting — secure the base properly. For a larger number of plants a fruit cage is the answer. Spray-on repellents are of limited value and are removed by rain. Mechanical scarers may be effective at first but they can lose their ability to frighten away birds.

CATS

Cats are a pest in the garden — seed beds and transplants are disturbed by their scratching and young trees may be damaged by their claws. Protection is not easy if a cat has chosen your vegetable plot as a toilet. You can try one of the newer cat repellent sprays or a sonic deterrent but there is no fool-proof method.

DEER

Deer can be a menace in rural areas close to woodland. Woody shoots are severed and bark may be rubbed away — rose buds are a favourite meal. Fencing at least 2 m (7 ft) high is the best answer but may not be practical. The trunks of trees can be protected with fine-mesh wire netting — deterrent sprays have limited value.

DOGS

Dogs, like cats, will disturb ground where plants are growing but the serious effect is the scorch caused by their urine. Conifers etc are damaged by dogs — lawns are disfigured by bitches. Copiously water the area as soon as you can but there is no satisfactory answer. The effect of deterrent dusts and sprays is short-lived.

FOXES

Foxes can be a nuisance in both town and country gardens. Dustbins are knocked over, plants are dug up and shrubs are scorched by their urine. There is no way of keeping foxes out of the average garden and there is no way of protecting the plants — conifers are especially vulnerable. Deterrents are of little value.

MICE & RATS

Mice will dig for planted peas, sweet corn, crocus corms etc — whole rows of large seeds may be removed. Between spring and autumn they will come indoors to attack stored fruit and vegetables. Proprietary mouse baits are available — mouse traps require some form of pet protection. Contact the council if rats are discovered.

MOLES

The tunnelling by moles can cause root damage and their hills are unsightly — a serious invasion can ruin a lawn. Unlike rabbits these pests are solitary creatures but the few which are present are difficult to eradicate. Try the simple ways first — smokes, sonic deterrents etc but call in a professional exterminator if all else fails.

RABBITS

A serious problem in rural areas — flowers and vegetables are nibbled, shrubs are attacked and tree bark may be gnawed in winter. Rabbit urine causes brown patches in the lawn. There is no easy answer — deterrents soon lose their power and ordinary fences are ineffective. Tree guards will protect individual plants.

SQUIRRELS

Nice to watch, but they can be a nuisance and their damage is often blamed on rabbits. They eat bulbs, nibble shoot tips, remove flower buds, carry away soft fruit and strip the bark off trees. As with rabbits there is no simple solution. Secure net-covered cages for groups of plants and individual tree guards are the only sure protection.

Lawn Problems

ALGAE

A coating of green or black slime which indicates poor drainage — it is encouraged by overrolling, underfeeding and mowing too closely. Algal growth is common under the drip-line of trees. Ferrous sulphate will kill algae, but the basic cause must be removed to prevent its return. Spike and top dress in autumn.

ANT

Unlike worm casts the hills made by ants are a feature of sandy soil and dry summer weather. They are not as harmful as the casts of earthworms but the hills can disfigure the surface if they occur in large numbers. Scatter with a besom before mowing — if numerous sprinkle an ant-killer over the affected area.

BITCH URINE

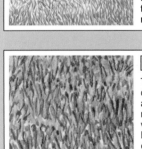

Bitch urine has a scorching effect on turf — the brown patches are roughly circular with a ring of dark lush grass around each one. The effect is worst in dry weather. There are no effective repellents to safeguard the whole lawn — the only thing you can do is to water the patches copiously. Reseed or returf if it is too unsightly.

BROWN TIPPING

There are a number of possible causes for the browning of cut tips after mowing. The most likely reason is using a rotary mower with dull blades — the grass is bruised instead of being cut cleanly. With a cylinder mower check the setting and inspect the bottom plate for damage. Another cause is mowing wet grass.

CHAFER GRUB

The curved grubs of the garden chafer gnaw at the roots in spring and summer — small brown patches of grass appear which can be pulled away quite easily. They are less troublesome than leatherjackets and control measures are rarely needed. In sandy soil they can be a nuisance — rolling in spring will crush the grubs.

CRACKING

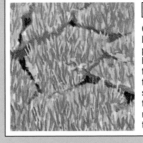

Cracks on the surface are due to lack of water — a common problem on April-sown lawns on heavy land. Water the whole lawn, top dress the cracked area and then sow a thin sprinkling of grass seed. It is much better to avoid trouble by remembering to water a new lawn in dry weather so that the soil does not dry out.

DOLLAR SPOT

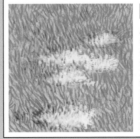

A disease of fine-leaved grasses such as creeping red fescue and cumberland turf. The straw-coloured patches are circular and 2.5-5 cm wide — they may join together and badly disfigure the lawn. Feed with a nitrogen-rich fertilizer in spring and spike the turf in autumn. Chemical sprays are no longer available.

EARTHWORM

Worm casts render the surface uneven and stifle fine grasses. The cast-forming species of earthworms are not efficient soil aerators, and they do attract moles. There are no chemicals to use these days — all you can do is to scatter the dry casts before mowing, remove clippings when mowing and apply lawn sand in spring.

FAIRY RING

A ring of toadstools which grows wider each year. The worst is produced by Marasmius — two dark green circles with a bare space between. The slender brown-capped toadstools are 5-10 cm high. Many cures have been proposed over the years but replacing the soil and returfing is the only satisfactory answer.

FERTILIZER SCORCH

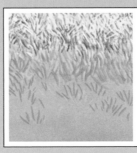

Overdosing is usually due to careless spreading by hand or by overlapping when a fertilizer distributor is used. The effect is either dark green or brown patches or stripes depending on the material and the degree of overdosing. The grass should recover in a few weeks — to speed up this recovery water the affected area copiously.

FUSARIUM PATCH

Fusarium patch (**snow mould**) is the most common lawn disease. In autumn or spring round patches of yellowing grass appear which spread to about 30 cm across and may merge. In damp weather the edges are covered with white mould. Do not use a nitrogen-rich fertilizer in autumn. The standard treatment is trifloxystrobin.

OPHIOBOLUS PATCH

It begins as a small sunken area which increases in size until it is a metre or more across. The edge is bleached and the central dead area is colonised by weeds and coarse grasses. Ophiobolus patch is often a feature of poor drainage, under-feeding and/or overliming — fortunately it is not common. Returf while the patch is still small.

LEATHERJACKET

The worst of all insect pests, especially in heavy soil after a wet autumn. The 3 cm brown grubs devour roots and stem bases in spring — the grass turns yellow or brown. Water in the evening and spread a plastic sheet over the surface. Remove next morning and brush away the grubs. Imidacloprid is a chemical treatment.

RED THREAD

Red thread (**corticium disease**) appears as irregular patches of bleached grass in late summer or autumn — these patches develop a pinkish tinge. Look closely in moist weather and you will find red needle-like growths on the leaves. This disease is a feature of starved lawns. Unsightly, but not fatal. Trifloxystrobin is a chemical treatment.

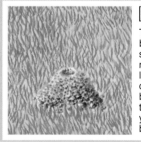

LICHEN

The upper surface of each leaf-like plate is nearly black when moist — the surface colour fades when dry and the edges curl upwards. Like moss it indicates poor growing conditions — too much shade, too little food and/or poor drainage. Lawn sand will kill it, but removal of the cause is the only way to prevent lichen from returning.

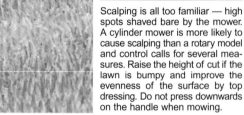

SCALPING

Scalping is all too familiar — high spots shaved bare by the mower. A cylinder mower is more likely to cause scalping than a rotary model and control calls for several measures. Raise the height of cut if the lawn is bumpy and improve the evenness of the surface by top dressing. Do not press downwards on the handle when mowing.

MINING BEE

This stingless bee makes its nest below the surface. The excavated soil is deposited as a small conical mound — at first glance it looks like an anthill, but there is a tell-tale crater at the top. Mining bees can be killed with an insecticide but they are useful pollinators and so you should just scatter the hills before mowing.

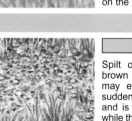

SPILT OIL

Spilt oil produces an irregular brown patch on the lawn which may eventually die. It appears suddenly a few days after mowing and is due to refuelling or oiling while the mower is standing on the lawn. Obviously the mower should be moved off the lawn before adding oil or filling with petrol. Returf the patch if necessary.

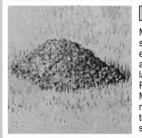

MOLE

Mole activity can destroy the even surface of the lawn. Large heaps of earth suddenly appear — attacks are most likely in sandy soil and lawns which receive little traffic. Remove the hills before mowing. Many remedies have been recommended but only traps offer long-term success. Employ a professional mole catcher if you can.

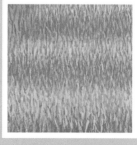

WASHBOARDING

A series of broad and regular corrugations about 15-30 cm (1-2 ft) apart run cross-wise along the mown strip. It is caused by always mowing in the same direction — this sets up a vibration pattern which eventually produces a ripple effect in the soil. The answer is simple — change the direction of the cut occasionally when you mow.

Garden weeds

Weeds are plants growing in the wrong place — they may be wild flowers, grasses, self-sown seedlings of garden plants etc. Last year's tulip growing through this year's wallflowers is a weed. There are various ways in which weeds can harm plants — they cast shade, harbour pests and diseases, and compete for water, nutrients and space. In addition they give an uncared-for look to the garden.

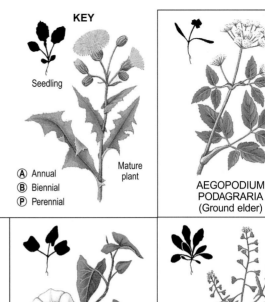

KEY

Seedling

Ⓐ Annual
Ⓑ Biennial
Ⓟ Perennial

Mature plant

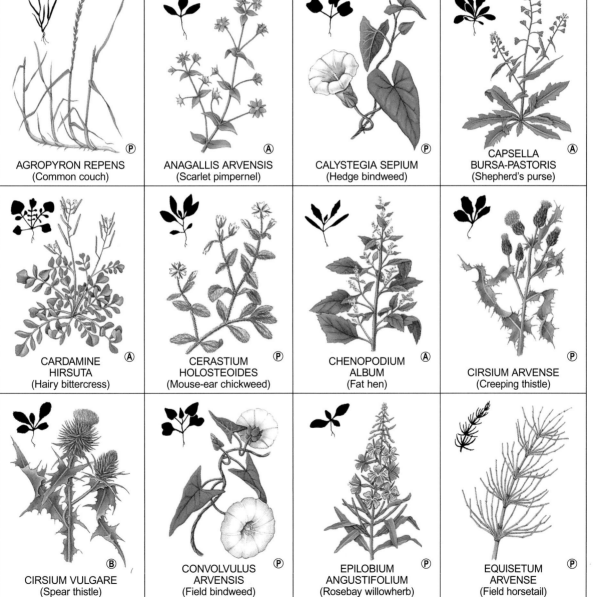

Ⓟ **AEGOPODIUM PODAGRARIA**
(Ground elder)

Ⓟ **AGROPYRON REPENS**
(Common couch)

Ⓐ **ANAGALLIS ARVENSIS**
(Scarlet pimpernel)

Ⓟ **CALYSTEGIA SEPIUM**
(Hedge bindweed)

Ⓐ **CAPSELLA BURSA-PASTORIS**
(Shepherd's purse)

Ⓐ **CARDAMINE HIRSUTA**
(Hairy bittercress)

Ⓟ **CERASTIUM HOLOSTEOIDES**
(Mouse-ear chickweed)

Ⓐ **CHENOPODIUM ALBUM**
(Fat hen)

Ⓟ **CIRSIUM ARVENSE**
(Creeping thistle)

Ⓑ **CIRSIUM VULGARE**
(Spear thistle)

Ⓟ **CONVOLVULUS ARVENSIS**
(Field bindweed)

Ⓟ **EPILOBIUM ANGUSTIFOLIUM**
(Rosebay willowherb)

Ⓟ **EQUISETUM ARVENSE**
(Field horsetail)

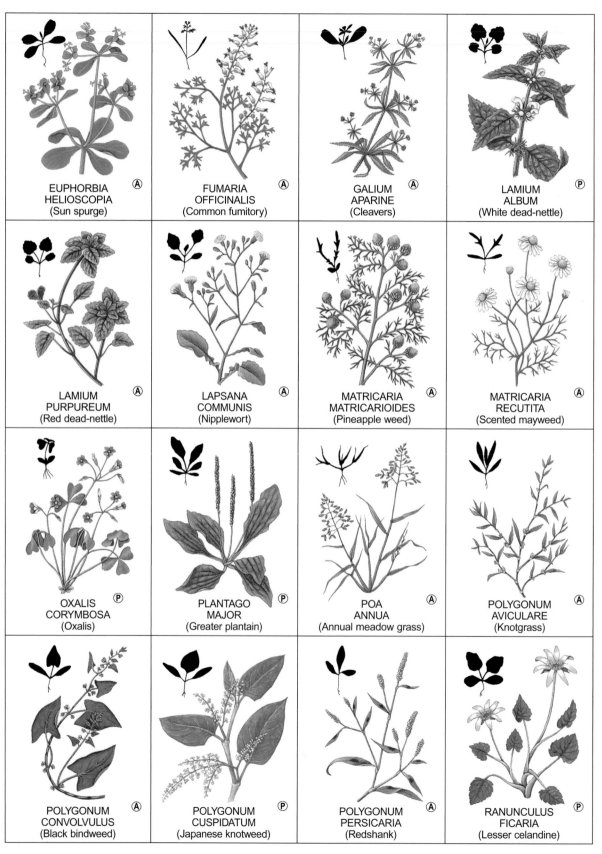

EUPHORBIA HELIOSCOPIA (Sun spurge) Ⓐ	FUMARIA OFFICINALIS (Common fumitory) Ⓐ	GALIUM APARINE (Cleavers) Ⓐ	LAMIUM ALBUM (White dead-nettle) Ⓟ
LAMIUM PURPUREUM (Red dead-nettle) Ⓐ	LAPSANA COMMUNIS (Nipplewort) Ⓐ	MATRICARIA MATRICARIOIDES (Pineapple weed) Ⓐ	MATRICARIA RECUTITA (Scented mayweed) Ⓐ
OXALIS CORYMBOSA (Oxalis) Ⓟ	PLANTAGO MAJOR (Greater plantain) Ⓟ	POA ANNUA (Annual meadow grass) Ⓐ	POLYGONUM AVICULARE (Knotgrass) Ⓐ
POLYGONUM CONVOLVULUS (Black bindweed) Ⓐ	POLYGONUM CUSPIDATUM (Japanese knotweed) Ⓟ	POLYGONUM PERSICARIA (Redshank) Ⓐ	RANUNCULUS FICARIA (Lesser celandine) Ⓟ

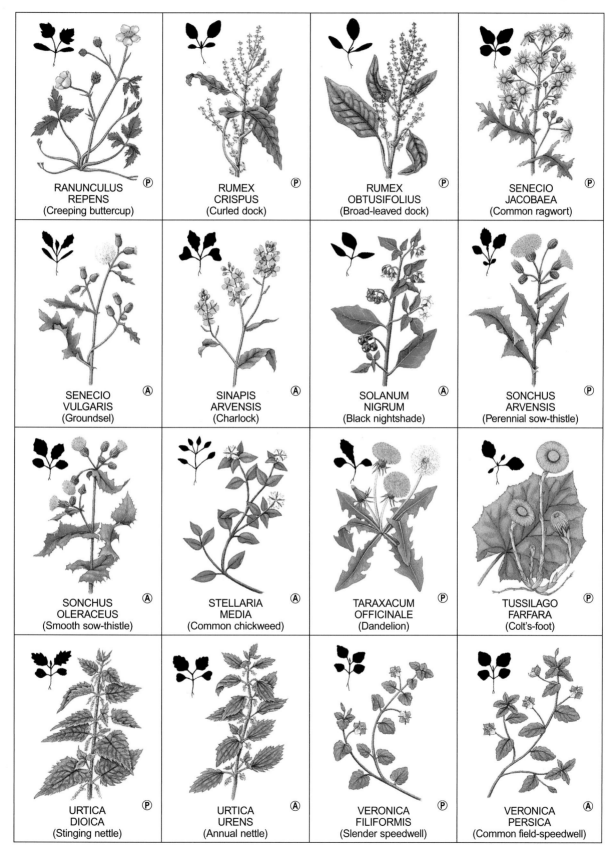

RANUNCULUS
REPENS
(Creeping buttercup) Ⓟ

RUMEX
CRISPUS
(Curled dock) Ⓟ

RUMEX
OBTUSIFOLIUS
(Broad-leaved dock) Ⓟ

SENECIO
JACOBAEA
(Common ragwort) Ⓟ

SENECIO
VULGARIS
(Groundsel) Ⓐ

SINAPIS
ARVENSIS
(Charlock) Ⓐ

SOLANUM
NIGRUM
(Black nightshade) Ⓐ

SONCHUS
ARVENSIS
(Perennial sow-thistle) Ⓟ

SONCHUS
OLERACEUS
(Smooth sow-thistle) Ⓐ

STELLARIA
MEDIA
(Common chickweed) Ⓐ

TARAXACUM
OFFICINALE
(Dandelion) Ⓟ

TUSSILAGO
FARFARA
(Colt's-foot) Ⓟ

URTICA
DIOICA
(Stinging nettle) Ⓟ

URTICA
URENS
(Annual nettle) Ⓐ

VERONICA
FILIFORMIS
(Slender speedwell) Ⓟ

VERONICA
PERSICA
(Common field-speedwell) Ⓐ

Garden weed control

Weeding is a season-long chore and in most gardens it is tackled badly. Little is done to prevent an infestation around the growing plants, and then we wait until the weeds are an eyesore. The garden owner then spends hours hoeing, forking out and hand pulling each bed and border in turn, only to find that the first bed is again full of weeds before the last bed or border is reached.

The answer is to follow a weed control programme which contains several steps. The first step is to remember that prevention is better than cure, so take action before the weeds appear. The next steps involve dealing with weeds which may appear despite the prevention techniques you have used. In all cases the job must be undertaken before annual weeds produce seed and before perennial ones spread.

Annual weeds

Annual weeds complete their life cycle during the season. They spread by seeding, and all fertile soils contain a large reserve of annual weed seeds. The golden rule is that emerged annual weeds must be killed before they produce seed — kill them by hand pulling, hoeing or using a systemic weedkiller (see below).

Perennial weeds

Perennial weeds survive over winter by means of underground stems or roots. Dig out the roots if you can. If you can't then the leaves must be regularly removed to starve out the underground storage organs or else a systemic weedkiller (see below) must be used which will kill these underground parts.

WEEDKILLERS

You must choose carefully to avoid the twin dangers of killing garden plants and not harming the weeds. There are touchweeders for dabbing into the crowns of persistent weeds and there are gel formulations for brushing on to the leaves of weeds growing close to garden plants. But the most popular formulation type is the liquid spray which is diluted before use or is applied from a ready-to-use spray gun. Choose a still day when the weeds are actively growing in spring or summer, and never use the spraying equipment for any other purpose.

Plant safety

A **selective weedkiller** is damaging to a wide range of weeds but is not harmful to the garden plants listed on the label, provided that the instructions are followed. The best known examples are the lawn weedkillers based on 2,4-D, mecoprop, dicamba, fluroxypyr, clopyralid etc.

A **non-selective** or **total weedkiller** damages or kills garden plants as well as weeds. Use it as an overall spray on uncultivated land or choose a brand which can be used as a directed spray between plants. Examples are glyphosate, ammonium sulphamate.

Types

Contact types kill only those parts which are touched, so complete leaf cover is required. These products are fast-acting and are excellent for dealing with annual weeds. But movement within the plant is either very limited or absent, so there is no long-lasting action against perennial weeds. Examples — fatty acids, glufosinate ammonium.

Residual types enter the plant through the roots. These products remain active in the soil for weeks or even years, depending on the chemical concentration, soil type etc. They tend to be unspectacular in action, killing the weeds below ground as they germinate. This chemical type is found in path weedkillers. Examples — dichlobenil, oxadiazon.

Systemic types move in the sap stream, so roots as well as leaves are affected after spraying. Complete leaf cover is not required. These products are effective against many annual and perennial weeds, but action is often slow and the result are often governed by timing, weather etc. Examples — glyphosate, ammonium sulphamate.

Prevent weeds from appearing

The basic reason why you have a weed problem is bare ground. You can hoe or hand pull the weeds around growing plants and in some cases they can be safely sprayed, but if the soil is uncovered then the problem will return as weed seeds on or near the surface and pieces of perennial weeds start to grow.

Digging is often an ineffectual way of controlling weeds on a long term basis. The annual types on the surface are buried, but a host of seeds are brought to the surface. With care some perennial weed roots and bulbs can be removed, but all too often the roots of dandelions, thistles etc and the bulbs of ground elder are spread around.

The real answer is to try to cover the surface around plants in beds and borders. You can use a non-living cover (a mulch or weed-proof blanket) or a living one (ground-cover plants). Use one of the following techniques:

Apply a non-living cover

One of the purposes of a humus mulch is to suppress weed germination and to make it easier to hand pull ones which may appear. This reduces but does not eliminate the problem.

The weed control mulch is much more effective — done properly it can mean that weeding beds and borders becomes a thing of the past. It is a layer of weed-proof material placed over the soil surface, which is then covered with gravel or pebbles — the best cover is bark chippings. Black polyethylene sheeting is widely available and inexpensive, but it is not long-lasting and water has to percolate through the edges of the sheets. Woven polypropylene available from your garden centre is a much better choice — the water seeps through the myriad holes between the threads, and it last for 6 years or more.

This type of mulching is perhaps most successful when you are making a new shrub border, although it can be used for a mixed border. It can also be used in the vegetable plot where growth is stimulated, potatoes no longer need earthing-up, and strawberries and courgettes are kept off the ground. Simply make cross cuts where the planting holes will be. Plant in the usual way — remove soil left on the surface after planting and finally cover the sheeting with gravel or bark.

Plant ground cover

With bedding plants you can solve the ground cover problem by planting them closer together than the usually recommended distance.

Creeping evergreens with leafy stems provide an excellent way of suppressing weed growth around clumps of perennials. Examples include ballota, pachysandra, polygonum, stachys and vinca. Deciduous ones include alchemilla, euphorbia and lysimachia.

Get rid of weeds promptly when they appear

Pull by hand

The simplest method for the removal of well-established but easily-uprooted annual weeds in beds and borders and the removal of all types of weeds in the rockery. Use a small fork to uproot perennial weeds — don't pull up by the stems.

Use a hoe

The hoe is the traditional enemy of the emerged weed and still remains the most popular control method around growing plants. It will kill large numbers of annual weeds if the surface is dry, the blade is sharp and the cut is kept shallow. Hoeing at regular intervals is needed to starve out the roots of perennial weeds. See page 59 for information on the proper way to hoe.

Use a weedkiller

Both contact and systemic weedkillers are available for use around growing plants — make sure you choose the right type for the job you want it to do — see page 170. Use one of the methods listed below:

SPOT TREATMENT

Application to a single weed or a group of weeds. An example is painting the leaves of a perennial weed growing next to a rose with a systemic weedkiller such as glyphosate. It is useful for dealing with isolated weeds not killed by a previous treatment.

DIRECTED TREATMENT

Application to a group of weeds, great care being taken to avoid contact with nearby garden plants. Choose a still day and use a watering can fitted with a dribble bar. An example is glyphosate around herbaceous perennials and shrubs.

OVERALL TREATMENT

Application to the whole area which has a weed problem. The weedkiller may be a non-selective one where the area is either a path or a patch of bare land, or a selective weedkiller where the land contains plants which are resistant to the chemical.

Lawn weeds

It is not unusual to find a wide variety of common garden weeds growing in a newly-sown lawn. When the grass is established, however, the routine of regular mowing brings about a spectacular change in the weed population. Most types cannot withstand being constantly cut down by the whirling blades and so they steadily disappear from the lawn. There remains a small group of weeds with a low-growing habit which are able to survive and spread below the height of the mower blades. These are the lawn weeds.

There are three basic reasons for a weedy lawn — poor site preparation, poor choice of turf and incorrect management of the grass. In even the best-tended lawn there is nothing you can do to prevent occasional weeds from appearing, but there is a lot you can do to prevent them spreading to form large patches. See the Lawn Weed Control section on page 174.

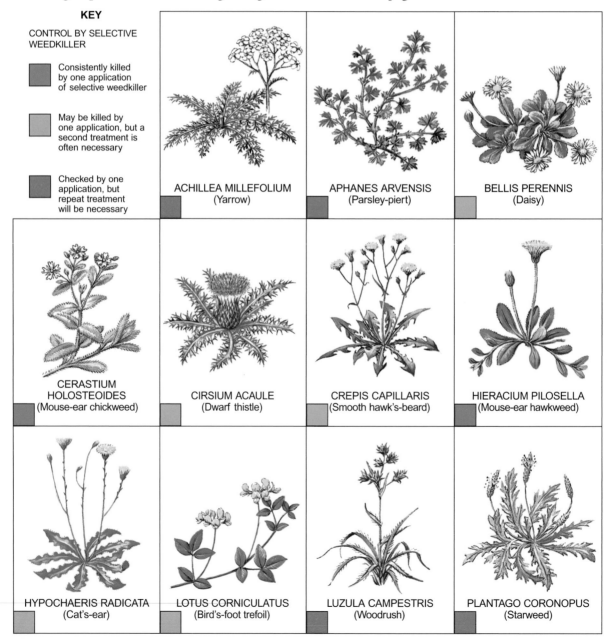

KEY

CONTROL BY SELECTIVE WEEDKILLER

Consistently killed by one application of selective weedkiller

May be killed by one application, but a second treatment is often necessary

Checked by one application, but repeat treatment will be necessary

ACHILLEA MILLEFOLIUM
(Yarrow)

APHANES ARVENSIS
(Parsley-piert)

BELLIS PERENNIS
(Daisy)

CERASTIUM HOLOSTEOIDES
(Mouse-ear chickweed)

CIRSIUM ACAULE
(Dwarf thistle)

CREPIS CAPILLARIS
(Smooth hawk's-beard)

HIERACIUM PILOSELLA
(Mouse-ear hawkweed)

HYPOCHAERIS RADICATA
(Cat's-ear)

LOTUS CORNICULATUS
(Bird's-foot trefoil)

LUZULA CAMPESTRIS
(Woodrush)

PLANTAGO CORONOPUS
(Starweed)

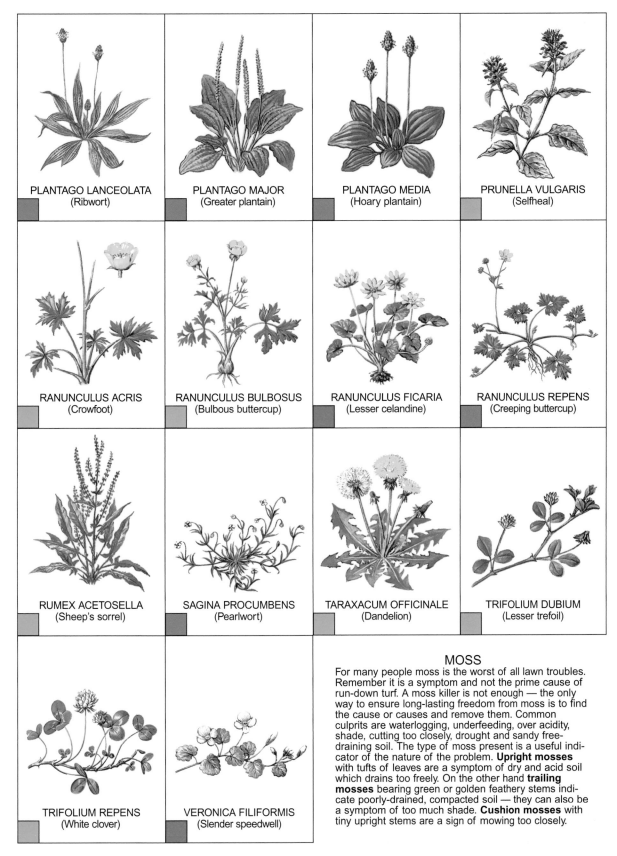

PLANTAGO LANCEOLATA
(Ribwort)

PLANTAGO MAJOR
(Greater plantain)

PLANTAGO MEDIA
(Hoary plantain)

PRUNELLA VULGARIS
(Selfheal)

RANUNCULUS ACRIS
(Crowfoot)

RANUNCULUS BULBOSUS
(Bulbous buttercup)

RANUNCULUS FICARIA
(Lesser celandine)

RANUNCULUS REPENS
(Creeping buttercup)

RUMEX ACETOSELLA
(Sheep's sorrel)

SAGINA PROCUMBENS
(Pearlwort)

TARAXACUM OFFICINALE
(Dandelion)

TRIFOLIUM DUBIUM
(Lesser trefoil)

TRIFOLIUM REPENS
(White clover)

VERONICA FILIFORMIS
(Slender speedwell)

MOSS

For many people moss is the worst of all lawn troubles. Remember it is a symptom and not the prime cause of run-down turf. A moss killer is not enough — the only way to ensure long-lasting freedom from moss is to find the cause or causes and remove them. Common culprits are waterlogging, underfeeding, over acidity, shade, cutting too closely, drought and sandy free-draining soil. The type of moss present is a useful indicator of the nature of the problem. **Upright mosses** with tufts of leaves are a symptom of dry and acid soil which drains too freely. On the other hand **trailing mosses** bearing green or golden feathery stems indicate poorly-drained, compacted soil — they can also be a symptom of too much shade. **Cushion mosses** with tiny upright stems are a sign of mowing too closely.

Lawn weed control

If the lawn has only a few weeds you may be tempted to ignore the problem — from a distance the turf may look uniformly green. It is wise, however, to tackle the problem before it gets out of hand — the visual effect gets worse when the weeds start to flower and the intruders can steadily take hold.

The correct method to use depends on the number and type of weed present. With isolated weeds grubbing out or spot treating with a weedkiller may be all that is needed, but if the trouble is widespread then an overall application of a suitable chemical will be necessary.

After the lawn has been freed from its unwelcome visitors it is necessary to follow the rules of proper lawn care to increase the vigour of the grass and so reduce the risk of re-invasion.

NON-CHEMICAL CONTROL

Non-chemical methods of control are much more effective at the prevention rather than at the eradication stage. Proper mowing is a key factor — cutting too closely or mowing at the correct height at infrequent intervals will weaken the grass and let in weeds. Raking the grass will help to control creeping weeds (see below) but do not overdo it — over-drastic raking can thin out the turf and allow weeds to take hold. Grass will generally recover after a period of summer drought, but if you fail to water then both weeds and moss will find a perfect breeding ground in the thin and open turf once the rains return.

Hand weeding
Scattered seedlings of annual weeds can be pulled by hand from the newly-seeded lawn. In the established lawn this technique of hand pulling will not do — the weed has to be dug out. Chose a day when the turf is actively growing. Use a hand fork or a knife and make sure you dig out the root. Keep the diameter of the hole as narrow as possible and fill it with compost when the weed has been removed. Firm down the surrounding turf.

Slashing
Clumps of coarse grass do not respond to lawn weedkillers. The recommended control method is to slash through the weed with a knife or edging iron before mowing.

Raking up
Before mowing rake upright the runners of creeping weeds, the stems of coarse grasses and the leaves of other weeds. In this way these stems and leaves will be cut off by the mower. Use the grass box on a weedy lawn and do not use the clippings for mulching around plants.

CHEMICAL CONTROL

The range of weedkillers is limited to just two types which are described below. They will not harm children or pets, but many garden plants are sensitive to them, so read the instructions and the precautions carefully before use. Put on the recommended amount . Use when the weeds are actively growing . Do not apply in windy weather nor when rain is forecast . Do not mow just before treatment . Store in a safe place away from plants and fertilizer.

Types

Ferrous sulphate destroys or reduces the top growth of many weeds — moss is checked.
Unlike the selective weedkillers the products containing ferrous sulphate can scorch fine grasses if carelessly applied, and they only kill top growth and not the roots. Ferrous sulphate is invariably sold as a mixture with fertilizer — when mixed with ammonium sulphate and sand it is sold as Lawn Sand.

Selective weedkillers destroy or reduce both the top growth as well as the roots of many weeds — moss is not checked.
These chemicals, sometimes wrongly called 'hormone weedkillers', are basic tools for the care of the lawn. They are selective in their action, killing susceptible weeds but sparing resistant plants such as grasses.
The product you buy will contain two or more active ingredients — popular ones include MCPA, dicamba, mecoprop-8 and clopyralid.
Selective weedkillers are sold in a variety of forms — the most popular is a weedkiller/fertilizer mix. This may be a powder, granule or liquid — a selective weedkiller works better when a nitrogen-rich fertilizer is used with it. A fertilizer distributor is the best method of application. Liquid formulations are the quickest way of killing weeds in the lawn — mixtures containing a fertilizer are available. Scattered rosette-type weeds can be spot-treated with a pinch of a powder product, but it is better to use one of the special products made for spot treatment. Ready-to-use weed guns and aerosols are squirted into the heart of each weed.
Wait 12 months after sowing seed or 6 months after laying turf before applying a selective weedkiller.

TACKLING MOSS

Small patches are not a problem, but large mossy areas are unsightly. Unfortunately there is no easy answer — it is necessary to follow a season-long moss control programme. In spring apply ferrous sulphate, either as Lawn Sand or as a proprietary granular or liquid fertilizer, hormone weedkiller/ferrous sulphate mix. Rake out the dead moss a couple of weeks later and reseed any bare patches. Feed the lawn in early summer and make sure that you mow regularly at the recommended height — closely shaving the lawn is one of the common causes of moss infestation. Remove shade if at all possible and in autumn rake and aerate the lawn by spiking.

CHAPTER 10

HERBS

There is no general agreement on the difference between a herb and a spice. According to some writers, if it is green and is either a stem or leaf then it is a herb, otherwise it is a spice. The definition here is even simpler — a herb is a flavouring plant which we traditionally think of as a herb and not as a spice. In the following pages the most popular home-grown herbs are described.

Herb growing is for everyone. If you don't have a garden or if open ground is short you can grow pots of chervil, marjoram, mint, parsley and thyme on the windowsill. Outdoors you can grow them in a mixed bed or border as in the cottage gardens of old. Best of all, however, is a raised herb bed. It is a good idea to grow them in compartments separated by permanent dividers of brick, wood, concrete slabs etc.

The standard requirements are some sun during the day, a well-drained soil, fairly regular picking to keep the plant compact and the replacement of perennials every three or four years. Rampant growers like mint must be kept in check. Most types can be raised from seed but it is better to buy them as small plants in pots from the garden centre. With shrubby herbs such as rosemary you will need only a single plant, but with smaller herbaceous types such as parsley you will require several specimens. Construct the herb garden as close as practical to the house — herb gathering tends to be neglected in wet weather when the bed is situated at the far end of the garden.

Harvest at the proper stage of growth — pick your requirements for immediate use when the plants are actively growing, and also pick some for drying. Most herbs can be dried for winter use, but wherever possible basil, parsley, mint, chives and chervil should be used fresh. Dry herbs by hanging them in branches or spreading them on a tray at about 26º-32ºC (80º-90ºF) for a day or two. The airing cupboard or green-house is a suitable spot — after this initial warm treatment they can be kept at ordinary room temperature for about a fortnight, turning them daily, until they are cornflake-crisp. Crush, discard chaff, and store in an airtight container in a cool, dark place.

Deep freezing has revolutionised the preserving of soft-leaved herbs with the ice-cube method. Fill the cups of an ice-cube tray with chopped and blanched herbs and top up with water. Freeze, then store in polythene bags in the freezer. To use, drop a herb cube in the dish or pan while cooking.

BASIL

The strong, clove-like flavour is an essential feature of many Italian recipes and its traditional partner is the tomato. It is also recommended for flavouring soups and salads.

This tender annual cannot stand frost. Sow under glass in March or April in a fibre pot and plant out in early June in a well-drained sunny spot. Space plants 30 cm (1 ft) apart and pinch out the tips regularly to produce bushy plants.

In summer gather leaves as required — preserve by the ice-cube method (page 175). Lift plants and pot up in September, placing the pots on the kitchen windowsill for use in winter.

CHERVIL

A delicate herb in many ways — its leaves are ferny, its life-span is short in hot weather and its subtle aniseed flavour is easily lost in cooking. Despite this it grows quickly with leaves ready for picking 8 weeks after sowing and it is hardy, which means that leaves are available in winter.

Sow in spring or summer where it is to grow. Thin the plants to 15 cm (6 in.) apart and water regularly in dry weather. Pick leaves from the outside of the plant. Remove flower heads at the same time.

Add just before serving soups, fish and egg dishes.

CHIVES

The grassy leaves of this mild member of the onion family can be cut from March to October.

Chives can be raised from seed sown in March, but it is easier to plant pot-grown specimens in spring or autumn. Space the clumps 25 cm (10 in.) apart and divide every 3 or 4 years. The ideal situation is moist soil and full sun — water regularly. Cut the leaves at 3 cm (1 in.) above ground level. Try to cut before the flower buds open.

Much of its value is lost by drying — grow a pot or two indoors or freeze-dry (page 175) for winter. Use in soups, salads, sauces, omelettes etc.

DILL

The 60 cm (2 ft) plant bears feathery leaves, and plates of small yellow flowers in July. Dill hates disturbance. Sow the seeds in April where the plants are to grow, and thin to 30 cm (1 ft) apart. Pick a sunny, well-drained spot, and water in dry weather.

To harvest seeds cut the stems when the flower heads have turned brown. Tie a paper bag over each head and hang stems upside down in bunches. Gather leaves for kitchen use when young — flavour is retained after drying.

Use chopped leaves as a garnish, and also in the cooking of fish. Seeds can be added to bread, cakes, fish etc.

FENNEL

Common fennel is a perennial growing about 1.5 m (5 ft) high with feathery foliage and yellow flowers. Do not confuse it with florence fennel — a vegetable grown for its swollen stem bases.

Choose a sunny, well-drained spot — it is more at home in a mixed border than in a herb bed. You can sow seed in spring, but it is much easier to buy a pot-grown plant from a garden centre. Pick leaves in summer — harvest the same way as described for dill.

It has a stronger flavour than dill with which it is interchangeable. The seeds are recommended for cooking with oily fish such as mackerel.

MARJORAM/OREGANO

There are many varieties of *Origanum* — most are referred to as marjoram but *O. vulgare* is called oregano. The usual type is sweet marjoram — a bushy plant grown as a half hardy annual.

Seeds are sown under glass in March and planted out in a sunny spot in late May, leaving 25 cm (10 in.) between the plants. Pick before the flowers open — lift plants in autumn and move indoors for winter use. The perennial pot marjoram is much easier to grow — just plant a pot-grown specimen in spring and it will grow as readily as mint.

The prime use is for sprinkling over meat or poultry before roasting.

MINT

Mint alongside parsley is our favourite herb. It will thrive in most garden soils. Keep it in check by growing in a container, sinking plastic sheets into the soil around the plants, or by lifting and replanting every year.

There are several types — spearmint (garden mint) is the usual one, but Bowles mint is highly recommended for mint sauce, and apple mint combines fragrance with a true minty flavour. Plant pieces of root 5 cm (2 in.) deep and 25 cm (10 in.) apart in autumn.

Sprigs are boiled with new potatoes or peas, but its most popular use is in mint sauce to accompany roast lamb.

PARSLEY

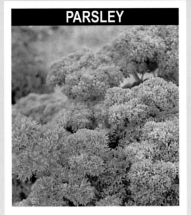

Curly-leaved parsley is the most decorative — the plain-leaved types have the most flavour.

Sow seed 1 cm (½ in.) deep in April for a summer and autumn crop, and again in August for winter use — germination may take up to 2 months. Thin to 25 cm (10 in.) and water in dry weather — cover overwintering plants with cloches or fleece. Remove flower stems as they appear. Pick regularly — dry sprigs by dipping in boiling water for 2 minutes and then placing in a cool oven until crisp.

The garnish *par excellence*, and an ingredient in *bouquet garni*.

ROSEMARY

This is an attractive evergreen shrub for the herb garden, mixed border or in a tub — it needs well-drained soil and a sunny, sheltered spot.

Regular picking and spring pruning should keep the bush about 60 cm (2 ft) high. You can sow seed in May but it is much more convenient to buy a pot-grown plant in spring. Winter frosts and icy winds in spring may kill some of the shoots but new growth will appear.

Both the needle-like leaves and the white or blue flowers are used. It is a traditional flavouring for lamb, pork and veal — insert sprigs before roasting and remove before serving.

SAGE

With its grey-green leaves and spikes of blue flowers, this herb is as useful in a mixed border as in the herb garden. A single plant should be enough.

Plant a pot-grown specimen in spring in a sunny, well-drained spot. Pick leaves regularly and prune lightly in July after flowering. Collect foliage for drying before the plant has flowered — sage takes a long time to dry but will keep for up to a year in a closed container.

Sage has a very strong flavour and you must take care not to use too much. It partners onions in the traditional stuffing for duck etc, and goes into sausages, tomato dishes etc.

TARRAGON

Make sure you buy French tarragon which is noted for its flavour, and not Russian tarragon which is practically tasteless. It is not completely hardy, so cover the plants with straw or fleece in the autumn. Despite this, tarragon can spread like mint.

Well-drained soil and a sheltered spot are needed. Plant a pot-grown specimen in March — remove flowering shoots to maintain the supply of fresh leaves. Pick from June to October for immediate use — the surplus can be dried or deep frozen (see page 175).

Tarragon is used in many classical chicken and fish dishes.

THYME

Thyme is a low-growing evergreen shrub — the aromatic leaves can be picked all year round so there is no need for drying. Common thyme has the strongest flavour, lemon thyme is less pungent, and caraway thyme has a pine/caraway aroma.

Plant pot-grown specimens 30 cm (1 ft) apart in a well-drained sunny spot in spring. Divide every 3 years and re-plant. Pick leaves as required — if you don't have a garden, thyme will grow quite happily in a pot on the windowsill.

This herb is the traditional partner for parsley in the stuffing for poultry. It is also widely used on its own.

CHAPTER 11
GARDEN STYLES

Pick up any textbook on the history of gardening and you will find a detailed account of the various styles which evolved over the centuries — Picturesque, Landscape, Dutch, Victorian, French etc. Around the country you will find superb examples of these styles, but these are the Grand Gardens and they have little or nothing to do with the styles of the ordinary garden — the home garden. An interesting example of the difference is the variance in the Landscape period (1730-1830). This was the time when fashion dictated that all flowering plants should be moved outside the gates .... where the villagers gathered them and planted them in the ground around their cottages!

Books dealing with home garden styles are much more difficult to find, and no garden designer has been clever enough (or foolish enough) to try to establish a generally acceptable classification of clear-cut styles. In the following pages six styles are described, and these cover the vast majority of British home gardens. There are about 15 million of them with an average size of 180 sq.m (2000 sq.ft). Somewhere in these statistics is your garden.

Within each of these styles there is an extremely wide range of options. Wildflower and Cottage Gardens are always informal, but the remainder can be formal filled with geometrical shapes, or informal with a more natural look. Within most styles different historical periods may be reflected — an Architectural Garden may be filled with classical statues and Victorian features in wood and stone, or it may be startlingly modern with stainless steel, glass and plastic. Unlike the Grand Garden owners in the past you can choose any style, provided that it meets the five requirements listed on page 200 — it must be right for you and also the situation.

In the majority of gardens there is one basic style, but this does not mean that the whole garden has to be given over to a single style. A Wildflower bed or border can sit comfortably in an informal Standard or Country House Garden, and an Architectural area may not be out of place in a formal Standard Garden around a modern house.

The six styles listed here could no doubt be extended — the Novelty Garden designed to amaze or amuse has been omitted. So has the Monoculture Garden devoted to a single plant — usually the rose. There are undoubtedly other fringe ones, but the six described here certainly represent the mainstream of home garden styles.

Town Garden

A Town Garden in a rural setting. Old-fashioned plants and subdued flower colours have been used so that the plot mirrors the verdant leafy surroundings — unity is a feature of good garden design. Green pots rather than earthenware ones have been chosen

Paving is one of the dominant features of the Town Garden and so making the right choice is important. It need not be a sea of plain slabs — in this garden there is a mixture of gravel, reconstituted stone slabs, brick and natural stone to accompany but not overwhelm the planting

The expression 'Town Garden' has no precise meaning. Some designers use it to mean any small plot in an urban area irrespective of whether grass is grown or not. In this book 'Town Garden' describes a small plot where paving material is used instead of a lawn. The key feature is the absence of grass rather than the size of the garden.

The creation of an attractive urban garden faces a number of difficulties. On the average plot there are walls which cast considerable shade. Traffic noise can be a problem and so can air pollution from cars etc, and there can be a lack of privacy. Finally, tool storage and waste plant disposal can pose problems.

The Town Garden approach is the recommended one as a lawn under these conditions would be a disappointment, and the design is usually formal. There is no point in aiming for a natural look. Clothe the walls and/or fence where you can with plants to increase privacy and cut down traffic noise. Use borders/beds and containers for planting — a liberal use of evergreens and variegated shrubs is recommended to give year-round living colour. Achieve a dramatic effect by growing architectural plants (see page 184) wherever you can. Raised beds and small water features are excellent items for a Town Garden.

Town Garden trees & shrubs

Salix exigua
Pinus mugo 'Gnom'
Rosa rugosa
Camellia japonica
Fatsia japonica
Stachys lanata
Magnolia stellata
Viburnum tinus
Choisya ternata
Lonicera americana
Mahonia 'Charity'
Dryopteris filix-mas
Buxus sempervirens
Arundinaria murielae
Pieris 'Forest Flame'
Prunus 'Amanogawa'
Acer negundo 'Flamingo'
Skimmia japonica 'Rubella'
Hydrangea macrophylla
Hedera helix 'Goldheart'
Aucuba japonica 'Variegata'
Jasminum nudiflorum

Is this style right for you?

If your plot is small and enclosed then a lawn-free Town Garden would be a good choice, especially if you like sitting outdoors.

Standard Garden

The small Standard Garden. The back garden may be no wider than the house and here there is little scope for flowing lines and an informal look. In these small plots a formal design is usually chosen. Circles and straight lines need not be dull — see the next page for ways to add interest

The large Standard Garden. The back garden may extend for an acre or more and numerous features may be present — pool, rockery, arches etc. A popular approach is to have a formal design near the house and an informal style with a winding path and curved borders at the outer reaches

The Standard style dominates the garden scene — mile after mile of these gardens can be seen from any railway carriage window. The front garden may be treated in several ways — grass is a common but by no means a general feature. It is the back garden which sets the style. There is a lawn which usually covers most of the area, and there is a selection of flowers, shrubs and/or trees to add colour and interest. At least one path or drive leads to the house and the property is totally or partly enclosed by a wall, fencing or hedge. These are the only features which all Standard-style Gardens have in common.

With no other features the garden could look dull. To add interest to your plot there are many optional extras — see the list on the right. Some should be included but don't overdo it. If you are changing your hackneyed Standard-style Garden then think about moving away from the central rectangular lawn and its frill of borders and scattering of beds. Consider curves and hidden areas to add interest. Think about the Bed System for growing vegetables the no-dig way — see the *Vegetable & Herb Expert* for details.

Finally, remember that all of these points are suggestions — if your ideal is a green handkerchief with a flowery edging then that is a good design.

Essential features

- Lawn
- Beds and/or borders
- Paths and/or drives
- Fencing, walls and/or hedges

Optional extras

- Play area (Sand box etc)
- Paved area (Table, chairs etc)
- Water area (Pond etc)
- Utility area (Shed, compost bin etc)
- Greenhouse
- Pergola/Archway
- Rock garden
- Steps
- Barbeque
- Ornaments (Sundial, birdtable etc)
- Vegetable plot
- Herb garden
- Containers (Pots, tubs etc)
- Lighting

Is this style right for you?

If you want your back garden to keep its lawn with a selection of flowers and shrubs then this is the style for you. Depending on your skill it can be restfully plain or outstandingly vibrant.

The Formal Approach

In the strictly formal garden there is a central axis and the right-hand side is a mirror image of the left side. Paths are straight and the shapes of beds, borders, pools etc are geometrical — squares, rectangles, circles, ovals etc. Trimmed hedges to divide beds and provide privacy are often key features. There are many examples in our great gardens, but for most people this approach is too sterile and quite unsuitable for a family garden.

The modern-day formal garden still relies on geometrical shapes but the requirement for one side of the garden or garden area to be just like the other has gone. So has the idea that the plants should be naturally neat or should be kept trimmed to avoid an untidy look. One of the ways to enliven a formal garden is to interlock some of the geometric shapes — a circular bed cutting into a circular paved area or square flower beds linked into a rectangular paved area.

The Informal Approach

In the informal garden there is no feeling of a collection of geometrical patterns — here the plants and not the shapes are the key feature. Winding paths and irregularly-shaped beds and borders are key features, and so is the use of tall plants and structures to hide the boundaries from view. Curves are paramount, but keep them simple and avoid wavy and fussy shapes at all costs.

It may seem strange but designing a 'natural' looking garden is more difficult than drawing up plans for a strictly formal one. In the informal garden one has to try to get a sense of balance with objects which are quite different in size and shape. One large plant may call for a group of small ones nearby to provide balance.

Borders are usually wider than the narrow straight strips of the formal garden, and where width is limited it is usually better to have a single side border. Beds in the centre of the lawn will make the garden look smaller.

The Basic Version

This is the back garden you will see everywhere — a square or rectangular plot with a central lawn and one or more borders at the edges. Bedding plants are in the flower beds and a mixture of plants is in the borders. There are few other features — the ones you are most likely to find are a vegetable plot at the bottom of the garden and containers close to the house. In most cases there is no call for change — the children play on the lawn, the beds provide a splash of colour, there is a place to sit in the sun and there are the vegetables to look after.

The De-luxe Version

Here the garden is more than a place for plants and most of the principles of good design have been incorporated. The use of formal and informal styles, hidden areas and clever use of focal points create what garden architects call 'tension' — a sudden increase in attention as you move from one part of the garden to the other. Materials are in keeping with the style of the house and there are adequate areas for sitting or entertaining. An important feature is the presence of year-round colour, and regular pruning and weeding ensure year-round admiration.

Country House Garden

The classical Country House Garden with a wrap-around lawn surrounding a large barn conversion. The plant beds are at some distance from the dwelling, and so are the outbuildings. The object here has been to give a feeling of open space around the house

The wrap-around lawn and a feeling of uncluttered space are not essential features of the Country House Garden. Deep borders and large beds surround this beautiful old manor house in East Anglia — here the lawns and not the flowers have been consigned to the outer reaches

The Country House Garden is usually found in a rural area, but they also occur in the suburbs. It is usually larger than the Standard model, but not always. Trees and large shrubs always play a key role, but they may also do so in a Standard plot. The basic difference is that a Country House Garden is a wrap-round plot which surrounds the house — there is no division into front and back garden. This means that here we have a single unit which offers great scope for creative landscaping.

There is often a touch of formal design close to the house (rectangular terrace, square flower beds flanking steps etc) and in the 'garden rooms' in the outer reaches of the garden (rose garden, box-edged knot garden, herb garden etc). The overall picture, however, is one of informal shapes and informal planting. The use of trees and large shrubs provides a woodland look and the main source of colour is traditionally a long and wide herbaceous border. Holding all the elements together is the large lawn with areas of less-manicured grassland in the large estate gardens.

There is great scope in the large wrap-round garden to have path-linked 'rooms' — a wildflower area, a mediterranean garden etc. The workaday regions (vegetable plot, compost heap etc) can be hidden away. Here we have the world's idea of a classic English garden.

Country Garden features

Extensive lawn (buttercups and daisies are acceptable)

Stone, brick or gravel paths (Concrete is not acceptable)

Stone ornaments (Urns, statues, sundial etc)

Wood or wrought iron seats

Shrub roses and old-fashioned climbers

Herbaceous plants grown in groups rather than single specimens

Summerhouse

Winding walkways

Beds surrounded by clipped box hedging

Specimen trees

Boundary fencing hidden by shrubs, hedging etc

Rhododendrons and azaleas if soil is acid

Is this style right for you?

Yes, if the garden is large and wraps around the house. Can look out of place around a contemporary style property.

Cottage Garden

Paths are generally straight and made of brick, stone or compressed earth — modern surfaces should be avoided. Edges are hidden by flanking plants

Plant clumps are large — perennials are not often divided. There is no planning — introductions are planted wherever there is room

Modern hard landscaping is avoided. Weathered pots, old sinks and low brick or stone walls form the framework

For centuries the Cottage Garden was the standard style to be found around the small dwellings in every village in the land, but that time is past. The true Cottage Garden is now quite a rarity, but it is still a welcome sight as a reminder of our horticultural heritage.

There are a number of key features. The basic one is a complete lack of formality — plants are crowded together to form a jumble of colours, shapes and sizes. A second feature is the use of old-fashioned plants. Modern roses and half-hardy annuals creep in these days, but they do not belong in the true Cottage Garden.

Floral colour should come from perennials, self-sown annuals, bulbs and some flowering shrubs — in addition there will be shrub roses in the beds and rambler roses on the house walls. Fragrance is important, and so is a kaleidoscope of colours.

The Cottage Garden has always had to work for a living. Vegetables such as cabbage, broad beans and onions fill the spaces between the flowers. Herbs like rosemary, mint and sage are another essential ingredient.

In the old days nothing was bought — seeds were saved, cuttings were rooted and plants were exchanged with neighbours. Things have changed, but even today the Cottage Garden owner is not the garden centre's favourite customer.

Favourite Cottage Garden plants

Lavender
Rose
Honeysuckle
Hollyhock
Shasta Daisy
Sunflower
Catmint
Geranium
Clematis
Pinks
Chives
Love-in-a-mist
Nasturtium
Daylily
Phlox
Hellebores
Aquilegia
Achillea
Pyracantha
Cotoneaster
Canterbury Bells
Lupin
Red-hot Poker
Parsley

Is this style right for you?

This style is at home on a moderate-sized plot around a rural house. It is decidedly unhappy in a modern suburban setting.

Architectural Garden

Starkly simple. The hard landscape is colourless and the planting is plain — architectural plants have not been used. Not for everybody's taste, of course, but it is much more eye-catching than the paved front gardens which are now such a common sight. The stone balls and cubes are effective focal points

The other end of the scale from the example on the left. There is no white to be seen and the large Agaves are a vital part of the garden. A garden made to impress lovers of modern design and to horrify traditionalists who believe that gardens are a place for plants

In the Architectural Garden the designer sets out to produce a non-living structure which looks attractive in summer and winter, and into which plants are introduced to add living colour and living shapes. Here paths, walls and containers are chosen for their decorative and not simply their functional role. Trees and shrubs are chosen for their shape and leaf colours just as much as their blooms. Flowers, if present, are in formal beds, borders or containers.

There is a growing trend these days to convert small front plots into Architectural Gardens for the purely practical purpose of providing off-the-street parking for the car — unfortunately the result is so often devoid of any worthwhile planting. Much better examples are to be seen in wall-enclosed courtyard gardens where attractive paving, wall features, ironwork, flower-filled pots etc are blended together.

Treating a large back garden in this way can be stunning, but be warned. Not only will it be expensive to create but it can be a definite deterrent to a would-be buyer if you decide to move house. It may be wonderful as an outdoor living or dining area when furnished with lighting, gas heaters, tables, chairs etc, but it is a horror for the keen and active traditional gardener.

Plants for the Architectural Garden

Palms
Bamboos
Grasses
Ferns
Conifers
Yucca gloriosa
Canna indica
Viburnum davidii
Agave americana
Myrtus communis
Phormium tenax
Cynara cardunculus
Musa basjoo
Agapanthus africanus
Aralia elata variegata
Citrus mitis
Rhus typhina
Zantedeschia aethiopica
Acer palmatum
Robinia pseudoacacia
Kalmia latifolia

Is this style right for you?

If this style really appeals to you then it is worth considering if the house is contemporary and you want an almost gardening-free life.

Wildflower Garden

This wildflower meadow provides a mass of colour in late spring — a reminder of the flower-filled fields of times gone by. Unfortunately weed grasses are a serious problem in most soils, and even when they are not present the area looks extremely dull when the flowers are absent

Clumps of wildflowers growing among rocks and/or native trees and shrubs are more appealing to many people than the wildflower meadow. Plant care is easier and the permanent residents of the plot provide some interest when the wildflower plants have died down

A Wildflower Garden seeks to look like an area of the countryside set next to your house — it may take up all of your property or just a section of it. The key feature is the flower-filled meadow planted with native species which produce their delicate, pastel-coloured blooms in spring and autumn. The design style is generally informal and its features should be in keeping — wattle fences, rural seating etc.

Creating a Wildflower Garden is not an easy option. First of all, it is necessary to remove the top 5 cm (2 in.) of soil as you need infertile soil for wild flowers. Kill re-emerging weeds and grasses with glyphosate before sowing with a wild flower mixture from your garden centre or specialist supplier — it is essential to choose a mix which is suitable for your soil type. On a small plot wildflower seedlings can be planted as an alternative to sowing seed.

Cutting takes place in July — trim down to about 10 cm (4 in.) and after a few weeks rake up the clippings. Never apply a fertilizer — in fertile soil the wildflowers may be quickly swamped by weeds such as couch grass and nettles.

A wild garden is not the same thing. It will contain a wildflower area, but its key feature is the provision of wildlife-attracting areas — nesting boxes, water, log piles, berry-bearing shrubs, native and cultivated plants which attract butterflies and so on.

Favourite wildflower species

White campion
Ragged robin
Betony
Crane's bill
Ox-eye daisy
Field poppy
Corncockle
Field scabious
Corn marigold
Meadow buttercup
Wild pansy
Musk mallow
Agrimony
Daffodil
Cat's ear
Primrose
Scentless mayweed
Bluebell
Vetch
Lily of the valley
Foxglove

Is this style right for you?

Yes, if you really want a natural look and accept that for much of the year it may not be attractive. Success is something of a gamble.

CHAPTER 12

FRUIT

Growing fruit in the garden is decorative and full of interest as each fruit progresses from bud to flower to the picking stage. It is also rewarding — the produce is picked straight from the tree or bush so that it is truly fresh, and you can grow varieties which are not available in shops. Above all, it is *your* apple or strawberry which you have grown with your own hands.

Despite the fascination of growing your own fruit, it was not until the Grow Your Own movement burst on the scene that this aspect of gardening began to cast off its Cinderella role. Only one U.K garden in three grew any fruit at all, and there were two basic reasons for this lack of interest. Firstly, there has been the view that all fruit is difficult and time consuming. It is true that there are some types which do require regular work, but a fruit garden once planted and established gives more for less effort than the vegetable plot. Perhaps some textbooks have been partly responsible for this negative view — there are descriptions of pruning which make it sound as complex as brain surgery, and it used to be fashionable to recommend a fungicide or insecticide for almost every unwelcome visitor.

Secondly, many people have regarded fruit growing as space-demanding with visions of ladders for picking tree fruit, and fruit cages for soft fruit.

Times have changed. The Grow Your Own movement has created the desire for home-grown produce, and the advances since World War II have made fruit growing practical for any garden.

Garden centres have container-grown trees, canes and bushes available for planting at any time of the year, and dwarfing stocks have produced apple and pear trees which are not much larger than rose bushes.

So fruit growing is for you, but a word or two of caution is necessary. Planting a fruit tree or bush is a long-term investment, so read this chapter and perhaps the *Fruit Expert* before going to the garden centre or ordering from a catalogue. Choose carefully, making sure that both the type and variety are suitable for your conditions. This should also include consideration of the time you devote to gardening. If time and interest are limited then choose the 'easy' ones such as dwarf apple bushes, autumn-fruiting raspberries and container-grown strawberries.

Tree Fruit

There is no exact definition of tree fruit — included here are the larger and stouter fruitbearing plants. Nearly all adopt a tree form (single main stem) in their natural state, but a few (e.g quince) are shrubs.

Most tree fruit belong to the rose family, and there is a vast range from which to make your choice. In this chapter you will find details of the four most popular ones — for others see the *Fruit Expert*. Remember that the trees will be with you for many years, so pick the site with care and prepare the soil properly.

The eventual height of the tree will be determined by type, growing conditions and by the rootstock on which the variety has been grafted. The growth pattern is determined by pruning and training.

Pick the sunniest spot available — full sun and a mild climate are essential for tender types. The soil should be reasonably deep and not prone to waterlogging.

There are a number of items to consider before choosing a variety. Go for dessert (eating) varieties rather than culinary (cooking) ones if space is limited — in the catalogues you may find one or more dual-purpose varieties. The variety on offer may be self-sterile and would require a suitable pollinating partner nearby. Further information on this subject is provided for each individual fruit. Consider buying a family tree (a plant grafted with several compatible varieties) if you intend to plant just one tree.

Once established the fruiting season usually lasts longer than with soft fruit. In addition the yield per plant is usually much higher — 4-180 kg (9-400 lb) compared with 200 gm-10 kg (8 oz-22 lb).

Rootstocks

The main factor controlling the eventual size of your tree is the rootstock which has been used.

Apples M27 is the very dwarfing rootstock. M9 and M26 are dwarfing stocks used for small bushes — MM106 is used for larger bushes, MM111 is the stock for half standards.

Pears Quince A is the most satisfactory rootstock.

Cherries Colt is the basic rootstock.

Plum Pixy is a semi-dwarfing stock — St. Julien A is used for half standards.

Planting material

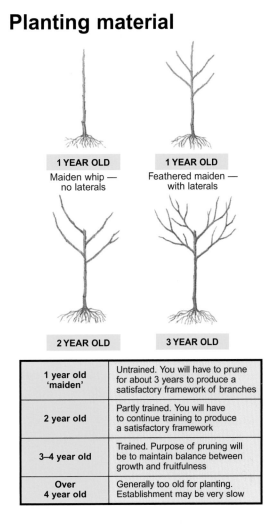

1 YEAR OLD	1 YEAR OLD
Maiden whip — no laterals	Feathered maiden — with laterals
2 YEAR OLD	3 YEAR OLD

1 year old 'maiden'	Untrained. You will have to prune for about 3 years to produce a satisfactory framework of branches
2 year old	Partly trained. You will have to continue training to produce a satisfactory framework
3–4 year old	Trained. Purpose of pruning will be to maintain balance between growth and fruitfulness
Over 4 year old	Generally too old for planting. Establishment may be very slow

Types

POME TREE varieties
Hardy trees which bear fleshy fruit which have a central cavity containing several small seeds (pips)
Apple
Pear
●

STONE TREE varieties
Hardy trees which bear fleshy fruit which have a central cavity containing a large hard seed (stone)
Plum
Cherry
●

OTHER OUTDOOR varieties
Hardy fruit-bearing trees which may be common in the countryside but not in the fruit garden
Mulberry
Elderberry
Quince
Sloe

TENDER varieties
Frost-sensitive plants which may be grown outdoors in sheltered localities but are more successful when grown under glass
Apricot
Peach
Nectarine
Fig

Apple

Apples are the most popular of all tree fruits — attractive in bloom and rewarding at cropping time. Most areas of Britain are quite suitable for apple cultivation, and there is a range of growth types. There is, of course, the standard or classic apple tree and this is dealt with below, but it is not for the average plot. It is much better to grow a bush if space is reasonably plentiful. If space is limited a dwarf bush, a row of cordons or a compact column is a much better choice. There are other types — the espalier, fan, spindlebush, step-over etc. See the *Fruit Expert* for details.

With all these growth types your apple variety will very likely need a pollination partner which flowers at approximately the same time. The standard advice is to plant a partner in your garden, but in urban areas there is generally an example nearby. If apple trees are scarce or absent in your neighbourhood, you can grow a self-fertile variety — 'Queen Cox', 'James Grieve' and 'Arthur Turner' are examples.

The final stage is picking the fruit. It is ready for picking when it comes away easily with stalk attached after being lifted and gently twisted. Store sound fruit by wrapping in newspaper, placing in wooden trays and keeping in a cool, dry place.

The catalogue words

Biennial bearer A variety which produces a good crop every other year with little or nothing in between. **Tip-bearing variety** A variety which bears most of its fruit at the ends of 1-year old shoots. **Spur-bearing variety** A variety which bears all or most of its fruit on very short branches.

Planting & Spacing

Lime the soil if it is very acid, and provide a windbreak if site is exposed. Follow the basic rules on pages 62-63. Plant to the old soil mark — the rootstock union should be 10 cm (4 in.) above ground.

Space half standards 5 m (16 ft) apart. Spacing for the other growth types below are bushes 4 m (13 ft), dwarf bushes 3 m (10 ft), dwarf bushes on M27 rootstock 2 m (7 ft), cordons 1 m (3 ft), and 60 cm (2 ft) between compact columns.

Fruit types

FRUIT SIZE	Diameter of fruit
Very Large	over 9 cm (3½ in.)
Large	6-9 cm (2¼-3½ in.)
Medium	5-6 cm (2-2¼ in.)
Small	less than 5 cm (2 in.)

FRUITING SEASON	Picking time	Storage period
Early	July — Early September	Nil — eat within 7 days
Mid-season	September — October	Limited — 2-3 weeks
Late	October — November	Prolonged — 1-6 months depending upon variety

Growth types

BUSH
The most popular type — bushes have an open centre and a short trunk — bushes 60-75 cm (2-2½ ft), dwarf bushes 45-60 cm (1½-2 ft). They soon come into fruit and are easy to maintain. The mature size depends on the rootstock — 2 m (7 ft) on M27 to 5.5 m (18 ft) on MM106. Not for lawn planting.

STANDARD
Large trees grown on semivigorous or vigorous rootstocks — they are only suitable where there is plenty of space and top yields are required. The standard has a 1.8-2 m (6-7 ft) high trunk — the half standard trunk is 1.2-1.4 m (4-4½ ft). These 4.5-7.5 m (15-25 ft) tall trees are difficult to care for.

CORDON
A single-stemmed tree which is planted at 45º and tied to a permanent support system such as a fence. A dwarfing rootstock is generally used and vigorous varieties are usually avoided. An excellent way of growing several varieties in a restricted space, but the summer pruning routine is tricky.

COMPACT COLUMN
The compact column was introduced in 1989 as the Ballerina tree. There is a single main stem with hardly any side branches, which means that no pruning is required. The height after 5 years is about 2 m (7 ft), and the unique growth habit makes it suitable for lawns, tubs and borders.

Pruning

It is necessary to prune bushes and standards between November and February — shown below is the easiest way to prune established trees. Espaliers, fans and cordons are pruned in mid July (southern districts) or early August (other areas). See the *Fruit Expert* for details.

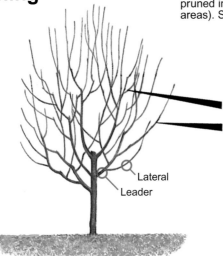

Lateral

Leader

Spur-bearing variety

Remove dead and badly diseased wood. Cut back crossing branches and vigorous laterals growing into the centre. Then:

Inside the head — leave leaders alone. Cut back each lateral which is growing into and beyond the branch leader

Outside the head — leave both leaders and laterals alone

Overcropping and undersized fruit may become a problem. If this has happened, thin some of the fruiting spurs and cut out some laterals

Tip-bearing variety

Remove dead, diseased and overcrowded wood. Then:

Cut back some leaders — leave alone all laterals with fruit buds at their tips

Varieties

ARTHUR TURNER Mid-season culinary variety. Green, flushed orange. Plus points include outstanding floral display, heavy yields and reliability in northern areas. Sets fruit without a partner.

ASHMEAD'S KERNEL Late dessert variety. Greenish-yellow, brown russet. Superb flavour is its only virtue — the apples are small and yields are light. Traditional season of use December-February.

BLENHEIM ORANGE Mid-season culinary/dessert variety. Orange, flushed and striped red. The best dual-purpose apple. Excellent nutty flavour — heavy yields. A biennial bearer prone to scab.

BRAEBURN Late dessert variety. Reddish-green. Britain's best-selling apple, but it has only recently entered the garden scene. Self-fertile, crisp, juicy — stores for up to 4 months.

BRAMLEY'S SEEDLING Mid-season culinary variety. Green. Our most popular cooking apple — but it is too vigorous for small gardens. A biennial- and partial tip-bearer.

COX'S ORANGE PIPPIN Mid-season dessert variety. Orange, flushed orange-red with russet patches. One for the shopping basket but not for the garden. Temperamental — susceptible to frost.

DISCOVERY Early dessert variety. Bright red. Better than its parent 'Worcester Pearmain', but its yields are moderate. Good choice for the smaller garden. It is a spur- and tip-bearer.

EGREMONT RUSSET Early dessert variety. Dull brown with russet patches. Fruit is rather small, but flavour is good — nutty and sweet.

FIESTA Mid-season dessert variety. Yellow, flushed and striped red. A variety for people who want a Cox-flavoured apple without the problem of growing the parent. Reliable — crops heavily.

GEORGE CAVE Early dessert variety. Green, flushed and striped red. A heavy-yielding apple which is ready in late July in favourable districts. A spur- and tip-bearer.

GREENSLEEVES Mid-season dessert variety. Green turning pale yellow. This is the one to grow if you are a 'Golden Delicious' fan. Heavy yields, but flavour fades in store. A spur- and tip-bearer.

GRENADIER Early culinary variety. Yellowish-green. The standard early cooking apple. It is a good apple to grow in the garden — hardy, compact, excellent flavour, but does not store well.

IDARED Late dessert/culinary variety. Yellow, flushed red. Outstanding keeping qualities — can last until April. It can be eaten fresh as well as used for cooking, but the flavour is nothing special.

JAMES GRIEVE Early dessert variety. Yellow, speckled and striped orange. A reliable and hardy apple which crops heavily and regularly. Fruit is juicy and tangy, but keeping quality is rather poor.

LORD LAMBOURNE Mid-season dessert variety. Greenish-yellow, flushed and striped red. It can be relied upon to crop heavily and regularly almost anywhere. A tip- and spur-bearer.

NEWTON WONDER Late culinary variety. Yellow, flushed and striped red. A vigorous apple not suitable for small gardens. The yields are heavy and the fruit stores well, but it is a biennial bearer.

ORLEANS REINETTE Late dessert variety. Yellow, flushed red with russet patches. An 18th century apple which does have its problems. Yields are low and it is a biennial bearer.

QUEEN COX Mid-season dessert variety. Orange, flushed orange-red with russet patches. This sport of 'Cox' is self-fertile and so does not need a pollinator.

RED FALSTAFF Late dessert variety. Red. This colourful sport of 'Falstaff' is self-fertile, and is highly recommended. Heavy yields, stores well, and it is a good pollinator for other varieties.

SUNSET Mid-season dessert variety. Orange, flushed and striped red with russet patches. This offspring of 'Cox' has all the good qualities of its parent, but with few of the bad points.

Pear

Pears are more temperamental than apples. They hate cold easterly winds — flowers open earlier than apple blossom and late spring frost can be very damaging. Choose from 'Conference', 'Beth' or 'Concorde' if your site is exposed and in a cool area. Pears are more susceptible to drought than apples, but generally less prone to disease and pests with one exception — bullfinches prefer pear fruit buds. Pears generally live longer — fifty years is the normal life span of an apple tree, but a pear should live for a century or more.

Pears have far fewer varieties in the catalogues and at the garden centre. Don't choose a culinary variety — use firm dessert fruit for cooking. Early-ripening varieties should be harvested when they are full-sized, but before they are fully ripe — cut the stalks and leave for 1-2 weeks to ripen. Follow the picking instructions for apples (see page 188) when harvesting late varieties — ripen unwrapped on wooden trays in a cool, dry place. Storage life is limited — hardly any dessert pears can be kept after Christmas.

Growth types

Pears can be grown as a **BUSH** or **CORDON** in the same way as apples — see page 188. They can also be grown as an **ESPALIER** or **FAN** — see below. Planting as a single row of cordons is perhaps the best way of growing pears in the average garden.

ESPALIER

The pairs of branches are stretched horizontally to form a series of tiers at 50 cm (1½ ft) intervals. It is more decorative than the cordon, but it takes up more space and it is more difficult to maintain. Buy trees which have already been trained.

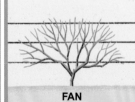

FAN

An attractive form when planted against a wall, but it needs space — a height of 2 m (7 ft) and a spread of 3 m (10 ft). Careful training is essential. Not a popular tree form for pears — the fan is much more widely used for cherries and plums.

Pollination

Pears are much less popular than apples, so you will probably have to provide a suitable pollination partner in your garden — ask your supplier for recommendations. The easiest plan here is to grow several different varieties as cordons. Alternatively grow 'Conference' which is partly self-fertile, or plant a family tree carrying 'Conference', 'Doyenne du Comice' and 'Williams' Bon Chrétien'.

Planting & Spacing

Choose the warmest spot in the garden. Pears can thrive in heavier soil than apples, but they dislike shallow soil, chalk and salt-laden air. Pears can be grown as bushes and cordons in the same way as apples and at the same spacings — see page 188. They can also be grown as fans and espaliers — leave 4 m (13 ft) between the plants when growing either of these growth types. For all these types follow the instructions on page 188. Do not plant standard or half standard trees unless you have a large garden — they are far too vigorous.

Pruning

See page 189 for details of a simple Regulation System to use on established trees in winter. For further details on pruning and for instructions on training young trees see the *Fruit Expert* (pages 22-23).

Varieties

BETH Dessert variety. Yellow, with russet spots. Pick in late August — use in September. Not a pear for shops, but a good one for you. Small fruit, but juicy and sweet. Yields are high.

BEURRE HARDY Dessert variety. Yellow, flushed red with russet patches. Pick in mid September — use in October. Sometimes recommended, but too vigorous for the average garden.

CONCORDE Dessert variety. Pale green. Pick in late October — use in November-December. One of the best — a compact plant which crops heavily with an early start to fruiting. Excellent flavour.

CONFERENCE Dessert variety. Olive green with large russet patches. Pick in late September — use in October-November. The No.1 choice because it is so reliable and partly self-fertile.

DOYENNE DU COMICE Dessert variety. Yellow, flushed brownish-red. Pick mid October — use in November-December. It has the best flavour, but a poor choice if conditions are unfavourable.

INVINCIBLE Dessert variety. Green, flushed with gold. Pick in October — use in November-December. It is partly self-fertile, so a partner is not essential. No grittiness — it is the 'butter pear'.

WILLIAMS' BON CHRETIEN Dessert variety. Pale yellow, striped and spotted red. Pick in September — use in September. A shop-bought favourite — excellent flavour, but storage quality is poor.

Plum

Plums are the most popular of the stone fruits and they are also the easiest to grow, but they are not for everyone. The first problem is that they flower very early in the season, and so cropping can be disappointing and irregular, especially in low-lying or exposed sites due to frost damage and/or poor pollination. Size can be another problem as plum trees and bushes are vigorous and wide-spreading — the recommendation given here is to plant a fan which has Pixy as its rootstock. Netting to keep off bullfinches is a simple matter with this growth form.

Cropping should start when the tree is about 5 years old. Thin out the fruits in June and provide support for branches if necessary. Pruning established trees is a relatively simple matter, but dealing with fan plums is rather more complex — see the *Fruit Expert* for details. Pick when the fruit parts easily from the tree. Harvest dessert varieties when thoroughly ripe but pick culinary types when the fruit is still slightly unripe. Dessert plums will keep for only a few days, but can be stored for 2-3 weeks in a cool place if picked unripe with stalks attached.

Types

DESSERT PLUM

Sweet — eaten fresh. Fleshy fruit — trees smaller and less hardy than culinary varieties. Most popular variety: 'Victoria'

●

GAGE

Smaller, rounder and sweeter than dessert plums. Yields are not high. Grow as a fan against a south wall

CULINARY PLUM

Rather tart — used for cooking. Fruit less fleshy than dessert varieties — trees more tolerant of poor conditions. Most popular variety: 'Czar'

●

DAMSON

Spicy tart flavour — used for cooking, jam- and wine-making. A hardy tree which succeeds where a plum would fail

Pollination

Many plums are self-fertile, including the most popular dessert variety ('Victoria') and the most widely-grown culinary variety ('Czar'). Others need a pollination partner, and you will have to plant one if plums are not grown in neighbouring gardens. Ask your supplier for recommendations.

Planting & Spacing

Plums need a moisture-retentive but free-draining soil. Light soils which easily dry out must be enriched with organic matter. Choose the highest spot in the garden, and an area which gets lots of sun if you plan to grow a dessert plum or gage.

A standard or half standard has no place in the average garden — they are far too vigorous. Even a bush grafted on to the dwarfing rootstock Pixy will reach 4-6 m (13-20 ft). The best plan is to grow your plum as a fan against a south-facing wall. The recommended distances are half standards on St. Julien A rootstock 5 m (16 ft), fans 4 m (13 ft) and bushes on Pixy 3 m (10 ft). November is the best time for planting.

Pruning

Pruning takes place in June-late July, not in winter. Keep pruning of an established tree to the minimum. Remove dead, broken and diseased branches and cut back overcrowded ones.

Varieties

CAMBRIDGE GAGE Culinary/dessert gage. Yellowish-green, flushed red. It will set some fruit without a partner, but it is not recommended for cold areas. Flavour is very good.

CZAR Culinary plum. Dark purple. The cooking variety most people choose. It is self-fertile and is one of the most reliable varieties when conditions are less than perfect.

MARJORIE'S SEEDLING Culinary/dessert plum. Purple. The blossom season is late enough to miss early frosts — picking starts end September. Large oval fruit, growth is vigorous and upright.

MERRYWEATHER Culinary damson. Blue-black. The most popular damson — an excellent all-round performer you will find in most catalogues. Self-fertile — large fruit.

OPAL Dessert plum. Reddish-purple. A partially self-fertile variety which is ready about 14 days before 'Victoria'. Flesh separates easily from the stone. Good flavour.

OULLIN'S GOLDEN GAGE Culinary/dessert gage. Yellow, spotted green and brown. A plum-like gage — large, yellow-fleshed and round. Self-fertile — growth is vigorous and upright.

VICTORIA Culinary/dessert plum. Pale red. The most popular variety — self-fertile, reliable and a heavy cropper. However, disease resistance is poor, thinning is necessary and flavour is only average.

Cherry

Both sweet dessert and sour culinary varieties are available. Until the mid 1970s sweet varieties were out of the question for the average garden — 12 m (40 ft) high trees made pruning, picking and bird protection quite impractical. Then along came the dwarfing rootstock Colt to make garden-sized plants a practical proposition, and the variety 'Stella' appeared — a self-fertile cherry which does not need a pollination partner.

Before this sweet cherry revolution it was traditional to choose an acid cherry variety. Growth is much more compact and the most popular variety ('Morello') is self-fertile. Trees begin to bear fruit after only 3 or 4 years and they grow quite happily in partial shade.

Protection against birds is essential — netting is the most satisfactory method and a fan cherry is the easiest type to protect.

Leave sweet cherries on the tree until they are ripe — try one or two for sweetness. Use scissors when harvesting acid cherries — pulling off fruits can encourage the entry of disease. Cut off with stalks attached. Harvest unnetted acid cherries at the red unripe stage to avoid the inevitable loss of ripe fruit to birds.

Types

SWEET (DESSERT) CHERRY

Sweet — eaten fresh. Flesh is either soft and very juicy or firm and moist. Skin colour ranges from pale yellow to near black. Traditionally very vigorous and self-sterile, but semi-vigorous and self-fertile trees are now available

●

ACID (SOUR or CULINARY) CHERRY

Sour — used for cooking, bottling, jam, wine-making etc. Flesh may be white, pink or red. 'Morello' is the usual choice, but other self-fertile acid varieties such as 'Nabella' are available

Pollination

All the varieties listed here, apart from 'Merton Glory' are self-fertile. Choose a plant with this property — others need a pollination partner.

Planting & Spacing

Sweet cherries need a sheltered, sunny site — acid varieties are less fussy. Ideally the soil should be moisture-retentive but free-draining — cherries fare badly in shallow or sandy soil.

Grow a bush or fan — the best plan is to plant a fan against a south-facing wall to provide sun and wind protection, plus making it easy to spread netting or fleece to prevent frost- and bird-damage.

The plant you will buy will almost certainly be on Colt rootstock. Bushes and fans should be about 5 m (16 ft) apart. Standards and half standards are grown on F12/1 rootstocks. A few suppliers offer bushes and fans on semi-dwarfing rootstocks such as Gisela 5 — here the spacing distance for bushes and fans is reduced to 3-4 m (10-13 ft). November is the best time for planting.

Pruning

Pruning takes place in June-late July, not in winter. Keep pruning of an established tree to the minimum. Remove dead, broken and diseased branches and cut back overcrowded ones. Dealing with fans is rather more complex — see the *Fruit Expert*.

Varieties

COMPACT STELLA Sweet cherry. Dark red. A compact form of 'Stella' which is less vigorous and less spreading. All the basic characteristics of its popular parent are present. Picking time: late July.

MERTON GLORY Sweet cherry. Yellow, flushed red. The one to choose if you want a white-fleshed cherry that is ready for picking in late June. Growth is upright. Requires a pollination partner.

MORELLO Acid cherry. Near black. By far the most popular of the culinary varieties — it is self-fertile. Tolerant and reliable, producing heavy crops in August and September.

REGINA Sweet cherry. Dark red. A late-season variety which bears heavy crops of large fruit in late July-early August. Noted for its flavour and its resistance to cracking.

STELLA Sweet cherry. Dark red. The first self-fertile sweet cherry — the No. 1 garden variety. Growth is vigorous and the flavour of the late July fruit is good. A good pollinator.

SUNBURST Sweet cherry. Near black. The first self-fertile black sweet cherry. The large fruits appear in early July. The growth habit and flavour are similar to 'Stella'.

SWEETHEART Sweet cherry. Dark red. A self-fertile variety which is similar in many ways to other modern dessert cherries, but it is ready in late August when others have finished.

Soft Fruit

'Soft fruit' is a term for a widely diverse group of plants which are generally head-high or smaller and which bear soft-skinned juicy fruit — but grapes can be tall and melons have a thick rind. In this chapter there are details of the five most popular ones — for others see the *Fruit Expert*.

Unlike vegetables you can harvest the plants year after year once they are established, and unlike tree fruit there is a place for at least one example in every garden. Plant gooseberry bushes and raspberry canes where space permits, but you only need a window box for strawberries.

The attraction of growing soft fruit is obvious, but there are two basic points which must not be ignored. First of all, soft fruit needs attention — you cannot neglect plants and still expect them to be long-living and to give high yields. Secondly, there are only a few general rules which apply to all plants. Enrich the soil with humus before planting, and feed every year after planting. Water thoroughly at planting time and when the fruit is swelling. A few general rules, but the differences in looking after the various types far outweigh the similarities.

Birds are a serious problem. Fruit buds are attacked in winter and spring — fruit is eaten as it ripens. Draped-over netting is the easiest answer — a cage is the best answer.

Buying

Avoid 'bargains' and go to a reputable supplier. Order early before the best varieties are sold out, and choose container-grown plants rather than bare-rooted ones if you have missed the autumn-spring planting period.

Do not plant gifts from other people's gardens. When buying from a nursery or garden centre you should inspect the plants carefully before buying. They should be clearly labelled with the name of the variety and details of certification if they are strawberries, raspberries or blackcurrants. The stems should be healthy and firm — there should be a green layer under the bark. If they are bare-rooted specimens you should check that the root system spreads in all directions and that there are no small white roots growing in the packing material.

Planting

Replacements will be necessary after a time — strawberries remain productive for 3-4 years and bush and cane fruit for 10-20 years. Never replace a plant with a bush or cane of the same type — raspberries should not follow raspberries etc.

Soft fruit should be grown in full sun, but nearly all types will do reasonably well in light shade.

Feeding & Mulching

A spring dressing of a general-purpose fertilizer has two functions — it promotes a good crop later in the season and also encourages the production of new growth which will bear next year's crop.

An organic mulch will help to keep down weeds, provide some nutrients and help to improve soil structure. See pages 14-16 for details.

Pests & Diseases

There are a large number of soft fruit enemies, ranging from tiny eelworms to large birds — see pages 159-161 for identification and control measures.

Types

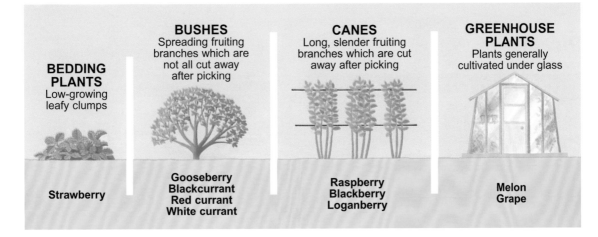

BEDDING PLANTS
Low-growing leafy clumps

Strawberry

BUSHES
Spreading fruiting branches which are not all cut away after picking

**Gooseberry
Blackcurrant
Red currant
White currant**

CANES
Long, slender fruiting branches which are cut away after picking

**Raspberry
Blackberry
Loganberry**

GREENHOUSE PLANTS
Plants generally cultivated under glass

**Melon
Grape**

Strawberry

It is not surprising that strawberries are the most popular home-grown fruit. There is the luscious taste, of course, but there are also the facts that you don't need much room and you also don't need much patience — plant in August and you can be picking fruit in June or July next year.

The problem is that the season is all too fleeting. If just one popular variety is grown, picking in June or July will last for two or three weeks and then it is over. But if you have the space and choose with care, it is possible to pick strawberries for six months of the year. The Earlies will provide fruit in late May-mid June, followed by the Mid-season ones with mid June-late July fruit. Finally the Late varieties are ready for picking in August. The baton is then picked up by the Perpetual varieties which fruit from September until the first frosts after having provided a previous crop in early summer.

As noted on page 193 the productive life of your strawberries is limited, after which you will have to create a new bed with stock you have raised yourself or with stock you have bought from a garden centre or nursery. There are alternatives to this pattern. Strawberries can be grown in tubs, pots, hanging baskets etc instead of in a bed — this makes picking easier and overcomes the slug problem. Alpine strawberries can be raised from seed — sow in autumn and keep in small pots over winter under glass. Plant out at 25 cm (10 in.) intervals in spring.

Picking

Inspect daily — pick fruit which is red all over. Do this in the morning when the fruit is dry. Nip the stalk between the forefinger and thumbnail — do not tug away from the stem.

Pruning

Do not cut back the leaves at planting time. The time to prune is when the last of the berries have been picked. With Summer fruiting varieties cut off all the leaves about 8 cm (3 in.) above the crown, and at the same time cut off unwanted runners. With Perpetual varieties remove only the old leaves.

Planting

A sunny, sheltered site is required — a little shade during the day is acceptable. The site should not have been used for growing potatoes, tomatoes, chrysanthemums nor strawberries for several years. Good drainage is essential. Incorporate a bucketful of compost or manure per sq.m (10 sq.ft) when preparing the bed a month before planting. Scatter a compound fertilizer over the ground just before planting. Leave 50 cm (1½ ft) between plants — 75 m (2½ ft) between rows.

Bare-rooted plants

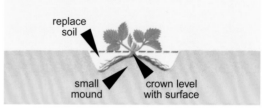

Plant in July-September. March-April planting is acceptable, but remove all flowers during the first season.

Container-grown plants
Specimens can be planted at any time of the year when the weather is suitable. See page 63 for details.

Types

SUMMER FRUITING STRAWBERRY

By far the most popular group. Largest and best quality fruits found here. Cropping time between late May and August. Single flush — a few varieties occasionally produce a second crop

•

PERPETUAL STRAWBERRY

Fruit is generally smaller and less sweet than Summer fruiting varieties — plants are less hardy. Cropping time June and again in late summer-autumn. Remove early flowers to increase the autumn crop

•

ALPINE STRAWBERRY

Fruit is very small — aromatic and sweet but not juicy. Grow in a container or as an edging. Cropping time midsummer to late autumn. Yellow, white and red varieties available — not eaten by birds

Caring for the plants

- Cover plants with fleece or newspaper if frost is expected when flowers are open — remove the cover during the day. Newly-planted strawberries must be watered regularly — so must established plants during dry weather. It is important to keep water off fruits — do this job in the morning so splashes can dry before nightfall.

- Strawberries are low-growing plants and yields can be seriously affected by weeds. Hoe regularly — do not go too deeply and keep away from the crowns. May is the usual time for mulching — see page 61. The soil must be moist and weed-free before putting down a mulch.

- Most varieties produce runners which bear plantlets. These runners can be removed or alternatively left to grow and root between the plants to form a matted row. The fruit tends to be smaller, but the total yield is higher.

- Spray against pests and diseases if necessary — see pages 159-161. After leaf removal at the end of the season it is necessary to hoe to remove weeds and excess runners.

- For a May crop grow an early variety such as 'Honeoye' and cover with cloches from late winter onwards. Partially open cloches during the day when flowers appear.

Raising new plants

New strawberries can be easily raised from runners, but you must make sure that the mother plant is healthy with leaves which are neither crinkled nor mottled. In June or July select four or five strong runners from each plant and proceed as shown below:

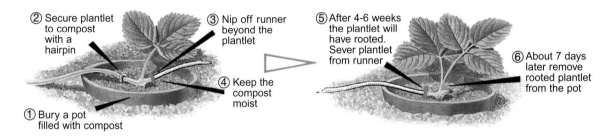

② Secure plantlet to compost with a hairpin

③ Nip off runner beyond the plantlet

④ Keep the compost moist

① Bury a pot filled with compost

⑤ After 4-6 weeks the plantlet will have rooted. Sever plantlet from runner

⑥ About 7 days later remove rooted plantlet from the pot

Some Perpetual varieties do not produce runners. Propagate by division — dig up the plant in early September and divide into a number of separate crowns. Plant each one immediately — the crown of each divided plant should be level with the soil surface after planting.

Varieties

ALEXANDRA Alpine variety. The fruit is bright red and the flavour is excellent. They are about 1 cm (½ in.) long, which is larger than other Alpine strawberries. Yields, however, are not high.

AROMEL Perpetual variety. The only virtue of this strawberry is its outstanding flavour. Drawbacks include moderate yields, poor disease resistance and fruits which are soft and misshapen.

CAMBRIDGE FAVOURITE Mid-season Summer fruiting variety. An old favourite which is reliable and crops well, but it is worth looking elsewhere. The flesh lacks flavour and virus is now a problem.

ELSANTA Mid-season Summer fruiting variety. An excellent replacement for 'Cambridge Favourite'. Yields are high and the fruit is attractive with an excellent flavour and a long shelf life.

FLAMENCO Perpetual variety. One of the newer strawberries which produces crops in early summer and again in autumn. Heavy yields, good flavour. May be listed as an 'everbearer'.

FLORENCE Late Summer fruiting variety. You will find this one in some of the popular catalogues. The fruits are large, firm and sweet — the resistance to verticillium wilt is outstanding.

HAPIL Mid-season Summer fruiting variety. This Belgian strawberry does much better than its rival 'Golden Delicious' in light soil and dry seasons. Good flavour, high yields.

HONEOYE Early Summer fruiting variety. An awful name but a good record — the bright red, medium-sized fruits have flavour and grey mould resistance which are better than average. Yields are high.

MAE Early Summer fruiting variety. Consider this one if you are looking for large strawberries in early June — you can grow it under cloches for a mid May crop. The berries are firm and sweet.

MARA DES BOIS Alpine variety. A rival to 'Alexandra'. As you would expect the fruits have the same wild strawberry flavour, but this one has outstanding resistance to powdery mildew.

PEGASUS Mid-season Summer fruiting variety. The fruits are large and the flavour is sweet, but there is nothing special here. Its outstanding feature is unmatched resistance to pests and diseases.

ROYAL SOVEREIGN Mid-season Summer fruiting variety. An old favourite still in some catalogues for sentimental reasons and its flavour — but yields are low and it soon falls prey to pests and diseases.

Raspberry

Raspberries are by far the most popular of the cane fruits, but they still play second fiddle to strawberries. They have drawbacks — strong supports are needed and annual pruning is necessary. But there are plus points — the canes remain productive for many years, the fruits freeze extremely well, frost is rarely a problem, and cool summers do not bother them.

The Summer fruiting varieties are the ones you are most likely to find. Fruit colours range from yellow to dark red, and these raspberries are borne on canes which developed last year. July and/or August is harvest time, protection against birds is essential, and so is a stout fence or a post-and-wire structure to support them.

Autumn fruiting varieties bear fruit from late August and may go on until the first frosts. These raspberries appear on the top of this year's canes. Compared to Summer fruiting types the yields are lower, and both support and bird protection are desirable but not essential.

Varieties

ALL GOLD Autumn fruiting variety. The fruits which appear from late August are large and golden yellow with a flavour which is claimed to beat any red raspberry. An excellent dessert raspberry.

AUTUMN BLISS Autumn fruiting variety. The parent of 'All Gold' which gave it many of its properties — large fruit, firm texture, excellent flavour — but not its red colour.

GLEN AMPLE Summer fruiting variety. A widely-available raspberry which has vigorous canes which are spine-free. The yields are very high — cropping begins in mid July.

GLEN MOY Summer fruiting variety. Plus points include no spines, large fruits and good aphid resistance. The picking season starts in early July and is quite short.

JOAN J Autumn fruiting variety. There are great claims for this one. Fruit is larger than 'Autumn Bliss' raspberries — picking starts at the beginning of August and goes on until October.

LEO Summer fruiting variety. Growth is vigorous and the stems are aphid- and grey mould-resistant. The major problems are the sparsity of canes and yields which are below average.

MALLING JEWEL Summer fruiting variety. An all-purpose and reliable variety which has been popular for many years. Fruits appear from early July onwards — the yields are not high.

Planting

Good drainage is essential for raspberries. They can thrive in heavier soil and shadier conditions than strawberries but they do need shelter from strong winds. Leave 50 cm (1½ ft) between plants and 2 m (7 ft) between rows of Summer fruiting varieties. Reduce to 1 m (3 ft) for rows of Autumn fruiting varieties.

Bare-rooted plants

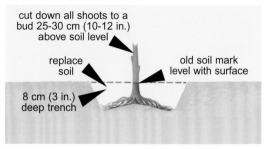

cut down all shoots to a bud 25-30 cm (10-12 in.) above soil level

replace soil

old soil mark level with surface

8 cm (3 in.) deep trench

Plant in October-November.

Container-grown plants
Canes can be planted at any time of the year when the weather is suitable. See page 63 for details. There is no need to cut back shoots.

Caring for the plants

- Water regularly during the first season if the weather is dry. Keep the soil moist when the fruit is swelling.
- Hoe regularly to keep down weeds — do not go too deeply nor too close to the stems. Mulch around the plants in May — see page 61. In summer remove suckers and any stems growing away from the row.
- With container-grown Summer fruiting varieties remove any flowers which may appear on the canes in the first summer after planting.
- Raspberry beetle is a serious pest. If this has been a problem in the past, spray when the fruits start to turn pink — see page 161.

Picking

The harvesting season should last for six weeks or more. Pick when the fruits are fully coloured but still firm. Pull each raspberry gently away from the stem, leaving the plug and stalk behind. Inspect the crop daily — try to harvest when the fruit is dry. Pick slightly unripe fruit for freezing.

Pruning

Summer fruiting varieties
Immediately after picking cut out all canes which have borne fruit. Retain best 8-10 young unfruited canes — tie to wires 8-10 cm (3-4 in.) apart. Remove tips in February.

Autumn fruiting varieties
In February cut all canes down to ground level.

Gooseberry

The gooseberry is a long-suffering plant — left unfed and unpruned a bush will continue to give some fruit for many years. Because of this it is sometimes called an 'easy' plant, but this is not true. Pruning in winter and summer is necessary to ensure a heavy crop which can be readily reached and which is not borne at ground level. Winter protection against birds is important in many areas, and failure to spray against american mildew can result in a totally mouldy crop.

The usual growth type is a 60 cm-1.5 m (2-5 ft) bush which is open-centred and is borne on a 10-15 cm (4-6 in.) bare stem. The bush is a permanent framework of young and mature branches. Alternatively gooseberries can be grown as cordons.

A bush should yield 3-5 kg (6½-11 lb) of fruit and it should remain productive for 10-15 years. Gooseberries are generally not troubled by virus.

Culinary varieties have a sharp taste and are not suitable for eating fresh. Dessert varieties are much less common in shops — they are larger, thinner-skinned and sweeter. The best plan is to buy a Culinary/Dessert variety. Pick unripe fruit in late May or June for cooking and then pick ripe fruit in July or August for eating fresh.

Varieties

CARELESS Culinary variety. The most popular cooking variety — it is reliable and not fussy about soil type. It is susceptible to american mildew — 'Invicta' is a better choice.

HINNONMAKI YELLOW Dessert variety. Something different — medium-sized greenish-yellow berries with a unique flavour and aroma. The spreading bushes are harvested in June-mid July.

INVICTA Culinary/dessert variety. The most widely available gooseberry — it is immune to american mildew, yields are heavy and it is excellent for cooking. Dessert quality, however, is less praiseworthy.

LEVELLER Culinary/dessert variety. The extra-large fruit is oval and downy, a standard choice for the exhibitor. Not just pretty — the flavour is exceptional. Picking starts late July.

WHINHAM'S INDUSTRY Culinary/dessert variety. An excellent all-rounder. The growth is upright, the flavour of the dark red fruit is excellent, and it is the one to grow if there is shade or the soil is heavy.

Planting

Gooseberries will thrive in a wide range of soil types, but they do require good drainage and shelter from strong winds — avoid frost pockets. Incorporate compost into the planting area at least a month before planting. Leave 1.5 m (5 ft) between the bushes — space cordons 1 m (3 ft) apart.

Bare-rooted plants

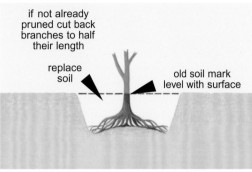

if not already pruned cut back branches to half their length

replace soil

old soil mark level with surface

Plant in October-November — plant in February-March if this is not possible.

Container-grown plants
Bushes and cordons can be planted at any time of the year when the weather is suitable. See page 63 for details. There is no need to cut back branches.

Caring for the plants

- Winter protection against birds is necessary — use netting to protect the buds. Drape fleece over the bushes if a late spring frost is expected. Firm down the soil with your feet if the plants have been lifted after a heavy frost.
- Keep weeds down by hand pulling — hoeing can damage surface roots. Pull suckers away from the roots during the dormant season.
- If the crop is heavy start to thin the fruits in May or June. Do this in stages — aim to have 3-5 cm (1-2 in.) between the gooseberries left for ripening. Cover the fruit with netting.

Picking

Begin picking gooseberries for cooking fresh or freezing in late May. You will have to wait for the fully ripe stage with dessert varieties which are to be eaten fresh. The fruit will be fully coloured and feel rather soft when gently squeezed. Not all will ripen at once — go over the bushes several times.

Pruning

For the first four years build up the framework. Cut back new growth by half each winter — keep the centre of the bush open. In later years, prune between November and March. Remove thin and overcrowded branches. Lightly prune back the new growth on remaining branches by about a half and reduce the side-shoots on the branches to about 5 cm (2 in.).

Blackberry

Blackberries are often regarded as wild fruit we pick in late summer from the brambles in the hedgerows. Not one for the garden — a rampant grower with vicious thorny stems. This generalisation is no longer true — there are compact hybrids and several thornless types. Consider a modern blackberry variety if you have a large trellis or fence to clothe. No soft fruit is less trouble — neither bird nor frost protection is necessary, the arching stems will grow against a north-facing wall and plants can remain productive for up to 20 years.

An increasing number of gardeners are turning to the hybrid berries which have been bred by crossing blackberries, raspberries, dewberries etc. Nearly all are less vigorous than the blackberry.

Varieties

ASHTON CROSS Blackberry variety. The picking season lasts for 6-8 weeks in August-September. The medium-sized fruits are carried in large clusters. Wild blackberry flavour.

FANTASIA Blackberry variety. Thorny, vigorous, cropping in August-September — nothing unusual there. The unique feature is the outstanding size of the fruit.

LOCH NESS Blackberry variety. Something different — the thornless stout stems are semi-erect and require little support. Train and prune like Summer fruiting raspberry.

MERTON THORNLESS Blackberry variety. A thornless blackberry to use where there is not enough space for 'Oregon Thornless' — the canes are shorter. Yields are not high.

OREGON THORNLESS Blackberry variety. A popular thorn-free blackberry — the fruit has a mild flavour and the stems are easy to train. Colourful autumn foliage.

BOYSENBERRY Hybrid berry. Prickly canes bear long, dark, raspberry-like fruits. The flavour, however, is much more like a wild blackberry. Remarkably drought-resistant.

LOGANBERRY Hybrid berry. A 19th century raspberry x dewberry cross which bears long, tangy fruit which is cooked rather than eaten raw. Moderately vigorous.

TAYBERRY Hybrid berry. This blackberry x raspberry cross is the one to choose — growth isn't rampant and the juicy, aromatic berries are large and sweet. Slightly thorny.

TUMMELBERRY Hybrid berry. A tayberry hybrid which is hardier than its parent, but some of the sweetness has been lost.

Planting

Strong supports are required — 1.5-2 m (5-7 ft) posts with horizontal wires or nylon cords stretched between them. The long, arching stems are trained along the wires.

The soil and situation requirements are the same as those for raspberries (see page 196) but the planting distances are greater — 2-5 m (7-16 ft) between plants, 2 m (7 ft) between rows.

Bare-rooted plants

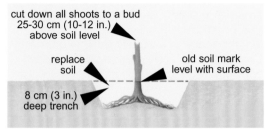

cut down all shoots to a bud 25-30 cm (10-12 in.) above soil level

replace soil

old soil mark level with surface

8 cm (3 in.) deep trench

Plant in November-December — plant in March if this is not possible.

Container-grown plants
Canes can be planted at any time of the year when the weather is suitable. See page 63 for details. There is no need to cut back shoots.

Caring for the plants

- Water in summer if the weather is dry when the fruit has started to develop — water the ground and not the stems.
- Hoe regularly — do not go too deeply or too close to the stems. Mulch around the plants in May — see page 61. In summer remove suckers, and stems growing away from the row.
- Remove any flowers which may appear on the canes in the first summer after planting.
- Raspberry beetle is a serious pest. If this has been a problem in the past, spray when the fruits start to colour — see page 161.

Picking

Pick when the fruits are fully coloured and soft. Pull each blackberry gently away from the stem — the plug generally comes away with the fruit. Pick when the fruit is dry — wet fruit soon starts to go mouldy.

Pruning

There are several ways of training blackberries and hybrid berries — the fan method, the weaving system, roping etc. For details of these methods see the *Fruit Expert*. The simplest but not the most productive method is roping. Immediately after picking has been completed cut out the canes which have borne fruit — the remainder will bear fruit in autumn. In spring and summer tie in the new canes which have appeared — tie 3 or 4 canes horizontally along each wire.

Blackcurrant

Blackcurrants are grown mainly for use in pies and puddings. They are also excellent for jam and jelly making, but are not popular for serving as fresh fruit. They are not difficult to grow, but you must know what to do at planting and pruning time. The reason is that most fruit is borne on last year's stems, and that means a regular supply of new growth from below ground level is required each year. To ensure this you must plant deeply with the root/shoot union well below the surface and you must cut out some old wood in winter.

Buy 2 year old certified plants bearing at least 3 shoots. The bush should eventually reach a height and spread of 1.5 m (5 ft), producing 4.5-7 kg (10-15 lb) of fruit each summer and staying productive for 10-20 years. Big bud mite or reversion may reduce this long and active life by a few years, but the real threat used to be frost. The older varieties bloom in early April and both flowers and small fruitlets are susceptible to frost damage. Fortunately plant breeders have produced a range of late-flowering and partially frost-hardy types — the 'Ben' group are a notable example. Some people claim that the modern varieties have lost the 'real' blackcurrant flavour, but there never has been a standard taste.

Varieties

BEN CONNAN A large-fruited Early variety with a tough constitution — good resistance against frost damage and american mildew. Compact growth habit. Good flavour.

BEN LOMOND The first of the 'Ben' series which have brought some mildew-resistance and heavy yields to blackcurrants. Growth is upright and reasonably compact.

BEN SAREK The main feature here is the dwarf growth habit — bushes reach 1 m (3 ft). Frost- and some mildew-resistance are present — the drawback is the need for branch support.

JOSTABERRY A blackcurrant x gooseberry cross which is grown like a blackcurrant. Resistant to mildew and very prolific — the currants are twice the normal size.

WELLINGTON XXX A pre-war variety which keeps its place in some catalogues because of its outstanding flavour. Crops are heavy but late frosts can be very damaging.

Planting

Blackcurrants will tolerate poor drainage better than other soft fruits, but they do need organic-rich soil with shelter from the wind. Full sun is preferred but light shade is not a problem — do not plant in a frost pocket. Space the bushes 1.5 m (5 ft) apart.

Bare-rooted plants

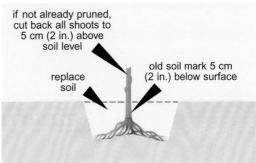

if not already pruned, cut back all shoots to 5 cm (2 in.) above soil level

replace soil

old soil mark 5 cm (2 in.) below surface

Plant in November — plant in February-March if this is not possible.

Container-grown plants

Bushes can be planted at any time of the year when the weather is suitable. See page 63 for details. Cut back shoots — see above.

Caring for the plants

- If a late spring frost is expected, drape fleece over the bushes. Tread down bushes which have been lifted by frost.

- Keep weeds under control. Never hoe more deeply than 1 cm (½ in.), otherwise the shallow root system may be damaged. It is better to keep weeds in check by hand pulling. Mulch in May with garden compost.

- Water regularly and thoroughly during dry weather — keep water off the stems. Bird protection is necessary — drape netting over the bushes when the fruits begin to change from green to purple.

- Blackcurrants do need feeding. Spread a general-purpose fertilizer around each bush in March.

Picking

Fruit is ripe and ready for picking about 7 days after it has turned blue-black. For immediate use you can pick individual currants — the fruits at the top of the fruit stalk are the first to ripen. Blackcurrants can be kept in the refrigerator for a week — for longer storage you should freeze or bottle.

Pruning

Prune between November and March. Cut out weak and diseased branches, then cut out to near ground level about one third of the branches which have fruited. Leave all the strong young shoots unpruned. No wood should be retained which is more than 4 years old.

CHAPTER 13
GARDEN DESIGN

This chapter is not a boiled-down version of a traditional garden design book. There are not pages and pages of garden plans and planting lists — these are readily available in gardening magazines and books. The purpose of this chapter is to explain the various steps you must take in order to move from a feeling of dissatisfaction with your present plot to a garden which delights you.

There are five elements which make up good design:

- The garden must appeal strongly to you and your family.
- The garden must be labour-saving unless you have lots of time and money.
- The garden must not cost more to create or maintain than you can afford.
- The garden must provide a suitable home for the plants you have chosen.
- The garden must not be truly objectionable to the people you like.

Think about your plot and read Chapter 11, then fill in the questionnaire below and carefully consider your answers. Now you are ready to begin — turn to Step 1 on the next page.

What have I got?

SOIL TYPE
Loam/heavy/light/acid/alkaline — see Chapter 2

PLOT SIZE
Tiny/small/average/large/country estate

STYLE
Happy/unhappy with all/part of the present style

CHANGE NEEDED
Start from scratch/major changes/minor changes

MONEY AVAILABLE
Hard landscaping (walls, paving etc) is expensive

LABOUR AVAILABLE
Self/ self+helpers /professional help

LIGHT & SHADE
Open and sunny/enclosed and shady

What is important?

WORK
Somewhere to relax/somewhere to work

PRIVACY
Privacy/open plan

STYLE
Traditional/modern/natural/off-beat design

PURPOSE
A garden for us/a garden to impress our friends

FAMILY
A place for children/pets

OUTDOOR LIVING
A place for entertaining/sitting/eating outdoors

FEATURES
Items which must be included — see pages 230-253

STEP 1 : PREPARE A SITE PLAN

1: Begin with a rough sketch

Start with a large piece of paper on a clip board. Make a rough sketch plan of the house and the boundaries of your property — use a pencil and not a pen as even the experts have to rub out and make corrections at this survey stage. Within this plan mark the main features of the garden and outside the plan draw an arrow indicating north. The features should include more than the obvious things like beds, borders, paths, garden sheds etc. If the site is a new one mark deep hollows left by the builder, dead trees and so on — in an established garden mark poorly-drained areas, frost pockets etc if these are known.

Having drawn in the features, look out of the windows of the rooms in which you spend or plan to spend much of your time. See if there are any attractive views beyond your boundary and mark them on the sketch — you will not want to block these views when you draw up your design. Now look for eyesores and make a note of them. Almost every garden has an eyesore — the neighbour's dilapidated garden shed or compost heap, a nearby factory chimney etc. In your final design it will be necessary to screen out these areas if possible.

On the rough drawing write down the distances between the corners of the site by running the tape from one to the other. It is a good idea to use a red pen if you have drawn in lots of features and your sketch is crowded with pencil lines. For features within the garden you will sometimes have to use the process known as triangulation (see page 202) when preparing the site plan. This involves taking two measurements in order to fix the position of the feature — one from each side of the house or from two other fixtures. See the sketch below for examples.

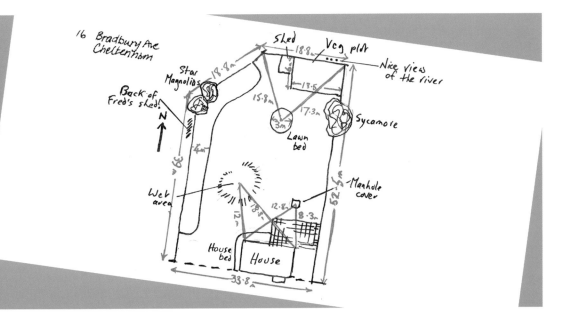

2: Draw the Site Plan

You are now ready to prepare a scale plan of your garden. Use graph paper and pick a scale which will allow the plan to fill most of the sheet — 1 : 50 and 1 : 100 are popular scales. Draw in the house to scale and then draw in each feature using the measurements noted on your rough sketch plan. Triangulation may be necessary — see below. Mark beds and borders in green, use a red pencil to show eyesores and a yellow one to highlight attractive vistas you wish to retain.

There is one more task. Pick a day when blue skies are forecast and in the morning mark the shaded area in blue on your plan. Repeat at noon and in the evening — the unshaded area is the 'full sun' zone.

Of course, Step 2 need only be carried out in full for a virgin site or where complete remodelling is planned. However, it is worthwhile even if only a minor change is intended. You will have a reference plan of your garden which can be used for future planning.

Triangulation

This technique will enable you to plot the in-garden features accurately on your site plan. Set the compasses to one of the distances marked on your rough sketch. Now place the point of the compasses on the relevant spot from which it was measured — the left hand corner of the house to fix the position of the manhole cover in the example on page 201. Draw an arc, and repeat the process from the second measuring point with the second distance — the right hand corner of the house in the rough sketch. Draw another arc, and the feature is at the point where the two arcs cross.

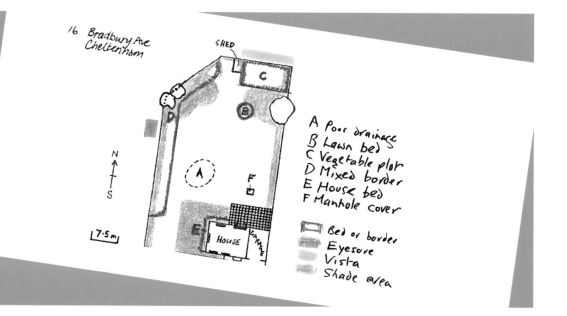

16 Bradbury Ave
Cheltenham

SHED

N
↑
S

7·5 m

A Poor drainage
B Lawn bed
C Vegetable plot
D Mixed border
E House bed
F Manhole cover

Bed or border
Eyesore
Vista
Shade area

HOUSE

STEP 2 : READ THE GOOD DESIGN RULES

You will be doing nothing 'wrong' if you choose to ignore the advice on this page and the other tips up to page 206. The principles set out here are what the professionals regard as good design — they are ways to ensure that the knowledgeable will recognise the presence of the accepted good design concepts in your garden. For many years these rules have been accepted as the proper way to do things, but it is your garden. The all-important factors which you have to follow are the five essential elements set out on page 200 and the rules for avoiding design pitfalls on page 207.

Basic principles

Simplicity

Professional landscapers generally aim for simplicity in their designs, but despite their advice over-fussy gardens outnumber the restrained ones. Before deciding to fill your plot with all sorts of shapes and features it is worth while looking at the advantages of the simple approach.

First of all, the work in an over-complex garden can be enormous. Mowing is a skilful operation when weaving between a complex of flower beds, while edging and weeding can be never-ending tasks. Dead-heading cannot be neglected and early watering of all those annuals you have planted is an essential job in dry weather. Secondly, a jumble of unlinked features will make your garden look smaller, and it will not have the restful feel of a garden which has simpler lines.

The professionals are right — it is not a good idea to fill a large garden with a collection of borders, beds, pathways etc which do not hang together, but we should not take this concept too far. Many people with tiny plots choose an over-fussy design so that they have the opportunity to potter outdoors for hours.

Balance

A garden should be balanced. This does not mean that it should be strictly symmetrical with the right hand side being a mirror image of the left. In fact clear-cut symmetry is generally not a good idea in the home garden and there should be marked differences in design between the two halves. But it still has to be balanced, and the easiest way to do this is to imagine the left and right side of the garden on an enormous scales — if one side would clearly outweigh the other then the garden is not balanced. This is not quite as easy as it sounds — a dense leafy evergreen such as lawson's cypress is 'heavier' than a taller, more spreading open tree such as silver birch.

Unity

This word is used by garden designers to describe the way they make sure that the various parts of the garden blend into a harmonious whole. This does not mean that the result should be dull or unexciting. All sorts of variations and patterns are possible within an old-world garden or a modern formal one, but a piece of abstract sculpture would be quite out of place in a garden of old urns and old-fashioned roses as would be a wildflower area in an architectural garden.

A useful way of promoting unity is to make sure that the materials used for building walls belong to the same family as the walls of the house. They need not be identical in shape or colour, but weathered brick walls linked with an old brick house will give a feeling of unity. Avoiding the use of too many types of paving materials is also important — mixing artificial stone slabs, bricks, crazy paving, grass and gravel would certainly create a feeling of disharmony!

Contrast

It must seem odd to have both unity and contrast in a list of the basic principles of good design and actually on the same page! They are after all direct opposites. Unity means that there should be a feeling of harmony in the garden — contrast means that there should be a marked difference between things in the garden.

There is actually no problem — both have a role to play. As described above, you should aim to give the overall design a basic feeling of unity without having features which do not belong. Within that scheme of things there is a place for contrast, and that applies especially to the plants in the beds and borders. Don't just aim to have contrasting flower colours to provide eye-catching interest — yellow next to violet, orange close to blue etc. There should also be contrast in plant and leaf shape — feathery foliage next to large-leaved plants and upright shrubs next to bushy ones.

Scale

Scale is a designer term for ensuring that the height, width and length of the various living and non-living elements of the garden are in proportion. It is usual to think first of all of the dangers of having items which are just too big. Make sure that the mature plant height of any tree or shrub you buy will be in keeping with the garden — a basic piece of advice which continues to be given and continues to be ignored. The main problem is impulse buying — a weeping willow or japanese larch is bought at the garden centre because it 'looks so nice'. In a few years time there is the constant need to prune back as the giant tries to get to its natural height.

Less obvious but equally important is the necessity to avoid features which are too small. A tiny patio attached to a large and impressive house will look all wrong as will a small bed in a large expanse of lawn. Not too big and not too small, but this should never be taken to mean that a standard height is the thing to aim for. Even in a tiny plot a large-leaved architectural plant can provide a welcome focal point.

Interest

This is a very simple principle — there should be items in the garden which will make the observer go over to look at them. The item may be an especially attractive flower, or a plant that the visitor has never seen before, a piece of statuary or a koi pond. The interest point may be obvious as soon as you step out in the garden, but your skill as a designer is to ensure that at least some of these interest points are not immediately in view. In designer terms there should be 'mystery' as you approach the point of interest, 'tension' as you get close, and finally 'surprise' when you at last reach the hidden focal point. For us it is much simpler — just make sure that you have several focal points in the garden which catch the eye, and make sure that you cannot see them all when you stand on the patio or at the entrance to the back garden.

Shape and size

The introduction to this chapter stressed the point that it is your garden and within reason the only thing that matters is that the design should appeal to you. It is important, however, that you should take the size and shape of the plot into consideration as these really do limit what you can do to make it attractive.

It is only natural for a keen gardener to try to fill the area with as many plants and features as possible. Garden design bureaux look with amazement at some of the wants lists sent to them. The essentials are there, of course – lawn, garden shed, flower beds etc. Then there is all the rest – rose bed, fish pond, vegetable plot, rockery, play area, sundial and ..... If you have an acre or two then it may be no problem, but on a small plot it really is out of the question. Something must go from the list – some open area is vital in an average-sized standard garden if it is not to suffer from horticultural indigestion.

You also have to adapt your ideas to the shape of the garden. A long and narrow plot needs to be divided into several areas if it is not to look like a long passageway. A square garden can be depressingly box-like. It will help if you have curved borders at the corners to break the line — circular beds or features also help.

Colour

In Step 6 on page 211 you will find a brief account on colour theory — the basic Colour Wheel and how it is used to guide you in the choice of colours which harmonise in a pleasing way. In some textbooks you will find long lists of do's and don'ts on the use of colour in the garden, but you really do not have to learn a long list of rules on what goes with what and how to avoid colour clashes — "never put pink next to orange or dark crimson" and so on. These purist rules are less important in the garden than is often supposed. The reason is quite simple. A solid sheet of colour placed directly next to another with which it clearly does not harmonise can clearly be distasteful and this is important in interior decoration, dress etc. In a garden, however, the various hues, shades and tints are broken up by green foliage and earthen shades which dilute the so-called colour clashes. The best idea is to read Step 6 and perhaps the suggestions in books, magazines etc and then use the information to produce colour schemes which fit in with your personal likes and dislikes.

Whites and greys have a special part to play in colour schemes in your garden. White on its own has a calming effect, and stands out on cloudy days and at dusk when purples and red fade out into dullness. The main purpose of greys and whites, however, is to bring out the best in other colours. Interest is added to monochromatic and pastel analogous schemes (see page 211) — the garishness of over-bright contrasting schemes is reduced.

Add height to the garden

The beauty of your garden will be enhanced if you have a mixture of heights. To some extent this can be achieved by having a range of plant sizes — column-like conifers, spreading shrubs, low-growing plants and carpeting ground covers. Remember that a tall feature reasonably close to the house will make the garden look longer. Planting climbers against the house wall is nearly always a good idea — the garden is extended upwards.

You will need more than a range of plant heights if you are to avoid the flat-earth policy which seems to affect so many plots. There should be some planted soil surfaces above the general ground level, and there are several ways of achieving this result. Planted tubs are an age-old method — as valuable as ever for providing colour and interest near the house. A rockery is another way of having living plants above ground level, but it must be properly constructed and maintained. If you have a sloping site the obvious answer is to create one or more terraces with brick or stone retaining walls. Spreading rockery perennials can be planted at the front of these terraces to cascade downwards and soften the lines of the wall.

On a level site the answer is to build one or more raised beds. These will help to relieve the monotony of a flat garden, but there are other important advantages — better drainage, easier weeding and planting etc. Retaining walls can be built from a variety of materials — stone, brick, wood etc. Using dry stone walling gives the added advantage of allowing plants to be grown in the crevices of the retaining wall.

Hide eyesores

For eyesores which cannot be removed you will have to employ some form of screening. The usual answer is a decorative wall, a fence covered with russian vine, ivy or climbing roses, or a line of quick-growing conifers. These methods of screening are not the only ways of hiding eyesores. In fact, flat screening can have its problems — if it is large and eye-catching it can serve as a focal point which draws attention to the partly-hidden eyesore. It is sometimes better to have an irregular-shaped and three-dimensional feature such as a wide-spreading bush between the window and the undesirable view.

Create a permanent skeleton

The garden should contain a fixed year-round frame-work rather than looking like an over-sized windowbox. There should be a definite feeling of maturity, and this calls for the presence of permanent objects. Ornaments are useful — arches, sundials, fountains, walled areas and the rest, but you have to turn to shrubs and trees to provide the basic skeleton. Lack of space is no excuse — there are compact woody plants which can provide winter tracery when the annuals and the stems of border plants have disappeared.

Have evergreen and deciduous woody plants

Garden books abound with photographs of the scene in full summer, but the appearance in mid winter is largely ignored. In many gardens, however, we have to look at the garden for several months when all the leaves and flowers have gone. Evergreens seem to be the answer and of course some evergreens with grey, yellow, green or purple leaves are necessary, but the deciduous shrubs and trees have an equally important role to play. Most of the beautiful flowering types belong here, and there is also seasonal change.

Beware of the pitfalls

Don't be over-ambitious

Before you draw up the Design Plan you must face up to your limitations in time, money, ability, garden knowledge and health. There is no point in planning for a heated greenhouse unless you accept the annual cost of heating it in winter and the year-round work involved in watering, ventilating and so on.

Changing levels always involves more work than the gardener expects. You can't just cart the excess soil from a high spot to raise the height of another area. The topsoil must be first removed, the subsoil graded and the topsoil then replaced.

Laying paving slabs, bricklaying, concreting and cutting down large trees are not jobs to be undertaken lightly if you have never tackled them before. Get a professional to do the work if you can afford it. If that is not possible then read about the technique, speak to a knowledgeable friend and get him (or her) to help.

Few aspects of gardening give more pleasure than growing vegetables successfully … and few take more time. If you have little time to spare do not incorporate a large vegetable patch in the design.

Don't commit the lawn sins

Just a patch of grass, perhaps, but a lot of thought should go into its design. The actual shape is up to you, but avoid tight or fussy curves and awkward corners. You should aim to have a surface free from bumps and hollows, but a gentle and even slope is acceptable. Grass will grow happily in sun or partial shade, but in deep shade it will never produce a satisfactory, tightly-knit turf.

The first sin is to extend the lawn into a completely sunless area. The second sin is to extend the lawn right up to a wall or path — a grass-free mowing strip should be maintained all round the lawn to make edging easier. The third sin is having a path which leads directly on to the lawn and stops at the edge. The regular traffic at this point will cause excessive wear and compaction. The fourth sin is to have narrow grass strips between beds and/or borders — the strips should be at least 75 cm (2½ ft) to facilitate easy mowing.

The upkeep of grass banks is quite practical with the advent of the hover mower, but you should not extend the lawn over a bank with a slope of more than 30°. Finally, do not clutter up the lawn with objects which will make mowing difficult — examples include heavy seats, large flower pots and leafy trees.

Don't choose the wrong plants

When drawing up your planting plan check on the characteristics of each tree, shrub and border perennial before making your choice. Do this by looking in books, catalogues or on the internet. You will want to know the plant's expected height at maturity, flowering season and the colour of the blooms, but you must also find out the expected spread of a tree or shrub and its light and soil type requirements.

Nearly all bedding plants and rockery perennials thrive best in full sun, but numerous shrubs and border plants will flourish in partial shade. Make sure that your plant list matches the conditions under which the plants will have to grow. Failure to do this is asking for trouble — for example some plants will thrive in chalky soil but many would fail miserably. Check the plants' needs before adding them to the plan.

STEP 3 : WRITE A REMOVALS LIST

You have decided on a style and you have a site plan of the garden. You will also have a rough idea of the sort of design you wish to create. If it is to be a standard garden then you will have thought whether you want it to be formal, informal or a mixture of both — a simple basic garden or an ornate de-luxe one.

Towards this end you should prepare a Removals List — things that are to go. This is usually a simple task if only a small amount of remodelling is planned — removing a garden shed, filling in a fussy flower bed on the lawn or getting rid of the sand-box now that the children have grown up. It is even easier when moving into a newly-built house — just get rid of the builders' rubbish!

Do think carefully before deciding to add a major item to your Removals List when remodelling an established garden. The removal of a large feature can leave a gaping bare patch which is much more extensive than you imagined it would be. Removing a path seems such a simple idea until you start trying to lift the stones. Old trees and ugly hedges are a special case. They may have reached the end of their useful life and then it is right to add them to your list, but in some cases renewal pruning by cutting stems back to half their height can turn an eyesore into a vigorous and attractive plant in a couple of seasons.

A golden rule is to try to fit outstanding plants and/or features into your plan. Trees provide a living skeleton for and a feeling of maturity to your garden, but there are times when some trees have to go, and here it is necessary to check that they are not subject to a Tree Preservation Order.

16 Bradbury Ave
Cheltenham

REMOVALS LIST

The narrow annual flower border around the house has to go — it is so dull all winter long.

The mixed border has to be changed. The present one is too long and too boring, but I do want a border and I want to keep as many of the plants as possible.

The round flower bed at the bottom of the lawn. It is such a formal feature at a spot where the garden should have a more informal look.

The vegetable plot has to be changed. I want to grow some vegetables but the present site is so much trouble.

The tall sycamore in front of the vegetable garden has to go — it is not attractive and casts too much shade.

STEP 4 : START THE DESIGN PLAN

You have prepared a Site Plan and made a note of the garden style you have chosen. Towards this goal you have listed the features you have decided to remove, and in Step 2 you have got to know something about the principles of good design.

It is now time to start work on the Design Plan. Make a tracing of the scale plan prepared in Step 1, leaving out the red, yellow and blue shaded areas. In addition omit the items on your Removals List. This will include both features which will not appear in the new design and also those which are to have a different shape. Include only the items which will remain unaltered. This new plan will eventually become your Design Plan. Take a photocopy and enlarge it to fill nearly all of the sheet of paper. Take a number of copies so you can develop your ideas — you will certainly have second thoughts after your first attempt!

If there are to be major changes or if you are starting from scratch there is much to do before you are ready to finalise the plan. It is necessary to draw up a Wants List — for each new feature you will have studied the advantages, limitations, price etc of the various items. You can use one or more of the photocopies to rough out a general idea of the form of your new garden, but it is too early to prepare a final Design Plan at this stage.

It may be that you are planning only a minor alteration and have a clear idea of just what you want. In that case you can draw the features on the plan and if the time is right you are ready to start work — move to Step 9.

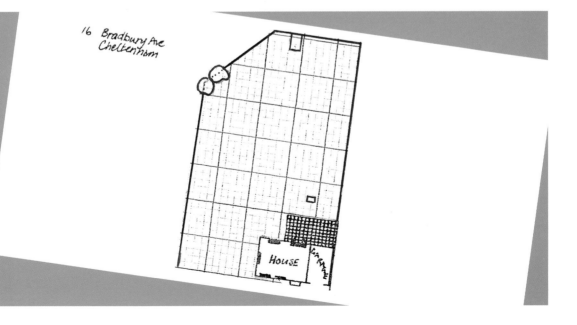

STEP 5 : WRITE A WANTS LIST

It is now time to draw up a Wants List so that you can get on with the Design Plan. Before beginning study the preliminary plan you have prepared to see what space you will have available once the items earmarked for removal have gone. Look at the site too, of course — some people find it useful to take photographs at this stage so that they have a picture of the garden when drawing up the Wants List and working on the Design Plan.

So off you go to prepare a list of the things you want to include. There will be basic garden features — rose bed, pond, paved sitting-out area or other desirable item which is missing. Add trees and shrubs you have seen and would like to include — weeping cherry, pampas grass etc. Finally, the non-living features — some attractive like a greenhouse, summer house or patio, and others mundane, such as a rotary washing line or a compost bin. It is not just a matter of deciding on the type of feature you would like in your garden — a greenhouse, sundial etc. As noted on page 209 you will have to decide on which ones you plan to buy. Read pages 230-253, look in the catalogues and magazines, watch the TV programmes and collect leaflets. Best of all, look at other people's gardens.

There are two general rules concerning the Wants List. Don't try to pack too much into your garden. It would be surprising if this list didn't need pruning once the first draft was completed. A garden should not look like a garden centre — there should be large plain areas to dramatise the busy and colourful spots. The second rule is that you should plan for the future. Include a play area even though the baby is still at the crawling stage. Include a much-wanted greenhouse even though funds will not be available for a couple of years. Simply add these as 'items to follow' to remind you to leave space on the Design Plan.

16 Bradbury Ave
Cheltenham

A decent sized lawn, free from hard-to-cut bits. Paths at the side but not through the middle.

A mixed border along the west fence with a more interesting slope than the present one.

A new vegetable garden.

The patio is fine, but it does need some pots, wall plants etc.

The overall design I should like is a standard garden with a formal area with beds close to the house and an informal feel towards the back.

Some more trees, especially near the back. It would be nice to have some conifers and other evergreens to give winter colour.

A pergola or arch on which I can grow a clematis or honeysuckle.

A hidden-away place for the compost heap.

Some nice paved paths.

STEP 6 : LEARN ABOUT COLOUR

This step shows you how to make colour work for you in the garden — the basic tool is the Colour Wheel. As you can see there is a division into warm and cool colours. To make a plot look longer use plants with warm-coloured flowers/leaves — the yellow, orange and red ones as close as you can to the point from which you view the garden, and put the cool-colour types — the blues and purples at the back. The weather has an effect on the appearance of these colours — pastel shades can look quite washed out in brilliant sunshine but their colour is heightened on dull days.

Within this span of warm and cool colours you will find a number of individual hues. In the feature on Colour on page 205 it is noted that some of these hues will clash when placed close to each other — although the danger of this is less in the garden than in interior decoration and putting items of clothing together. To be sure that colours will not clash you can use one of the three classic types of harmonious colour schemes set out below.

- The **MONOCHROMATIC SCHEME** uses the various tints and shades of a single hue.
- The **ANALOGOUS SCHEME** uses two, three or four colours which are all neighbours on the wheel.
- The **CONTRASTING SCHEME** uses colours which are directly across from each other on the Colour Wheel.

Colour Wheel

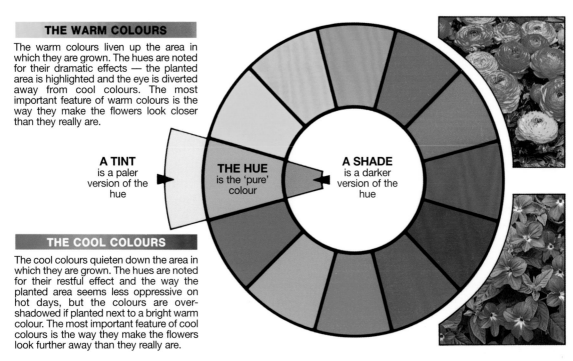

THE WARM COLOURS

The warm colours liven up the area in which they are grown. The hues are noted for their dramatic effects — the planted area is highlighted and the eye is diverted away from cool colours. The most important feature of warm colours is the way they make the flowers look closer than they really are.

A TINT
is a paler version of the hue

THE HUE
is the 'pure' colour

A SHADE
is a darker version of the hue

THE COOL COLOURS

The cool colours quieten down the area in which they are grown. The hues are noted for their restful effect and the way the planted area seems less oppressive on hot days, but the colours are over-shadowed if planted next to a bright warm colour. The most important feature of cool colours is the way they make the flowers look further away than they really are.

STEP 7 : COMPLETE THE DESIGN PLAN

We have at last reached the stage where a detailed plan has to be prepared, using the notes and drawings collected during Steps 1 - 6. It is a good idea to have collected photographs of gardens and features which appeal — these can be taken by you or cut from magazines.

It is now decision time — who is going to prepare this plan? For nearly everyone it is a simple choice — you will be your own designer. If so, go on to page 214 and carry on from there. As an aid you can try one of the many Garden Designer CD-ROMs which are available. Fun to use if you are a computer fan and many are very informative, but they do not give you the flexibility and freedom of a pencil and piece of graph paper. You can copy an example from a book of garden plans, but none of them will fit your site and aspect exactly.

You may feel that you do not have the necessary experience and/or expertise to create your own plan, in which case you will need professional help. The less expensive route is to use a Garden Planning Service — several magazines and organisations run such a service. There will not be a site visit, so send the lists and plans you have prepared so far. A better alternative is to employ a garden designer who will come to your garden. Here it is not necessary to have prepared a Site Plan or to have started the Design Plan, but it is a useful exercise in order to give a detailed summary of what you have and what you want, and to enable you and the designer to speak the same language. Under no circumstances should you merely hand over a few vague thoughts on a scrap of paper.

16 Bradbury Ave
Cheltenham

DESIGN PLAN

The garden design at 16 Bradbury Avenue was developed to give a clean and simple feel with the minimum of reorganisation of the garden spaces. This latter point is important as the clients will be doing the work in their spare time. Two lawns are included — a play lawn to the side and the main lawn to the rear. Both are bounded by mowing strips for ease of maintenance. A previously damp low area has been utilised to create a formal pool and a brick path sweeps around the western lawn edge. A new patio has been included at the sunny end of the garden and a pergola cuts through the mixed border to a secluded seating area. The vegetable plot now has formal paths and smaller, easy-to-manage beds. A bird table to disguise the manhole cover and two raised beds complete the scheme.

paul dracott garden designs

THE DESIGNER APPROACH

To find a designer you can ask a garden centre or look in your local telephone directory, but it is better to choose someone who has been recommended to you. Do look through the portfolio of work which has been done for other people and ask for a quote before work begins. The design below was prepared by Paul Dracott who was given the plans and lists from Steps 1 - 6. The reasons why he chose this design are given on the previous page.

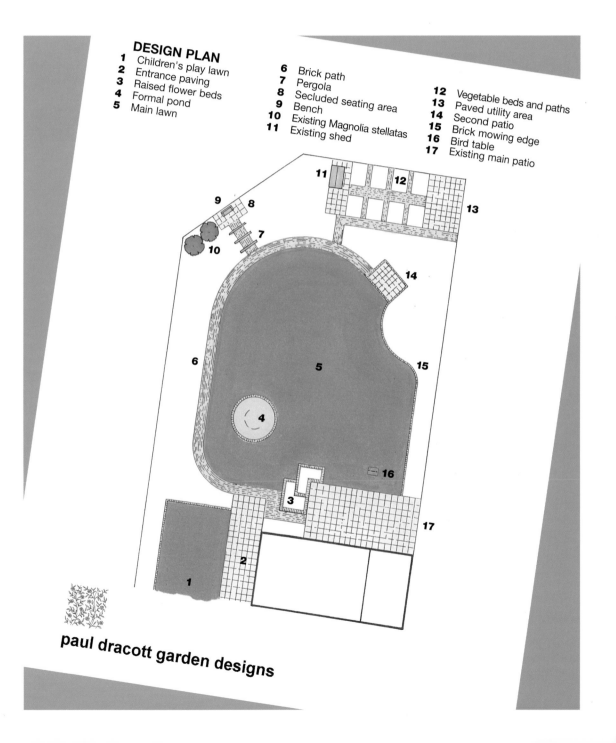

DESIGN PLAN

1 Children's play lawn
2 Entrance paving
3 Raised flower beds
4 Formal pond
5 Main lawn

6 Brick path
7 Pergola
8 Secluded seating area
9 Bench
10 Existing Magnolia stellatas
11 Existing shed

12 Vegetable beds and paths
13 Paved utility area
14 Second patio
15 Brick mowing edge
16 Bird table
17 Existing main patio

paul dracott garden designs

THE DIY APPROACH

Doing it yourself is, of course, the cheapest planning route but that is not the only advantage. You can spend much more time on the task than a professional, and you know better than anyone else what you like. Finally, there is the feeling of pride in having created a new garden from scratch.

1: Begin with a rough plan

Look at the questionnaire you filled in on page 200 and the Wants List you prepared at Step 5 (page 210). Now write down a 'must have' list and a 'like to have' one. In the example we have been working on the must-haves would include the large lawn, the altered mixed border, a vegetable plot, patio etc. Since preparing the original Wants List there may be other features you have decided to add — a pergola perhaps, or a swing for the children. A word of warning — do not make this list too large. The 'like to have' list can be longer — a pond in the wet area on the lawn perhaps, a rockery at the far end of the garden or maybe an extra sitting-out area.

Use one of the photocopies prepared at Step 4 (page 209) to start your rough plan. You will have decided on the style of garden and also whether it is to be formal or informal (page 181). Moving from a formal approach to a more informal feel at the back of the garden is an accepted good design technique, but to mix formal and informal features in the same area is rarely a good idea. At this stage you should map out the must-have features — the lawn, border, vegetable plot etc. Do not add any detail at this stage and do not try to fix definite dimensions. Just allocate space for all the major features and the like-to-haves you wish to include, walk around the garden with the plan to make sure you are happy and then get on with the finished plan. Don't rush this stage. You will no doubt change your mind several times and have to prepare several versions until you are ready to get on to that finished drawing.

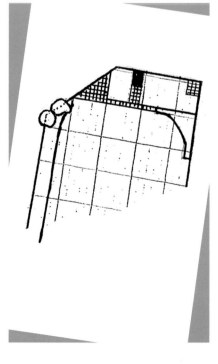

2: Draw the finished plan

It is now time to make a scale drawing using one of the photocopies from Step 4 (page 209) and the rough plan you have just prepared. In making your plans you should have kept both construction cost and maintenance time in mind. A koi pond may be highly desirable, but the cost may be prohibitive. A warm, large greenhouse would be a joy in winter, but the year-round work involved can make it a burden.

With the features which are to be included there are two important considerations before deciding on size and exact position. The first point to think about is that it is much cheaper to enlarge or reduce the size of some features (beds, borders, lawns etc) than to move them from one place to another. The second point to consider is aspect. Ponds, rockeries, greenhouses and beds for annuals need sunny sites away from trees. Turf grasses fail in deep shade — patios should be in sunshine for at least part of the day. Play areas and herb gardens are best sited close to the house. Whether you hide away the vegetable plot or leave it prominently exposed as your pride and joy is up to you.

Everything now has a place and a size, and the features can be drawn on the plan. You have remembered to avoid blocking attractive views and have made provision to hide eyesores either at this stage or in the Planting Scheme (page 216). Check that the family is happy. You have reached the stage when there is nothing more you can do, so take several photocopies and start work on the Planting Scheme.

Awkward shapes

Long and narrow

Long and narrow plots are not uncommon and so many people have a garden which poses a problem. A long unbroken lawn bounded by straight borders along the sides will give the property an unappealing tube-like look, with the eye being drawn immediately to the far distance. The photograph shows the standard way to provide interest — turn the plot into a series of rooms. These can be separated by hedges or low fences, or you can have an open plan as illustrated

L-shaped

The usual answer is to continue the garden design around the corner as in the example shown here, and leave the owner to feel disappointed that the display has been shortened. It is generally a better idea to create a quite different arrangement in all or part of the leg around the corner so as to provide a surprise item

Small and square

Low planting in a small and square garden which is surrounded by a close-board wooden fence can have a depressing box-like appearance. One of the answers is to have shrubs which hide the fence and have curved or irregular planting areas in the corners to hide the geometrical lines. Theoretically this dense planting should make the garden look smaller, but if there are tall trees and shrubs in the surrounding gardens the overall effect may be to enhance the size of the plot

STEP 8 : ADD THE PLANTING SCHEME

You have produced a detailed outline of the non-living structures in the garden. The Design Plan shows the position of the lawn, but there are beds, borders, boundaries and perhaps other areas for which it is necessary to prepare a Planting Scheme. This will show how you propose to clothe the garden with the elements which will give it colour, variety, seasonal interest and life — the plants.

As with the preparation of the Design Plan it is once again decision time — who is going to prepare this scheme? The answer is the same — for nearly everyone it is the garden owner who puts the Planting Scheme together. This is a worrying prospect for many people but help is on hand if you lack experience. You can copy or adapt the planting schemes in gardening books — collections plus the necessary plans are offered in magazines. Be guided by others if you must but the basic rule remains that you should check the requirements of each plant in a reliable garden book and make sure that it will be happy in the conditions to be provided. If you propose to do your own thing and not use someone else's plan then it is vital to gather information. Cuttings from magazines, watching TV programmes and using internet sites are fine, but nothing can match looking around gardens to see what plants you like.

If you have used a designer for the Design Plan then he or she will be responsible for the Planting Scheme. If you are just creating a new border in an existing garden you can use a Garden Planning Service run by a magazine or horticultural organisation if you feel the job is beyond you.

16 Bradbury Ave Cheltenham

PLANTING SCHEME

To achieve a balanced design the amount of planting has been increased. The main mixed border has been refurbished and extended towards the house with a border of spring bulbs and summer flowering perennials. The mixed border has been backed by climbers and a hedge of Lawson's cypress planted to screen an ugly view. At the foot of the garden a deep tree and shrub border has been added to give the garden depth and to separate the second patio from the vegetable garden. This flows into an herbaceous border designed to give a long season of interest, combining flowers with varied shapes. Close to the house the raised beds and small border will be planted with spring and summer hardy annuals to give year round interest.

paul dracott garden designs

THE DESIGNER APPROACH

The Outline Planting Scheme prepared by Paul Dracott is shown below — the reason why he has chosen the various bed and border types is explained. In addition a Detailed Planting Scheme for the west-facing herbaceous border (6) is included to show how designers present individual bed and border schemes.

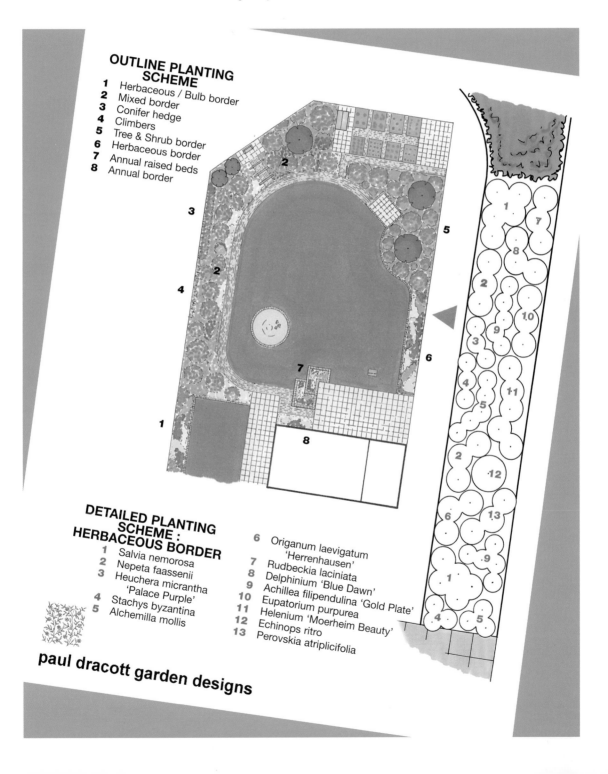

OUTLINE PLANTING SCHEME

1 Herbaceous / Bulb border
2 Mixed border
3 Conifer hedge
4 Climbers
5 Tree & Shrub border
6 Herbaceous border
7 Annual raised beds
8 Annual border

DETAILED PLANTING SCHEME : HERBACEOUS BORDER

1 Salvia nemorosa
2 Nepeta faassenii
3 Heuchera micrantha 'Palace Purple'
4 Stachys byzantina
5 Alchemilla mollis
6 Origanum laevigatum 'Herrenhausen'
7 Rudbeckia laciniata
8 Delphinium 'Blue Dawn'
9 Achillea filipendulina 'Gold Plate'
10 Eupatorium purpurea
11 Helenium 'Moerheim Beauty'
12 Echinops ritro
13 Perovskia atriplicifolia

paul dracott garden designs

THE DIY APPROACH

The guidelines below should help you to plan your new garden or new border. At the outset you should follow the most important rule of all — never buy a collection of plants because you like them at the garden centre and then try to find a home for them. Plan first on paper — buy later.

1: Prepare an outline scheme

The outline scheme covers the whole garden and it shows the structural planting. This includes trees and large shrubs, climbers on walls, arches, pergolas etc and any new hedges you propose to introduce. The planting plans for beds and borders are not included in this outline scheme.

Have a list of candidate plants before you begin. This will include 'must-haves' and old favourites. Include some unusual ones by all means, but avoid the danger of a garden filled with rarities unless you are a keen plantsman. Remember that the common-or-garden ones are generally the most reliable.

Start your scheme with one of the photocopies from Step 7 which will contain the plants which are to remain. With a pencil mark up the position of the trees, shrubs and hedges which you plan to have in your new garden. Check the expected height and spread at maturity of each variety and also check that its soil and light requirements are right for the situation. A small cross or dot is used to indicate where the stem of a tree or shrub will be and a ring is drawn round it to show the anticipated spread of the plant when mature. Where there are to be several specimens of the variety as with a hedge, draw an outline of the expected mature shape and put dots or crosses within to represent the planting stations. Check that you have followed the good design rules on pages 203-207 — make any changes before inking in the plant symbols.

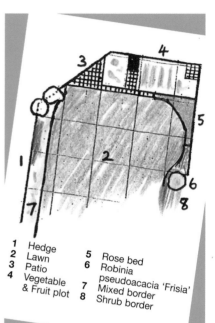

1	Hedge	5	Rose bed
2	Lawn	6	Robinia
3	Patio		pseudoacacia 'Frisia'
4	Vegetable	7	Mixed border
	& Fruit plot	8	Shrub border

2: Prepare detailed schemes

It is now time to prepare detailed schemes for the beds and borders. For each area draw its shape on a piece of graph paper — the scale will, of course, be greater than the one used for the outline scheme.

Follow the same convention — circles for individual plants, and overall spread areas where a large number of the same variety is to be planted. Use interlocking circles where a small number of border perennials is to be planted. Write the name of each plant next to each circle if not too many plants are involved — for a large bed or border it is usually better to give each circle a number and then have a separate plant list. Finally you may wish to colour the circles and areas to indicate the flower or leaf colour.

Planning a successful border takes a lot of thought. The tallest plants are generally at the back and the smallest at the front, but there should be some variation to avoid an over-regimented look. Be careful not to choose too many different types — border perennials should be planted in groups of three to five, not singly. It is age-old advice to go through your proposed list and cross out half of them.

Leaving sufficient space between the plants on your plan is another important point, especially for trees and shrubs — see page 70 for recommended distances. Following these rules means that there will be an empty feel for a few years — you can overcome this by temporary planting with some cheap shrubs or annuals and bulbs. Once you have finished take photocopies of both the outline scheme and the detailed ones — you will need them once you start work.

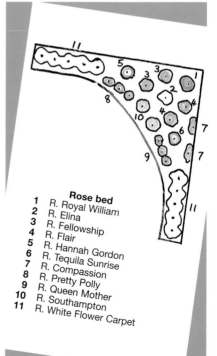

Rose bed
1   R. Royal William
2   R. Elina
3   R. Fellowship
4   R. Flair
5   R. Hannah Gordon
6   R. Tequila Sunrise
7   R. Compassion
8   R. Pretty Polly
9   R. Queen Mother
10 R. Southampton
11 R. White Flower Carpet

STEP 9 : NOW GET TO WORK

The Design Plan and Planting Scheme are finished and it is now time to begin work if the season and weather are right. The plans may have been prepared by a person or company which will be responsible for the creation of the new garden and so there is nothing more for you to do, but for most people this final step calls for a decision.

You will most likely have prepared your own design or you may have used the service of a professional — you must now decide who is going to carry out the actual work. Having to begin from scratch can be really hard work, and there is a lot to be said for using a landscape contractor if you can afford it. These people know where to go for materials, plants and so on, and they have the necessary equipment, skill and experience to do the work. You may not have the money to hand the whole job over, but do consider using a landscaper for the most strenuous parts of the project such as levelling, paving, bricklaying etc.

Pick your landscaper with care — mistakes at the garden-making stage cannot be simply rubbed out and changed like faults at the design stage. Personal recommendation is best — ask your designer if you used one, your local garden centre or a friend who has been satisfied with the work done by a contractor. Get more than one quote (fixed price, not estimate) and check a job they have done, their membership of a trade body and the cover provided by their insurance. Make sure you know exactly what is included in the quote. Fix a start date, and hand over all the plans well before that time.

For most people creating a new garden is a DIY job. Professional help may be too expensive, the garden may be very small or only a part of it may have to be changed. Whatever the reason for doing it yourself, forget the 48-hour makeover miracles you see on TV. Creating a garden is a lengthy job which may well take more than one season. It is usual to begin at the back of the garden, then the sides and finally the front garden. Don't try to do everything at once — tackle the work in a logical order. Listed below is a standard sequel of events followed by landscape contractors.

Garden making step by step

1. **SITE CLEARANCE** Remove builders' rubble in a brand new garden — unwanted trees and shrubs etc in a garden to be changed.

2. **EARTHWORKS** Establish new levels if necessary. Remember that topsoil must never be buried — move it away for later use.

3. **MARKING OUT** The distances shown on the plans must be translated to the garden and the areas marked out accordingly. Use canes and white string. If you have a change of heart when working on the site, make sure that the plan is altered.

4. **WALL & FENCE BUILDING**

5. **PAVING** First lay down lighting cables and water pipes if they are to be installed.

6. **SOIL PREPARATION** Beds and borders need levelling — bring in topsoil if necessary. Allow soil to settle.

7. **PLANTING** Now is the time for putting in the trees, shrubs and border perennials.

8. **LAWN AREA PREPARATION** Level — prepare surface for seeding or turf laying. Allow soil to settle.

9. **GRASSING** Sow grass seed or put down turves.

HARD LANDSCAPING HINTS

Laying bricks

The first job is to use pegs with string stretched tightly between them to mark out the width of the foundation trench. Dig out the earth to the depth and width shown below. If the bottom of the trench is not firm, remove the soft earth and replace with hardcore.

Pour in concrete to the recommended depth and leave to set for at least 4 days. Spread a 1 cm thick layer of mortar along the concrete and lay the first brick. Lay a second brick 6 brick-lengths away — use a straightedge and spirit level to check the level. Repeat until the far end is reached — lay additional bricks to fill in the gaps between the widely-spaced bricks. Check both vertical and horizontal levels regularly.

(1) Spread a 1 cm thick layer of mortar over about 3 bricks

(2) Press down brick. Scrape off excess mortar

(3) 'Butter' 1 cm thick layer of mortar on to head of next brick

(4) Press down brick so that it is firmly bedded below and on the buttered side. Scrape off excess mortar. Check horizontal level. Tap with trowel handle if necessary

(5) Check vertical level with straightedge. Tap side of brick with trowel handle if necessary

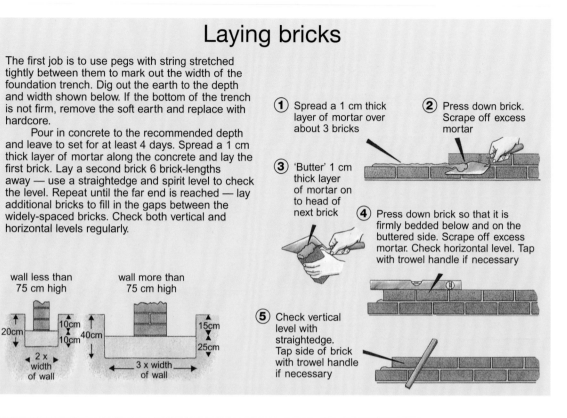

wall less than 75 cm high

wall more than 75 cm high

20cm 10cm 10cm 40cm 15cm 25cm

2 x width of wall

3 x width of wall

Erecting fence panels

Erect a post ① and then attach a panel to it. Support this panel on bricks ②. Now erect the next post at the other end of the panel — again fix the panel to the post as shown ③. Attach the next panel to this post, supporting it with the bricks removed from the previous section ④. Carry on with this post-panel-post-panel-post routine ⑤ until the fence is finished.

Metal post spikes are an easy-to-use alternative to digging holes. Place a wood block in the cup and hammer into the ground. Remove block and insert post when only the cup is visible.

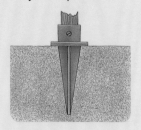

or

Panel clips avoid the problem of frame splitting which occurs when nailing is done badly

Nailing is the traditional method. Three 75 mm long galvanized nails are needed

Laying paving slabs

(5) Finish the path using the technique outlined in Step 4. Use a spirit level to make sure that the desired slope is achieved. Pull out the spacers and leave the mortar to set

(6) The path is ready for jointing (pointing) after 2 days. Point with moist mortar and a trowel

(4) Place the first line of slabs along a string which marks the edge. Lift the first slab and place 5 blobs of mortar on the sand below. Replace and bed down using a block of wood and club hammer. Repeat to finish the row. Insert two wooden spacers (5 mm thick) between each slab

(3) A 5 cm layer of sharp sand is the next step. Level and press down this sand with a screeding board

(2) Put down a layer of hardcore. For an ordinary path or patio a 5 cm layer is enough, but for a driveway have a depth of 10 cm. Mix the hardcore with some ballast to fill all the spaces between the broken bricks and stones. Ram down

(1) Remove earth to the depth and width required for the foundations and the paving slabs. Consolidate the bottom of the trench firmly

Building steps

(1) Carefully measure the height from the top of the bank to the bottom and then work out the number of steps you will need. Study the diagram — remove the earth as shown. Note that the base stones will require a foundation of an 8 cm deep layer of hardcore and an 8 cm layer of concrete. Firm the earth steps

(4) Continue building risers, infilling with hardcore and bedding down treads in mortar until the final tread is laid level with the upper surface of the bank. Replace earth to fill the gaps at the sides and foot of the steps. Cover the edges with plants and/or large stones

(3) Fill the space behind the riser with hardcore and ram down until it is firm and level with the top of the riser. Spread a layer of mortar and bed down the paving slabs to make the first tread

(2) When the concrete has set, bed the base stones into a thin layer of mortar and build the first riser with concrete blocks or Special Quality bricks

CHAPTER 14

ROSES

More than one thousand rose varieties are offered for sale in Britain. Nearly all are grown for the beauty and/or the fragrance of the flowers, but there are varieties noted for their decorative hips, colourful leaves and even for their beautiful thorns. The plant may struggle to reach the height of a teacup or it may tower to the top of a house. Colours range from purest white to darkest red with a rainbow of colours in between, apart from pure blue.

We sometimes regard this great variety of rose types, shapes and colours as part of our heritage, but the story is surprisingly recent. In regency times the roses were either large shrubs or climbers with a limited colour range and a limited flowering season.

Things changed during Queen Victoria's reign — the tough European varieties were crossed with repeat-flowering types from the East, and hybridisation with Persian roses brought in bright yellow and orange shades. It is not surprising that the new roses became Britain's most popular garden plants in the early years of the 20th century.

Some roses are trouble-free and are easy to grow — R. *rugosa* varieties and ground-cover types like White Carpet are examples. But for most gardeners roses mean Hybrid Teas and Floribundas with their repeat-flowering habit and unsurpassed floral display. This choice comes at a price — you have to prune before growth starts and to dead-head when blooms fade. Feeding is necessary for top-quality blooms and worst of all are the pests and diseases which make roses their favourite host. So producing a fine-looking rose bush with show-quality blooms may be a challenge, but that for many people is part of its charm.

New varieties appear every year and they get the largest photographs and the most alluring descriptions in the catalogues, but this does not make them the best choice. For the gardener who just wants a few reliable and attractive bushes it is sometimes better to wait a year or two to see how the new ones have fared in other people's gardens.

A list of varieties appears at the end of this chapter. There has been no attempt to list the author's favourites. The ones selected have been chosen on their popularity and their widespread availability at garden centres and in catalogues, and also on their appearance in the reliability and popularity polls conducted by the Royal National Rose Society.

Flower types

SINGLE

less than 8 petals
Examples: Ballerina
Dortmund
Fred Loads
Mermaid

SEMI-DOUBLE

8-20 petals
Examples: Boy's Brigade
Joseph's Coat
Masquerade
Sweet Magic

DOUBLE

MODERATELY FULL
21-29 petals
Example: Pascali

FULL
30-39 petals
Example: Dearest

VERY FULL
40 petals and over
Example: Peace

SINGLE COLOUR
Petals similarly coloured throughout, although some changes may occur as blooms get older
Example: Iceberg

BI-COLOUR
Colour of the outside of each petal distinctly different from the inside hue
Example: Piccadilly

MULTI-COLOUR
Colour of the petals changes distinctly with age. Flower trusses have several colours at the same time.
Example: Masquerade

BLEND
Two or more distinct colours merge on the inside of each petal.
Example: Peace

STRIPED
Two or more different colours on each petal, one of which is in the form of distinct bands.
Example: Rosa Mundi

HAND PAINTED
Silvery petals with red blotched and feathered over the surface, leaving a white eye at the base
Example: Regensberg

Flowering period

REPEAT FLOWERING ROSES produce two or more flushes of blooms during the flowering season. Modern roses generally produce blooms at intervals throughout the summer months and into the autumn — one of the main reasons for the unrivalled popularity of Hybrid Teas and Floribundas. Repeat flowering varieties, also known as recurrent and remontant varieties, may produce some flowers between the main flushes. When this feature is strongly marked the descriptions perpetual and continuous flowering are sometimes used, but they are not strictly correct.

ONCE FLOWERING ROSES produce a single flush of blooms which usually lasts for several weeks. Occasionally a few flowers may appear in autumn, but this flowering is far too sporadic to be considered a second flush. The once flowering roses most frequently bloom in June/July (summer flowering varieties), but there are varieties of Shrubs and Ramblers which bloom in late spring, early summer or late summer.

HIGH-CENTRED
Classical shape of the Hybrid Tea — long inner petals forming a regular central cone.

SPLIT-CENTRED
Inner petals confused, forming an irregular central area.

BLOWN
Normally well-shaped bloom past its best — opened wide to reveal stamens.

GLOBULAR
Bloom possessing many petals forming a ball-like arrangement with a closed centre.

OPEN-CUPPED
Bloom possessing many petals forming a cup-like arrangement with an open centre.

QUARTERED
Inner petals folded into 4 distinct sections rather than forming a cone.

FLAT
Flat, low-centred bloom with a small number of petals.

ROSETTE
Flat, low-centred bloom with many short petals regularly arranged.

POMPON
Rounded bloom with many short petals regularly arranged.

The right spot for planting

Roses will not thrive in poor soil. Ideally it should be a medium loam, slightly acid and reasonably rich in plant foods and humus. Fortunately this ideal situation is desirable but not essential, but there are two areas where roses will struggle. Heavy clay soil must be improved by adding organic matter, and a soil with a high lime content is harmful.

Reasonably free drainage is necessary, and so is a sunny or slight shady site. Finally, shelter from cold winds is helpful, but bushes do not like being shut in by overhanging trees or nearby walls.

Getting the plant ready

There is little to do if you have chosen a container-grown plant. Water thoroughly before removing from the pot — keep the soil intact when planting.

A bare-rooted plant should be carefully unpacked and very long roots cut back to about 30 cm (1 ft). Remove any leaves, buds and hips which may be present. Plunge roots in a bucket of water if they appear dry or stems are shrivelled. If planting is to be delayed you can keep the unopened package in an unheated shed or garage. Heel in the plants in a shallow V-shaped trench if the delay is to be over 10 days.

Spacing

Rose Type	Distance Apart
Miniature roses	30 cm (1 ft)
Patio roses	45 cm (1½ ft)
HT & Floribunda bushes Compact varieties	45 cm (1½ ft)
HT & Floribunda bushes Average varieties	60 cm (2 ft)
HT & Floribunda bushes Tall varieties	75 cm (2½ ft)
Standards	1.2 m (4 ft)
Ground cover roses	expected spread
Shrubs	half expected height
Weeping standards	2 m (7 ft)
Climbers	2 m (7 ft)

Planting

Container-grown bushes

These roses can be planted at any time of the year, but some times are better than others. The soil must be in the right condition — autumn or spring planting allows some root development before dry weather in summer. See page 63 for planting details.

Bare-rooted bushes

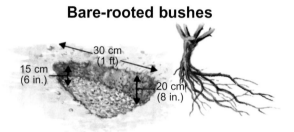

30 cm (1 ft)

15 cm (6 in.)

20 cm (8 in.)

Plant between late October and late March. November is the best time in most gardens — plant in March if the soil is very heavy. The ground should be neither frozen nor waterlogged. Squeeze a handful — it should form a ball and yet be dry enough to shatter when dropped. Dig a fan-shaped hole where roots run along in one direction — see above. See page 62 for planting details.

Bare-rooted climbers

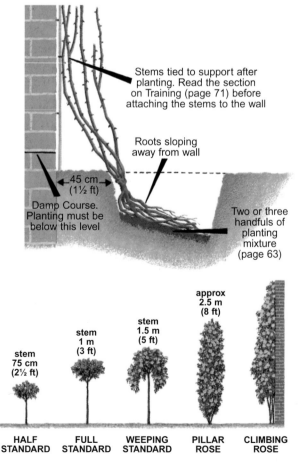

Stems tied to support after planting. Read the section on Training (page 71) before attaching the stems to the wall

Roots sloping away from wall

45 cm (1½ ft)

Damp Course. Planting must be below this level

Two or three handfuls of planting mixture (page 63)

Growth types

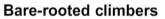

30 cm (1 ft) or less	45 cm (1½ ft) or less	stem 30 cm (1 ft)	60 cm (2 ft) or less	over 60 cm (2 ft)	stem 75 cm (2½ ft)	stem 1 m (3 ft)	stem 1.5 m (5 ft)	approx 2.5 m (8 ft)	
PROSTRATE ROSE	MINIATURE BUSH	MINIATURE STANDARD	DWARF BUSH	BUSH	HALF STANDARD	FULL STANDARD	WEEPING STANDARD	PILLAR ROSE	CLIMBING ROSE

Plant care

Roses, like most other garden plants, make heavy demands on the reserves of plant food in the soil. If one or more of the vital elements run short, then hunger signs appear on the leaves or flowers and both vigour and display are affected. The standard answer is to apply a small handful of rose fertilizer around each plant when the soil is moist in spring before the leaves are fully open. Hoe in lightly.

The value of mulching has already been described several times on earlier pages — see page 61 for the list of benefits. The time to mulch is in May or June. The main purpose of hoeing is to keep down weeds, such as couch grass, which are not suppressed by mulching. For this purpose hoeing must be carried out at regular and frequent intervals. Hoeing must not go deeper than 2-3 cm (1 in.) below the surface, or rose roots may be damaged.

The rose is perhaps the most widely used of all flowers cut for indoor decoration. A certain amount of care is necessary to avoid weakening the plants. Do not take more than one-third of the flowering stem. Cutting blooms from newly-planted roses is not recommended.

One of the blessings of roses is the deep-rooting habit of growth. This means that watering of established plants is not vital in some seasons. Some roses, however, may need watering after a week of dry weather in summer — newly-planted roses, climbers growing against walls, and bushes in sandy soil. All roses will need water during a period of drought in late spring or summer.

There is, unfortunately, the disfiguring duo of fungal diseases — black spot with its yellow-edged dark spots on the leaves which fall prematurely, and mildew which distorts leaves, shoots and buds, covering them with white mould. Read page 151 for guidance. Many Ramblers and Shrub roses have little or no resistance, and it is always wise to check resistance to disease on the label or in the catalogue before buying one of these plants.

The regular removal of dead blooms from Floribundas and Hybrid Teas is an important task. When the flowers have faded remove the whole truss, cutting the stem just above the second or third leaf down. By doing this the energy which would have gone into fruit production is conserved. Faded flowers on first year roses should be removed with very little stem. Do not dead-head varieties grown for their decorative hips.

Pruning
Hybrid Teas • Floribundas Patio roses

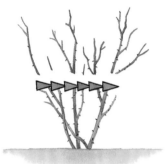

Nothing could be easier — the bush is cut to half its height with secateurs or a hedge trimmer. Leave the twiggy growth — cut out dead wood at the base if it is unsightly.

It comes as a surprise to many experts that this easy-care way of pruning has proved to be so successful compared to the traditional method described in the textbooks. The blooms are sometimes larger and more numerous, and the bushes are at least as healthy as plants pruned in the standard way.

Miniatures • Shrub roses

Don't cut back these roses by the method recommended for Hybrid Teas and Floribundas. Very little pruning is required — cut out dead wood and sickly growth and then merely trim to shape as necessary to avoid overcrowding. Secateurs are the usual tools for pruning, but Ground Cover roses are trimmed with garden shears.

When to prune

Early spring pruning is recommended for autumn- and winter-planted roses and for established plants. The best time to prune is when growth is just beginning. The uppermost buds will have begun to swell but no leaves will have appeared. Prune just before planting if the bushes or standards are to be put in the bed or border in spring.

Rose groups

HYBRID TEA (HT)

The most popular class — the flower stems are upright and the flowers are shapely. The typical Hybrid Tea bears blooms which are medium-sized or large, with petals forming a distinct central cone. The flowers are borne singly or with several side buds. The top choice for the flower vase, but the HT will not put up with neglect like many Shrubs and Floribundas.

FLORIBUNDA (F)

Second only to the Hybrid Tea in popularity. The Floribunda bears its flowers in clusters or trusses, and several blooms open at one time in each truss. This class is unsurpassed for providing a colourful and long-lasting bedding display, but in general the flower form is inferior to that of the HT. Both petal size and number vary greatly from one variety to another.

PATIO (P)

In the 1980s the low-growing varieties of Floribunda roses were separated and given their own name — the Patio roses. These neat 45 cm (1½ ft) high bushes have become popular and there are many fine types. They make excellent tub plants — hence the name, but they are also widely used for the front of the border. The continuity of bloom is generally very good.

MINIATURE (Min)

This class has increased in popularity due to its novelty and versatility. Both leaves and flowers are small, and under normal conditions the maximum height is less than 45 cm (1½ ft) — many varieties are considerably shorter. Miniature roses can be used for edging, growing in tubs and in rockeries and for bringing indoors as temporary pot plants.

SHRUB (Sh)

A large and highly varied class of roses with only one feature in common — they do not fit neatly into any other group. The typical Shrub is taller than the types used for bedding and is a Species variety (clearly related to a wild rose), an Old Garden rose (dating back to pre-HT days) or a Modern Shrub rose (mostly repeat flowering).

CLIMBER (Cl)

A class of roses which if tied to a support can be made to climb. There are two groups. Ramblers have long pliable stems which need to be cut back each year and there is only one flush of flowers. Choose instead a stiff-stemmed Climber. The easy-care ones have a repeat flowering habit plus good disease resistance.

GROUND COVER (GC)

Shrub roses with a distinctly spreading or trailing growth habit have been moved to a class of their own — the Ground Cover roses. The leafy mounds are useful for covering banks or manhole covers, but nearly all varieties can grow to 60 cm (2 ft) or more when mature. There are a few which reach only 45 cm (1½ ft) or less.

Silver Jubilee

Congratulations

Elina

Remember Me

Varieties

NAME	TYPE	COLOUR	NOTES	HEIGHT
ABRAHAM DARBY	Sh	Pink	A vigorous bush with leathery foliage. The large blooms have a strong fruity aroma	1.5 m (5 ft)
ALBERIC BARBIER	Cl	Cream	An old favourite which can flourish in difficult situations. The double blooms appear in June or July	5 m (16 ft)
ALBERTINE	Cl	Pale pink	A vigorous Rambler which blooms in June — the flowers are fragrant. Mildew can be a problem	5 m (16 ft)
ALEC'S RED	HT	Cherry red	Large, globular and fragrant blooms which have good rain resistance. Vigorous, healthy growth	1 m (3 ft)
ALEXANDER	HT	Vermilion red	A tall bush which needs space. Blooms are medium-sized and only moderately full	1.5 m (5 ft)
ALOHA	Cl	Rose pink	The flowers are very full and sweetly scented — a good choice where space is restricted	2.5 m (8 ft)
AMBER QUEEN	F	Amber yellow	The bush is neat and compact — the blooms are large, cup-shaped and fragrant	60 cm (2 ft)
ANGELA RIPPON	Min	Carmine pink	A popular Miniature — compact and bushy with lots of fragrant double blooms above healthy foliage	50 cm (1½ ft)
ANNA FORD	P	Deep orange	Trusses of small, semi-double flowers are borne above healthy glossy foliage	50 cm (1½ ft)
ARTHUR BELL	F	Golden yellow	Flowering starts very early — the blooms are large and very fragrant. Unfortunately colour fades to pale cream	1 m (3 ft)
BALLERINA	Sh	Pale pink	Tiny, white-eyed single flowers are borne in hydrangea-like heads above small, glossy leaves	1 m (3 ft)
BONICA	GC	Pink	A domed bush with arching stems bearing semi-double slightly fragrant blooms	1 m (3 ft)
BUFF BEAUTY	Sh	Pale apricot	Double, rather shapeless flowers are carried on arching stems. Prone to mildew. Good autumn display	1 m (3 ft)
BUXOM BEAUTY	HT	Pink	The large blooms have the classic high-centred shape and the fragrance is strong. Good disease resistance	1 m (3 ft)
CANARY BIRD	Sh	Yellow	The rose to grow to herald in the flowering season — blooms in May. Good for hedging. Prone to die-back	2 m (7 ft)
CHAMPAGNE MOMENTS	F	Ivory	The apricot-centred blooms appear profusely all summer long. Rose of the Year 2006. Good disease resistance	60 cm (2 ft)
CLIMBING ICEBERG	Cl	White	The usual choice for clothing a wall with glossy foliage and large trusses of flat white blooms. Reliable	3 m (10 ft)
COMPASSION	Cl	Apricot pink	Free-flowering and fragrant — the double blooms are borne on stiff stems. An excellent pillar rose	3 m (10 ft)
CONGRATULATIONS	HT	Rose pink	The medium-sized blooms are high-centred and moderately fragrant. Good disease resistance	1 m (3 ft)
DAWN CHORUS	HT	Deep orange	The high-centred, medium-sized blooms are borne in clusters. Long flowering period — good disease resistance	1 m (3 ft)
DOUBLE DELIGHT	HT	Cream/ red	The queen of the bi-colours with very large flowers. They are strongly scented and are freely produced	1 m (3 ft)
DUBLIN BAY	Cl	Deep red	Attractive double blooms on healthy stems. Unfortunately may remain as an upright bush	2 m (7 ft)

Amber Queen

Queen Elizabeth

Iceberg

Trumpeter

NAME	TYPE	COLOUR	NOTES	HEIGHT
ELINA	HT	Ivory	The yellow-centred flowers are large and fragrant, growth is upright. Delicate appearance, but stands up well to poor weather	1 m (3 ft)
FALSTAFF	Sh	Dark red	The large flowers are cup-shaped with a strong old rose fragrance. Colour changes to purple with age	1.5 m (5 ft)
FELICITE PERPETUE	Cl	Creamy white	In July there are clusters of small, rosette shaped blooms. Vigorous and reliable in less-than-perfect situations	5 m (16 ft)
FLOWER CARPET	GC	Pink	A great favourite in the 1990s — perhaps less so now. Abundant small flowers — outstanding disease resistance	50 cm (1½ ft)
GENTLE TOUCH	P	Pale pink	This popular compact variety has high-centred HT-shaped small flowers in large trusses. Long flowering season	50 cm (1½ ft)
GOLDEN SHOWERS	Cl	Golden yellow	The double, fragrant blooms appear from June until the frosts arrive. Blooms soon become loose — growth is bushy at first	3 m (10 ft)
GRAHAM THOMAS	Sh	Deep yellow	Paeony-shaped blooms appear over an unusually long flowering period on arching stems. The fragrance is pleasant but unusual	1 m (3 ft)
GREAT EXPECTATIONS	F	Apricot	Fragrance is an outstanding feature of this variety which was judged Rose of the Year in 2001. Good disease resistance	1 m (3 ft)
HANDEL	Cl	Cream/ pink	The bi-coloured blooms are the outstanding feature. Stems are relatively thornless — prone to mildew and black spot	3 m (10 ft)
HOT CHOCOLATE	F.	Brownish red	Colour of the medium-sized blooms is hard to describe — won top Novelty Award. Average disease resistance	75 cm (2½ ft)
ICEBERG	F	White	The most popular white Floribunda — the quantity and quality of the medium-sized flat blooms are outstanding	1.5 m (5 ft)
IRISH EYES	F	Yellow/ red	The red-eyed yellow flowers are fully double and cupped. Growth habit is upright and there is good disease resistance	75 cm (2½ ft)
KORRESIA	F	Yellow	A favourite Floribunda grown for its large double, fragrant blooms. Unfading blooms appear for a long period	75 cm (2½ ft)
LOVING MEMORY	HT	Red	An excellent choice for cutting and exhibiting. The large blooms are borne on long, straight stems	1 m (3 ft)
MAIGOLD	Cl	Bronze yellow	This variety starts to bloom early and the fragrance is strong, but the flowers are unshapely and the flowering period is short	2.5 m (8 ft)
MARGARET MERRIL	F	Pearly white	The rival to Iceberg — lacks flower abundance but the flower form is better and the fragrance is strong	1 m (3 ft)
MERMAID	Cl	Primrose yellow	One to choose if you want to cover a large area. Very large fragrant flowers, but can be killed by frost	7 m (23 ft)
MOUNTBATTEN	F	Yellow	Healthy, easy to grow, but it does need space — useful as a hedge. The flowers are large and fragrant	1.5 m (5 ft)
NEVADA	Sh	Creamy white	In June the thornless stems and small leaves are covered with large semi-double blooms. Prone to black spot	2.5 m (8 ft)
NEW DAWN	Cl	Shell pink	Small flowers appear throughout the summer — grow as a hedge, specimen bush or climber	3 m (10 ft)
NOSTALGIA	HT	White/ red	The compact bush has large bi-coloured flowers which are cup-shaped. There is some fragrance	50 cm (1½ ft)
PAUL SHERVILLE	HT	Pink/ peach	Growth is leafy and spreading — flowers are double, high-centred and very fragrant. Prone to black spot	1 m (3 ft)

Dublin Bay

Felicite Perpetue

Mermaid

Handel

NAME	TYPE	COLOUR	NOTES	HEIGHT
PEACE	HT	Pink/ yellow	It was once the world's most popular rose, despite the lack of fragrance and late start to flowering. Prone to black spot	1.5 m (5 ft)
PENELOPE	Sh	Shell pink	A large, spreading bush if lightly pruned — use for hedging. Blooms appear in June — prune for repeat flowering	1.5 m (5 ft)
PENNY LANE	Cl	Pink	High-centred large blooms with a strong fragrance. They appear from spring until late summer — good disease resistance	4 m (13 ft)
PRETTY POLLY	P	Pale pink	More than just another pink dwarf — the blooms are borne in large numbers and are extremely attractive	50 cm (1½ ft)
QUEEN ELIZABETH	F	Pale pink	Give it space. Fine foliage, lovely large blooms which keep well in water — an outstanding rose	1.5 m (5 ft)
RAMBLING RECTOR	Cl	Creamy white	One of the best roses for covering walls. Flower trusses are large, will grow on a north wall and the leaves are healthy	8 m (26 ft)
REMEMBER ME	HT	Orange/ yellow	Each large bloom is borne in a wide-spreading truss — growth is vigorous and upright. Good disease resistance	1 m (3 ft)
ROSA MUNDI	Sh	Pink/ crimson	Still in most catalogues after 400 years. The flowers are distinctly striped, appearing in midsummer. Prone to disease	2 m (7 ft)
ROSA RUGOSA ALBA	Sh	Greenish white	A typical Rugosa — wrinkled disease-free leaves, fragrant blooms, attractive hips and an iron constitution	2 m (7 ft)
ROSERAIE DE L'HAY	Sh	Wine red	One of the best Rugosas — excellent for hedging. Large, fragrant blooms — extremely tolerant of poor conditions. No hip display	2 m (7 ft)
ROYAL WILLIAM	HT	Deep crimson	One of the best dark reds — large, fragrant blooms on stout stems. Leaves large and healthy. Recommended for flower arrangers	1 m (3 ft)
SALLY HOLMES	Sh	Creamy white	Large open flowers are borne on clusters which stand above the foliage. Take care — it is temperamental	2 m (7 ft)
SEXY REXY	F	Rose pink	The abundance of the floral display has made this variety a popular choice. The camellia-shaped blooms are borne in large trusses	75 cm (2½ ft)
SILVER JUBILEE	HT	Pink/ peach	This classic rose still keeps its place in the catalogues. The shapely blooms are on short stems — the long petals keep their colour	1 m (3 ft)
SUMMERTIME	P	Yellow	This Rose of the Year 2005 produces an abundant display of fragrant double flowers. Good disease resistance	25 cm (10 in.)
SWEET DREAM	P	Apricot	Its advantages made it one of the Patio stars. Colour does not fade with age, blooms stand up to rain and growth is neat	50 cm (1½ ft)
THE FAIRY	Sh	Pink	The rosette-shaped flowers are very small but are borne in large clusters. Flowering does not start until late July	75 cm (2½ ft)
TRUMPETER	F	Vermillion	A bright red, low-growing Floribunda which bears a continuous show throughout the summer. Unfortunately heads bow down in rain	1 m (3 ft)
WARM WISHES	HT	Peach	The flowers are not particularly large — its popularity is due to the abundance of the blooms which stand up to wind and rain	75 cm (2½ ft)
WILLIAM SHAKESPEARE	Sh	Dark red	William Shakespeare 2000 is one of the English Rose group — the quartered blooms are highly fragrant. Good disease resistance	1 m (3 ft)
WINCHESTER CATHEDRAL	Sh	White	A free-flowering English Rose variety — the double blooms are fragrant. Early flowering is the outstanding feature	1 m (3 ft)
ZEPHIRINE DROUHIN	Cl	Carmine pink	More than 100 years old but still in many catalogues. Grow as a Climber or tall Shrub — dead-head regularly. Prone to disease	3 m (10 ft)

Penelope

Nevada

Roseraie de l'Hay

Ballerina

CHAPTER 15
GARDEN FEATURES

What is a garden? The definition in our standard dictionaries is not very helpful. 'An enclosed piece of ground devoted to the cultivation of flowers, fruits and vegetables' would include countless arable farms and exclude the millions of unenclosed gardens in America and Scandinavia. 'A piece of ground in which flowers etc are cultivated' is not much better as it would include every plant nursery in the country.

A better description, perhaps, is 'an area of land on which plants are grown for their decorative and/or culinary value and not for commercial gain.' It isn't perfect, of course, but it does highlight two key elements — land and plants which are grown for pleasure rather than profit. However, a third vital element is missing — the presence of features.

A plot containing attractive plants and nothing else is not what we would really regard as a garden — there are no features. In the history of Grand Gardens, features arrived before plants — gardens began as areas of tiles and tinkling water rather than sites for growing flowers. To those early Persians the pots of flowers and bushes which arrived later were incidental to the coolness of the courtyard. Even Le Nôtre, the designer of Versailles, was quite happy to use coloured glass beads rather than plants in his complex beds.

In today's gardens we find a wide variety of features, with just one being universal. There must be a pathway of some type for foot traffic. Next, there is a small group of features which appear in the majority of gardens — walls, fences and gates where open-plan gardening is not practical, beds and borders for plants, a lawn as a centrepiece and paved areas for a variety of purposes. Other common features include a garage for the car, a shed for tools etc and various containers for plants close to the house. Apart from these basic features there are a number of non-essential ones which have been popular features for generations — arches, pergolas, rockeries, ponds, greenhouses and ornaments. Finally there are a small group of features which have grown in popularity in recent years. The number of vegetable plots has dramatically increased with the grow-your-own boom — the presence of barbeques, furniture, outdoor lighting and patios has become much more popular with the growing use of the garden as an outdoor living area. In addition there are the wildflower plots, which represent the increased interest in the environment. However big, however small, a garden is not a garden without its features.

Arches & Pergolas

An arch is a relatively narrow walk-through structure — a pergola is an extended archway or a series of linked arches. There are three basic rules. The first one is that an arch or pergola should have a definite purpose — do not use it as an isolated feature in the lawn at the side of a flower bed. The classical use is to cover part or all of a pathway with plant-bedecked vertical and overhead supports. Next, make sure that material and design fit in with the house and garden style — rustic poles look attractive in a traditional setting but would look out of place in ultra-modern surroundings. The third vital rule is that the structure must be strong enough and sufficiently well-anchored to withstand gale-force winds.

You can make a wooden arch from scratch using rustic poles or sawn timber, but it is much more usual these days to buy a kit or ready-made one. Use preservative-treated wood and rust-proof nails and screws. Wood, of course, is not the only material — a wide range of plastic-coated and all-metal arches are available. Make sure it is large enough — the height should be at least 2 m (7 ft) and the width 1.25 m (4 ft) or more.

The pergola was once a feature of the country estate, but now you will find them everywhere. There are two reasons for this increase in popularity — there is a wide variety of prefabricated kits nowadays and the patio boom has created a widespread need for a semi-enclosed spot which links house and garden. Some people prefer the oriental pergola to the traditional one — here the cross beams have bevelled rather than square-cut edges.

A typical arch — apex-topped, trellis-sided and flanked by a simple picket fence. Make sure that the posts are set firmly in the ground

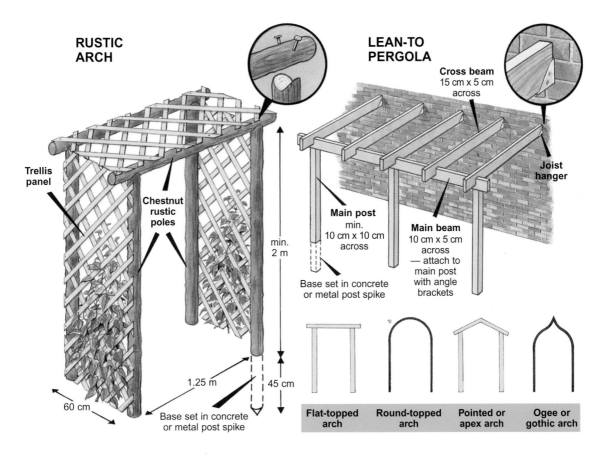

RUSTIC ARCH

Trellis panel

Chestnut rustic poles

min. 2 m

1.25 m

45 cm

60 cm

Base set in concrete or metal post spike

LEAN-TO PERGOLA

Cross beam 15 cm x 5 cm across

Joist hanger

Main post min. 10 cm x 10 cm across

Main beam 10 cm x 5 cm across — attach to main post with angle brackets

Base set in concrete or metal post spike

Flat-topped arch **Round-topped arch** **Pointed or apex arch** **Ogee or gothic arch**

Barbeque

Annual sales of barbeques in Britain now exceed over one million, so no longer is it strange to be invited to lunch in summer and find the host in the garden cooking the food. The range of barbeques now on offer is extensive in both price and variety. You can pay as little as a few pounds or more than £600. Sizes range from a tiny disposable tray and the standard **brazier** model to the **kettle** barbeque which has a domed lid which can be closed to retain heat. Another sophisticated form is the **wagon** barbeque which is a wheeled trolley with work surfaces.

Charcoal is the most popular but not the only fuel — both electric and gas models are available with a firebox containing re-usable lava rock. Finally, there is the permanent barbeque built with brick or stone.

A few points to remember. Practise on the family first before trying out new techniques and foods at a party, and try to keep it at a reasonable distance away from neighbours and trees. Finally, do not cater for more people than your skill and temper will allow — it is more difficult than cooking in the kitchen!

Bird table

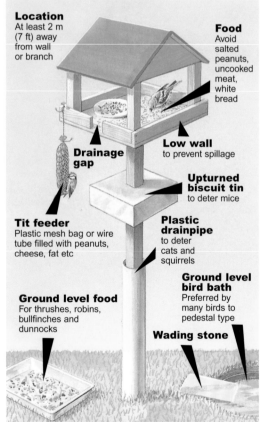

Location
At least 2 m (7 ft) away from wall or branch

Food
Avoid salted peanuts, uncooked meat, white bread

Drainage gap

Low wall
to prevent spillage

Upturned biscuit tin
to deter mice

Tit feeder
Plastic mesh bag or wire tube filled with peanuts, cheese, fat etc

Plastic drainpipe
to deter cats and squirrels

Ground level food
For thrushes, robins, bullfinches and dunnocks

Ground level bird bath
Preferred by many birds to pedestal type

Wading stone

Beds

A bed is a planted area which is designed to be viewed from all sides. The **flower bed** is the traditional home for annuals, biennials, bulbs and half-hardy perennials — the occupants are usually bedded out in autumn or late spring. An **island bed** is surrounded by lawn or paving — this term is sometimes used to describe a border perennial bed. In a **raised bed** there is a solid surround to support the soil above the surrounding level — a **sunken bed** has its surface below the surrounding level. In a **formal bed** the outline and planting are strictly geometrical. Finally there is the **scree bed**, which is a deep and sloping bed filled with a mixture of stone chippings and loam to house alpines.

Borders

A border is a planted area which is designed to be viewed from one, two or three sides but not from all angles. The **herbaceous border** was an essential feature of the larger garden 100 years ago, but is less popular these days. It is long and narrow with a backcloth of a wall or clipped hedge and a variety of border perennials planted in tiers. The **shrub border** is a labour saving alternative, but it can be dull for part of the year. The **mixed border** is a fairly recent innovation and is now the favourite type. There is a framework of flowering shrubs and decorative evergreens — roses and border perennials form colourful patches and remaining pockets are filled with bulbs and annuals.

Buildings

Buildings have been a feature of British gardens right from the beginning. Some of these early garden buildings were impressive creations in brick and stone, but here we are concerned with more modest structures.

Greenhouses are primarily designed for the cultivation of plants and have the entrance sited in the garden. Conservatories are also primarily designed for the cultivation and enjoyment of plants, but they are usually more ornate than greenhouses and there is an entrance within the house. The remaining garden structures which you can enter are classed as 'buildings'.

There are four basic types. The most popular one is the **Shed** — a building which is primarily used for storage. It may also serve as a place for a variety of gardening and non-gardening jobs and it can provide shelter from rain, but it is a practical rather than an ornamental structure. The **Summerhouse** differs in two respects — it is an ornamental building to be admired from the outside, and it also should have an aspect which allows the garden to be admired from the inside. This means that proper siting, attractive appearance and the presence of an adequate number of windows are all-important. The **Gazebo** and **Arbour** are rather similar in purpose to the summerhouse, but the sides are open or latticed. Finally there is the **Playhouse** for children, which can be as grand as a miniature chalet with veranda to a simple bedsheet stretched between two chairs on the lawn.

Choice is very difficult these days as so many types are available. Wood is no longer the only material and all sorts of clever variations are to be found, but the basic rules remain. Firstly, study the catalogues if you wish, but you should inspect the actual buildings before buying — go through the basic checklist below. Secondly, clarify what is included in the price before deciding between one supplier and another. The quote may or may not include floor, glass, lining, delivery and erection.

Find out if planning permission is necessary — larger buildings and those to be erected close to the boundary do need permission. In addition, look at your insurance policy and include your new shed or summerhouse if such a structure is not covered.

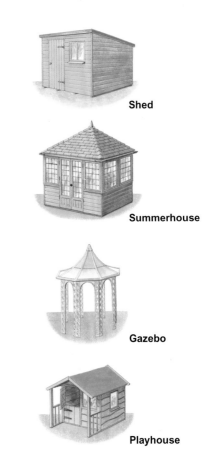

Shed

Summerhouse

Gazebo

Playhouse

CHOOSING A BUILDING

- **Floor** Sound construction is essential. Both sides should be treated with a preservative — tongued-and-grooved boards are much better than plywood or hardboard.

- **Bearers** These should be heavy-duty timbers, pressure-treated and at least 5x5 cm (2x2 in.) across.

- **Framework** The upright frames should be no more than 60 cm (2 ft) apart and there should be stout cross braces between them.

- **Door** Make sure it is wide enough for your needs. With a shed it must allow ready access for the mower, wheelbarrow etc. It should be soundly constructed with at least 3 ledges and 2 braces. A strong lock with key is essential. Hinges and all other metal parts should be rust-proof.

- **Windows** At least one window is essential if you intend to work or sit in the building. A single window will do in a small shed, but you will need more windows if you intend to use it for potting. In a summerhouse for garden viewing you will need extensive windows which are both well-fitting and attractive. A top-hung window can be left open when it is raining. A sloping sill with a drip groove on the underside is necessary.

- **Eaves** There should be sufficient overhang to make sure that rainwater from the roof is kept well away from the walls.

- **Roof** Choose one made of tongued-and-grooved boards rather than plywood if you can afford it. Roofing felt should be thick and it should cover the eaves beams completely. Make sure that the headroom is high enough for the tallest member of the family.

- **Cladding** The boards must be weatherproof and rot-proof — softwood should have been pressure-treated with a preservative. Feather-edged and waney-edged weatherboarding is the cheapest, but it is the least weatherproof. It is better to choose tongued-and-grooved or shiplap cladding. Whichever type you choose, make sure that it is free from cracks or numerous knot holes.

Containers

As shown below there are places all round the garden for containers. Wherever you need a compact splash of colour or a green focal point there is a type of container to fill the bill. The increased use of containers is not difficult to understand. The dramatic growth in the number of patios has meant that there are now more bare paved areas to clothe in millions of gardens, and people are now more aware than ever of the benefits of container gardening. Ground is not needed and plants can be put right next to the house. Plants not suited to your soil can be grown, tender plants can be put outside in summer and there is less chance of pest damage. Finally, plants can be moved away once the flowering season is over.

Many advantages, but there is one important disadvantage. Frequent watering is essential in summer and this may mean using a watering can or hose daily during a dry spell. Containers with vertical sides will need less frequent watering than those with sharply sloping sides. In addition feeding is required at regular intervals.

Containers are usually bought as such from garden centres, hardware sheds or mail order companies, but there are kits for wooden containers and a wide range of non-garden items can be used — kitchen sinks, chimney pots etc. In a tiny garden the container display may be more extensive than the open ground features, but in most cases the troughs and pots are restricted to just a few well-defined areas. When grouping containers it is generally wise to have a single or a limited range of types (wood, plastic etc) but a decent range of sizes.

Making the right choice is not easy. Obviously you will be influenced by your personal taste and the depth of your pocket, but there are some general guidelines. Make sure it is large enough. Large containers do not have to be watered as frequently as small ones. On an exposed site you will need a tub which is at least 50 cm (1½ ft) across and 30 cm (1 ft) high if tall plants are to be grown. Make sure that size and material are in keeping with the house and garden — an ornate pot may be out of place in a modern garden. Finally, check that there is at least one drainage hole (2 cm/1 in. or more across) every 10-15 cm (4-6 in.)

The same plant in the same pot. A line of evenly-spaced terracotta pots planted with hydrangeas provides a feeling of unity

The muted colour of the unstained Versailles tub gives an extra brilliance to this spring display of wallflowers and pansies

Front door & Porch
An excellent place for containers — either singly or as a pair of matched pots. Careful selection and maintenance are essential as the display must always be in first-class condition

Path or Steps liner
A line of identical pots or troughs can enhance the appearance of a plain walkway or flight of steps

Focal point
A large container or a group of smaller containers can be used to provide a focal point. Attractive trees and shrubs have an important role to play here — pots and plants must be in scale with the surroundings

Patio
The favourite place these days for free-standing containers. The starkness of bare walls and paving slabs is relieved by the presence of plants. Bedding plants and bulbs are the usual planting material

Balcony
Trailing plants to grow over the container and climbers to clothe the railings are widely grown. Use a lightweight container and a peat-based compost. Exposure to strong winds can be a problem

Hanging basket
A popular feature these days — about a third of gardens have one. The best site is partly sunny during the day and is protected from strong winds. Remember daily watering may be necessary in summer

Window sill
Window boxes add colour and interest to dull walls and windows. The construction material and its colour should not detract from the plants — make sure that the box is firmly attached

Greenhouse
Planting vegetables in the border soil can create all sorts of problems — the greenhouse is usually filled with pots and growing bags which contain suitable growing media

Fences

A fence provides the quickest and usually the easiest way to mark the boundary of your property — if privacy is important a solid fence is the answer. Fences are more than boundary markers — they can be used to hide unsightly objects, separate sections of the garden, provide protection against the wind, act as supports for climbing plants and provide a way to keep children in (or out).

The range of materials for and the styles of fencing are much greater than for walling. Shown below are some of the more popular styles, but there are many others — closeboard fencing, wattle panels, chain link fencing, post and chain fencing etc. The basic choice of construction material is wood or concrete for the posts and wood or metal for the fence itself — for low-level fencing there are plastic fences. The fencing you pick should be in keeping with the style of both house and garden. Chestnut paling around a modern house is as much out of place as a chain-link fence around a cottage garden.

Where possible inspect both posts and panels before buying and check the following points. Posts should be made of hardwood or pressure-impregnated softwood. The pales should be neither bowed nor warped and all nails and staples should be rust-proof. There should be very few knots, and they should not measure more than 3 cm (1 in.) across. Post caps and panel capping rails are necessary.

One final point. Seek planning permission from your local authority before building a boundary wall or fence which is more than 2 m (7 ft) high — or 1 m (3 ft) high if it is to be erected adjacent to the road.

Ordinary trellis fencing without plants can look rather plain. Decorative types such as these wave-shaped panels are available

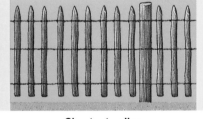

Interwoven panel
The most popular of the solid panel fences, made from thin strips of wood woven between a number of vertical stiffeners. Make sure that the wood strips fit closely together and are attached to the stiffeners

Chestnut paling
Bought as a roll and is attached to 2 or 3 strong wires stretched between posts at 2 m intervals. Not a thing of beauty but it is cheap, easy to erect and an effective barrier. Camouflage with shrubs and climbers

Lap panel
An alternative to the ever-popular interwoven panel — more expensive but more durable. The pales may be horizontal or vertical. Make sure that the overlap is adequate (about 2 cm)

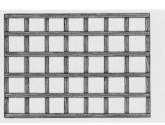

Picket fence
The stout pales are rarely more than 1 m high and are attached to horizontal rails. Leave about 8 - 10 cm between the pales. The bottom of these pales should be 5 - 8 cm above the ground to prevent rotting

Trellis
Trellis made from thin strips of wood (laths) or larch poles (rustic work) arranged in a square or diamond pattern. It requires a stout holding frame and is rarely used as a boundary fence

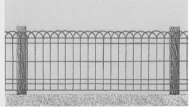

Wire picket fence
Nearly all the fences shown here are stout structures — wire picket fencing is at the other end of the scale. A series of small loops of plastic-coated wire are linked together to form a low fence for beds

Furniture

In the early years of the 1980s an idea took hold — small gardens as well as large ones are for living in and are not merely places for working in and admiring. As a result the sales of outdoor tables and chairs increased dramatically, and now two-thirds of all gardens have outdoor furniture.

There are basically two types of garden furniture — permanent and foldaway. Permanent types stay outdoors throughout the summer, although cushions may have to be brought in at night. In winter most of these tables and chairs are left in the garden, but the lighter ones in plastic or resin may be stacked and stored in the garage or shed. All fitted furniture such as brick-and-wood patio benches and tree seats belong to this permanent group, of course, and so do all the heavy items such as cast iron chairs.

Where outdoor space is very limited or when seating is required for only a short time then foldaway furniture is the obvious choice. The deck chair is the traditional example, but folding metal chairs and recliners are now the best sellers.

The usual plan in furnishing the garden is to begin with enough foldaway chairs and recliners for the family to use on the patio or lawn, and then a patio set (table, chairs and a sunshade as an optional extra) is bought. The standard routine is to buy ready-made furniture — kit-made tables and chairs are much less popular and DIY furniture is quite rare.

No longer need you settle for a group of deck chairs and a folding table. Nowadays there is furniture for all tastes and all pockets, so you can relax in a deeply-cushioned recliner with a built-in sunshade, adjustable foot stool and detachable table with drinks holder.

Garden chair   Director's chair   Tub chair

Deck chair   Folding chair   Recliner

Tree seat   Bench   Hammock

Sun lounger   Picnic table   Garden table

The long dominance of the simple chair and the slatted wooden table on the lawn has gone. Now we can buy resin furniture with a degree of comfort and an air of luxury which may surpass the dining room suite indoors!

Greenhouse

Here you can raise plants, keep half-hardy perennials over winter and grow tomatoes. In addition it is a cosy retreat from workaday worries and the weather. Unfortunately greenhouse growing is perhaps the most labour-intensive of all aspects of gardening — consider having as much automatic equipment as you can afford.

SIZE

The minimum satisfactory size is 2.5 m x 2 m (8 ft x 6½ ft) — it is much more difficult to control the temperature and avoid draughts in a small house than in a large one. The ventilation area in the roof should be at least 20% of the floor space.

SITE

Choose a sunny site, away from buildings. Avoid erecting a greenhouse close to trees — 10 m (33 ft) is the recommended distance.

CONSTRUCTION MATERIALS

Wood is the most attractive material, but cheap soft-wood may rot after a few years if it has not been pressure-treated. Choose rot-proof wood such as teak or western red cedar, but it is expensive and so aluminium has taken over as the most popular material. It loses slightly more heat than wood at night and aluminium houses are more difficult to erect than wooden ones, but these drawbacks are minor. On the credit side it needs no maintenance, more light is admitted, re-glazing is a simple matter and warping does not occur. uPVC requires nothing more than an occasional washing down.

HEATING

A cold house is unheated. It is used for tomatoes and cucumbers in summer, chrysanthemums in autumn, and alpines and bulbs in winter. In a cool house you can grow greenhouse plants such as Azalea, Cineraria etc and half-hardy bedding plants for the garden. You will need some form of heating — electricity is generally considered the best choice. It is clean, easily controlled and disease-promoting humidity is not produced. With a warm house you can grow semi-tropical plants, but costs are high.

COLD GREENHOUSE
Unheated except by the sun

**minimum temperature -2° C (28° F)
when outside temperature falls to -7° C (19° F)**

COOL GREENHOUSE
Heater required during the cooler months

minimum temperature 7° C (45° F)

WARM GREENHOUSE
Heater required during most months

minimum temperature 13° C (55° F)

Span roof
The traditional style has vertical sides. Efficient use of space and heat. Winter heat loss is reduced if lower part is enclosed. Choose an all-glass version for growing-bag and border crops

Lean-to
Useful for a south- or west-facing wall. The house wall stores heat so the fuel bill is reduced. This is the usual conservatory pattern — an interconnecting door makes it part of the home

Dutch light
Sloping sides and an even span roof — the angled glass makes it warmer and brighter than a traditional span roof house. Also more stable, but support-ing upright plants from floor to roof is more difficult

Three-quarter span
More airy and more comfortable to work in than a lean-to — useful for growing wall plants such as grapes and figs. Expensive, so it is usual to choose between a span roof house or a lean-to

USING YOUR GREENHOUSE

Far too many greenhouses are used to grow a few Tomato plants in summer and a tray or two of seedlings in spring. For the rest of the year there is an array of empty pots, bags of fertilizer, trowels and assorted tools. Make your greenhouse earn its keep every day of the year — below is a calendar to illustrate the many ways you can use an average-sized house.

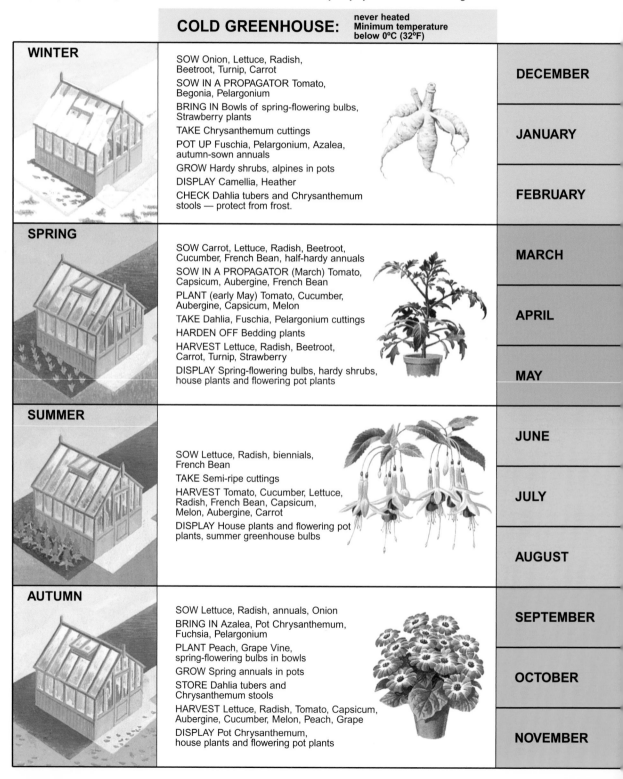

COLD GREENHOUSE: never heated
Minimum temperature below 0°C (32°F)

WINTER

SOW Onion, Lettuce, Radish, Beetroot, Turnip, Carrot

SOW IN A PROPAGATOR Tomato, Begonia, Pelargonium

BRING IN Bowls of spring-flowering bulbs, Strawberry plants

TAKE Chrysanthemum cuttings

POT UP Fuschia, Pelargonium, Azalea, autumn-sown annuals

GROW Hardy shrubs, alpines in pots

DISPLAY Camellia, Heather

CHECK Dahlia tubers and Chrysanthemum stools — protect from frost.

DECEMBER

JANUARY

FEBRUARY

SPRING

SOW Carrot, Lettuce, Radish, Beetroot, Cucumber, French Bean, half-hardy annuals

SOW IN A PROPAGATOR (March) Tomato, Capsicum, Aubergine, French Bean

PLANT (early May) Tomato, Cucumber, Aubergine, Capsicum, Melon

TAKE Dahlia, Fuschia, Pelargonium cuttings

HARDEN OFF Bedding plants

HARVEST Lettuce, Radish, Beetroot, Carrot, Turnip, Strawberry

DISPLAY Spring-flowering bulbs, hardy shrubs, house plants and flowering pot plants

MARCH

APRIL

MAY

SUMMER

SOW Lettuce, Radish, biennials, French Bean

TAKE Semi-ripe cuttings

HARVEST Tomato, Cucumber, Lettuce, Radish, French Bean, Capsicum, Melon, Aubergine, Carrot

DISPLAY House plants and flowering pot plants, summer greenhouse bulbs

JUNE

JULY

AUGUST

AUTUMN

SOW Lettuce, Radish, annuals, Onion

BRING IN Azalea, Pot Chrysanthemum, Fuchsia, Pelargonium

PLANT Peach, Grape Vine, spring-flowering bulbs in bowls

GROW Spring annuals in pots

STORE Dahlia tubers and Chrysanthemum stools

HARVEST Lettuce, Radish, Tomato, Capsicum, Aubergine, Cucumber, Melon, Peach, Grape

DISPLAY Pot Chrysanthemum, house plants and flowering pot plants

SEPTEMBER

OCTOBER

NOVEMBER

COOL GREENHOUSE:

heated during the colder months
Minimum temperature 7°C (45°F)

This is the best general-purpose greenhouse. Instal a maximum/minimum thermometer and try to keep the temperature within the range shown here:

21°C (70°F)	7°C (45°F)	27°C (80°F)	16°C (60°F)
WINTER		SUMMER	

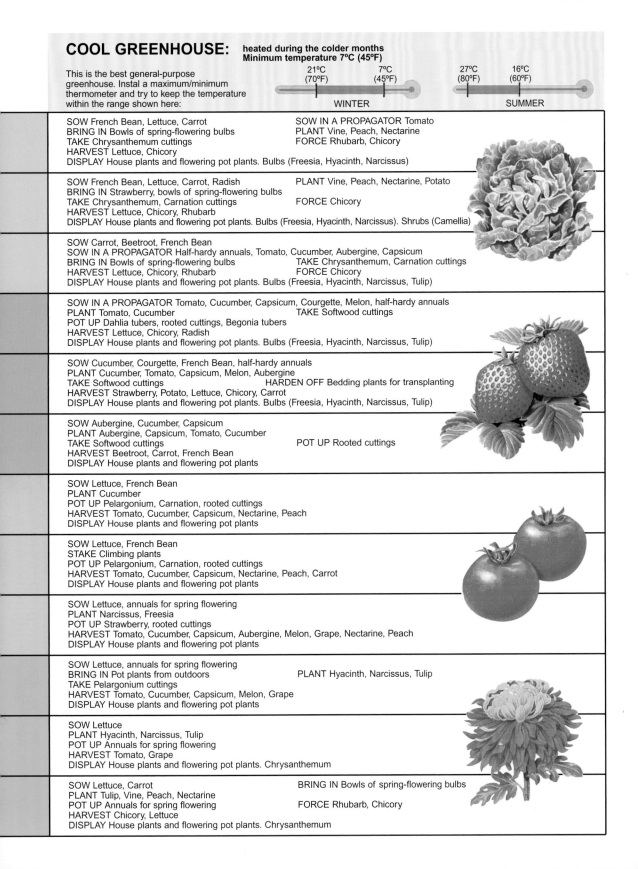

SOW French Bean, Lettuce, Carrot
BRING IN Bowls of spring-flowering bulbs
TAKE Chrysanthemum cuttings
HARVEST Lettuce, Chicory
DISPLAY House plants and flowering pot plants. Bulbs (Freesia, Hyacinth, Narcissus)

SOW IN A PROPAGATOR Tomato
PLANT Vine, Peach, Nectarine
FORCE Rhubarb, Chicory

SOW French Bean, Lettuce, Carrot, Radish
BRING IN Strawberry, bowls of spring-flowering bulbs
TAKE Chrysanthemum, Carnation cuttings
HARVEST Lettuce, Chicory, Rhubarb
DISPLAY House plants and flowering pot plants. Bulbs (Freesia, Hyacinth, Narcissus). Shrubs (Camellia)

PLANT Vine, Peach, Nectarine, Potato
FORCE Chicory

SOW Carrot, Beetroot, French Bean
SOW IN A PROPAGATOR Half-hardy annuals, Tomato, Cucumber, Aubergine, Capsicum
BRING IN Bowls of spring-flowering bulbs
HARVEST Lettuce, Chicory, Rhubarb
DISPLAY House plants and flowering pot plants. Bulbs (Freesia, Hyacinth, Narcissus, Tulip)

TAKE Chrysanthemum, Carnation cuttings
FORCE Chicory

SOW IN A PROPAGATOR Tomato, Cucumber, Capsicum, Courgette, Melon, half-hardy annuals
PLANT Tomato, Cucumber
POT UP Dahlia tubers, rooted cuttings, Begonia tubers
HARVEST Lettuce, Chicory, Radish
DISPLAY House plants and flowering pot plants. Bulbs (Freesia, Hyacinth, Narcissus, Tulip)

TAKE Softwood cuttings

SOW Cucumber, Courgette, French Bean, half-hardy annuals
PLANT Cucumber, Tomato, Capsicum, Melon, Aubergine
TAKE Softwood cuttings
HARVEST Strawberry, Potato, Lettuce, Chicory, Carrot
DISPLAY House plants and flowering pot plants. Bulbs (Freesia, Hyacinth, Narcissus, Tulip)

HARDEN OFF Bedding plants for transplanting

SOW Aubergine, Cucumber, Capsicum
PLANT Aubergine, Capsicum, Tomato, Cucumber
TAKE Softwood cuttings
HARVEST Beetroot, Carrot, French Bean
DISPLAY House plants and flowering pot plants

POT UP Rooted cuttings

SOW Lettuce, French Bean
PLANT Cucumber
POT UP Pelargonium, Carnation, rooted cuttings
HARVEST Tomato, Cucumber, Capsicum, Nectarine, Peach
DISPLAY House plants and flowering pot plants

SOW Lettuce, French Bean
STAKE Climbing plants
POT UP Pelargonium, Carnation, rooted cuttings
HARVEST Tomato, Cucumber, Capsicum, Nectarine, Peach, Carrot
DISPLAY House plants and flowering pot plants

SOW Lettuce, annuals for spring flowering
PLANT Narcissus, Freesia
POT UP Strawberry, rooted cuttings
HARVEST Tomato, Cucumber, Capsicum, Aubergine, Melon, Grape, Nectarine, Peach
DISPLAY House plants and flowering pot plants

SOW Lettuce, annuals for spring flowering
BRING IN Pot plants from outdoors
TAKE Pelargonium cuttings
HARVEST Tomato, Cucumber, Capsicum, Melon, Grape
DISPLAY House plants and flowering pot plants

PLANT Hyacinth, Narcissus, Tulip

SOW Lettuce
PLANT Hyacinth, Narcissus, Tulip
POT UP Annuals for spring flowering
HARVEST Tomato, Grape
DISPLAY House plants and flowering pot plants. Chrysanthemum

SOW Lettuce, Carrot
PLANT Tulip, Vine, Peach, Nectarine
POT UP Annuals for spring flowering
HARVEST Chicory, Lettuce
DISPLAY House plants and flowering pot plants. Chrysanthemum

BRING IN Bowls of spring-flowering bulbs

FORCE Rhubarb, Chicory

LOOKING AFTER THE GREENHOUSE

WATERING & DAMPING DOWN

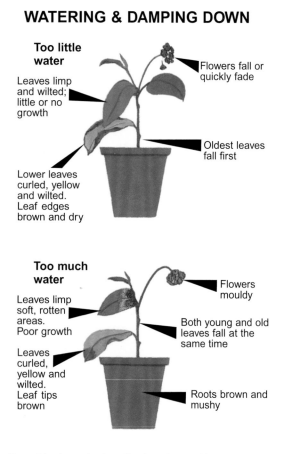

Too little water

Leaves limp and wilted; little or no growth

Flowers fall or quickly fade

Oldest leaves fall first

Lower leaves curled, yellow and wilted. Leaf edges brown and dry

Too much water

Leaves limp soft, rotten areas. Poor growth

Flowers mouldy

Both young and old leaves fall at the same time

Leaves curled, yellow and wilted. Leaf tips brown

Roots brown and mushy

Do not try to water to a fixed routine — in summer some plants may require watering twice a day, and in winter water may be needed only once a fortnight. Use the finger test to see if water is required. Insert your forefinger into the compost to the full depth of your fingernail — watering is required if the fingertip remains dry. Growing bags have their own rules — these are printed on the pack.

On hot days the house should be damped down by spraying the floor and staging with water. The plants should be misted with a fine spray.

How to water:

You will need a can with a long spout. Use the spout when watering established plants — fit a fine rose for seedlings. A hose pipe will be necessary if the house is large — keep the pressure low to avoid disturbing the plants and washing away compost.

The water to use:

Tap water is suitable for nearly all plants, but for delicate types it should be left to stand overnight. Do not use hard water on lime haters such as azalea, orchids, cyclamen and hydrangea. Rainwater is excellent, but it must be clean and not stagnant. Water softened with salt must not be used, but osmosis-filtered water is suitable.

FEEDING

As clearly described on page 57 plants require food in order to maintain healthy and productive growth. With a high-yielding crop such as tomatoes and cucumbers this need is even more pronounced. This does not mean constant feeding — too much can be as harmful as too little. Commercial composts contain the essential elements and should last for 6-8 weeks after planting — after that feeding should start.

Slow-growing and dormant plants need little or no food — actively-growing ones need regular feeding. Follow the manufacturer's instructions — as a general rule use a fertilizer in which nitrogen, phosphates and potash are in approximately equal proportions. Keen growers, however, use a potash-rich feed when tomatoes and cucumbers reach the flowering and fruiting stage. Make sure the compost is moist before feeding.

PESTS & DISEASES

The warm and moist conditions in a greenhouse encourage the rapid spread of plant pests and diseases. Troubles often start under the leaves and can multiply unnoticed until a serious infestation has built up. Inspect plants regularly — consult the *Greenhouse Expert* for advice. Take action as soon as possible and when spraying do carefully follow the recommendations and precautions.

VENTILATING & SHADING

Even a small house needs at least one roof ventilator and one side ventilator. In a well-stocked house ventilation will be required almost all year round. In winter the roof ventilator should be opened 3-5 cm (1-2 in.) around midday in dry weather — increase the opening in spring, and in summer side ventilators are opened.

In high summer the door may have to be opened, but this may not be enough to keep the temperature below the plant-damaging 30°C (86°F) mark. Some form of shading will be necessary — the best answer is a set of outdoor blinds. Most people use simpler methods of shading — covering pots with newspaper, or applying a proprietary shading paint to the glass.

Lawn

For generations the lawn has been the centrepiece of the garden. In both small and large plots the area of grass has traditionally been the place where deck chairs were opened, children played their games and adults laid in the sun. Nowadays the patio next to the house has become the living area for many people, but the lawn still retains its unique charm.

Regular work is unavoidable — mowing, edge trimming, leaf removal etc. The golden rule is to avoid trying to create a Luxury lawn with a bowling green look — far too much work is involved. Aim instead for a Utility lawn which is much easier to maintain.

The **LUXURY LAWN** has a velvety look. Two factors are responsible for this appearance — the turf is made up of Bent and Fescue grasses which have very narrow leaves and the lawn is mown at frequent intervals (twice a week in summer) so that it is kept at a height of 1 cm (½ in.). The beauty of a first rate Luxury lawn is unmatched by any other type but it has too many drawbacks for the gardener with little time to spare. Seed and turf are more expensive than for a Utility lawn and establishment from seed takes a long time. In addition the Luxury lawn will not stand up to heavy wear and it quickly deteriorates if there is a period of neglect.

The **UTILITY LAWN** has a lush and low-growing leafy look. It is a pleasure to see and walk on when well-grown — this is the lawn for you. It is not a second-rate Luxury lawn — it is a different type of turf with its own merits and appeal. The basic difference from its closely-cut sister is that it is the broad-leaved lawn grasses which are dominant. This means that the native coarse grasses which invade lawns are hidden, but they would stand out as weeds in a Luxury lawn. The velvet look is missing, but you can easily create a striped effect by using a mower with a roller. If you are starting from scratch with seed, choose a mixture which is described as slow growing.

The **ROUGH LAWN** has a natural look. The grass is allowed to grow about 8-10 cm (3-4 in.) high and the place for this type of grassland is in the semi-wild areas on the fringes of a large garden. Here is the place where bulbs can be naturalised and left to die down after they have bloomed. The first cut is made when the bulb foliage has withered away in spring and then the grass is mown every 2-3 weeks until October. A useful technique is to mow a strip at weekly intervals through this area of Rough lawn so as to create a Utility lawn path which leads to various points of interest within the 'natural' part of the garden. When starting from scratch use a Ryegrass seed mixture or meadow turf.

The **WILDFLOWER MEADOW** has a colourful look. A mixture of fine-leaved grasses is sown in infertile but free-draining soil and a selection of wildflower seeds is sown at the same time. Cutting is an occasional rather than a regular task and there are no hard-and-fast rules. A popular maintenance plan for an established wildflower meadow is to make the first cut when the spring flowers have died down and then repeat the mowing about a month later. The final cut is made in September. It all sounds so simple and desirable, but there are problems. Scything is necessary if your mower will not cut at 8-10 cm (3-4 in.), and the 'flowery meadow' so often turns into a weed-ridden untidy eyesore.

LAWN DESIGN

Don't let your lawn be an obstacle course for the mower or a near-impossible test for the edging shears. Of course it doesn't have to be a strictly geometrical rectangle or oval bare of all objects, but an area of grass strewn with isolated trees, island beds, narrow paths and items of furniture can take twice as long to cut as a well-designed lawn.

DON'T

DO

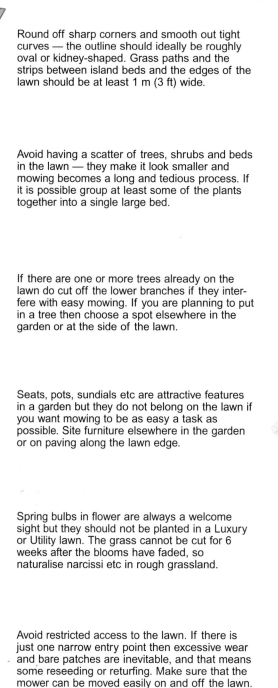

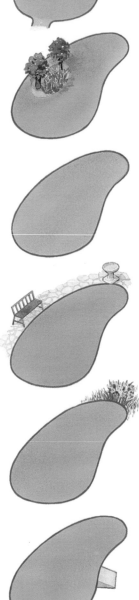

Round off sharp corners and smooth out tight curves — the outline should ideally be roughly oval or kidney-shaped. Grass paths and the strips between island beds and the edges of the lawn should be at least 1 m (3 ft) wide.

Avoid having a scatter of trees, shrubs and beds in the lawn — they make it look smaller and mowing becomes a long and tedious process. If it is possible group at least some of the plants together into a single large bed.

If there are one or more trees already on the lawn do cut off the lower branches if they interfere with easy mowing. If you are planning to put in a tree then choose a spot elsewhere in the garden or at the side of the lawn.

Seats, pots, sundials etc are attractive features in a garden but they do not belong on the lawn if you want mowing to be as easy a task as possible. Site furniture elsewhere in the garden or on paving along the lawn edge.

Spring bulbs in flower are always a welcome sight but they should not be planted in a Luxury or Utility lawn. The grass cannot be cut for 6 weeks after the blooms have faded, so naturalise narcissi etc in rough grassland.

Avoid restricted access to the lawn. If there is just one narrow entry point then excessive wear and bare patches are inevitable, and that means some reseeding or returfing. Make sure that the mower can be moved easily on and off the lawn.

LOOKING AFTER THE LAWN

FEEDING

Every gardening textbook with a chapter on lawns will tell you to feed the grass with fertilizer at least once a year. This must seem strange advice for people who want to spend less time tending to their lawns. The purpose of feeding is to make the grass grow more quickly, and they want the grass to grow more slowly! Actually it is good advice, as feeding does more than make the grass grow more quickly. It also builds up the density of the grass covering the surface and increases the resistance of the turf to drought and disease. Weeds and moss find it more difficult to get a foothold in closely-knit turf.

WATERING

During a period of drought there is at first a loss of springiness in the turf and a general dullness over the surface. Later on the grass turns straw-coloured and unsightly. You will have to choose between two courses of action. First, you can decide to leave it to nature. Lawn grasses are very rarely killed by drought and recover quite quickly once the rains return. Furthermore, water is often banned for garden use in times of prolonged drought. The problem with leaving it to nature is that drought-resistant weeds such as yarrow and clover can spread rapidly and the lawn has a mottled appearance for some time once the drought is over. So watering is the alternative course of action, but it must be thorough. This calls for applying at least 20 litres per sq.m (4 gallons per 10 sq.ft) once a week until the dry spell ends. Do not use a watering can or a hose pipe propped on the handle of a spade — water with a rotary, pulse-jet or oscillating sprinkler so that a large area is covered.

ROTARY SPRINKLER

Rotating arms produce a circle of fine droplets. Very popular and many brands are available. Some are adjustable for fineness of spray and area covered

PULSE-JET SPRINKLER

A single jet produces a narrow arc of fine droplets. This jet rotates as a series of pulses, spraying an even circle of turf. Covers a larger area than other sprinklers

TRIMMING

Horizontal trimming

There may be several places where the mower cannot reach, such as around trees, along walls and under large shrubs. For long grass in these areas you will need a horizontal trimmer, and by far the best choice is an electric strimmer which cuts by means of a replaceable nylon cord — using long-handled shears is a laborious job if the area is large. In nearly all situations this need to trim can be eliminated by leaving a space between the grass and the obstacle — see below for details.

Vertical trimming

Vertical trimming, or edging, is the removal of grass from the edge of the lawn to give a neat appearance. The traditional method is to use a half-moon edging iron at the start of the season, cutting along a plank of wood to give a straight edge. Then, after each mowing an edging tool is used to trim the grass left by the mower. Ordinary hand shears are not suitable — long-handled edging shears can be used but few people enjoy this back-aching job. A variety of power-driven tools is available — strimmers, electric edgers etc, but all involve an extra job after mowing.

Do consider doing away with the need for edging by installing a **mowing strip**. This consists of a line of slabs, bricks, tiles or blocks between the lawn edge and the path, bed, border or wall. The top of this mowing strip is set slightly below the surface of the turf so that the mower can be taken over the top of the hard surface. For a perfect job the slabs should be fixed with blobs of mortar on to a foundation of compacted sand, but this is not vital.

Instead of using a mowing strip a narrow trench is sometimes left around the lawn. This uncovered trench can allow the mower to go over the edge, but it is usually necessary to install an edging strip as shown below.

Flexible strip — metal or plastic

Wooden strip held by stakes

MOWING
See page 60.

SCARIFYING & AERATING

Scarifying means taking up debris and dead grass with a rake or rake-like implement — aerating means making holes or slits in the surface. The correct time for this work is in autumn and not in spring. You can hire a power-driven rake or aerator.

Lighting

Nothing quite matches the drama of well-planned lighting. You have seen how a building which looks drab in daylight can be transformed by floodlighting, and how a thoroughfare may look much more exciting at night when the lights and signs are switched on.

The secret of good lighting design is to highlight certain areas and features, and to leave duller and unused places in the shadows. The lights should not all be set at the same height and you should use more than one type of lighting. Spotlighting is used to illuminate a specific feature whereas floodlighting is used to light up an area. Downlighting illuminates paths, steps and low-growing pants — uplighting produces dramatic shadows and backlighting forms spectacular silhouettes.

There are a number of cardinal rules. First of all, don't overdo it — too much light means that shadows and mystery are lost — too much use of coloured rather than plain lights can produce bizarre and unnatural effects. Correct placing is also vital — wherever possible ensure that the lights shine on the objects to be illuminated and not in the eyes of the viewer. And remember your neighbour — spotlights shining into next door's windows have caused many an argument!

The popularity of garden lighting has grown in recent years as more DIY kits have appeared and the garden has been increasingly used as an outdoor living area. But there is a long way to go — for a million or more people, outdoor lighting remains a string of coloured bulbs around an evergreen close to the house at Christmas time. There are non-electrical systems but for nearly all purposes you will need an electric cable. This, or course, deters many people and a mains electric cable will certainly have to be buried deep in the ground. But low-voltage systems are now widely available, and cable laying here is a simple task.

TYPES

Non-cable lighting

Candle lanterns have long been used — fragrant and insect-repelling candles are available. Oil-fuelled lanterns and flares are also sold, and all may pose a fire risk. A popular item in mail-order catalogues is the **solar-powered floodlight** — it costs nothing to run, but do not expect too much illumination.

Cable lighting

The **wall-mounted light** is the usual choice for illuminating the patio or front of the house. Mains rather than a low-voltage circuit is the usual choice, and there is a choice of shades — bulkhead, lantern, globe or rectangular floodlight. At the other end of the scale from these wall-mounted lights is the **spiked light** which is easily moved from one spot to another. The **post globe** is a version for lighting pathways — a more permanent type of pathway light is the **lamp-post** which has a solid fixed post and a lantern shade. The **bollard** has a cylindrical shade as an integral part of the post. The **string light** is a familiar sight at Christmas time — a long mains or LV cable bearing coloured lights at regular intervals. There is no need to leave it in the box until next Christmas — string lights fitted with plain bulbs give a festive touch to an evening patio party. **Water lights** can be operated on a mains or low-voltage circuit — there are floating lamps and submerged floodlights. Fountains fitted with underwater lights which shine through the spray are quite spectacular.

In most cases some form of shade is required. A **bulkhead** is made of glass or plastic and fits against the wall — a **globe shade** may be frosted, or clear, plain or coloured. The **rectangular floodlight** has a textured glass face, and the **lantern** is based on the carriage lamp of old. **Tiered shades** are used as post lights and bear a series of narrow metal diffusers which direct the light downwards. The metal or plastic-topped **mushroom shade** directs all the light downwards to light up steps and pathways.

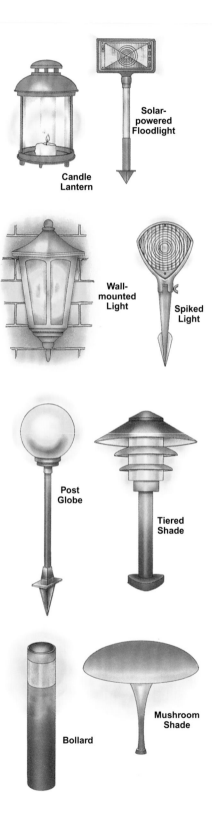

Candle Lantern

Solar-powered Floodlight

Wall-mounted Light

Spiked Light

Post Globe

Tiered Shade

Bollard

Mushroom Shade

Ornaments

The dividing lines between ornaments, containers and furniture are blurred. Is a stone urn filled with geraniums an ornament or a container? The definition of an ornament in this book is simple — perhaps too simple. Objects are classed as ornaments if they are distinctly ornamental when not in use. So a large and decorated urn filled with geraniums is indeed an ornament, whereas a tub or plastic pot filled with geraniums is a container.

The range of ornaments is vast. Six basic groups are described here, but there are others — Victorian lamp-posts, bird baths, iron weather-vanes and so on. The proper home for large ornaments such as life-sized statues is the Grand Garden, and some styles (French, Italianate etc) demand the presence of such objects. But there is a place for ornaments in the ordinary home garden provided that the basic rule is followed — not too big and not too many.

The two main sites are in and around the pond for added interest and at the end of vistas to serve as focal points. Finding suitable ornaments is part of their charm — the easiest way is to study the catalogue of garden centres which specialise in water gardening. You will also find them listed in the catalogues of specialist suppliers who advertise in gardening and countryside magazines. Garden ornaments can sometimes be found tucked away in junk shops, car boot sales, antique shops and fairs and even in scrap yards.

Remember the effect of weathering. Cast iron becomes more brittle with age and rust can be a problem. Lead does not rust but it is easily damaged. Rough stone becomes crusted with lichens more quickly than the smooth type, and soft limestone is damaged by rain and frost.

There has been an increase in interest in ornaments, but millions of people continue to dislike the idea of having such things in their garden. Ornaments are not essential unless you are trying to build a Japanese garden, but many plots can be improved by careful choice with regard to style and size of a suitable ornament.

STATUES & FIGURES

There is no clear cut distinction between statues and figures — the word 'statue' here is used for a figure, design or bust which is borne on a stand or plinth. Size should be in keeping with the house, and so should the style. Consider a piece of abstract sculpture if the house is modern. A 'figure' is a portrayal in stone, terracotta, metal etc of a living thing. The garden gnome and the painted donkey belong here, but so does a range of attractive animal figures which can provide an amusing touch.

SUNDIALS

Sundials have been in gardens for a long time — 400 years ago they were the most popular way of telling the time. These days, however, their role is ornamental. Sundial plates are generally made of brass or bronze. The pedestals are bought or made on site from brick or stone — make sure that the top slab is perfectly level. Before beginning construction decide how the sundial will have to be positioned. This is simple to do — mark out a N-S line using a compass and note that the gnomon (the upright part) must point due N.

URNS & JAPANESE FEATURES

It was the Victorians who had the novel idea of using urns and plant containers. This is how they are used in gardens today and you can buy reasonably-priced ones in terracotta or reconstituted stone — designs are usually based on funerary urns of Ancient Rome and Greece. Ornaments are essential if you want to give your garden a Japanese look. First come the lanterns, squat and broad topped or tall and ornate. Small pagodas and carved stepping stones are acceptable, but don't overdo it with Buddhas and Oriental maidens.

WATER FEATURES

It is quite smart these days to have a fountain which emerges from the pool surface, but for many people a fountain is a stone figure or statue from which a jet or spray emerges. Fountains of real stone belong in the Grand Gardens — for your pond look for a reconstituted stone one. Do make sure it is in keeping — it should enhance but not overwhelm the pond. Designs range from cherubs to abstract modern sculpture. Some fountains are self-contained and are suitable patio ornaments.

Patio

A patio is a hard-surfaced area which is usually but not always attached to the house and is used for relaxation, enjoyment and perhaps entertaining. There may be just a small area of paving slabs with a plastic table and a couple of chairs, or it may be a multi-tiered structure with beds, pond, pergolas and permanent features.

The size should generally be in keeping with the size of the garden. Aim for at least 4 sq.m (43 sq.ft) for each person who will eat or lounge on it — modify the dimensions slightly so that the need to cut slabs, blocks etc is kept to a minimum. The usual shape is a rectangle — an irregular shape may be more interesting but slab-cutting to fit curves is a laborious job.

The best place is adjoining the back of the house, especially if there are patio doors — the task of taking out food and drink and bringing in cushions is greatly simplified. It is not the only place — afternoon sun and protection from the prevailing wind are even more important than saving labour.

For suitable paving materials, see page 248. A single paving material should dominate the patio, and this should be in keeping with nearby paths and walls. Some designers like to introduce a second paving material, but do resist a patchwork quilt effect.

Mark out the proposed area with canes and string before work begins. Sit in the space, walk about, bring in chairs and tables. Is it really the right size? Remember that if you don't have the necessary skill, strength or time it will be necessary to bring in a landscaping company — as stressed on page 219 you should obtain quotes before work starts. Enrol a willing helper if it is to be a DIY job.

Basic patio

Designer patio

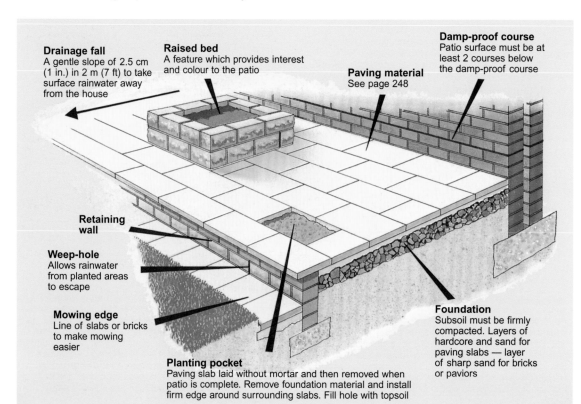

Drainage fall
A gentle slope of 2.5 cm (1 in.) in 2 m (7 ft) to take surface rainwater away from the house

Raised bed
A feature which provides interest and colour to the patio

Paving material
See page 248

Damp-proof course
Patio surface must be at least 2 courses below the damp-proof course

Retaining wall

Weep-hole
Allows rainwater from planted areas to escape

Mowing edge
Line of slabs or bricks to make mowing easier

Planting pocket
Paving slab laid without mortar and then removed when patio is complete. Remove foundation material and install firm edge around surrounding slabs. Fill hole with topsoil

Foundation
Subsoil must be firmly compacted. Layers of hardcore and sand for paving slabs — layer of sharp sand for bricks or paviors

Paths & Drives

A hard surface is required between A and B when regular traffic occurs between the two points. A path is designed for two-footed and two-wheeled traffic — a drive carries four-wheeled traffic. Nowadays there is a host of different paving materials and this makes selection difficult. For out-of-the-way walkways as in the vegetable garden you can use purely functional materials such as compacted earth, concrete and bark chippings, but in nearly all cases the paths and drives have a decorative as well as a utilitarian purpose. The drive is the first part of the garden the visitor may see, and paths often form a clearly visible skeleton to the garden. So choose with care — see below. Combining different materials can reduce the danger of dullness (see illustration) but take care not to mix too many paving materials.

Path shape is another factor you must consider. In informal gardens, curving paths are generally more attractive than straight ones, but bends should be gentle. Shape can affect your choice of paving material.

A few rules. Make the path wide enough — 60 cm (2 ft) is the minimum for the average garden but 1 m (3 ft) is better. It should slope (minimum 1 in 100) to prevent water standing after rain. If constructed next to the house, the surface must be at least 15 cm (6 in.) below the damp-proof course. Finally, seek planning permission if you propose to create a drive which will make a new access on to the road.

BRICKS or BLOCKS		No heavy lifting is necessary. Bricks make an excellent path where an old-world look is required. Don't use ordinary bricks — ask for paving ones. As an alternative you can use brick-like blocks (paviors) made of clay or concrete
STONE or SLABS		Natural stone gives an air of luxury, but slate, sandstone, yorkstone etc are very expensive. Slabs made of concrete or reconstituted stone are a much more popular and inexpensive alternative these days
MACADAM		This mixture of stone chippings with tar or bitumen is the favourite material for drives and has several names — asphalt, black top, 'Tarmac' etc. This is not a job for an amateur — choose your contractor with care
CRAZY PAVING		Laying flagstones or paving slabs can be heavy work and you generally have to keep to straight lines — with crazy paving the pieces are smaller and the informal effect means that you don't have to aim for a perfect fit
CONCRETE		Concrete is criticised by many for its austere look, but it remains a popular material for both paths and drives. It is durable, fairly inexpensive and suitable for curving or irregular pathways. Laying concrete is for the fit, strong and knowledgeable
WOOD or BARK		Pulverised or shredded bark is a popular material for paths in woodland — it is soft underfoot but requires topping up every few years. Sawn log rounds are sometimes set in the shredded bark. Decking (see page 248) is sometimes used
GRAVEL or PEBBLES		Gravel is by far the cheapest material. Shingle (small stones smoothed by water) and true gravel (stone chips from a quarry) are the types available. Large rounded pebbles are sometimes used for small decorative areas
PATTERN-PRINTED CONCRETE		A post-war development for paths, drives and patios. A concrete-based mix is poured over the area and a roller is taken over the surface before it has set. The roller leaves an embossed pattern in the form of blocks, slabs or crazy paving

Paved areas

The dividing line between paths and paved areas is a narrow one. The essential difference is that paths are designed for foot or light vehicle traffic and so have a practical purpose — a paved area is basically to support sitting or standing people and so the decorative element is more important.

Not surprisingly most of the materials used for the construction of paths and drives (see page 247) can be used for paving, but there are two restrictions if the area is to be used as a patio. Loose material such as gravel or bark should be avoided for overall surfacing and so should items like cobblestones and granite setts which feel uncomfortable underfoot.

A single material should be used for paving a patio, and this should be in keeping with nearby paths and walls. The introduction of a second paving material can sometimes be attractive — popular examples are a line of paviors around large expanses of paving slabs or a patch of cobblestones set within a stone or paving slab patio.

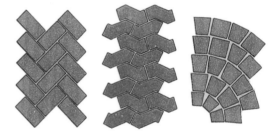

PAVING SLABS

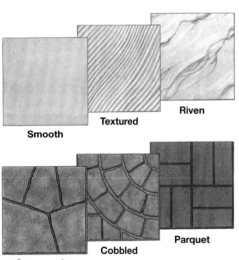

Smooth

Textured

Riven

Crazy paving

Cobbled

Parquet

Colour and arrangement are a matter of taste, but most designers advise against multicoloured and chessboard schemes. A mixture of square and rectangular slabs tends to give a more interesting surface than one made up entirely of squares, and unnatural colours are best avoided. The cheapest slabs are 4 cm (1½ in.) thick concrete ones, but it really is worth investing in reconstituted stone slabs.

DECKING

Wooden paving blends in well with surrounding trees and shrubs, and its popularity continues to grow. Use western red cedar — an alternative is an ordinary softwood which has been pressure-impregnated with a preservative. For DIY decking fix planks to stout wooden joists which are stood on brick supports — a 10 mm (½ in.) gap is left between the planks. It is much easier to lay 60 cm x 1 m (2 ft x 3 ft) timber tiles which are laid on sand over gravel.

BRICKS & PAVIORS

Bricks (Special Quality grade) are a good choice in old-world and informal settings — their great advantage is the way they can be used for irregular or curved areas without the need for cutting. Concrete and clay-based paviors (blocks) have similar advantages and are available in several colours and shapes.

CRAZY PAVING

A favourite surface until concrete and reconstituted stone slabs came along. It is worth considering if you want an informal look — yorkstone is the popular type but there are others. Broken concrete slabs are an inexpensive alternative — some paving suppliers have them available at a very low price.

STONE

Natural stone is expensive, difficult to lay and not too easy to find. It is, however, still the only paving choice for many traditionalists and you may feel that the special and unique charm of yorkstone outweighs the disadvantages.

TILES

Square tiles which are about 2.5 cm (1 in.) thick are an easy-to-handle paving material for patios. Concrete ones are available in several sizes and colours — some too bright for the average garden. For the architectural or mediterranean-style garden there are colourful ceramic tiles.

Pond

A garden pond provides so much interest for most of the year, but only if the pond is constructed and stocked in the right way. All too often we see murky green water which is overrun by weeds. The cause is generally a combination of doing the wrong things at the start and then failing to do the few necessary things once the pond has become established. Read the paragraphs below — consult the *Rock & Water Garden Expert* if you decide to have a pond.

Small formal pond

SIZE

You will need a surface area of at least 4 sq.m (43 sq.ft) if the water is to stay clear — the depth will have to be 60 cm (2 ft) or more if you plan to have several types of fish.

SITE

Choose a sunny spot away from trees — dead leaves decompose to produce salts and gases which are harmful to fish and encourage green algae.

STYLE

There are two basic styles. The formal pond outline is clearly defined and the shape is either geometrical (square, oblong etc) or gently curved. It is separated from other garden features and is often used as a centrepiece. The informal pond outline is not clearly defined — it merges into an adjoining feature or features. The shape is irregular.

CONSTRUCTION MATERIALS

There are three basic materials. Concrete was once the basic material but its time has now passed. The rigid or moulded pool makes pond-making a much easier task. Vacuum-formed plastic ones are fairly short-lived and are only semi-rigid — it is better to choose a fibreglass one. To make a larger pond and/or one of your own design you must use a flexible liner. Polyethylene sheeting was the original material but it is no longer a good choice. PVC is a better choice, but for life-long reliability you should choose butyl — a synthetic rubber sheeting.

Large informal pond

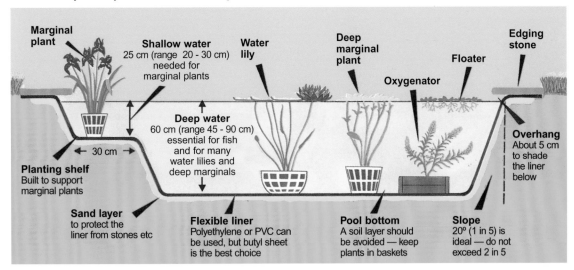

Marginal plant

Shallow water
25 cm (range 20 - 30 cm) needed for marginal plants

Water lily

Deep marginal plant

Oxygenator

Floater

Edging stone

Deep water
60 cm (range 45 - 90 cm) essential for fish and for many water lilies and deep marginals

← 30 cm →

Planting shelf
Built to support marginal plants

Overhang
About 5 cm to shade the liner below

Sand layer
to protect the liner from stones etc

Flexible liner
Polyethylene or PVC can be used, but butyl sheet is the best choice

Pool bottom
A soil layer should be avoided — keep plants in baskets

Slope
20° (1 in 5) is ideal — do not exceed 2 in 5

POND PLANTS

Latin name	Common name	Height	Distance between crown and surface	Flowering period	Notes
DEEP WATER AQUATICS					
Roots submerged — leaves and flowers on or just above the surface. Important for keeping the water clear — the leaves provide shade and this discourages algae					
NYMPHAEA	Water Lily	Surface	10 cm-1 m (4 in.-3 ft), depending on the variety — usual depth 30-60 cm (1-2 ft)	June - September	Dwarfs cover 900-1800 sq. cm (1-2 sq. ft) — crown 10-23 cm (4-9 in.) below surface. Other extreme is the V. Strong Grower group — 5.5 sq.m (60 sq. ft) across — crown 1 m (3 ft) below surface. Check the size group before buying
APONOGETON DISTACHYUS	Water Hawthorn	Surface	30-60 cm (1-2 ft)	April and October	White petals, black anthers. Oval, glossy leaves. Not fully hardy in North
NYMPHOIDES PELTATA	Water Fringe	5-8 cm (2-3 in.)	30 cm (1 ft)	July - September	Deep yellow flowers. Miniature Water Lily-like leaves 4 cm (1½ in.) across
OXYGENATORS					
Leaves, stems and roots submerged — flowers may be above the surface. Important for keeping the water clear. The leaves absorb minerals and carbon dioxide, and this discourages algae					
ELODEA CRISPA	Goldfish Weed	Below surface	Not critical	—	Upright brittle stems — narrow curled leaves. Very effective
TILLAEA RECURVA	Tillaea	Below surface	Not critical	June - August	Dense green mat — used by fish as food. Insignificant white flowers
RANUNCULUS AQUATILIS	Water Buttercup	3 cm (1 in.)	Not critical	June	Surface leaves Clover-like, submerged leaves finely divided. White flowers just above surface
HOTTONIA PALUSTRIS	Water Violet	15 cm (6 in.)	Not critical	June	Ferny leaves — whorls of pale lavender flowers on emerged stems
MYRIOPHYLLUM SPICATUM	Water Milfoil	Below surface	Not critical	—	Bronzy-green feathery leaves on long reddish stems
FONTINALIS ANTIPYRETICA	Willow Moss	Below surface	Not critical	—	Tangled masses of stems covered with dark green, mossy leaves. Grows in shade
FLOATERS					
Leaves, stems and flowers on, just below or just above the surface. Important for providing shade if Water Lilies are not present					
AZOLLA CAROLINIANA	Fairy Moss	Surface	Floating	—	Dense green mat of ferny leaves — turns red in autumn
EICHHORNIA CRASSIPES	Water Hyacinth	15 cm (6 in.)	Floating	August - September	Very attractive, but not hardy. Glossy leaves, feathery roots and spikes of lavender flowers
STRATIOTES ALOIDES	Water Soldier	Surface	Floating	July - August	Rosettes of spiny leaves rise to the surface at flowering time
LEMNA TRISULCA	Ivy-Leaved Duckweed	Surface	Floating	—	Small translucent leaves — the only Duckweed which will not take over the pond
HYDROCHARIS MORSUS-RANAE	Frog-bit	Surface	Floating	May	Good choice — small Water Lily-like pads and small white flowers
MARGINAL PLANTS					
Roots submerged — leaves and flowers clearly above the surface. Purely ornamental. Not required to maintain balance					
ALISMA PLANTAGO	Water Plantain	60 cm (2 ft)	0-15 cm (0-6 in.)	April - June	Oval leaves — spikes of small pink and white flowers. Remove seed heads
IRIS LAEVIGATA	Blue Water Iris	60 cm (2 ft)	5-10 cm (2-4 in.)	June - September	Excellent choice — typical Iris flowers in white, blue, purple and pink
MYOSOTIS PALUSTRIS	Water Forget-me-not	22 cm (9 in.)	0-8 cm (0-3 in.)	May - July	Pale green leaves — bright blue flowers are yellow-eyed
PONTEDERIA CORDATA	Pickerel	45 cm (1½ ft)	8-12 cm (3-5 in.)	June - October	Spear-shaped leaves — blue flowers borne on spikes
RANUNCULUS LINGUA GRANDIFLORA	Spearwort	60 cm (2 ft)	5-10 cm (2-4 in.)	June - August	Dark green, narrow leaves — large Buttercup-like flowers
SAGITTARIA JAPONICA PLENA	Arrowhead	30 cm (1 ft)	8-12 cm (3-5 in.)	July - August	Arrow-shaped leaves — whorls of white Stock-like double flowers
SCIRPUS ZEBRINUS	Bulrush	1 m (3 ft)	8-12 cm (3-5 in.)	June - July	An attractive Bulrush with stout stems which are striped green and white
TYPHA MINIMA	Dwarf Reedmace	45 cm (1½ ft)	2-10 cm (1-4 in.)	May - September	Brown heads on Reed-like stems. Good for small pools
BOG PLANTS					
Roots in moist but not waterlogged soil. Can be useful around an informal pool, but only if damp conditions exist. There is no place for bog plants near modern watertight pools					

Examples include **ASTILBE ARENDSII, CALTHA PALUSTRIS, DICENTRA SPECTABILIS, GUNNERA MANICATA, HEMEROCALLIS VARIETIES, HOSTA VARIETIES, IRIS KAEMPFERI, PRIMULA JAPONICA and TROLLIUS VARIETIES** — see The Flower Expert for details

Rockery

The sight of alpine plants tumbling over well-laid stones is indeed an attractive one, but do think twice before deciding to make a rockery. The simple truth is that no other aspect of the garden combines the need for such a high degree of design sense with an equally high level of sheer hard work.

Considering the design side first, most of the rockeries we see in home gardens miss the point. A rock garden should have a natural feel to it, as if it could be an actual outcrop even though we are not fooled for a moment. Instead we so often see overgrown and wholly unnatural rocks sticking out of the ground. The problem here is that we cannot just look up a rockery plan in a book and then go out and order the bits as we can for a fence or patio. With a rockery the final result is governed by the shapes and sizes of the stones and no two loads of stones are alike. The answer is to read the general principles of construction in this section, go and see one or more examples of good design in a botanical garden and then draw up a rough plan once the stone is delivered. There are a few basic rules — use stones of different sizes but all of the same type, do not use too many and keep the slopes fairly gentle.

Now for the hard work. Moving stone and then setting out rocks at different levels are strenuous tasks. The hard work story doesn't end there — the rock garden is labour intensive as hand weeding, dead-heading and trimming have to be carried out regularly.

There is, of course, a credit side to creating a rock garden, and that is what makes the feature worthwhile for so many gardeners. A bank with a pond at the base makes a rockery almost obligatory, and a flat uninteresting site can be enlivened by this feature. There are two basic types. The **Sloping Rockery** is the more satisfactory — a series of tiers rising backwards gently until the highest point is reached on an artificial or natural bank. The **Island Bed Rockery** is more difficult to create and usually appears less natural — earth and stones are laid on a flat bed to create an outcrop — aim for a series of irregular and broken tiers leading up to a flat plateau at the top.

PLANTS

Rockery perennials ('alpines') are the most important plants in the average rock garden. The general rule is to use some bold plants such as dwarf conifers and shrubs as single specimen plants and to grow smaller plants in groups.

Rockery perennials Be careful if you use the most popular types — Cerastium, Alyssum saxatile, Aubretia, Arabis and Saponaria. They are easy to grow but they are also invasive. Fill cracks with rock-hugging plants such as Saxifrage, Sempervivum, Draba, Thymus etc. Bolder plants such as Hypericum, Primula and Pulsatilla can be used to produce colourful drifts.

Conifers Make sure that the varieties are classed as 'dwarf' or 'slow-growing medium'. Aim for variety — for example blue upright (Juniperus virginiana 'Sky-rocket'), golden upright (Chamaecyparis lawsoniana 'Ellwood's Gold') and green upright (Juniperus communis 'Compressa'). There are also blue prostrate (Juniperus horizontalis 'Glauca') and green globular (Pinus mugo 'Gnom').

Shrubs Popular ones include Acer (Japanese maple), Hebe, Pieris, miniature rose, Deutzia, Daphne, Rosmarinus, Azalea, Skimmia, Erica and Calluna.

Other plants Dwarf bulbs, ferns, grasses and even bedding plants can be included.

Site
Pick an unshaded spot — rockery perennials are sun lovers. Keep well away from overhanging trees — the drips from wet foliage in summer and fallen leaves in winter can be fatal. Clear away all perennial weeds before construction begins

Grain (Strata)
These lines should all run the same way — never have a mixture of horizontal and vertical

Key stone
A large and attractive stone. This is the first rock to be laid

Small stones
Wedge together into a group — plant alpines in the crevices

Joints
These should run vertically — do not stagger the joints as if you were building a wall

Grouping
Place rocks in groups rather than in a continuous line one stone high

Grit mulch
Place a layer of small stones around the plants. This mulch will conserve moisture, suppress weeds and keep roots cool

Planting pocket
This area should slope slightly backwards. Consolidate the planting mixture firmly

First tier
The starting point of the rockery. Each stone should tilt slightly backwards and ⅓-½ should be buried. Firm the soil at the base and back of the stone — do not leave air pockets

Planting mixture
2 parts soil
1 part peat or bark
1 part grit or coarse sand

Drainage layer
Good drainage is essential. In free-draining land this layer is not needed — in heavy soil remove the topsoil and add rubble topped with gravel

A 3m x 1.5 m rockery requires 1-2 tons of stone

Vegetable plot

The Vegetable chapter beginning on page 74 is devoted to the way to grow the popular types — when to sow, what varieties to choose, how to care for the plants etc. On this page we deal with the various ways to grow vegetables, ranging from the traditional plot at the back of the garden to a collection of pots and growing bags at the back of the house.

Here you will find the virtues of the non-standard methods. Growing them among ornamental plants in mixed beds and borders began long before the allotment method, and it means that an extra plot of land is not required. Of course yields will be low, as they are with the container method where the actual area devoted to the vegetables is relatively small. The drawback does not apply to the bed method — here the yield from the plot matches the amount harvested from the traditional plot. As noted below digging is no longer needed, and weeds are a minor problem.

Despite these points, the traditional allotment method for growing vegetables will remain the favourite way. It is hard work, but for many people that is part of the fascination!

The **ALLOTMENT METHOD** is the standard way and for most gardeners the only method of growing vegetables. The whole of the plot is cultivated and the plants are grown in rows. Strips of bare earth are left between each row or group of rows so that the gardener can walk along for watering, cultivating, picking etc. By the allotment method the longest beans and the heaviest potatoes are produced, but it is extremely laborious. There is the chore of digging each autumn and both the bare pathways and the large spaces left between the plants encourage weeds. In addition the long rows often result in a glut so some produce may be wasted.

The **COTTAGE GARDEN METHOD** is the best way to grow vegetables if you don't want to devote a separate area of ground to them. They are planted among the flowers, bulbs, roses and shrubs in the mixed beds and borders. Ordinary vegetables can be grown, of course, but there are some types which are ornamental as well as useful. There is the red-veined ruby chard or the red-leaved beetroot and lettuce 'Lollo-Rossa'. Best of all are the climbing beans — scarlet runners or the purple-podded French ones.

The **CONTAINER METHOD** is the best way to grow vegetables if you don't have a garden. Any tub, pot or trough which is deeper than 20 cm (8 in.) can be used, but the favourite container these days is the growing bag. All sorts of vegetables apart from the bulky ones like Brussels sprouts, broccoli etc can be grown, but there is little point in growing 'ordinary' ones. Choose unusual or decorative ones, or grow rather tender vegetables such as aubergine, capsicum or tomato against a sheltered south-facing wall. Still, there are no rules and many people without a vegetable plot use a variety of pots and bags to grow salad crops.

The **BED METHOD** is the best way to grow vegetables if you want an appreciable amount of produce. Yields are higher than you would obtain by the allotment method, but the size of each harvested vegetable is usually smaller. The reason for the high yields is that each vegetable is sown or planted in a block so that all the plants are the same distance from each other — the spacing is quite close so that the leaves of adjacent plants touch when the plants are mature. There are several distinct advantages. General maintenance is much easier — closely-planted vegetables smother most weeds and there are soil-free walkways between rows. And, of course, no digging is needed next year.

Walls

The basic difference between a wall and a fence is that there is a firm foundation along the entire length of a wall. Boundary walls are chosen rather than fencing when maximum privacy, permanence and noise reduction are required. A high wall may seem a good idea, but there are problems — cost, bye-law restrictions, creation of turbulence in windy weather etc. Internal walls are an important feature in many gardens. There are screen walls to enclose areas or hide unsightly views and there are retaining walls as shown below.

BRICKS

Clay bricks are available in all sorts of colours and textures — choose Special Quality ones for exposed situations, wall tops etc. Concrete bricks are much less popular — they are lighter to lift than blocks but are more difficult to lay.

BLOCKS

Blocks made from natural stone, concrete and reconstituted stone are much larger than a brick. Laying time is reduced, and blocks with a 'natural' face mask minor imperfections. As with bricks a sound foundation is vital.

Stone blocks Constructing a wall of limestone, granite or sandstone is not a practical idea.

Decorative concrete blocks These blocks have a moulded face and can be used to build a head-high wall without piers. Cheaper than reconstituted stone blocks, but they look less natural. The standard thickness is 10 cm (4 in.).

Screen blocks Square concrete blocks are available which are pierced with a variety of patterns, and are made in numerous colours. They are stack bonded with each vertical mortar joint lining up with the one above and the one below.

Reconstituted stone blocks These blocks are the favourite garden walling material. Surface textures range from the near-smooth to the deeply-hewn pitched face. Low walls can be built on firm paving as well as on concrete footings. For dry (mortar-free) walling there are 15 cm (6 in.) wide blocks.

Most walls are now built with reconstituted stone blocks rather than bricks. An advantage is that units of various sizes can be used

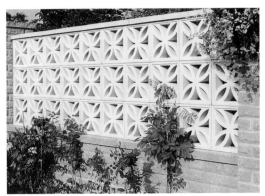

Screen walls can provide an attractive feature. Here the screen is incorporated in a solid block wall

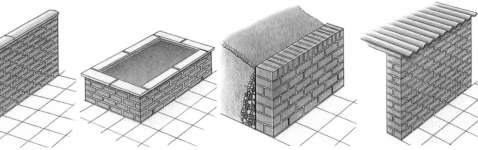

Free-standing wall

Basic example is the boundary wall. Maximum height of a brick wall without piers is 45 cm (10 cm thick wall) or 135 cm (21 cm thick wall). Higher walls need piers at 1 - 1½ m intervals

Light-duty retaining wall

The wall around a modest raised bed. The blocks are vertical and not sloping backwards. The wall should be just one block thick. Leave weep-holes at the base and paint inside with bituminous paint

Heavy-duty retaining wall

This wall has to withstand a great deal of pressure — it should be at least 21 cm thick. Make sure it slopes slightly backwards and has weep-holes near the base. Line inside with plastic sheeting

Load-bearing wall

Not a common garden feature — but is required if you plan to erect a carport or brick conservatory. The simple rule is that you should leave this work to a professional if you do not have the necessary skill

CHAPTER 16
PLANT INDEX

Acknowledgements

It would be quite impossible to acknowledge all of the people who have helped to create the Garden Expert over the past 50 years. Sadly the small group who were involved with me right at the beginning are no longer with us — artist Henry Barber, designer John Woodbridge, Denis Nahum and my dear wife Joan.

In the middle period there were many others, some helping for a year or two and a few people, such as John Adkins, Paul Norris and Barry Highland, who were part of the team for many years.

And so on to today, with this enlarged edition which covers all the aspects of the garden. Photographs from Garden World Images, Georgia Norris and Mark Whitman, artworks from Christine Wilson, proof-reading by Angelina Gibbs, repro skills from Ian Harris, and finally my long serving (and long suffering) Girl Friday — Gill Jackson.

This book, however, would be in a storeroom somewhere if it was not for the marketing and sales efforts of the people at Transworld Publishers — notably M.D. Larry Finlay, Gareth Pottle, Martin Higgins, Ed Christie, Janine Giovanni and Claire Evans.

To all these people and many more, past and present, I owe a great debt of gratitude. And also to my father, who gave me my first packet of seeds.